A Field Guide to the Plants and Animals
of the Middle Rio Grande Bosque

A Field Guide to the Plants and Animals of the Middle Rio Grande Bosque

Jean-Luc E. Cartron

David C. Lightfoot

Jane E. Mygatt

Sandra L. Brantley

Timothy K. Lowrey

Drylands Institute

Museum of Southwestern Biology

University of New Mexico Press | Albuquerque

Printed and bound in China by Everbest Printing
Company Ltd. through Four Colour Imports, Ltd.

13   12   11   10   09   08   1   2   3   4   5   6

Library of Congress Cataloging-in-Publication Data

A field guide to the plants and animals of the Middle Rio
Grande bosque / Jean-Luc E. Cartron . . . [et al.].
    p. cm.
Includes bibliographical references and index.
ISBN 978-0-8263-4269-0 (pbk. : alk. paper)
1. Natural history—New Mexico—Middle Rio
Grande Conservancy District. 2. Riparian plants—
New Mexico—Middle Rio Grande Conservancy
District—Identification. 3. Riparian animals—New
Mexico—Middle Rio Grande Conservancy District—
Identification. I. Cartron, Jean-Luc E.
QH105.N6F54 2008
508.789—dc22
                    2008009099

Book design and type composition by Melissa Tandysh
Composed in 9.75/12 Utopia Std : Display type is
Frutiger LT Std

In memory of

JOHN P. TAYLOR JR. (1954–2004) and

THOMAS H. WOOTTEN (1939–2007).

May their extraordinary dedication to the preservation of New Mexico's

native plants and animals be a source of inspiration for generations to come.

CONTENTS

Extending from the spillway below Cochiti Dam to the headwaters of Elephant Butte Reservoir, the Middle Rio Grande bosque is more than a cottonwood woodland or forest. It is a whole riparian (or riverside) ecosystem that also includes wetlands, ponds, moist meadows, and willow stands. Riverside drains, saltcedar thickets, and areas recently burned by wildfires are also part of today's ecosystem. These habitats did not exist historically, but rather were created by or resulted from human activities.

In the arid American Southwest, riparian ecosystems cover less than 2% of the landscape, but they harbor very large numbers of plants and animals. The heart of a riparian ecosystem is its river, a source of water that is otherwise scarce in the region. The abundance of water directly sustains many species and supports the growth of trees. Trees in turn offer shade and vertical structure, both important for providing suitable habitat otherwise not available in the surrounding lowlands.

Southwestern riparian ecosystems are fragile, and many have been severely impacted by humans. Groundwater pumping, water diversion and storage, woodcutting, and overgrazing have all contributed to the demise of some southwestern rivers and their associated riparian ecosystems. Even the Middle Rio Grande bosque is at risk today, as many of its cottonwoods are dying of old age and not naturally regenerating. The stands of large cottonwoods that we see today may not be here in another 100 years.

The field guide is intended as a tool for all those interested in nature who visit the bosque. Whether you are walking, riding your bike, or birding any-where along the river, there is much to discover by simply looking around. This field guide will allow you to more easily name the plants and animals you see while providing information on the status and natural history of each species. In writing this field guide, we hope to increase your awareness of the bosque as an important part of New Mexico's natural heritage.

ACKNOWLEDGMENTS

Many individuals and organizations contributed to make this field guide possible. We are grateful to the staff at the Bosque del Apache National Wildlife Refuge and the Rio Grande Nature Center, who granted us special access to gather some of the information contained in the book. We are especially indebted to all those who provided additional information for the species accounts or reviewed draft sections of the field guide: Kelly Allred, Heather Bateman, Ruth Bronson, Steve Cary, Yvonne Chauvin, Alice Chung-MacCoubrey, Cliff Crawford, Bill Degenhardt, Gina Dello Russo, Rob Doster, Kim Eichhorst-Mitchell, Dave Ferguson, Jim Findley, Karen Gaines, Gail Garber, Rebecca Gracey, Jake Grandy, Ben Hanelt, David Hanson, Dave Hawksworth, Bill Howe, Ondrea Hummel, Colin Lee, Manuel Molles, Yasmeen Najmi, Charlie Painter, Christopher Rustay, Robert Sivinski, Max Smith, Scott Stoleson, Jim Stuart, Phil Tonne, Ernie Valdez, Joran Viers, John Vradenburg, Owen William, Sondra Williamson, and Rob Yaksich. All made an important contribution, but Rob Doster, Dave Hawksworth, Charlie Painter, and Christopher Rustay in particular proved invaluable sources of information. Thank you also to Sandra Brown, Mike Gustin, and Joddi Hedderig for information on access to the bosque; and to Lolly Jones for field assistance. Our deep appreciation goes to the many photographers whose images so greatly enhance the field guide: A. S. Ahl, Patrick Alexander, Scott Altenbach, Wynn Anderson, Heather Bateman, Rick and Nora Bowers, Doug Boykin, Larry Brock, Doug Brown, John V. Brown, Andrea Capanella, Sharyn Davidson, Rich Ditch, Diana Doan-Crider, Rob Doster, Jerry Dragoo, Jon Dunnum, Dave Ferguson, Richard B. Forbes, Gordon French, Jennifer Frey, Ralph Giles, Bill Gorum, Joseph V. Higbee, Patty Hoban, Gene Jercinovic, Tom Kennedy, Karen Krebbs, Greg W. Lasley, Colin Leslie, Patrick O'Brien, Charlie Painter, Dave Rintoul, Bill Schmoker, Robert Shantz, Steve Shoup, Robert Sivinski, Lisa Spray, C. S. St. Clair, Ken Steiner, Phil Tonne, Matias Vega, Gordon Warrick, Mike Yip, Lee Zieger, and Dale and Marian Zimmerman. Thank you in particular to Doug Brown and Gordon French, who went out of their way to photograph some of the bosque fauna for the field guide. Thank you also to the established professional photographers who depend on the sales of their photos for their livelihood yet contributed to the project without financial compensation. Their generosity is much appreciated, as is that of the American Society of Mammalogists, which kindly provided us with several of the mammal photos. Likewise, our gratitude goes to the Bureau of Reclamation for giving us permission to use historical images of the Middle Rio Grande. Special thanks also to Melissa Tandysh (UNM Press), who expertly designed the layout of the field guide; Karen Taschek, who copyedited the text; and Teri Neville (Natural Heritage New Mexico), who crafted the map. The project received generous financial support from the Middle Rio Grande Bosque Initiative (U.S. Fish and Wildlife Service); the Friends of the Bosque del Apache National Wildlife Refuge; the Rocky Mountain Research Station (RMRS); Intel; the Public Service Company of New Mexico (PNM); the University of New Mexico (UNM) Department of Biology; SWCA, Inc.; Daniel B. Stephens and Associates; T&E, Inc.; the Rotary Club of Socorro, New Mexico; the Albuquerque Chapter of the Native Plant Society of New Mexico; the New Mexico Ornithological Society; and Jack and Martha Carter. We are grateful to Catherine Conran (PNM), Deb Finch (RMRS), Sam Loker (UNM Department of Biology), Tom Wootten (T&E, Inc.), Jerry Oldenettel, and Cyndie Abeyta (Middle Rio Grande Bosque Initiative, U.S. Fish and Wildlife Service) for their assistance in securing financial sponsors. Michael Wilson at the Drylands Institute, Inc., diligently processed grants for the project. Special thanks finally to UNM Press, Cyndie Abeyta, Cliff Crawford (Bosque Ecological Monitoring Program), Michael Wilson, and Manuel Molles (UNM) for their early encouragements and sustained belief in the merits of the project.

COLLABORATORS

SPONSORS

Rotary Club of Socorro,
New Mexico

New Mexico
Ornithological
Society

T & E, Inc.

ENVIRONMENTAL CONSULTANTS

Sound Science. Creative Solutions.

A personal commitment
to New Mexico

Daniel B. Stephens
& Associates, Inc.

TECHNICAL ADVISORS

Kelly Allred
Heather Bateman
Ruth Bronson
Alice Chung-MacCoubrey
Cliff Crawford
Bill Degenhardt
Gina Dello Russo
Rob Doster
Kim Eichhorst-Mitchell
Jim Findley
Karen Gaines
Ben Hanelt
David Hanson

David Hawksworth
Colin Lee
Yasmeen Najmi
Charlie Painter
Christopher Rustay
Robert Sivinski
Max Smith
Jim Stuart
Phil Tonne
Ernie Valdez
John Vradenburg
Rob Yaksich

Proceeds from sales of this book will be used to purchase additional copies for schools and environmental education programs.

PROLOGUE
Clifford S. Crawford

The Middle Rio Grande bosque is a work in progress, constantly changing in form and function. Spend time in it with this field guide and you'll begin to appreciate both the causes and the effects of this change. As you enter the bosque, keep your eye on the river, the historical cause of the bosque's existence. Today would you say the river is flowing high or low, and how long has it been that way? Note the season and the time of day. Expand your thoughts to the regional climate, which still influences river flow but less directly than in the past. Was there much of a snowpack in the upper basin last winter? If so, did a warm spring melt it unusually fast? Are we in a drought? With these questions in mind, scan the vegetation around you. What, if any, trees dominate the scene? Is there evidence of recent clearing or burning? Clearing and fire are recent drivers of change in the bosque. Might there be others as well?

With the help of your informative field guide, turn your attention to the bosque's plants and animals and to the habitats they occupy. From your observations you can start to make inferences about why what you see is there. Let's say you're walking along one of the main bosque trails on a late spring morning. There's been a little rain in the past week. A knocking sound comes from high up in a dead cottonwood some distance from the trail, toward the river. Could be a woodpecker—but what kind? Move carefully in that direction; fallen branches and uneven ground can trip you. The bird turns out to be a flicker. A surprising number of trees in the vicinity are Siberian elms. Some are as tall as a line of cottonwoods growing on a long ridge paralleling the river but separated from it by a stand of young summer cypresses and old sunflower stalks. A swale covered by low grasses borders one side of the stand, while a clump of coyote willows lines the other side and merges with an impassible thicket of Russian olives crowding the riverbank. Only a few young cottonwoods are present; their leaves are shredded by leaf beetles. Swallows occasionally swoop over the bank, and other small passerine birds move quietly in its dense vegetation. One is a wren, several are warblers, but most are sparrows.

Looking down as you pick your way back to the trail, you notice a series of freshly made pocket gopher mounds and a conical harvester ant nest among the abundant tansy mustards. Seed husks line the periphery of the nest. Wander over to a large decaying cottonwood stump. Pads of shelf fungi adhere to an intact part of the trunk. Where the bark has peeled, there's an accumulation of sawdust made by carpenter ants. As you lift an adjacent log, ground beetles scatter and pill bugs roll up. It's a busy time of year.

Back on the trail and reflecting on what you've just seen, you might ask yourself, "What's going on in the bosque?" That's a question asked increasingly by bosque visitors, students, resource managers, and researchers—all of whom can benefit greatly by consulting this carefully crafted field guide. The guide is truly a comprehensive work containing an immense amount of easy-to-retrieve information. It's also beautifully illustrated. Finally, it presents everything in an ecosystem context, one that mirrors society's past, present, and future expectations of Middle Rio Grande water—what's going on in the bosque?

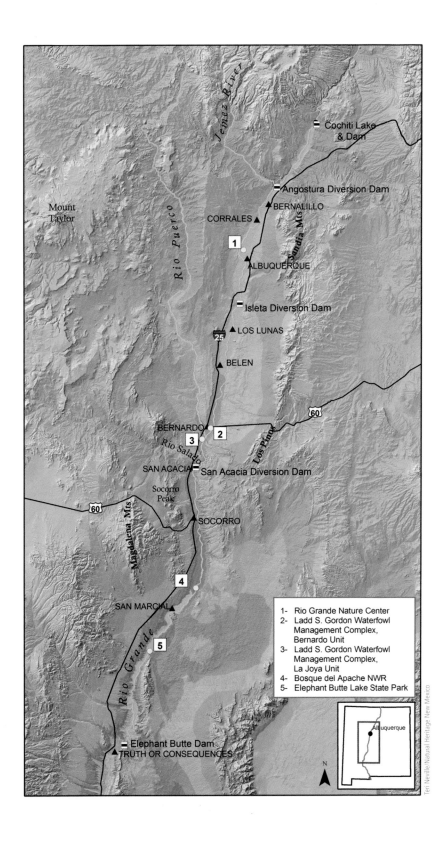

1- Rio Grande Nature Center
2- Ladd S. Gordon Waterfowl Management Complex, Bernardo Unit
3- Ladd S. Gordon Waterfowl Management Complex, La Joya Unit
4- Bosque del Apache NWR
5- Elephant Butte Lake State Park

Cochiti Lake & Dam

Angostura Diversion Dam

BERNALILLO

Mount Taylor

CORRALES

ALBUQUERQUE

Isleta Diversion Dam

LOS LUNAS

BELEN

Rio Puerco

Jemez River

Sandia Mts

BERNARDO

Rio Salado

SAN ACACIA

San Acacia Diversion Dam

Los Pinos

Socorro Peak

SOCORRO

Magdalena Mts

SAN MARCIAL

Rio Grande

Elephant Butte Dam
TRUTH OR CONSEQUENCES

Albuquerque

N

MAIN PLACES TO VISIT, ACCESS POINTS, AND VISITOR INFORMATION

The Middle Rio Grande bosque is under the administrative oversight of several agencies and tribes, including the Middle Rio Grande Conservancy District (MRGCD), the U.S. Bureau of Reclamation, state and federal wildlife refuges, municipalities, and six Pueblos (Cochiti, Santo Domingo, San Felipe, Sandia, Santa Ana, and Isleta). Below is a list of places to visit and primary public access points, from north to south. Please heed signs barring or limiting access.

RIO RANCHO AND CORRALES AREA

Rio Rancho Bosque Preserve
Access to the bosque is a turnoff from State Highway 528, north of the Village of Corrales. Additional information, including a bird checklist, is available at the Friends of Rio Rancho Open Space.

   www.forros.org

Corrales Bosque Nature Preserve
Access points are at Alameda Bridge, via Romero Road, and at the northern end of the village. A bird checklist and other information are available at the Corrales Visitor Center.

   505-897-0502

ALBUQUERQUE AREA

Most bridge areas in Albuquerque provide access to the river, the bosque, and the Paseo del Bosque Bike Trail.

Paseo del Bosque Bike Trail
The 16-mile, paved bike trail goes through the bosque from Alameda Bridge south to Rio Bravo Bridge.

   www.cabq.gov/openspace/paseodelbosquetrail.html

Rio Grande Nature Center, 2901 Candelaria NW
The Nature Center is part of the New Mexico State Park system. It is open throughout the year (except for Thanksgiving, Christmas, and New Year's days), Monday through Sunday from 8:00 a.m. to 5:00 p.m. The center has checklists of birds and dragonflies, guides group tours (including full moon walks on a few summer nights), and hosts a variety of local events about New Mexico's natural

history. Viewing access to the main pond is easy. The visitor center has a small bookstore and exhibits. There is a parking fee of $3.00 for cars and $15.00 for buses and small vans.

www.rgnc.org

Open Space Visitor Center

Located at 6500 Coors Blvd. NW, the Open Space Visitor Center features interpretive and art exhibits, wildlife viewing, a prehistoric pueblo, guided tours, special talks, and demonstrations and is part of the City of Albuquerque Major Public Open Space system. Open throughout the year (except for Thanksgiving, Christmas, and New Year's days), Tuesday through Saturday from 9:00 a.m. to 5:00 p.m.

www.cabq.gov/openspace

Tingley Beach

In Albuquerque, Tingley Beach offers fishing, biking, ponds for model boats, and trail access to the bosque.

www.cabq.gov/biopark/tingley/

Bridge at Rio Bravo Blvd./Rio Bravo Riverside Picnic Area

Rio Bravo Blvd. is a major intersection with I-25 in the South Valley of Albuquerque. The bridge area has parking and a fully accessible fishing pier and trail leading to the river. Access is via Poco Loco Rd.

LOS LUNAS AND BELEN AREA

Los Lunas River Park

This park has a nature trail and fishing and picnic areas.

1660 Main St. SE

Belen Bridge

The river crossing at the south side of town has ample parking and access to the river for birding and exploring wetland habitat.

BERNARDO AREA

Ladd S. Gordon Waterfowl Management Complex, Bernardo Unit

These 1600 acres near the river at Highway 60 and I-25 provide areas for hunting, fishing, and wildlife viewing. Several access points are east and north of Bernardo, most requiring special permits through the MRGCD. One access point from the frontage road north of Bernardo is open to all visitors, with a tour loop, viewing platforms, and a birding trail. The best time of year to visit is winter, when the area is flooded to create seasonal ponds for waterfowl. Check with the New Mexico Department of Game and Fish offices for more information.

http://www.wildlife.state.nm.us

Ladd S. Gordon Waterfowl Management Complex, La Joya Unit

Located at I-25, exit 169, on the east side of the freeway, the refuge was established in 1957 and is a 3500-acre network of ponds for waterfowl, shorebirds, and nearby desert bird species as well. The waterfowl hunting season runs from September through mid-January. Check with the New Mexico Department of Game and Fish offices for more information.

www.wildlife.state.nm.us

SOCORRO AREA

Escondida Lake Park

Access is off I-25 at exit 152, 2 miles north of Socorro. Go east at the stop sign until the road turns, then go north 6 miles to the Escondida Lake Park sign. The park is mainly for fishing and camping, but it is right next to the levee and can be used to access the bosque. Facilities include RV hookups, tent sites, bathrooms, and water.

505-835-0424 or 505-835-2041

Socorro Valley Riverine Parks

Between La Joya and the Bosque del Apache National Wildlife Refuge are over a dozen smaller river parks with trails and picnic areas. Contact the Save Our Bosque Taskforce at PO Box 1527, Socorro, NM 87801.

Bosque del Apache National Wildlife Refuge (NWR)

This refuge is a major stopping place for migrating birds. It is open every day of the year from 1 hour before sunrise to 1 hour after sunset. From Socorro, drive 8 miles south on I-25 to exit 139, continue east one-quarter mile on US 380 to Old Highway 1, turn right, and continue south 9 miles to the visitor center. The tour loop has viewing platforms overlooking ponds that are accessible to people with disabilities. Hiking trails offer additional opportunities to view wildlife. Some ponds are drained during the summer for vegetation management. Stop by the visitor center (with small bookstore and exhibits) for additional information. The web page below is a link to more information, including a bird species checklist.

www.fws.gov/southwest/refuges/newmex/bosque/

TRUTH OR CONSEQUENCES AREA

Elephant Butte Lake State Park

Public access to the lake is described in a special section of this field guide. The northernmost section of the park (both part of the Middle Rio Grande bosque and within the reservoir pool) has restricted access.

PHYSICAL SETTING AND ENVIRONMENTAL HISTORY

The Rio Grande is the third-longest river in the United States, extending 1885 miles from its headwaters in the San Juan Mountains of southwestern Colorado to its mouth in the Gulf of Mexico near Brownsville, Texas. The reach from the outflow of Cochiti Dam to the headwaters of Elephant Butte Reservoir is known as the Middle Rio Grande. It extends approximately 175 river miles. The Middle Rio Grande bosque (*bosque* is the Spanish word for "woods") refers to the cottonwood woodland along the river and, by extension, the entire Middle Rio Grande riparian (riverside) ecosystem.

The river receives most of its water from the mountains of southern Colorado and northern New Mexico. Flows in the Rio Grande, like those of other regional rivers, are strongly influenced by climate and geology. Seasonal runoff from mountain snowmelt generally causes such flows to peak in late spring and early summer.

The Rio Grande Rift Valley was formed 25 million years ago when the earth's crust thinned and separated into a gap 40 miles wide and several miles deep. The tension and uplifting of the crust formed several mountain ranges to the east, including the Sandia, Manzano, Oscura, and Fra Cristobal ranges. The Rio Grande has flowed through this valley for more than a million years. Sediments from erosion of nearby mountains (alluvial deposits) as well as those transported by the river are slowly filling the rift. Typical riparian soil textures in the valley floodplain range from sandy channel and bar deposits to clay-rich deposits above the main riverbanks.

Warm summers and cool winters characterize the climate of the Middle Rio Grande. In the last 10,000 years most of New Mexico has been semi-arid, with numerous drought and wet cycles. In the last 600 years the climate has been relatively stable, with a cool period from about 1450 to 1850. Tree ring data reveal that at least 52 droughts have occurred in the past 450 years. The region is also strongly affected by the El Niño Southern Oscillation weather pattern of the southern Pacific Ocean. El Niño influences the timing and amount of flow in the Rio Grande. In addition, climate change may be contributing to a shift in peak flow rates because of snowmelt occurring earlier in the spring.

During the course of a year most valley precipitation arrives in late summer from thunderstorms generated by airflow from the Gulf of Mexico. The variable and localized nature of these storms causes flash flooding in tributaries that drain into the Rio Grande. Winter precipitation comes mostly from Pacific frontal systems.

In the Albuquerque area, long-term annual average precipitation is 9.5 inches. Summer high air temperatures tend to be in the mid-80s (degrees Fahrenheit, F) to low 90s (F), occurring from June to September; average minimum temperatures of low to mid-20s (F) occur from December to February. The seasonal patterns of winter and summer rains, along with a hot, dry early summer period, produce distinct spring and late summer assemblages of plants and animals.

The rich biological diversity of plants and animals in the Middle Rio Grande bosque (and New Mexico in general) comes from its proximity to geographically distinct regions in North America, with influences from the Rocky Mountains, Colorado Plateau, Great Plains, and Chihuahuan Desert. In addition, the Middle Rio Grande is situated along major north-south migration routes for many bird and several butterfly species. The combined effects of climate and biogeography ensure interesting observations of plants and animals throughout the year.

ONCE A FREE-FLOWING RIVER

Historically, as the Rio Grande wound its way across its central New Mexico floodplain, the appearance and location of its riparian ecological communities kept changing. Oxbow lakes, wetlands, and woodlands (bosques) of cottonwoods and willows came and went. The river flowed freely, meandering and changing course. Spring floods were at times common and extreme, as were periods of drought. Flooding added nutrients and sediments to the soil while sweeping away woody debris.

After the end of the last ice age (approximately 10,000 years ago), nomadic hunter-gatherer Paleo-Indians lived in the region. Their numbers being small, they had little impact on the river environments. By approximately 2000 years ago Native American pueblo peoples established settlements in the Middle Rio Grande Valley. These early settlers were farmers, irrigating small tracts of land with water from natural high flows and overbank flooding. Their impact on the river and its floodplain was negligible; however, seasonal floods occasionally destroyed their villages.

From the 16th to the 19th centuries the Spanish settlers cleared land and developed complex irrigation techniques, among them a system of canals and ditches called acequias. Throughout this time they introduced a variety of domestic agricultural plants and animals from the Old World and Latin America. Even so, their impacts on the riparian environments were relatively small and localized. The river and adjacent habitats continued to change with flooding events and natural succession. Native cottonwoods and willows thrived in the bosque, and the river still dominated the landscape.

A HUMAN-REGULATED RIVER

Anglo immigration and settlement increased through the 1800s, bringing a cultural shift to the area based on larger-scale agriculture and irrigation. By the 1890s extensive livestock grazing and logging in the uplands of northern and central New Mexico resulted in increased soil erosion, which drastically added sediment loads to the river. By the early 1900s increased sediment loads raised the level of the riverbed, intensifying flooding of communities and farmlands. Repeated flooding events led to increased salt buildup and reduced the productivity of floodplain farmlands. Throughout the Middle Rio Grande Valley and downstream there was a need for flood control and a reliable and readily available source of water for irrigation. In 1905 the secretary of the interior authorized the Rio Grande Project to address these problems and to produce hydropower and irrigation systems. As part of this project, Elephant Butte Dam was completed in 1916.

The most significant environmental impacts on the Middle Rio Grande took place during the early to mid-20th century. In 1923 the New Mexico legislature created the Middle Rio Grande Conservancy District to control flooding, drain marshlands, and provide a system of canals and ditches for irrigation. Over the next several decades a series of diversion and water storage dams and hundreds of miles of canals and levees were constructed. The river was straightened by dredging and confined to a narrow channel. Beginning in the 1950s, thousands of large steel crosslike structures called jetty jacks were installed by the U.S. Army Corps of Engineers and the U.S. Bureau of Reclamation to trap sediments and stabilize the riverbanks in case of flooding. River flow rates fell

Herman E. Carter/U.S. Bureau of Reclamation

Excavation of the western half of the river channel near Socorro, March 27, 1957. Sediment material dredged up from the riverbed is added to the levee.

James Weese/U.S. Bureau of Reclamation

Jetty jacks in the river channel south of Belen, April 25, 1956.

to one-sixth of predam levels, affecting the supply, movement, and deposition of sediments.

Cochiti Dam, completed in 1973, became the largest and most influential of the Middle Rio Grande dams. It ended natural flooding in the river valley, preventing the regeneration of native cottonwoods and willows in many parts of the bosque. Along the realigned Rio Grande, resulting from bank stabilization, the once scattered cottonwood stands turned into a nonregenerating but continuous woodland confined between the levees. Beginning in the 1910s, 1920s, and 1930s, non-native vegetation such as saltcedar, Siberian elm, Russian olive, Russian thistle, and kochia invaded the bosque rapidly. In less than a century the once free-flowing Middle Rio Grande became a regulated river with a bosque dominated by exotic plants.

AN ENDANGERED ECOSYSTEM

Native trees such as Rio Grande cottonwood, Goodding's willow, and coyote willow evolved to germinate on flooded soils and require abundant groundwater for their establishment and survival. Since sections of the bosque are hydrologically less connected to the river than they were in the past, incomplete soil saturation above the water table inhibits these trees' germination and establishment. Furthermore, continuing tree growth and maintenance

Wildfire near San Marcial, 2006.

depends on groundwater remaining above a depth of about 10 feet. The relationship of bosque groundwater and adjacent surface water flows is complex and poorly understood. However, during prolonged periods of very low flows, bosque groundwater connected to the river drops, potentially killing the trees. Monitoring has shown that valley groundwater levels have been dropping as water is removed for agricultural and municipal purposes.

Wildfires are another environmental threat to native trees in the bosque. Historically, fire played a minor role because the woodlands were interspersed with wetlands and open areas acting as natural firebreaks. Today the bosque floodplain is predominantly dry, with an increased accumulation of leaf litter due to lack of scouring floods and slowed decomposition. That, combined with extensive stands of saltcedar and other introduced plants, creates an ample fuel source for fires increasingly set by humans. Unlike the Rio Grande cottonwood, saltcedar and Russian olive generally resprout and survive well following intense bosque wildfires.

The combined environmental changes of river regulation, introduced species, and increased occurrence of fire profoundly affect the survival of native riparian species. Introduced species generally outcompete native species in the bosque for ecological, physiological, and life history reasons. Under current conditions, native woody vegetation in the bosque will continue to decline and disappear.

The Rio Grande (top) and the adjacent low-flow conveyance channel near Bernardo
(bottom), September 2003. The two photos illustrate cumulative human impacts
on the Middle Rio Grande and its bosque. Note that the low-flow conveyance channel
is full, while the river is essentially dry and the bosque has been scorched by wildfire.

PRESERVATION OF THE BOSQUE

One early and important conservation effort along the Middle Rio Grande was the creation of the Bosque del Apache National Wildlife Refuge in 1939. The damming and diversion of the river along with draining of marshlands had by that time resulted in the loss of critical habitat for aquatic and wetland species such as sandhill cranes. Today the refuge consists of extensive wetlands, agricultural fields, and cottonwood stands. Managed by the U.S. Fish and Wildlife Service, the refuge grows corn and other crops to provide food for wintering migratory birds, including geese and cranes. The success of the refuge is apparent: myriads of birds inhabit the refuge every year, including thousands of sandhill cranes.

Since the 1980s, and as public awareness increased, efforts to preserve the bosque have intensified. Government agencies at federal, state, tribal, and local levels, along with private organizations, are involved in protecting endangered species, restoring habitat, and removing exotic vegetation. The Bosque del Apache National Wildlife Refuge in particular has been instrumental in developing new ways to control invasive saltcedar. Projects aimed at reducing invasive saltcedar often include replanting with Rio Grande cottonwood saplings and other native plants. Some areas of the bosque are being flooded experimentally in an effort to duplicate the historical pattern of seasonal flooding. Although these efforts are having a positive effect on native species, non-natives are generally better adapted to man-made environmental changes. As human needs for water continue to increase for agriculture and urban uses, the preservation of biodiversity in the bosque will remain a challenge. Ultimately, the availability of water in the Rio Grande will determine the future environmental integrity of the Middle Rio Grande bosque.

KEY TO SYMBOLS

[INT]   Introduced

✳   Hypothetical, irregular, or very rare breeding in the bosque

✳✳   Regular breeding occurs in the bosque

HABITAT ASSOCIATIONS

 Cottonwood woodland

 River channel, including open riverbanks, sandbars, and islands

 Drains, canals, and ditches

 Saltcedar stands

 Open areas

 Wetlands

SEASONALITY

Vascular plants—Unless otherwise indicated months given represent the blooming season.

Invertebrates—Seasons (Sp: spring, March–May; Su: summer, June–August; F: fall, September–November; W: winter, December–February) given indicate the time of year when the adults are active aboveground.

Amphibians, Reptiles, and Mammals—Months given indicate time of occurrence or activity aboveground. Months in capital letters represent the main period of year when the species can be encountered.

Birds—Months given in brackets indicate time of occurrence. Months in capital letters indicate that the species is abundant, common, or uncommon; months in lowercase letters indicate that the species is occasional or rare.

For the purpose of this field guide, the Middle Rio Grande bosque is divided into six easily recognizable, main habitat types: cottonwood woodland; saltcedar stands; the river channel, including open riverbanks, sandbars, and islands; wetlands; drains, canals, and ditches, together with their side banks; and open areas, often the result of fire or human disturbance. These habitat types are based on a combination of physical environmental features such as landforms, soils, and water availability and also on overall vegetation species composition and physical structure. All of them interface with one another and can overlap. Included by us as part of the Middle Rio Grande bosque, the northern section of the Elephant Butte Reservoir pool is no longer underwater (due to receding water levels) and has become revegetated with a mix of Goodding's willow (*Salix gooddingii*), Rio Grande cottonwood (*Populus deltoides* ssp. *wislizenii*), Russian olive (*Elaeagnus angustifolia*), and saltcedar (*Tamarix* spp.). This brushy vegetation is mentioned in a few species accounts, but because it generally will not be seen by visitors, it is not described here.

COTTONWOOD WOODLAND

The native cottonwood woodland along the Middle Rio Grande is typically composed of mature Rio Grande cottonwood trees, together with understory shrubs and herbaceous vegetation. It is nearly restricted to a narrow corridor between the levees that parallel the river. The lack of flooding has produced a woodland floor with large amounts of accumulated dead branches and logs amid a thick layer of dead leaves. Lack of natural flooding also has reduced cottonwood reproduction, so that most of the trees seen today are mature or even senescent. In the southern part of the region, Goodding's willow may co-dominate the overstory (tree foliage canopy) with Rio Grande cottonwood. In many areas, the understory tends to be shaded and lacks herbaceous vegetation. It often supports a mixture of native shrubs, such as New Mexico desert-olive (*Forestiera pubescens*), Torrey's wolfberry (*Lycium torreyi*), screwbean mesquite (*Prosopis pubescens*), coyote willow (*Salix exigua*), and seep-willow (*Baccharis* spp). More typically, however, the understory is dominated by saltcedar and Russian olive, two exotic species that can form nearly impenetrable thickets and contribute greatly to elevate the risk of wildfire. Other common exotic tree species found in cottonwood woodland include Siberian elm (*Ulmus pumila*), mulberry (*Morus alba*), honey locust (*Gleditsia triacanthos*), and tree of heaven (*Ailanthus altissima*). Small clearings occur naturally in this woodland habitat, and here herbaceous plants can be common. Ephemeral

Mature cottonwood woodland after thinning of the understory vegetation. In the background are saltcedar and Russian olive thickets. The ground is characterized by a thick layer of dead organic matter (dead branches and other woody debris).

Open cottonwood woodland with mature cottonwood trees and a ground cover of fall aster and other annuals.

pools may form in response to groundwater seepage or, more rarely, from overbank flooding. Recently, restoration and postfire rehabilitation projects have focused on the removal of saltcedar and Russian olive in the cottonwood woodland and replanting with cottonwoods and willows. Where saltcedar and Russian olive are removed with no follow-up effort to plant native vegetation, weeds such as kochia (*Kochia scoparia*) can become established in very high densities.

SALTCEDAR STANDS

Saltcedar is an exotic deciduous tree or large shrub that was introduced as an ornamental into the Middle Rio Grande Valley in the early 20th century. By the 1940s it had invaded thousands of acres along the river. It is now a dominant species in the bosque and spreads rapidly via wind-dispersed seeds that are able to germinate in moist silt within 24 hours. Prior to the introduction of saltcedar, native woody species such as Goodding's willow, coyote willow, and seep-willow dominated the vegetation along the Rio Grande, together with Rio Grande cottonwood. Those species are often present in saltcedar stands, but where saltcedar forms thickets, it is associated with little or no understory plants, native or introduced. Saltcedar communities also tend to produce

Jean-Luc Cartron

Saltcedar thickets near San Marcial.

dense layers of leaf litter covering the ground up to several centimeters deep. The dense saltcedar foliage and the ground-surface litter layers do provide habitat for both vertebrate and invertebrate animals, albeit many of them more typical of upland habitats.

RIVER CHANNEL (OPEN RIVERBANKS, SANDBARS, AND ISLANDS)

The Rio Grande from Cochiti to Elephant Butte has been highly modified throughout the 20th century. River channels were dredged to control water flow and Cochiti Dam was constructed primarily for flood and sediment control. In addition, a system of levees and jetty jacks was built in an effort to minimize flooding and sediment flow. Historically, the Middle Rio Grande had a wider channel and the river meandered, creating numerous oxbow lakes. The landscape was a mosaic—a shifting succession of marshlands and forests. Today the riverbanks are often steep and uniformly lined with trees that extend to the river's edge. Only where flash flooding creates frequent disturbance are the riverbanks open and characterized by bare soils, grasses, and shrubs. These open riverbanks, together with sandbars (sediment bars that become exposed in the channel during low-flow periods) and islands (vegetated bars), create a distinctive terrestrial river habitat. Sandbars can be seen

River channel south of San Marcial, characterized by a swift current and recent entrenchment.

River channel with sandbars at Los Lunas Bridge.

anywhere along the margins of the river or in the river channel. They can shift due to flooding during spring snowmelt or as a result of flash flooding during heavy thunderstorm activity.

The riverbanks, sandbars, and islands support a variety of native and exotic species that are tolerant of occasional flooding. Large and more permanent sandbars support a variety of shrub species, including coyote willow, Goodding's willow, Russian olive, and saltcedar. The herbaceous vegetation along the moist margins of the riverbanks and sandbars include American licorice (*Glycyrrhiza lepidota*), ragweed (*Ambrosia* spp.), rough cocklebur (*Xanthium strumarium* var. *canadense*), and sweetclover (*Melilotus* spp.) in addition to Canada wild rye (*Elymus canadensis*), bearded sprangletop (*Leptochloa fusca* ssp. *fascicularis*), saltgrass (*Distichlis spicata* var. *stricta*), common reed (*Phragmites australis*), and numerous rushes and sedges (Cyperaceae).

WETLANDS

Wetland vegetation in the Middle Rio Grande bosque occurs where standing water has formed and sun exposure is high. There are seasonal wetlands, which exhibit annual wet and dry cycles, and semipermanent or "persistent" wetlands. The main habitat type at the Bosque del Apache NWR is seasonal wetlands. Part of the refuge management program is to drain and fill tracks of land

Discovery Pond at the Rio Grande Nature Center.

Wetland near Tingley Beach in Albuquerque.

to mimic the historic flooding cycles of the river to create seasonal wetland conditions. Persistent wetlands consist of swampy areas dominated by herbaceous perennials, less often by shrubs. All wetlands have plants with their roots periodically or continually submerged in water. They may form in narrow strands along the main river channel, along in-filled channels severed from the river, at the confluences of tributaries with the Rio Grande, or along drains. The plant species are mainly emergent aquatics, meaning only the roots are covered by water rather than having all plant parts submerged. Seep-willow and coyote willow are shrubby perennial species commonly occurring in wetlands. Perennial herbaceous plants include sedges and bulrushes (Cyperaceae), rushes (*Juncus* spp.), cattails (*Typha* spp.), yerba mansa (*Anemopsis californica*), and horsetail (*Equisetum laevigatum*). Many of these plants are important food for wintering ducks and geese. Wetlands can become overgrown with cattails, reducing the amount of open water for aquatic birds. At the Bosque del Apache NWR, wetlands with mats of rank cattail have to be drained, followed by prescribed fire.

DRAINS, CANALS, AND DITCHES

A system of drains, canals, and ditches was created along the Middle Rio Grande to provide flood control, drainage of marshlands, and irrigation for

Overgrown riverside drain in the South Valley of Albuquerque.

Jean-Luc Cartron

Typical riverside drain with associated bank vegetation.

agriculture. In nature preserves such as the Bosque del Apache NWR, canals and drains now also serve for the establishment of ponds and wetlands. The artificial waterways closest to the river, among them the riverside drains (typically marking the edge of the cottonwood woodland on the levee side), all now represent an important component of the Middle Rio Grande bosque. Water may be present seasonally or year-round. Drains, canals, and ditches with permanent water support aquatic and facultative wetland species, including parrot's feather (*Myriophyllum aquaticum*), common duckweed (*Lemna* spp.), cattail, and many rushes and sedges. The saturated soils near the waterline support a variety of mesic (requiring a moderate amount of water) vegetation, including rabbitfoot grass (*Polypogon monspeliensis*), common reed, and horsetail. The ground along the sides and tops of the drains, canals, and ditches is occasionally mowed. The periodic soil disturbance in and around the drain, canal, and ditch system creates ideal conditions for the establishment of exotic and native weedy species. Exotic species such as saltcedar, Russian olive, inland saltgrass, London rocket (*Sisymbrium irio*), broad-leaf pepperweed (*Lepidium latifolium*), flixweed (*Descurainia sophia*), kochia, and tumbleweed (*Salsola tragus*) grow alongside native plants, including coyote willow, American licorice, copper globemallow (*Sphaeralcea angustifolia*), Mexican devilweed (*Chloracantha spinosa*), and annual sunflower (*Helianthus annuus*).

OPEN AREAS

In addition to wetlands, the river channel, and some drain, canal, and ditch side banks, there are other large open areas in the bosque that lack an overstory. Many result from fire, while others are drained wetlands or areas where trees have been removed for various reasons, including areas along roads, trails, and levees. Available soil moisture can be low and soils vary depending on location but are typically sandy or silty. The vegetation is often characterized by native shrubs and grasses such as four-wing saltbush (*Atriplex canescens*), screwbean mesquite, and alkali sacaton (*Sporobolus airoides*) in addition to weedy invasive species, including yellow sweetclover, kochia, and tumbleweed. Exotic tree species such as tree of heaven, Russian olive, Siberian elm, and saltcedar are able to establish or recover quickly in areas opened by fire. Unless managed, these weedy exotic species threaten to completely dominate the Middle Rio Grande floodplain. At the Bosque del Apache NWR, open areas near seasonal and permanent ponds consist of mesic meadows that support a fairly lush carpet of plants tolerant of alkaline soils, including inland saltgrass, foxtail barley (*Hordeum jubatum*), alkali mallow (*Malvella leprosa*), and red bladder vetch (*Sphaerophysa salsula*). Also present are assemblages of wetland species, including cattail, and various rushes and sedges.

Jean-Luc Cartron

Burned area in the South Valley of Albuquerque.

Jean-Luc Cartron

Drained, seasonal wetland area at the Bosque del Apache National Wildlife Refuge.

NONVASCULAR PLANTS, LICHENS, AND FUNGI

SCOPE FOR THIS GUIDE

Nonvascular plants do not fall into the other, larger groups covered in this guide and are represented by few members in the bosque, but at certain times and places they may be abundant. These plants include mosses, liverworts, and hornworts. Most do not have true roots or stems that can transport water and nutrients internally (see Vascular Plants section). Instead, when a stem-like structure is present, it primarily provides support, and the cells wick water and nutrients from their substrates. As a result, the plants usually do not extend more than a few centimeters above the soil surface and live in damp habitats. Nonvascular plants have rootlike structures that extend only a short way into the soil and serve as an anchor. They reproduce with spores rather than seeds.

Lichens are formed by a symbiosis (mutually beneficial interrelationship) of algae and fungi. Algae are classified in the kingdom Protoctista (single-celled organisms), and the mushrooms and their relatives are in the kingdom Fungi. The algae, which contain chlorophyll as plants do, make their own sugars and other nutrients. The fungi do not make their own food but resist drying out quickly in arid conditions. The fungi encase the algae and get some of their nutrients, while the algae are protected from drying out. Lichens contain a variety of protective acidic chemicals, which are useful in identification and give lichens their often bright colors of green, yellow, orange, and red. They are named for the fungal partner and reproduce by spores.

The familiar mushroom is the fruiting body (reproductive structure) of fungi, but most fungal tissue is within wood, roots, or the soil as threadlike structures called *mycelia*. The mycelia act like roots and absorb water and nutrients from the soil or roots for the growth of the fungus. Mycelia associated with tree roots are called mycorrhizae and greatly increase the plant's ability to gather water and nutrients. This association is ancient and may well be responsible for trees becoming one of earth's dominant life-forms.

DIVERSITY AND ECOLOGY IN NEW MEXICO

These organisms are generally associated with damp habitats; in New Mexico most occur in riparian areas and at high elevations where there are forests and meadows. Lichens grow on decaying wood but are also well adapted to extreme habitats, such as rocky outcrops exposed to wind, heat, and cold. Cryptobiotic crusts, which contain mosses, algae, lichens, and fungi, also can form in dry open areas in woodlands and grasslands. These soil crusts are no more than a few centimeters thick but bind soil particles together and help prevent erosion. They can also increase the amount of rainwater that penetrates and stays in soils and contributes nitrogen to soils, which is in limited supply in arid systems. Estimated species numbers in New Mexico are 300 for mosses, 50 for liverworts and hornworts, more than 500 for lichens, and more than 700 for fungi.

Riccia Liverwort (*Riccia* sp.)

Sp Su F

Taxonomy—Phylum: Bryophyta; Class: Hepatocopsida; Order: Marchantiales; Family: Ricciaceae.

Identification—Inconspicuous, green, flat, strap-shaped thallus (a leaflike structure) that is usually bilobed (has a Y shape), 1–5 cm long. When growing on soil, the thallus is broader and the whole liverwort grows in a rosette form. The spore-producing reproductive structures are embedded in cavities within the thallus and often appear as dark spots when viewed from above.

David Lightfoot

Natural history—Float in shallow water in ponds or along the river or grow on damp soil in these habitats. If the area dries out, the liverwort darkens and shrivels but can revive when conditions become wetter, although it will die if dry periods are too long or severe. Liverworts are among the oldest of terrestrial plant forms.

Status—Widespread, uncommon.

Rosette Lichen (*Physcia* sp.)

Sp Su F W

Taxonomy—Phylum: Ascomycota; Class: Lecanoromycetes; Order: Lecanorales; Family: Physciaceae.

Identification—Surface pale gray to almost white with a lobed or leafy outline; underside usually pale but can also be brown or black. Fungal reproductive structures are cuplike, green to dark brown in the center. The several species of *Physcia* in the Middle Rio Grande bosque are difficult to differentiate.

David Lightfoot

Natural history—Found on the bark of cottonwood and elm trees in areas of open canopy.

Status—Widespread, common.

Hooded Sunburst Lichen

(Xanthoria fallax)

Sp Su F W

Taxonomy—Phylum: Ascomycota; Class: Lecanoromycetes; Order: Teloschistales; Family: Teloschistaceae.

Identification—Bright yellow-orange to dark orange with a lobed or leafy outline; underside white. Fungal reproductive structures are green-yellow at the tips of the lobes and form a small hood. There are a few other species of *Xanthoria* in the Middle Rio Grande bosque, with a very similar appearance.

Natural history—Found on the bark of cottonwood and elm trees in areas of open canopy.

Status—Widespread, common.

Fairy Ring Mushroom

(Marasmius orades)

Sp Su F

Taxonomy—Phylum: Basidiomycota; Class: Basidiomycetes; Order: Agaricales; Family: Marasmiaceae.

Identification—Height of fruiting bodies up to 10 cm; white to tan in color; tend to grow in rings in flat open areas (often in parks and yards); can withstand dry conditions and will revive with rainfall. Species other than *Marasmius* often grow in rings as well.

Natural history—Often associated with grass roots; the ring grows outward over time as the fungus uses up nutrients from the center.

Status—Widespread, common.

Polypore Bracket Fungus

Sp Su F W

Taxonomy—Phylum: Basidiomycota; Class: Basidiomycetes; Order: Polyporales; Family: Polyporaceae.

Identification—Polypore fungi grow on wood, have a shelf-like appearance and tough texture, and live several years; the underside has coarse-to-fine pores rather than the more familiar lamellae or gills, through which spores are released. A common genus is *Pleurotus*, whose species grow as overlapping fans on downed elm and cottonwood trees.

Natural history—These fungi are important decomposers of wood, capable of persisting during dry periods or through winters. Growth occurs mostly during the summers and wet periods, when new rings appear on the outer edges.

Status—Widespread, common.

CRYPTOBIOTIC SOIL CRUSTS

Cryptobiotic crusts are mats of vegetation made up of many kinds of organisms that have traditionally been considered plants. Crusts made of mosses, hornworts, and liverworts are familiar green carpets in damp forests or along mountain streams. In arid regions, they are often overlooked because they are not green unless they have received recent rain or snow. Instead, they are dark brown or black and look like part of the (inorganic) soil. The primary components of crusts are green algae, fungi, blue-green algae, and lichens. The base layer is often a green alga, *Microcoleus vaginatus*, which provides some structure for the lichens or blue-green algae to grow on. A network of fungal threads (mycelia) extends into the soil for a few centimeters, loosely connecting the crust to the soil. Crusts provide a microhabitat for many small arthropods, such as pseudoscorpions and free-living (nonparasitic) mites. Bits of crust are easily dislodged and transported by wind, water, or large animals to new locations.

David Lightfoot

VASCULAR PLANTS

ORGANIZATION AND SCOPE FOR THIS GUIDE

Vascular plants are plants with specialized conducting tissues, xylem and phloem, which transport water and nutrients throughout the plant. The classification of vascular plants follows a scheme similar to that for most multicellular organisms on earth, with the main ranks including phylum, class, order, family, genus, and species. In this guide, there are only two phyla: the Monilophyta (ferns and fern allies) and the Magnoliophyta or Anthophyta (flowering plants). The Magnoliophyta contains two classes of flowering plants that represent major evolutionary lineages: Monocotyledonae (Monocots) and Dicotyledonae (Dicots). Within the Monocots and Dicots three ranks are emphasized: families, genera, and species. The families are arranged alphabetically within each class, as are the genera and species within each family. Common names have been provided, but since they vary in usage, scientific names are emphasized; they are standardized throughout the world.

TAXONOMIC SCOPE

This guide includes 203 species of vascular plants, including 1 fern ally, 56 Monocots, and 146 Dicots. The family with the most species is the Asteraceae, with 44 species, followed by the Poaceae with 41 and the Fabaceae with 13. Introduced plants account for 26% (52) of the entries, indicative of their importance in the bosque flora. The population size and ground cover of exotic species can be much greater than that of native species in parts of the bosque.

VASCULAR PLANT DIVERSITY AND ECOLOGY

There are more than 3600 species of vascular plants in New Mexico, so the 203 species in this field guide represent only 5% of the total species diversity in New Mexico. Many of the plant species are riparian (living along riverbanks or lakes), semi-aquatic, or aquatic and also can be observed at other watercourses, lakes, and ponds in New Mexico. In addition, a majority of the floodplain is dry for most of the year and highly disturbed, ideal conditions exist for weedy native and exotic species. We include many common species that are well adapted to these environments. Therefore the field guide will be useful for identification of plants within many other habitats in New Mexico.

Plants are the primary producers in most ecosystems due to their ability to carry out photosynthesis. They are able to convert sunlight, water, basic nutrients, and carbon dioxide into sugars, starches, oils, and proteins. Plants provide basic foods that support the food chains in ecosystems and are used as shelter and nesting sites for the animal species that form the links in the food chain. Any major change or disruption of the plant communities and their constituent species generally leads to major changes in the animal communities.

PLANT STRUCTURE AND LIFE HISTORY

Plants have three basic life history forms in the bosque: they can be annual, biennial, or perennial. Annual plants complete their life cycles within 1 year, beginning with seed germination, through flowering, fruiting, shedding their seeds or spores, and ending with senescence and death. Biennials take 2 years to complete their life cycle, in which the first year consists mostly of vegetative growth, followed by overwintering, with flowering, fruiting, and death in the second year. Perennial plants are able to grow, flower, and fruit for 3 or more years. Trees and shrubs may live for decades or centuries. Plant species in the Rio Grande bosque are a mixture of the three life history types. The woody perennial trees and shrubs, such as Rio Grande cottonwood, saltcedar, Russian olive, and willows, provide the most visible structure of the riparian communities, while the non-woody perennial cattails, grasses, and rushes dominate the wetlands.

Plants are modular structures consisting of three basic organs: roots, stems, and leaves. Flowers are simply modified stems and leaves that have assumed the function of sexual reproduction. Plants have specialized tissues called meristems that consist of cells capable of producing new plant organs throughout the life of the individual. In fact, many plants are capable of vegetative reproduction (cloning) via root sprouts, runners, and rhizomes. Plants commonly have the ability to reproduce both vegetatively and sexually, such as sod-forming grasses, cattails, and willows. Sexual reproduction in flowering plants is not so simple or well defined as in animals. The majority of plants are bisexual (hermaphrodites), having both male and female organs present in a flower. Or they may be unisexual, having either male or female organs in a flower. Common sex expressions involving unisexual flowers are monoecy (male and female flowers separated but on the same plant), as in cattails, and dioecy (separate male and female plants), as in cottonwoods and willows.

FLOWERS AND POLLINATION

Sexual reproduction in flowering plants begins with pollination within or between flowers. Pollination is the transport of pollen produced by the stamens (male organ) to the stigma on the pistil (female organ). There are a wide variety of transport mechanisms for pollen. The most familiar modes of pollen transport involve animals such as bees, butterflies, and hummingbirds, but many plants have their pollen moved by the wind. Plants that have animals involved in pollinating their flowers must have some type of attraction to induce the pollinator to visit the flowers and thereby move the pollen. The attractants include showy petals, nectar, and scent. Plants with brightly colored flowers or floral displays are therefore commonly animal-pollinated. Wind-pollinated plants, on the other hand, do not offer pollinator attractants such as bright color or nectar. Their flowers are inconspicuous, the petals often reduced or lacking. Wind-pollinated plants produce much more pollen than animal-pollinated plants. They often form large or dense communities (e.g., grasslands and conifer forests) where the random dispersal of pollen is more effective in producing large-scale pollination. Nearly all plants whose pollen causes allergies in humans are wind-pollinated. All grasses and many of the weeds in the bosque, such as ragweed and kochia, are wind-pollinated. They are the culprits responsible for causing "hay fever." The showy goldenrods in the bosque are animal-pollinated and do not cause hay fever despite an undeserved reputation for doing so.

STEM AND FLOWER MORPHOLOGY

Morphology is the study of the form and external structure of organisms. The morphology of stems and flowers provides a majority of the characteristics used to identify and classify flowering plants.

The fundamental unit of the stem is the node. A node consists of a leaf, an axillary bud, and that portion of stem where the leaf and bud are attached. The part of the stem between nodes without leaves is called the internode. A stem is really just a series of nodes connected by internodes. The length of the internode determines whether the leaves are crowded together or are spread out along the stem. The leaf arrangement at nodes is an important identifying feature, and the common arrangements are alternate (1 leaf per node alternate

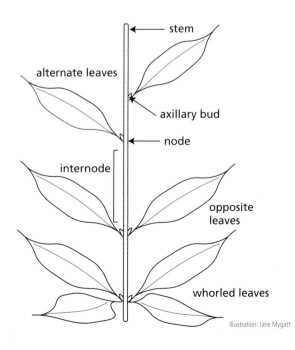

Illustration: Jane Mygatt

upward on stem), opposite (two leaves opposite each other at the node, each leaf with a bud), and whorled (three or more leaves per node). The branching of stems results from the growth of the axillary buds at nodes into new side stems. Flowers are also produced by axillary buds at nodes.

Leaf shape and leaf division are important characteristics for identifying plants. Leaf shape is one of the more variable features of plants, depending on growth conditions, position on the stem, and growth stage (juvenile versus mature). However, each species does have a specific and limited range of leaf shapes that is identifiable. Leaf shape names are derived from those used to describe geometric shapes. The most common leaf shapes are linear, lanceolate, oblanceolate, oblong, and ovate. Leaf division is the result of the leaf blade being divided into smaller leaflets, as in most ferns and beans. An undivided leaf is called simple, whereas a divided leaf is compound. Certain plants in the bosque such as those in the Legume family are characterized by having compound leaves.

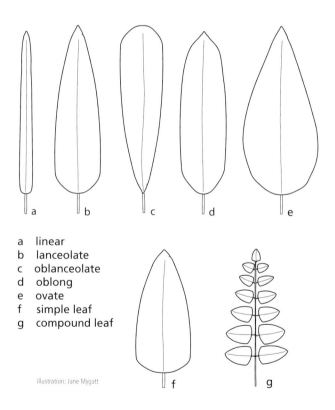

a   linear
b   lanceolate
c   oblanceolate
d   oblong
e   ovate
f   simple leaf
g   compound leaf

Illustration: Jane Mygatt

The flower is actually a modified branch or shoot with extremely short internodes. The leaves have been modified into the parts of the flowers. The floral parts are arranged in whorls, indicating that the leaf arrangement from which they were derived was also whorled. Starting from the outside, a typical flower

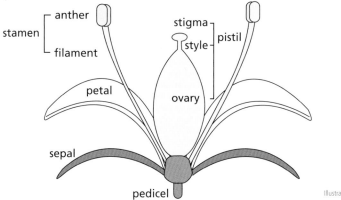

Illustration: Jane Mygatt

consists of sepals, which are generally green but sometimes colored; petals, which are usually brightly colored (in animal-pollinated plants or lacking in wind-pollinated plants); stamens, which are the male organs and produce pollen; and the pistil, which is the female organ of the flower. The pistil is made up of the stigma (where the pollen lands and germinates), the style, and the ovary, which contains the ovules. Flowers have undergone an enormous amount of evolutionary modification, and most have altered the regular pattern of a typical flower in some way. The greatest differences in flower morphology result from changes in size, shape, and symmetry or the addition, reduction, or fusion of floral components. For example, a cactus flower has numerous large and colorful sepals, which resemble petals. The sepals and petals of grasses are reduced to a few scalelike parts called the lemma and palea. Changes in symmetry are seen in many bee-pollinated plants such as mints and legumes. The Aster family is so highly modified that many individual flowers are combined into a "head," or inflorescence, that resembles a single flower. Some heads have

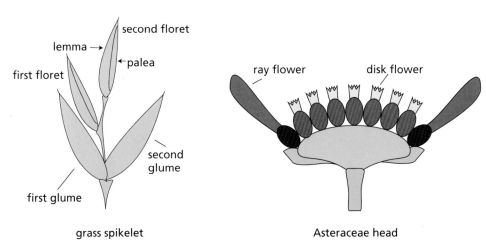

grass spikelet   Asteraceae head

Illustration: Jane Mygatt

an outer series of ray florets and an inner series of disk florets. Others may have heads composed only of ray florets or only of disk florets.

After pollination of the flowers, the pistil ripens into a fruit containing the seeds. There is a great diversity of fruit types, such as legumes, drupes, berries, and capsules. All of the stem, leaf, flower, and fruit characteristics can be used to define the species, genera, and families presented in this field guide. The "seasonality" information at the beginning of each species description reflects the typical blooming period, but it is not uncommon to find early or late blooming individuals in a population.

Ferns and Fern Allies (Monilophyta)

Ferns and fern allies (Monilophyta, formerly Pteridophyta) are the seedless vascular plants. This group consists of true ferns, horsetails, and club mosses. Ferns and their allies produce spores rather than seeds and require moist conditions to reproduce. Reproduction in the Monilophyta is more complicated than in seed plants. There is a free-living stage, the gametophyte, that grows from spores. The gametophyte contains the reproductive structures called archegonia (producing eggs) and antheridia (producing sperm). This free-living stage sets this group apart from the Anthophyta, the seed-producing plants, which dominate current landscapes. In the bosque, the only fern ally commonly seen is the horsetail.

Smooth Horsetail   (*Equisetum laevigatum*)

Taxonomy—Horsetail Family: Equisetaceae.

Identification—Perennial herb to 1 m tall; stems erect, green, hollow (except at nodes), jointed, smooth, and usually unbranched; leaf sheath green, elongate, divergent toward the apex; leaves reduced to 10–32 very small black teeth appearing as a single dark band; reproductive stems with terminal conical spore-producing structures (stroboli) up to 2.5 cm long.

Natural history—Smooth horsetail grows in moist, sandy soils. Reproduces by spores and vegetatively by rhizomes. Due to their high silica content, horsetails were once used for cleaning pots; hence their other vernacular name, scouring rush. Stroboli mature in spring through early summer.

Status—Widespread and common.

Robert Sivinski

Monocots (Monocotyledons)

Monocots form a natural evolutionary group of seed plants. The group is easily recognized by the parallel-veined leaves (grasslike), flower parts in threes or multiples thereof, and fibrous root systems. Other characteristics include pollen grains with one aperture or furrow and scattered vascular bundles in the stem, but these are best observed in the laboratory. All of the species in the bosque are herbaceous. *Monocotyledon* refers to only one initial leaf (seed leaf or cotyledon) being produced during germination.

Cosmopolitan Bulrush   (*Bolboschoenus maritimus*)

Jul–Sep

Taxonomy—Sedge Family: Cyperaceae;
Synonymy: *Schoenoplectus maritimus, Scirpus maritimus.*

Identification—Perennial grasslike herb, rhizomatous (horizontal stems belowground); stems triangular to 1.5 m tall; leaves sheathing to midstem; involucral bracts 1–4, leaflike, extending beyond the inflorescence, widest bract 1–6 mm wide; inflorescences with spikelets solitary or in compact clusters of 2–10 on 1–4 stalks; spikelets 2–40, ovoid, scales loosely overlapping.

Natural history—Cosmopolitan bulrush is a wetlands species growing in muddy flats and marshy areas. How compact or congested the inflorescences are varies considerably.

Status—Widespread and common.

Jane Mygatt

Emory's Sedge   (*Carex emoryi*)

Apr–Jul

Taxonomy—Sedge Family: Cyperaceae.

Identification—Perennial grasslike herb from long, scaly rhizomes; stems triangular, 30–110 cm long, rough; leaves 3–6 mm wide, sheathing the stem, leaf bases fringed; subtending bract leaflike, approximately the same length as the inflorescence, 3–5 mm wide; spikes erect, 5–8, the terminal 2–3 staminate, 2–4.5 cm long, lateral ones pistillate, 2–10 cm long.

Natural history—Emory's sedge is an obligate wetland species growing in calcareous (alkaline) muddy soils near riverbanks, ditches, and wetlands.

Status—Widespread and common.

Photographs: Jane Mygatt

Porcupine Sedge
(*Carex hystericina*)

May–Jul

Taxonomy—Sedge Family: Cyperaceae.

Identification—Perennial grasslike herb from short, stout rhizomes; stems triangular, 20–100 cm tall; leaves alternate, 3–7, the blades flat, 2–10 mm wide, yellow-green; leaf margins slightly curled; inflorescence of several green spikes, the terminal spike staminate 1–5 cm long × 2.5–4 mm wide, lateral spikes pistillate, 1–4, oblong, 1–6 cm long × 10–15 mm wide.

Natural history—Porcupine sedge is an obligate wetland species found in marshy areas, ditches, and other wet open sites.

Status—Widespread and common.

Jane Mygatt

Woolly Sedge
(*Carex pellita*)

Jun–Aug

Taxonomy—Sedge Family: Cyperaceae; Synonymy: *Carex lanuginosa*.

Identification—Perennial grasslike herb to 1 m tall; stems tufted from creeping rhizomes; leaves to 20 cm long, hairless, flat with a prominent ridge; inflorescence of separate male and female spikes; lower 1–3 spikes pistillate, ascending; terminal 1–3 spikes staminate, erect; seed pouch hairy.

Natural history—Woolly sedge is an obligate wetland species growing in moist calcareous (alkaline) soils, often in shallow water.

Status—Widespread and common.

Photographs: Jane Mygatt

Flat-sedges
(*Cyperus* sp.)

Jun–Sep

Taxonomy—Sedge Family: Cyperaceae.

Identification—Annual or perennial grasslike herbs, often from rhizomes; stems solid, 3-angled, unbranched, solitary or few; leaves usually basal, flat; bracts 1–7, leaflike, long, subtending the inflorescence; inflorescences on stem tips in numerous outwardly radiating spikelets.

Natural history—Flat-sedges grow in moist disturbed soil or on silty riverbanks.

Status—Widespread and common.

Jane Mygatt

Marshy Spike-rush

(Eleocharis palustris)

Jun–Sep

Taxonomy—Sedge Family: Cyperaceae; Synonymy: *Scirpus palustris.*

Identification—Perennial grasslike herb, from rhizomes, mat forming; stems solid, triangular, 30–115 cm tall; leaves reduced to sheaths; spikelets ovoid to lance shaped, 5–25 mm × 3–7 mm, brown, only 1 at the end of the stem.

Natural history—Several species of *Eleocharis* grow in New Mexico, but they all have solitary spikelets. The minute floral features require the use of keys and dissecting scopes for proper identification. Identification is almost impossible without mature achenes.

Status—Widespread and common.

Jane Mygatt

Hardstem Bulrush

(Schoenoplectus acutus)

Jun–Sep

Taxonomy—Sedge Family: Cyperaceae; Synonymy: *Scirpus acutus.*

Identification—Perennial grasslike herb, 1–3 m tall; stems 4–12 mm wide, dark olive green when fresh; leaf sheath fronts with fine featherlike fibers; inflorescence branched, often drooping; spikelets with peduncles, numerous, 6–24 mm long × 4 mm wide.

Natural history—Hardstem bulrush is a wetland obligate species and is abundant in wetlands (fresh and brackish); it often grows emergent in shallow water. Very similar to softstem bulrush (*Schoenoplectus tabernaemontani*), which also occurs in this range.

Status—Widespread and common.

Photographs: Jane Mygatt

Three-square Bulrush

(Schoenoplectus pungens)

Jun–Sep

Taxonomy—Sedge Family: Cyperaceae; Synonymy: *Scirpus pungens.*

Identification—Perennial grasslike herb, 10–200 cm tall; stems sharply triangular; inflorescence in clusters of 1–5 spikelets; bract below inflorescence looks like a continuation of the stem above the inflorescence, up to 12 cm long; spikelets cone shaped, sessile to 2 cm long.

Natural history—Three-square bulrush is an obligate wetland species, growing in marshes (fresh and brackish) and along pond margins, sandbars, and ditches, often emergent in shallow water. Very similar in appearance to *Schoenoplectus americanus*, which also has triangular stems.

Status—Widespread and common.

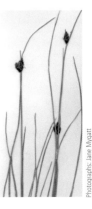

Photographs: Jane Mygatt

Yellow Flag Water Iris   (*Iris pseudacorus*) [INT]

Apr–Jun

Taxonomy—Iris Family: Iridaceae.

Identification—Perennial herb to 1.5 m tall, from rhizomes; leaves erect, swordlike, 90 cm long × 3 cm wide; flowers bright yellow, 7–10 cm across; sepals 3, spreading downward, petal-like, yellow; petals 3, beardless, upright; fruit a cylindrical 3-valved capsule, 4–8 cm long.

Natural history—Yellow flag water iris is a wetland species that grows in ditches with permanent water. It is easy to identify, being the only yellow-flowered water iris in the U.S. Introduced from Eurasia as an ornamental for water gardens, the plant has escaped cultivation and has become a noxious weed in some states. The populations along the Rio Grande ditches do not appear to be invasive.

Status—Localized and uncommon. Several permanent populations are found in the irrigation ditch near the Rio Grande Nature Center, to the north and south of I-40 paralleling the paved bike path trail.

Toad Rush   (*Juncus bufonius*)

May–Aug

Taxonomy—Rush Family: Juncaceae.

Identification—Annual tufted grasslike herbs, 5–40 cm tall; stems numerous, branching near the base; leaves basal and along the stems, flat, linear to 0.3–1.5 mm wide; inflorescences open and diffuse, usually a third or more as tall as plant; subtending bract shorter than inflorescence.

Natural history—Toad rush is an obligate wetland species growing in moist sandy to clay soil, in open areas or on muddy banks.

Status—Widespread and common.

Dudley's Rush   (*Juncus dudleyi*)

May–Aug

Taxonomy—Rush Family: Juncaceae.

Identification—Perennial tufted grasslike herb; stems 20–100 cm tall; leaves mostly basal; leaf auricles short, 0.5 mm long, yellowish; inflorescences compact and few flowered, a fifth or less as tall as the plant, 1–5 cm long; subtending bract longer than the inflorescence.

Natural history—Dudley's rush is an obligate wetland species and grows in moist sandy to clay soil.

Status—Widespread and common.

Torrey's Rush
(*Juncus torreyi*)

Jun–Sep

Taxonomy—Rush Family: Juncaceae.

Identification—Perennial grasslike herbs from creeping rhizomes; rhizomes tuberous at the nodes; stems solitary, erect, 40–100 cm tall; stem leaves 1–4; leaf sheaths with rounded auricles; inflorescence at the ends of the stem in clusters of 1–20 spherical heads, 10–15 mm wide.

Natural history—Torrey's rush grows in open wet habitats in sandy or muddy soils along the edges of ponds, ditches, and rivers. Torrey's rush is easy to identify because of its round cluster of flowers.

Status—Widespread and common.

Jennifer Anderson @USDA-NRCS PLANTS Database

Duckweed
(*Lemna* sp.)

Taxonomy—Duckweed Family: Lemnaceae.

Identification—Aquatic perennial herbs, minute, 5 mm long; colonies forming a solid cover floating on the surface of water; stems and leaves merged into a single structure called a frond; fronds flat, rounded, with a single filamentous root.

Natural history—Duckweed is found in slow-moving waters of ponds and ditches. Reproduction is nearly always vegetative: 2 daughter plants bud off from the adult plant. This allows very rapid colonization of new water. Duckweeds are flowering plants, but the flowers are exceedingly small. Nearly all species are known to reproduce sexually in appropriate conditions.

The rapid growth of duckweeds is useful for bioremediation of polluted waters. The plants are an important food for waterfowl.

Status—Widespread and common in perennial sources of slow-moving water.

Robert H. Mohlenbrock @ USDA-NRCS PLANTS Database

Indian Ricegrass
(*Achnatherum hymenoides*)

May–Aug

Taxonomy—Grass Family: Poaceae;
Synonymy: *Oryzopsis hymenoides, Stipa hymenoides.*

Identification—Perennial grass to 60 cm tall; leaf margins rolled inward; inflorescence a diffuse panicle; spikelets 1-flowered, round, disarticulation above the glumes; glumes subequal, 6–8 mm long, ovate, narrowing to a slender point, thin and papery; lemmas 3 mm long, ending in a terminal straight or twisted awn.

Natural history—Indian ricegrass was used by Native Americans, who would grind the grain into flour to make bread. The plants only grow in very sandy soils.

Status—Widespread and common.

Jane Mygatt

Redtop

(*Agrostis gigantea*) [INT]

Apr–Sep

Taxonomy—Grass Family: Poaceae.

Identification—Perennial grass to 1 m tall; leaves to 20 cm long × 3-7 mm wide; inflorescence an open panicle of 1-flowered spikelets; spikelets 2–3 mm long with 2 glumes and a single fertile lemma; glumes and lemmas awnless; disarticulation above the glumes; glumes spreading widely when mature.

Natural history—Redtop prefers moist soils in full sun. When the panicle is fully open, redtop has an airy appearance and an overall reddish purple cast to the spikelets. Commonly planted as a pasture grass, it was introduced from Europe.

Status—Widespread and common.

Threeawn

(*Aristida purpurea*)

May–Sep

Taxonomy—Grass Family: Poaceae; Synonymy: *Aristida glauca*.

Identification—Perennial bunchgrass to 75 cm tall; leaf margins curling inward; inflorescence a narrow panicle; glumes unequal in length; spikelets 1-flowered; florets with 3 awns; awns equal in length, 15-25 mm long.

Natural history—Threeawn grows in dry, open habitats, often on disturbed soils. The three-awned fruits can cause eye, nose, and mouth injuries to animals and attach easily to their fur. A morphologically variable species, several varieties of threeawn are found in New Mexico.

Status—Widespread and common.

Silver Bluestem

(*Bothriochloa laguroides* ssp. *torreyana*)

Jun–Oct

Taxonomy—Grass Family: Poaceae.

Identification—Perennial bunchgrass to 1 m tall; leaf blades smooth, 3-6 mm wide; inflorescence a silvery panicle of racemes; spikelets silky hairy, in pairs, 1 fertile, the other sterile; fertile spikelet sessile with a bent, twisted awn; sterile spikelet with long silky hairs.

Natural history—Silver bluestem grows in sandy, well-drained soils. Seed heads contain aromatic oils, and chewing is reputed to give a strong blueberry taste.

Status—Widespread and occasionally seen.

Needle Grama   (*Bouteloua aristidoides*)

Jun–Oct

Taxonomy—Grass Family: Poaceae.

Identification—Annual grass to 30 cm tall; inflorescence of 8–12 spikes, narrow, spreading to reflexed; spikelets 2–4 per spike.

Natural history—Needle grama grows in disturbed, dry, sandy soils.

Status—Widespread and common.

Six-weeks Grama   (*Bouteloua barbata*)

Jul–Sep

Taxonomy—Grass Family: Poaceae.

Identification—Annual bunchgrass to 30 cm tall, prostrate to erect; leaf blade to 6 cm long; inflorescence of 4–6 spikes in comblike array, to 25 mm long; spikelets 20–40 per spike, spreading to ascending.

Natural history—Six-weeks grama grows in open areas in sandy, often disturbed soils. Six-weeks grama is a short-lived, warm season grass.

Status—Widespread and common.

Sideoats Grama   (*Bouteloua curtipendula*)

May–Oct

Taxonomy—Grass Family: Poaceae.

Identification—Perennial grass to 75 cm tall; inflorescence of 30–50 spikes, arranged on 1 side of the main axis; spikelets 5–8 per spike; anthers red, orange, or yellow.

Natural history—Sideoats grama grows in sandy, well-drained soils and in disturbed habitats. Excellent forage grass that is tolerant of grazing.

Status—Widespread and abundant.

Blue Grama   (*Bouteloua gracilis*)

Jul–Oct

Taxonomy—Grass Family: Poaceae.

Identification—Perennial tufted grass to 50 cm tall; inflorescence of 1–3 spikes, curved at maturity; spikelets 50–70 per spike; glumes with several long hairs.

Natural history—Blue grama grows in well-drained sandy soils. Being drought tolerant, the roots are in the upper soil layers, where they can efficiently extract water, making them an effective competitor able to resist displacement by non-natives. Blue grama is commonly used in xeriscaping as a replacement for water-thirsty Kentucky bluegrass.

Status—Widespread and abundant throughout the state. Blue grama is the state grass of New Mexico.

Japanese Brome   (*Bromus japonicus*) [INT]

Jun–Sep

Taxonomy—Grass Family: Poaceae.

Identification—Annual grass to 1 m tall; leaf blade and sheath hairy; inflorescence an open, slightly nodding panicle to 30 cm long; spikelets 5–9 per spike, 1–2 cm long; lemma awn 8–10 mm long, twisted and bent at maturity.

Natural history—Japanese brome is tolerant of a variety of soil types and habitats, including disturbed ground. It can grow in semishade to full sun and in moist or dry soil. Introduced from Eurasia.

Status—Widespread and abundant.

Cheatgrass   (*Bromus tectorum*) [INT]

Apr–Jun

Taxonomy—Grass Family: Poaceae.

Identification—Annual tufted grass to 60 cm tall; leaf blade and sheath soft hairy; inflorescence an open, slightly nodding panicle, 5–20 cm long, branches with hairs; lemma with soft hairs, awn 12–15 mm long, straight.

Natural history—Cheatgrass readily spreads into open areas of high disturbance, including cultivated fields and burned areas and along the tops of ditches. An indicator of disturbed and abused land, dense populations of cheatgrass present fire hazards in the summer and fall. Introduced from Eurasia.

Status—Widespread and abundant.

Coastal Sandbur   (*Cenchrus spinifex*)

Jul–Oct

Taxonomy—Grass Family: Poaceae;
Synonymy: *Cenchrus incertus*.

Identification—Annual grass to 80 cm tall; spikelets hidden within the spiny burs; burs 4-6 mm wide with 2 spikelets; burs with 8-40 spines.

Natural history—Although a native, coastal sandbur, with its barbed spines, is considered a noxious weed in many states. The burs can inflict painful wounds and attach to clothing and the fur of animals.

Status—Widespread and common.

Showy Windmillgrass   (*Chloris virgata*)

Jun–Sep

Taxonomy—Grass Family: Poaceae.

Identification—Annual grass to 1 m tall; leaf blades flat, 10-30 cm long, 2-6 mm wide; inflorescence of 4–12 spikes arranged in a single terminal whorl; spikes 2–10 cm long.

Natural history—Showy windmillgrass grows in cultivated fields and open disturbed areas.

Status—Widespread and common.

Bermudagrass   (*Cynodon dactylon*) [INT]

Jun–Aug

Taxonomy—Grass Family: Poaceae.

Identification—Perennial grass from rhizomes; culms to 40 cm tall; inflorescence a panicle of 4 or 5 spikes; spikes 3-5 cm long; spikelets 1-flowered, borne in 2 rows along 1 side of the axis, 2-2.5 mm long.

Natural history—Bermudagrass is a very invasive weed and is common in open areas near ditches and paths. The vernacular name refers to its being introduced to the U.S. from the island of Bermuda. It can cause hay fever and dermatitis in susceptible individuals. Native to Africa.

Status—Widespread and common.

Inland Saltgrass　　　　　　　　　(*Distichlis spicata* var. *stricta*)

Jun–Oct

Taxonomy—Grass Family: Poaceae.

Identification—Perennial, dioecious grass to 30 cm tall from vigorous rhizomes; leaf blades in 2 opposite vertical rows to 10 cm long; inflorescence a dense panicle; pistillate spikelets 5–9 flowered; staminate spikelets 4–15 flowered.

Natural history—Inland saltgrass is a sod-forming grass that grows in floodplains and along irrigation ditches and tolerates saline and alkaline soils. The plants excrete salt from special glands on their leaves, and the salt crystals are easily observed. Plants are dioecious, but spikelets on both sexes are similar in appearance. The foliage of inland saltgrass can be confused with *Muhlenbergia asperifolia*, but the hairs on the upper leaf surface of inland saltgrass are lacking in *Muhlenbergia*.

Status—Widespread and abundant.

Large Barnyardgrass　　　　　　　(*Echinochloa crus-galli*) [INT]

Jul–Oct

Taxonomy—Grass Family: Poaceae.

Identification—Annual tufted grass 80–150 cm tall; stem nodes bending at abrupt angles; inflorescence a panicle of green or purple spikelets 10–30 cm long; spikelets crowded, arranged along 1 side of the axis.

Natural history—Large barnyardgrass is very weedy and is an invasive weed in some states. Prefers moist to wet sandy soils in disturbed areas.

Status—Widespread and common.

Canada Wildrye　　　　　　　　　　(*Elymus canadensis*)

Jul–Oct

Taxonomy—Grass Family: Poaceae.

Identification—Perennial grass to 1 m tall; inflorescence of dense arching spikes up to 15 cm long; spikelets of 2–4 florets at each node of the axis; lemma awns 2–4 cm long, curved.

Natural history—Canada wildrye grows in moist soils near water sources. It is non-aggressive, and large populations are uncommon.

Status—Widespread and common.

Longleaf Squirreltail
(*Elymus longifolius*)

Jun–Sep

Taxonomy—Grass Family: Poaceae; Synonymy: *Sitanion hystrix.*

Identification—Tufted perennial grass to 50 cm tall; inflorescence of bristly spikes; spikes up to 8 cm long; spikelets 2–4 flowered, sessile, in pairs at the axis; glumes linear-lanceolate, 1–2 nerved, each nerve extending into an awn up to 8 cm long.

Natural history—Longleaf squirreltail grows in sandy soils throughout the bosque in a variety of open and shaded habitats. Easily confused with foxtail barley (*Hordeum jubatum*), which has spikelets in 3s, the middle spikelet sessile and perfect, the lateral spikelets pedicellate and sterile.

Status—Widespread and abundant.

Stinkgrass
(*Eragrostis cilianensis*) [INT]

Jun–Sep

Taxonomy—Grass Family: Poaceae.

Identification—Annual grass to 40 cm tall; stems spreading to ascending, branching from the base; leaf blades 20 cm long × 7 mm wide, flat; leaf margins with minute glands; leaf bases with a fringe of hairs; inflorescence a panicle of spikelets; spikelets to 15 mm long × 2–4 mm wide, oblong-lanceolate; lemmas keeled, with minute glands along the midvein.

Natural history—Stinkgrass grows in moist sandy soil, particularly common beneath *Tamarix*. Stinkgrass produces a foul odor from the minute glands when the leaves are crushed. The tufts of hairs at the base of the leaves and the small glands on the leaf margins are diagnostic features. Introduced from Europe.

Status—Widespread and uncommon.

Tall Fescue
(*Festuca arundinacea*) [INT]

Jun–Aug

Taxonomy—Grass Family: Poaceae.

Identification—Perennial tufted grass to 75 cm tall; leaf blade 11–30 cm long, stiff; leaf base auriculate with soft hairs; inflorescence a panicle 10–35 cm long; spikelets arranged toward the ends of branches; florets 3–6 per spikelet.

Natural history—Tall fescue grows in moist to wet soils in the bosque but especially along the shaded riverbanks and ditches. Introduced to the U.S. from Europe as a cultivated crop and for lawns.

Status—Widespread and common.

Foxtail Barley   (*Hordeum jubatum*)

Apr–Sep

Taxonomy—Grass Family: Poaceae.

Identification—Perennial grass 15–30 cm tall; inflorescence a bristly spike 5–10 cm long, breaking apart when mature; spikelets in 3s, the middle spikelet sessile and perfect, the lateral spikelets pedicellate and sterile; glumes 25–150 mm long; awns of the lemmas to 60 mm long.

Natural history—Foxtail barley grows in moist, calcareous (alkaline) soils with a high water table. The seed heads with their long awns can penetrate the flesh of grazing wildlife, causing abscesses and infection. Easily confused with *Elymus longifolius*, which generally has 2–4 sessile (without pedicels) spikelets.

Status—Widespread and abundant.

Jane Mygatt

Wall Barley   (*Hordeum murinum* ssp. *glaucum*) [INT]

Apr–Jun

Taxonomy—Grass Family: Poaceae.

Identification—Loosely tufted annual grass 15–40 cm tall; leaves and nodes without hairs; sheaths often surrounding the culm, without hairs; auricles well developed to 8 mm; spikes 3–8 cm long × 7–16 mm wide, green to reddish; spikelets in 3s, the middle spikelet on a short stalk, lateral spikelets staminate (anthers only); glume margins fringed with hairs; lemmas 8–14 mm long with awns 20–50 mm long.

Natural history—Wall barley is a weedy species in disturbed, arid, sandy soils. It grows in full sun and semishaded areas. Native to the Mediterranean.

Status—Widespread and abundant.

Jane Mygatt

Rice Cutgrass   (*Leersia oryzoides*)

Jun–Sep

Taxonomy—Grass Family: Poaceae.

Identification—Rhizomatous perennial to 1 m tall; leaf blades to 23 cm long × 1 cm wide, rough on both surfaces; leaf margins rough and sharply toothed; culm nodes swollen, hairy; inflorescence a panicle of contiguous spikelets; spikelets 1-flowered, arranged on one side of the axis; glumes lacking; lemma oblong, hairy.

Natural history—Rice cutgrass may form thick patches around ponds or along riverbanks and ditches. The rough leaves snag clothes and scrape or cut skin. The seeds and rhizomes are a favorite food of waterfowl.

Status—Widespread and common.

Patrick Alexander

Bearded Sprangletop   (*Leptochloa fusca* ssp. *fascicularis*)

Jul–Sep

Taxonomy—Grass Family: Poaceae;
Synonymy: *Leptochloa fascicularis*.

Identification—Annual, with rather coarse, erect stems, 50 to 100 cm tall, forming rather large clumps, in strongly saline or alkaline soils the plants may reach only 15 cm; leaf blades firm and narrow; inflorescence a panicle of spikelike branches, panicles usually partially enclosed in the sheath and overtopped by the leaf blades; spikelets 6–10 mm long, maturing with a bluish or grayish, rarely violet, coloration; lemmas with 3 prominent nerves, the central nerve extended into a short awn 0.5–3 mm long.

Natural history—Bearded sprangletop is weedy and grows in moist or marshy soils in wetlands, often in saline or alkaline soils.

Status—Widespread and common particularly at the Bosque del Apache NWR.

Jane Mygatt

Scratchgrass   (*Muhlenbergia asperifolia*)

Jun–Oct

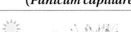

Taxonomy—Grass Family: Poaceae.

Identification—Perennial grass 10–60 cm tall, from rhizomes; leaf blade 2–6 cm long × 1–2.8 mm wide, flat and rough; inflorescence an open airy panicle, 5–15 cm; spikelets 2 mm long.

Natural history—Scratchgrass grows in dry or moist sandy soil, often in the cottonwood understory. Plants branch profusely and become bushy. The foliage may be confused with inland saltgrass (*Distichlis spicata* var. *stricta*).

Status—Widespread and abundant.

Jane Mygatt

Witchgrass   (*Panicum capillare*)

Jul–Oct

Taxonomy—Grass Family: Poaceae.

Identification—Annual tufted grass 20–60 cm tall from fibrous roots; leaf blades and sheaths with long soft hairs; ligule with a fringe of fine hairs; inflorescence a dense panicle that opens to an airy array 30 cm long; spikelets minute, 2–2.5 mm long.

Natural history—Witchgrass grows in moist soil in waste and cultivated lands, along irrigation ditches and in wet sandy places near riverbanks. The entire panicle can separate from the plant and, like a tumbleweed, reseed itself by distributing the grains as it tumbles in the wind.

Status—Widespread and common.

Jane Mygatt

Vine Mesquite   (*Panicum obtusum*)

Jun–Oct

Taxonomy—Grass Family: Poaceae.

Identification—Perennial grass to 60 cm tall from extensive array of aboveground stems; stem nodes swollen, with long hairs; leaf blade 5–20 cm long × 3–7 mm wide, mostly hairless; inflorescence of dense spikelets often in pairs along 1 side of the axis, 3–12 cm long × 1 cm wide; spikelets 3–4 mm long, ovoid, green, turning brown with age.

Natural history—Vine mesquite grows in sandy soils in full sun and semishaded areas.

Status—Widespread and common.

Jane Mygatt

Western Wheatgrass   (*Pascopyrum smithii*)

Apr–Jun

Taxonomy—Grass Family: Poaceae;
Synonymy: *Elymus smithii, Agropyron smithii.*

Identification—Perennial sod-forming grass from creeping rhizomes; culms erect, hairless; leaves often bluish, rough above, growing at a 45° angle from the stem; leaf base with small auricle, purplish; inflorescence a spike, 7–12 cm long; spikelets 6–10 flowered, closely overlapping along either side of the axis.

Natural history—Western wheatgrass can form large colonies along riverbanks, wetlands, and the moist soils near ditches.

Status—Widespread and occasional.

Photographs: Jane Mygatt

Common Reed   (*Phragmites australis*)

Aug–Oct

Taxonomy—Grass Family: Poaceae.

Identification—Perennial grass 2–4 m tall with extensive rhizomes; leaf blades broad, flat, glabrous, green or glaucous, the sheaths overlapping; inflorescence a densely flowered panicle, 15–40 cm long, tawny or purplish; spikelets 10–17 mm long, the hairs on the axis extending beyond the florets.

Natural history—Common reed tolerates moderate salinity. It is distinctive due to its colonial habit and large plumelike inflorescence. Plants parts were used for cordage, nets, mats, screens, prayer sticks, pipes, and thatching. Thick beds of reeds are effective biofilters of waterborne pollutants.

Status—Widespread and common in most of the warmer parts of the world.

Jane Mygatt

Galleta

(Pleuraphis jamesii)

Jun–Sep

Taxonomy—Grass Family: Poaceae; Synonymy: *Hilaria jamesii*.

Identification—Perennial grass 15–40 cm tall; leaves basal, stiff, and curling inward, the inside base of leaves with long hairs; inflorescence of terminal spikes 3–7 cm long, with long silky hairs; glumes of lateral spikelets bearing an awn.

Natural history—Galleta grows in well-drained, moderately alkaline soils. It prefers higher levels of moisture and is commonly found growing along the paved bike path near the Rio Grande Nature Center.

Status—Widespread and common.

Kentucky Bluegrass

(Poa pratensis) [INT]

Jun–Aug

Taxonomy—Grass Family: Poaceae.

Identification—Perennial tufted grass 20–80 cm tall; leaf tips boat shaped; inflorescence an open panicle, pyramidal or ovoid, branches whorled in groups of 3–5; spikelets 4–6 mm long.

Natural history—Kentucky bluegrass requires moist soil and is intolerant of drought. A cool season perennial, it is a common lawn grass. Native to Eurasia.

Status—Widespread and common.

Rabbitfoot Grass

(Polypogon monspeliensis) [INT]

May–Sep

Taxonomy—Grass Family: Poaceae.

Identification—Annual tufted grass to 50 cm tall; leaf blades flat, rough; inflorescence densely flowered, plumelike, 3–15 cm long; spikelets with long soft bristles.

Natural history—Rabbitfoot grass grows on wet sandy soils in sunny areas. The velvety soft inflorescence is the distinctive feature of this grass. Rabbitfoot grass produces many seeds, which are eaten by birds. Introduced from Europe.

Status—Widespread and common.

Ravenna Grass (*Saccharum ravennae*) [INT]

Aug–Oct

Taxonomy—Grass Family: Poaceae.

Identification—Perennial tufted grass to 4 m tall; leaf blades 100–150 cm long, 2 cm wide; inflorescence densely flowered, plumelike; spikelets with long soft bristles, pinkish, turning silver.

Natural history—Ravenna grass grows commonly around the riverbanks, sandbars, and marshy areas in the Albuquerque area near Tingley Beach and the Rio Grande Nature Center as far north as the Alameda Bridge. Ravenna grass can become noxious and invasive in some areas and may be confused with pampas grass (*Cortaderia*). A native to North Africa and the Mediterranean that escaped to the Middle Rio Grande bosque from plantings at the Rio Grande Zoo in Albuquerque.

Status—Localized and uncommon.

Jane Mygatt

Arabian Mediterraneangrass (*Schismus arabicus*) [INT]

Apr–Jun

Taxonomy—Grass Family: Poaceae.

Identification—Annual grass 6–16 cm tall; culms without hairs; leaf sheaths with tufts of hairs at the collar, auricles lacking; the terminal inflorescence of few-flowered panicles, 2–3.5 cm long; spikelets several flowered, 5–7 mm long.

Natural history—Arabian Mediterraneangrass is found throughout the Albuquerque bosque in open areas along the tops of ditches in highly disturbed soils. Native to southwestern Asia.

Status—Widespread and abundant.

Jane Mygatt

Patrick Alexander

Plains Bristlegrass (*Setaria leucopila*)

Jun–Oct

Taxonomy—Grass Family: Poaceae; Synonymy: *Setaria macrostachya*.

Identification—Perennial grass to 1 m tall; leaf blades flat or folded, 2–5 mm wide; leaf sheath margins with fine hairs; inflorescence terminal, spikelike, 10–25 cm long; spikelets subtended by 1–3 bristles; spikelets 2–2.7 mm long.

Natural history—Plains bristlegrass grows in dry soils. This species is often merged with *Setaria macrostachya*, which has minor differences in spikelet length and shape and has wider leaf blades.

Status—Widespread and common.

Phil Tonne

Green Bristlegrass

(Setaria viridis) [INT]

Jun–Sep

Taxonomy—Grass Family: Poaceae.

Identification—Annual grass to 1 m tall; culms branching from the base; leaf blades to 40 cm long × 2.5 cm wide, flat; leaf and sheath margins with fine hairs, often purple at the leaf base; inflorescence terminal, spikelike, to 20 cm long, erect or nodding at the tip; spikelets subtended by 1–3 stiff bristles; spikelets to 2.5 mm long.

Natural history—Green bristlegrass grows in disturbed moist soils on the edges of agriculture fields and along ditches and rivers. Native to Eurasia. Similar to plains bristlegrass (*Setaria leucopila*), which is perennial, has shorter bristles, and occurs in drier habitats in the bosque.

Status—Widespread and common.

Indiangrass

(Sorghastrum nutans)

Aug–Oct

Taxonomy—Grass Family: Poaceae.

Identification—Perennial bunched grass to 2 m tall; stem nodes with soft hairs; leaf blades flat, smooth, narrower at the base; inflorescence a plumelike panicle 10–30 cm long, coppery; spikelets in pairs at nodes of the axis; sessile spikelet perfect, sterile spikelet reduced to a hairy pedicel; fertile lemma with a bent and twisted awn, 10–15 mm.

Natural history—Indiangrass was 1 of the prominent grasses of tall-grass prairies in the central U.S. In the bosque it occurs on riverbanks or in moist swales near the river. It is an important forage grass in the Midwest and some areas of New Mexico such as the Sacramento Mountains.

Status—Widespread and common.

Johnsongrass

(Sorghum halepense) [INT]

Jun–Oct

Taxonomy—Grass Family: Poaceae.

Identification—Perennial grass to 1.5 m tall; stem nodes with short hairs; leaves attaching along the stem, 1–1.5 cm wide; inflorescence an open panicle 15–50 cm long × 3–25 cm wide; spikelets in pairs, 1 sessile and perfect, the other on a short stalk (pedicle) and sterile (stamens only); sessile spikelet with silky hairs, awned (though falling early), 10–15 mm long.

Natural history—Johnsongrass grows in moist to wet soils along ditches, riverbanks, and at the edges of irrigated fields. It is able to spread aggressively by rhizomes and is hard to eradicate once established. This species hybridizes with cultivated sorghum. Wilted Johnsongrass leaves are poisonous to livestock. Introduced from Eurasia.

Status—Widespread and abundant.

Alkali Sacaton · (*Sporobolus airoides*)

May–Oct

Taxonomy—Grass Family: Poaceae.

Identification—Perennial bunchgrass to 1 m tall × 1 m wide; leaf blades flat or curled inward, 2–4 mm wide; leaf sheath sometimes with hairs at the top; inflorescence an open panicle, 30–40 cm long, often purplish; spikelets 1-flowered, small.

Natural history—Alkali sacaton grows in various soil types and can cover large expanses of floodplains and flats. Similar to sand dropseed (*Sporobolus cryptandrus*), which has tufts of hairs at the summit of the leaf sheath. Hairs of alkali sacaton are not very obvious.

Status—Widespread and abundant.

Phil Tonne

Spike Dropseed · (*Sporobolus contractus*)

Jun–Sep

Taxonomy—Grass Family: Poaceae.

Identification—Perennial tufted grass to 40–100 cm tall; stems 1.5–3.5 mm wide at the base; leaf blade flat or curled inward, 3–6 mm wide; leaf sheaths with a cluster of white hairs at the top; inflorescence spikelike, dense, 15–50 cm long, less than 1 cm wide.

Natural history—Spike dropseed grows in sandy soils. Very similar in appearance to giant dropseed (*Sporobolus giganteus*), which is more robust at 1–2 m tall, has wider stems at the base, 2–7 mm, and generally has an inflorescence longer than 50 cm.

Status—Widespread and uncommon.

Jane Mygatt

Sand Dropseed · (*Sporobolus cryptandrus*)

May–Sep

Taxonomy—Grass Family: Poaceae.

Identification—Perennial tufted grass to 40–100 cm tall; leaf blade 6–15 cm long × 2–5 mm wide; leaf sheaths with a tuft of white hairs at the top; inflorescence an open panicle (often seen contracted or included in the sheath) 12–20 cm long; spikelets 1-flowered, 2–2.5 mm long, with-out awns.

Natural history—Sand dropseed is very drought tolerant and grows on sandy soils. The grains provide food for birds.

Status—Widespread and common.

Jane Mygatt

Giant Sacaton (*Sporobolus wrightii*)

Jun–Aug

Taxonomy—Grass Family: Poaceae;
Synonymy: *Sporobolus airoides* var. *wrightii*.

Identification—Perennial grass more than 1 m tall; leaf blade flat, 3-8 mm wide; inflorescence an open panicle, branchlets densely flowered to the base, straight, spreading; spikelets 1-flowered, 2 mm long.

Natural history—Giant sacaton grows in sandy moist soils, often in arroyo bottoms, where it forms large dense colonies. It is used as an ornamental grass in Albuquerque.

Status—Widespread and common.

Southern Cattail (*Typha domingensis*)

May–Jul

Taxonomy—Cattail Family: Typhaceae.

Identification—Perennial aquatic or semi-aquatic herb to 3 m tall; leaves basal, erect, linear, and flat; leaf sheaths gland dotted on the inside near the base; inflorescence a dense, cylindrical spike 15–25 mm wide, brown; separation between male and female sections 1-8 cm long.

Natural history—Cattails are emergent wetland species. They have separate staminate (male) and pistillate (female) flowers on the same axis, with staminate flowers above, pistillate flowers below. Similar to the broadleaf cattail, southern cattail differs in generally having a bare section of stem between the pistillate and staminate flowers, and the inside of the leaf sheath is dotted with brown glands.

Status—Widespread and abundant.

Broadleaf Cattail (*Typha latifolia*)

May–Jul

Taxonomy—Cattail Family: Typhaceae.

Identification—Perennial aquatic or semi-aquatic herb to 3 m tall; leaves basal, erect, linear, and flat; inflorescence a dense, dark brown cylindrical spike, 28–36 mm wide; usually no separation between male and female sections, staminate portion above pistillate portion.

Natural history—Cattails form the major component of early successional stages in wetlands. Spreading rapidly by rhizomes, cattails also produce copious amounts of seeds that are dispersed by wind and water. Cattail stands provide important food and cover for wildlife. Red-winged blackbirds, common yellowthroats, and American bitterns nest in cattail in the bosque.

Status—Widespread and abundant.

Dicots (Dicotyledons)

The sister group to the Monocots, Dicots have net-veined leaves, flower parts in fours or fives or multiples thereof, and taproots. They can be either woody or herbaceous. The pollen grains have three apertures or furrows, and the vascular bundles in the stem are arranged in rings. *Dicotyledon* refers to two initial leaves (seed leaves, or cotyledons) being produced during germination. The cotyledons eventually wither and the stem leaves develop.

Desert Horsepurslane (*Trianthema portulacastrum*)

Jun–Sep

Taxonomy—Stone Plant Family: Aizoaceae.

Identification—Annual succulent herb; stems prostrate to 1 m long; leaves opposite and unequal in size, leaf blade elliptic to round, to 4 cm long, petioles often as long as leaf blade; inflorescence solitary in leaf axils, flowers without petals, the 5 calyx lobes pink-purple on the inner surface.

Natural history—Desert horsepurslane grows in sandy, dry soils around waste grounds, the dry tops of ditches, and agricultural fields.

Status—Widespread and common.

Smooth Amaranth (*Amaranthus hybridus*) [INT]

Jul–Oct

Taxonomy—Amaranth Family: Amaranthaceae.

Identification—Annual herb, male and female flowers on the same plant; stems green or reddish, with or without hairs; leaves 15–30 mm long with long petioles, lanceolate, ovate, or rhombic-ovate; inflorescence in panicles of slender terminal or axillary spikes, occasionally drooping; floral bracts approximately 2 times as long as the sepals, spine tipped; male flowers at the tips of the inflorescence.

Natural history—Smooth amaranth grows in disturbed soils and waste areas throughout the bosque. Several species of *Amaranthus* look similar to *A. hybridus*, and the species is highly variable. Positive identification requires a close look at the floral structures with the use of a dissecting microscope. Similar species in the range are *Amaranthus palmeri* and *Amaranthus retroflexus*.

Status—Widespread and abundant.

Woolly Honeysweet   (*Tidestromia lanuginosa*)

Jul–Oct

Taxonomy—Amaranth Family: Amaranthaceae.

Identification—Annual herb to 50 cm long; stems generally sprawling and covered with fine white hairs; stems often reddish; leaves ovate to rounded, gray-green; inflorescences axillary, 1–3 flowered, the yellow flowers in small clusters among numerous small bracts.

Natural history—Woolly honeysweet grows in irrigated fields at the Bosque del Apache NWR and around the Elephant Butte lakeshore area. The reddish stems contrast conspicuously with the silvery leaves.

Status—Widespread and common.

Skunkbush Sumac   (*Rhus trilobata*)

Apr–Jun

Taxonomy—Sumac Family: Anacardiaceae.

Identification—Deciduous shrub to 3 m tall; leaves alternate, compound with 3 leaflets, margins coarsely toothed; flowers in dense clusters, yellowish, appearing before the leaves; fruits red at maturity with short glandular hairs, 5–7 mm wide.

Natural history—Skunkbush sumac grows in sun or semishaded areas of the bosque. In spring the small flowers appear before the leaves. In summer the foliage is green, turning to a red-orange in autumn. The fruits are sticky to the touch. The common name skunkbush refers to the foul smell released when the leaves are crushed.

Status—Widespread and common.

Water-parsnip   (*Berula erecta*)

Jun–Aug

Taxonomy—Carrot Family: Apiaceae.

Identification—Perennial aquatic herb to 1 m tall; stems grooved and hollow; leaves pinnately compound, 5–9 pairs of leaflets, leaflets oblong, leaf margins serrate; flowers white, in flat-topped arrays.

Natural history—Water-parsnip requires moist or wet soils and can grow in either semishade or full sun. Roots are poisonous.

Status—Widespread and common.

Indian-hemp   (*Apocynum cannabinum*)

May–Sep

Taxonomy—Dogbane Family: Apocynaceae.

Identification—Perennial herb to 1 m; stems reddish purple; leaves opposite, oblong, sessile, or short petioled; inflorescence greenish white, in terminal and axillary cymes, each flower subtended by small lanceolate bract, corolla small, tubular, petals 5; fruit a pair of follicles to 20 cm long, spreading or erect; seeds with tufts of silky hairs.

Natural history—Indian-hemp stems and leaves exude a milky sap that is considered toxic, but the plant was used in folk medicine and for medical purposes. The sap contains cardiac glycosides and is a deterrent to herbivores. The specific epithet *cannabinum* refers to the hemplike fibrous stems, and Indian-hemp once was used to make a strong rope by weaving together the stem's long fibers. Flowers are attractive to butterflies and many small insect pollinators.

Status—Widespread and common.

Jane Mygatt

Showy Milkweed   (*Asclepias speciosa*)

Jun–Aug

Taxonomy—Milkweed Family: Asclepiadaceae.

Identification—Perennial herb to 150 cm tall; herbage without hairs to velvety hairy; leaves gray-green, opposite, 8–20 cm long, broadly oblong to ovate, thickened; inflorescence of terminal or axillary hemispherical arrays to 8 cm wide, pink to greenish purple; calyx lobes 4–5 mm long; corolla 9–12 mm long, spreading to reflexed; corona star shaped, composed of 5 segments, known as the hoods and horns; hoods pink to whitish, spreading; horns short, inflexed; fruit of follicles 7–12 cm long, white hairy; seeds with long silky hairs.

Natural history—Showy milkweed grows in cultivated fields, wet meadows, and wet alkali soils. This species has the largest flowers of any milkweed in the bosque. Highly fragrant flowers are a nectar source for many butterflies, and the leaves are a source of food for monarch butterfly larvae. The leaves and stems contain a poisonous milky sap, which the monarch caterpillars ingest to protect themselves from predators.

Status—Widespread and frequently encountered.

Robert Sivinski

Horsetail Milkweed

(*Asclepias subverticillata*)

May–Sep

Taxonomy—Milkweed Family: Asclepiadaceae.

Identification—Perennial herb to 1 m tall; stems erect with short axillary branches; leaves linear, green, in whorls of 3 to 5 leaves at the joints, margins rolled backward; flowers in terminal hemi-spherical arrays, white to cream; flowers have 5 downward-pointing petals below a central column; fruit a follicle 2.5–7.5 cm long; seeds with tufts of silky hairs.

Natural history—Horsetail milkweed grows in sandy flats and seepage areas along wetlands, ditches, and riverbanks. The milky sap of this species and other milkweeds contains digitalis-like glycosides, which cause cardiac arrhythmias, and is toxic to animals, particularly livestock.

Status—Widespread and frequently encountered.

Robert Sivinski

Bur Ragweed

(*Ambrosia acanthicarpa*)

Jul–Sep

Taxonomy—Aster Family: Asteraceae;
Synonymy: *Franseria acanthicarpa*.

Identification—Annual herb to 80 cm tall; stems erect, branched near the base; leaves mostly alternate (opposite toward the bottom of the stem), 1–2 pinnately lobed; leaf margins entire to toothed, lower leaf surfaces with stiff hairs and glandular dotted; inflorescence of disk florets only; female heads clustered, 1-flowered in upper leaf axils; male heads 6–12, stalked, clustered along the ends of the branches; burs spiny.

Gene Jercinovic

Natural history—Bur ragweed is very common in sandy, disturbed soils in sunny areas near ditches and along the river. The species is known to cause contact dermatitis.

Status—Widespread and common.

Perennial Ragweed

(*Ambrosia psilostachya*)

Jul–Oct

Taxonomy—Aster Family: Asteraceae.

Identification—Annual or perennial herb to 1 m tall, forming extensive colonies from runnerlike roots; leaves pinnatifid, the segments toothed or shallowly lobed; flowers inconspicuous, greenish yellow, male and female flowers borne on the same inflorescence; staminate heads of 5–20 flowers above pistillate heads of 1 flower.

Natural history—Perennial ragweed grows on sandy, disturbed soils. Male flowers produce large amounts of windborne pollen, causing hay fever.

Status—Widespread and common. Although a native plant, it is considered a noxious-weed seed in several states.

Jane Mygatt

Tarragon
(Artemisia dracunculus)

Jul–Sep

Taxonomy—Aster Family: Asteraceae.

Identification—Perennial herb to 120 cm tall, often tarragon scented; stems without hairs; leaves linear to oblong, bright green to gray green; leaf margins mostly entire, others irregularly lobed; inflorescence of small clusters of nodding heads along the flowering stem; ray florets absent; disk florets pale yellow.

Natural history—Tarragon grows on sandy, well-drained alkaline soils. It grows in full sun and tolerates drought. The crushed leaves are aromatic and are used in cooking.

Status—Widespread and common.

Louisiana Wormwood
(Artemisia ludoviciana)

Jul–Sep

Taxonomy—Aster Family: Asteraceae.

Identification—Perennial aromatic herb to 80 cm tall, from rhizomes; stems gray-green, simple to widely branched, white hairy; leaves along the stem, gray-green, hairy; leaf blades linear to oblong; leaf margins entire to deeply lobed; inflorescence of small clusters of erect or nodding heads; ray florets absent; disk florets yellow, often red tinged.

Natural history—Louisiana wormwood grows in well-drained sandy soils and waste places in full sun. The leaves are aromatic, and the windborne pollen can cause hay fever.

Status—Widespread and common.

Willow Baccharis
(Baccharis salicifolia)

Jun–Sep

Taxonomy—Aster Family: Asteraceae.

Identification—Perennial dioecious shrub to 4 m tall; stems angled, branched, ascending, smooth, and leafy; leaves sticky-glutinous, alternate, entire to slightly toothed, linear-lanceolate, to 12 cm long, 4–15 mm wide, 3-nerved, nearly sessile; inflorescence in rounded terminal panicles of whitish yellow disk florets.

Natural history—Willow baccharis grows in moist alkaline soils and can form thickets along ditches. *Salicifolia* means "willow leaved," referring to the shape of the leaves.

Status—Widespread and frequently encountered.

Great Plains Seep-willow · (*Baccharis salicina*)

May–Sep

Taxonomy—Aster Family: Asteraceae.

Identification—Perennial dioecious shrub to 2 m tall; stems much branched, glabrous and glutinous; leaves oblong to oblanceolate, 3–4 cm long, 0.5–1.0 cm wide, margins entire to slightly toothed; inflorescence of terminal pyramid-like clusters; female heads of 25–30 disk florets, the corolla hidden by long, white hairlike bristles; the male heads have shorter bristles that extend barely above the involucral bracts.

Natural history—Great Plains seep-willow usually grows in disturbed soils, often in moist or dry, sandy, subsaline soils.

Status—Localized and frequently encountered.

Jane Mygatt

Desert Marigold · (*Baileya multiradiata*)

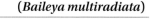

May–Oct

Taxonomy—Aster Family: Asteraceae.

Identification—Perennial herb to 40 cm tall; herbage densely woolly-hairy; leaves alternate, deeply lobed; peduncles 10–30 cm long; flower heads solitary with ray and disk florets, bright yellow.

Natural history—Desert marigold grows in sandy soils in full sun and is drought tolerant. Commonly used in wildflower seed mixes and very useful for xeriscaping.

Status—Widespread and occasionally encountered.

Jane Mygatt

Chocolate Flower, Greeneyes · (*Berlandiera lyrata*)

May–Oct

Taxonomy—Aster Family: Asteraceae.

Identification—Perennial herb to 40 cm tall; herbage hairy; leaves deeply lobed to 14 cm long with long petioles; inflorescence of ray and disk florets; ray florets yellow with darker veins, 10–15 mm long; disk florets yellowish with dark stamens.

Natural history—Chocolate flower grows in sandy soils and dry, open areas. The unopened disk florets are bright green and the source of another common name, greeneyes. Flowers are strongly chocolate scented. The flowers were mixed with sausage as seasoning at Acoma and Laguna pueblos.

Status—Widespread and occasionally encountered.

Jane Mygatt

Nodding Beggarticks

(Bidens cernua)

Aug–Oct

Taxonomy—Aster Family: Asteraceae.

Identification—Annual herb to 1 m tall; stems with short, stiff hairs; leaves lanceolate to 20 cm long, margins entire to serrate; inflorescence of radiate (occasionally all discoid) heads, nodding in fruit; ray florets yellow, ovate, 10–15 mm long; disk florets yellow; phyllaries leafy, 5–10, spreading or reflexed to 25 mm long; fruit an achene with 4 barbed awns.

Natural history—Nodding beggarticks grow in moist muddy ground and seepage areas along the banks of ponds, ditches, and rivers. The barbed fruits readily attach to clothing and the fur of animals.

Status—Widespread and frequently encountered.

Patrick Alexander

Mexican Devilweed

(Chloracantha spinosa)

Jun–Sep

Taxonomy—Aster Family: Asteraceae; Synonymy: *Aster spinosus.*

Identification—Perennial herb, colonial by rhizomes; stems erect, glabrous, nearly leafless, green, to 1 m tall, axillary branches often transformed to thorns; leaves early deciduous, stem leaves reduced to a few minute scales, spines often present in or above leaf axils; heads radiate, solitary at ends of short branches.

Natural history—Mexican devilweed grows in sandy, disturbed soil and is abundant along the tops of ditch banks.

Status—Widespread and common.

Photographs: Jane Mygatt

Canadian Horseweed

(Conyza canadensis)

Jun–Oct

Taxonomy—Aster Family: Asteraceae.

Identification—Annual or biennial herb to 1 m tall; leaves alternate, linear to oblanceolate, 2–10 cm long, margins entire to coarsely few toothed, hispid; inflorescence in narrow panicles; ray florets white, minute, disk florets yellow to light pink.

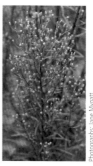

Natural history—Canadian horseweed grows in sandy, disturbed soil and waste areas. This native plant is considered an invasive species in several states.

Status—Widespread and abundant.

Photographs: Jane Mygatt

Sand-daisy   (*Dieteria canescens*)

Jul–Oct

Taxonomy—Aster Family: Asteraceae; Synonymy: *Machaeranthera canescens*.

Identification—Annual, biennial, or short-lived perennial herb to 70 cm tall; herbage variable, from smooth, to finely hairy, to glandular; leaf blades linear to lance shaped; leaf margin entire to toothed; heads numerous, ray florets 10–25, blue-purple.

Natural history—Sand-daisy grows in dry, sandy soil, often in the cottonwood understory or in waste ground. Other purple-flowered daisies in the bosque look similar to the sand-daisy, including Tahoka-daisy (*Machaeranthera tanacetifolia*) and small-flower spine-aster (*Arida parviflora*).

Status—Widespread and common.

Robert Sivinski

False Daisy   (*Eclipta prostrata*) [INT]

May–Oct

Taxonomy—Aster Family: Asteraceae.

Identification—Annual herb to 50 cm; stems erect or sprawling, reddish purple with short, flat, upturned hairs; leaves opposite, the leaf blades 1- or 3-nerved, linear to lance shaped, with widely spaced teeth; inflorescence of white ray and disk florets, occurring alone or in clusters of 2–3.

Natural history—False daisy grows in mud at the edges of water sources. Introduced from Asia, now a widespread weed.

Status—Widespread and occasionally encountered.

Patrick Alexander

Rabbitbrush   (*Ericameria nauseosa*)

Aug–Oct

Taxonomy—Aster Family: Asteraceae.

Identification—Shrub to 1 m tall; stems erect, white to green, with a dense covering of woolly hairs; leaves linear and entire, gray-green, with or without hairs; flowers in large clusters, yellow; heads discoid.

Natural history—Rabbitbrush grows in open, dry areas in the bosque and is very showy when it blooms. The plant has a variety of medicinal and miscellaneous uses. The flowers produce a yellow dye, and the plant is a source of latex, used for making rubber.

Status—Widespread and common.

Robert Sivinski

Spreading Fleabane   (*Erigeron divergens*)

May–Sep

Top photographs: Patrick Alexander

Taxonomy—Aster Family: Asteraceae.

Identification—Annual to short-lived perennial herb to 50 cm tall; stems erect to ascending with dense spreading hairs; basal leaves spatulate to oblanceolate, falling early; stem leaves linear to oblanceolate, 1–2 cm long, margin entire or with 2–3 pairs of teeth, upper surface hairy, sometimes sparsely glandular; inflorescence solitary or few (nodding as buds), ray florets more than 100, white to purple; disk florets yellow.

Natural history—Spreading fleabane grows in dry, sandy waste ground or disturbed areas. Other species of *Erigeron* occur in the Middle Rio Grande, including *E. flagellaris*, *E. bellidiastrum*, and *E. philadelphicus*. *Erigeron flagellaris* can be distinguished by its small size (to 15 cm) and the leafy, prostrate runners that form dense matted clones. *Erigeron philadelphicus* can be distinguished by the many (3–35) flower heads per stalk. *Erigeron bellidiastrum* is recognized by the up-curved hairs of the stem, (which are spreading in *E. divergens*) and relatively few (22–70) ray florets.

Status—Widespread and common.

Jane Mygatt

Western Goldentop   (*Euthamia occidentalis*)

Aug–Oct

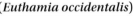

Taxonomy—Aster Family: Asteraceae; Synonymy: *Solidago occidentalis*.

Identification—Perennial herb from rhizomes; stems much branched, erect to 2 m tall, glabrous, resinous-glutinous above; leaves linear-lanceolate, sessile, entire, 3–5 nerved, glandular-punctate; inflorescence in small cymose clusters, heads contain 15–25 ray florets and 7–14 disk florets, yellow, conspicuous.

Jane Mygatt

Natural history—Western goldentop grows in moist to wet soils. *Euthamia* was formerly included with the genus *Solidago*, but the arrangement of heads and gland-dotted leaves distinguish it from *Solidago*.

Status—Widespread and frequently encountered.

Indian Blanket (*Gaillardia pulchella*)

Jun–Aug

Taxonomy—Aster Family: Asteraceae.

Identification—Annual herb to 60 cm tall; leaves alternate, basal and along the stem; leaves linear to oblong, leaf margins entire to toothed or wavy; heads radiate, rays 10–20 mm long, yellow, often reddish toward the center, disk florets reddish purple.

Natural history—Indian blanket grows in sandy, well-drained soils in sunny areas and is drought tolerant. Attractive to a variety of butterfly and other insect pollinators.

Status—Widespread and frequently encountered.

Jane Mygatt

Curlycup Gumweed (*Grindelia squarrosa*)

Jul–Oct

Taxonomy—Aster Family: Asteraceae.

Identification—Biennial or perennial herbs to 100 cm tall; stems erect, often reddish, without hairs; leaf shape variable, ranging from linear to oval; leaf margins usually toothed; leaf surfaces glandular dotted and sticky; heads radiate or discoid, outer bracts recurved and very gummy, florets bright yellow.

Natural history—Curlycup gumweed grows in dry, disturbed ground, especially old fields or arroyo bottoms, and is easily recognized by the gummy, recurved bracts. Gumweed shows promise as a source for industrial resins.

Status—Widespread and frequently encountered.

Gene Jercinovic

Broom Snakeweed (*Gutierrezia sarothrae*)

Jun–Oct

Taxonomy—Aster Family: Asteraceae.

Identification—Small shrub to 60 cm; stems erect, branched; leaves basal and on stems, basal and lower stem leaves falling before flowering, upper stem leaves linear and sometimes clustered in bundles; flowers in compact cymes; ray florets 3–8 per head, yellow; disk florets 3–9 per head, yellow.

Natural history—Broom snakeweed grows in dry, open habitats. It responds well to disturbance such as overgrazing. A great deal of money has been spent in New Mexico on snakeweed control; however, it is not a problem on land with little disturbance.

Status—Widespread and common.

Patrick Alexander

Robert Sivinski

Annual Sunflower   (*Helianthus annuus*)

Jul–Sep

Taxonomy—Aster Family: Asteraceae.

Identification—Annual herb; stems coarse and hispid, simple or branched to 3 m tall; leaves alternate above, opposite below, ovate to ovate-lanceolate, serrate, long petioled; heads radiate, ray florets yellow and sterile, disk florets brownish yellow.

Natural history—Annual sunflower grows in dry or moist soil and can tolerate drought and full sun or semishaded locations. The plants are pollinated by bees and flies, and the seeds provide food for birds.

Status—Widespread and common.

Blueweed   (*Helianthus ciliaris*)

Jun–Oct

Taxonomy—Aster Family: Asteraceae.

Identification—Perennial herb to 70 cm tall, from rhizomes, often forming large colonies; stems smooth, with a bluish waxy coat; leaves opposite, blue-green, 1- or 3-nerved, linear to lanceolate, leaf margins wavy; heads radiate, ray florets 10–18, golden yellow, disk florets 35+, reddish.

Natural history—Blueweed grows in moist, alkaline soil or irrigated fields in and around the disturbed regions near the ditches. It can propagate vegetatively from pieces of rhizome and, although native, is considered a noxious weed in some states.

Status—Widespread and common.

Pecos Sunflower (*Helianthus paradoxus*)

Aug–Oct

Taxonomy—Aster Family: Asteraceae.

Identification—Annual herb to 2 m tall; stems branched above, usually with short stiff hairs; leaves opposite below, alternate above, lanceolate with 3 prominent veins, the surface rough; leaf base tapers to a short petiole; leaf margin entire to few toothed on larger leaves; flower heads solitary; ray florets 12–20, yellow.

Natural history—Pecos sunflower requires brackish, water-saturated soils and grows only in a few wetland habitats in New Mexico. Two other annual sunflowers in the Middle Rio Grande are similar in appearance. Pecos sunflower is an ancient hybrid species whose parents are annual sunflower (*Helianthus annuus*) and prairie sunflower (*H. petiolaris*), both annual species. Pecos sunflower differs from annual sunflower in having narrower leaves and smaller flower heads. Pecos sunflower differs from prairie sunflower in having shorter petioles and differences in small floral characters.

Status—Restricted distribution and rare. Pecos sunflower is listed as a federally threatened species, which automatically makes it a New Mexico state endangered species. Activities leading to the degradation or destruction of habitat include groundwater depletion, water diversion, and saltcedar invasion.

Hairy Golden-aster (*Heterotheca villosa*)

May–Oct

Taxonomy—Aster Family: Asteraceae; Synonymy: *Chrysopsis villosa*.

Identification—Perennial herb to 50 cm tall; herbage variously hairy, often sparsely glandular; leaves alternate, entire; leaf blade variable in shape from linear to spatulate to oblong; heads cymose, ray and disk florets yellow.

Natural history—Hairy golden-aster grows in open sunny habitats in sandy soil.

Status—Widespread and frequently encountered.

Yellow Woollywhite (*Hymenopappus flavescens* var. *canotomentosus*)

Jul–Aug

Taxonomy—Aster Family: Asteraceae.

Identification—Biennial herb 30–90 cm tall; stems erect, herbage variously woolly; leaves basal and along the stem, twice pinnate with linear segments, the ultimate segments 1–2 mm wide; heads many per stem, discoid; corolla glandular, yellow.

Natural history—Yellow woollywhite grows in dry, sandy soils in full sun or semishaded areas.

Status—Widespread and occasionally encountered.

Goldenweed, Southern Jimmyweed (*Isocoma pluriflora*)

July–Oct

Taxonomy—Aster Family: Asteraceae;
Synonymy: *Haplopappus pluriflorus*.

Identification—Perennial subshrub; stems erect, glabrous, or finely pubescent, 20-120 cm tall; leaves crowded on the stems, alternate, sessile, oblanceolate to nearly linear, 10-40 mm long, often with glandular hairs, margins entire; heads discoid only, in terminal flat-topped clusters, disk florets bright yellow.

Natural history—Goldenweed grows in calcareous, sandy, or silty soils, commonly on roadsides or mesquite flats. It also grows on gypsum outcrops in moist habitats. Although it begins flowering in midsummer, the height of the blooming season is in late summer and early fall. It is particularly common south from Bernardo.

Status—Widespread and common.

Prickly Lettuce (*Lactuca serriola*) [INT]

Jul–Oct

Taxonomy—Aster Family: Asteraceae.

Identification—Annual or biennial herb to 2 m tall with milky sap in stems, leaves, and roots; stems branched above and sparsely bristled below; leaves alternate, the lobes arrowhead shaped, clasping at the base, to 20 cm long, midribs of the lower surface prickly; flowers yellow.

Natural history—Prickly lettuce grows in dry or moist, sandy soils. Readily hybridizes with cultivated lettuce (*Lactuca sativa*). The young leaves can be used in salads. Introduced from Europe.

Status—Widespread and abundant.

Tansyleaf Aster (*Machaeranthera tanacetifolia*)

Apr–Oct

Taxonomy—Aster Family: Asteraceae;
Synonymy: *Aster tanacetifolius*.

Identification—Annual herb to 50 cm tall; herbage glandular-hairy; leaves alternate, pinnately divided 2-3 times into linear to oblong segments, spine tipped; inflorescence of solitary heads, 2.5 cm wide; ray florets 15-25, usually 10-15 mm long, purple; disk florets yellow.

Natural history—Tansyleaf aster grows in open, dry, well-drained sandy soils.

Status—Widespread and common.

Blue Lettuce   (*Mulgedium pulchellum*)

Jun–Sep

Taxonomy—Aster Family: Asteraceae;
Synonymy: *Lactuca tatarica* var. *pulchella*.

Identification—Annual or biennial herb to 1 m tall; stems single, erect, branching from the base; stems and leaves with milky sap when crushed; leaves basal and along the stem; leaf blades ovate to lanceolate, the margins entire to toothed to pinnately lobed; heads in open clusters, ray florets blue.

Natural history—Blue lettuce grows in moist, well-drained soil in full sun or semishaded edges of ditches and the river.

Status—Widespread and uncommon.

Gene Jercinovic

Cottonbatting Plant   (*Pseudognaphalium stramineum*)

Jun–Sep

Taxonomy—Aster Family: Asteraceae;
Synonymy: *Gnaphalium stramineum, Gnaphalium chilense.*

Identification—Annual or biennial herb to 60 cm tall; herbage white woolly; leaves narrowly lanceolate to linear, 2–8 cm long × 2–5 mm wide; heads in terminal round clusters 1–2 cm wide; flowers yellow.

Natural history—Cottonbatting plant grows in disturbed sites but prefers sandy, moist soil.

Status—Widespread and occasionally encountered.

Jane Mygatt

Woolly Paperflower   (*Psilostrophe tagetina*)

May–Aug

Taxonomy—Aster Family: Asteraceae.

Identification—Perennial herb to 50 cm tall; herbage with long silky hairs; leaves basal and along the stem; basal leaves generally ovate to lanceolate, to 10 cm long; stem leaves linear to lanceolate; heads in cymes; ray florets 3 (may be up to 5), 5–9 mm long, 3-lobed, yellow.

Natural history—Woolly paperflower grows in sandy, compact, silty soils in dry, open, disturbed sites. The common name, paperflower, refers to the dry, papery appearance of the ray flowers that remain long after the plant has finished flowering.

Status—Widespread and frequently encountered.

Photographs: Jane Mygatt

Green Mexican-hat, Short-rayed Coneflower (*Ratibida tagetes*)

Jun–Sep

Taxonomy—Aster Family: Asteraceae.

Identification—Perennial herb to 50 cm tall; leaves usually once or twice pinnately divided into linear segments, glandular dotted; heads radiate; ray florets 5-10, yellow or reddish, reflexed; disk florets greenish yellow to purplish, stamens dark.

Natural history—Green Mexican-hat grows in sandy, moist, or dry, well-drained soil. Tolerant of drought and alkaline soils and prefers full sun.

Status—Widespread and occasionally encountered.

Jane Mygatt

Abert's Creeping Zinnia (*Sanvitalia abertii*)

Aug–Sep

Taxonomy—Aster Family: Asteraceae.

Identification—Annual herb to 30 cm tall; leaves opposite, leaf blade lanceolate; heads solitary, with ray and disk florets; ray florets with notched tips, yellow; disk florets greenish yellow.

Natural history—Abert's creeping zinnia grows in sandy soils, particularly in arroyos. It is used medicinally by the Navajo people for colds, fever, and toothache.

Status—Widespread and occasionally encountered.

Patrick Alexander

False Salsify (*Scorzonera laciniata*) [INT]

May–Aug

Taxonomy—Aster Family: Asteraceae.

Identification—Annual, biennial, or perennial herb; stems erect, with milky juice; leaves basal and along stems; basal leaves linear to ovate, often deeply divided into linear segments, upper leaves reduced; flowers solitary, composed of ray florets, yellow.

Natural history—False salsify grows in sandy, well-drained soils in open and semishaded areas and is spreading quickly throughout the bosque. Recently introduced into New Mexico; originally from the Mediterranean.

Status—Widespread and common.

Jane Mygatt

Threadleaf Groundsel

(*Senecio flaccidus*)

Jun–Oct

Taxonomy—Aster Family: Asteraceae; Synonymy: *Senecio douglasii* var. *longilobus*, *Senecio filifolius*, *Senecio longilobus*.

Identification—Perennial herb to 120 cm tall; stems and leaves with white woolly hairs; leaves pinnately divided into linear segments; flower heads numerous, composed of ray and disk florets, yellow; phyllaries (subtending bracts of the flower head) in a single series and equal in length, subtended by small bracts.

Natural history—Threadleaf groundsel grows in dry, open habitats. All species of *Senecio* contain a poisonous alkaloid that is a potent liver toxin. Toxic to humans and livestock.

Status—Widespread and common.

Photographs: Jane Mygatt

Riddell's Groundsel

(*Senecio riddellii*)

Jun–Oct

Taxonomy—Aster Family: Asteraceae.

Identification—Perennial herb or subshrub to 100 cm tall; stems and leaves green, without hairs; leaves linear or pinnately divided into linear segments; flower heads numerous, composed of ray and disk florets, yellow; phyllaries in single series and equal in length, subtended by small bracts.

Natural history—Riddell's groundsel grows in sandy soils in open or semishaded areas. It differs from threadleaf groundsel in being glabrous (no hairs on herbage). Riddell's groundsel is very similar to *Senecio spartioides*, with minor differences in the shape of the base of the inflorescence and size of the subtending bracts. Like all groundsels, it is toxic to humans and livestock if eaten.

Status—Widespread and frequently encountered.

Photographs: Phil Tonne

Tall Goldenrod

(*Solidago altissima* ssp. *gilvocanescens*)

Jul–Oct

Taxonomy—Aster Family: Asteraceae; Synonymy: *Solidago canadensis* var. *gilvocanescens*.

Identification—Perennial herb to 2 m, from rhizomes; stems with short hairs throughout; leaves alternate, leaf blades oblanceolate, entire to toothed, 3-nerved; inflorescence of numerous heads in pyramidal arrays; heads radiate; ray florets 8–13 per head, yellow; disk florets 3–6 per head, yellow.

Natural history—Tall goldenrod grows in moist, sandy soils. Goldenrod is insect pollinated and not a source of pollen that causes hay fever.

Status—Widespread and common.

Jane Mygatt

Spiny-leaf Sowthistle

(*Sonchus asper*) [INT]

May–Oct

Taxonomy—Aster Family: Asteraceae.

Identification—Annual herb to 120 cm; stems erect, hollow, with milky juice; leaves lanceolate to oblong, leaf bases auriculate, auricles often curled and rounded, leaf margins pinnately lobed, prickly toothed; heads loosely cymose, of ligulate florets (no disk florets), yellow to orange.

Natural history—Spiny-leaf sowthistle is common on moist or wet sandy and muddy soils and also tolerates drier, disturbed habitats. A weedy species introduced from Europe.

Status—Widespread and common.

Photographs: Jane Mygatt

White Heath Aster

(*Symphyotrichum ericoides*)

Jul–Oct

Taxonomy—Aster Family: Asteraceae; Synonymy: *Aster ericoides*.

Identification—Perennial herb to 80 cm with creeping rhizomes; herbage with stiff hairs; leaves linear to oblong, most of the lower leaves withered by flowering time; leaf blades and margins with hairs; flower stalks with many spreading leaflike bracts; heads numerous in crowded arrays; ray florets 10–18 per head, 6–12 mm long, white; disk florets yellow.

Natural history—White heath aster grows in sandy, moist soil. Very similar to prairie aster (*Symphyotrichum falcatum* var. *commutatum*), which has 20–35 ray florets per head and longer rays, 18–30 mm long.

Status—Widespread and frequently encountered.

Jane Mygatt

Common Dandelion   (*Taraxacum officinale*) [INT]

May–Sep

Taxonomy—Aster Family: Asteraceae.

Identification—Perennial herbs to 30 cm; leaves all basal in mounded rosettes, deeply triangular lobed, toothed, with milky latex; heads solitary, ligulate, yellow; seeds with hairs that are easily dispersed by wind.

Natural history—Common dandelion is a weedy species that grows in a variety of disturbed habitat types. The young leaves are edible and used in salads. Often used in herbal medicine. Introduced from Eurasia.

Status—Widespread and common.

Photographs: Patrick Alexander

Navajo Tea, Greenthread   (*Thelesperma megapotamicum*)

May–Oct

Taxonomy—Aster Family: Asteraceae.

Identification—Perennial herb to 80 cm; leaves opposite, pinnately dissected into linear segments; heads on long peduncles; flowers discoid, yellow brownish.

Natural history—Navajo tea grows in dry, semishaded or open habitats. The stems, leaves, and flowering heads are collected and used for brewing tea. Reputed to have medicinal properties.

Status—Widespread and occasionally encountered.

Jane Mygatt

Annual Townsend Aster   (*Townsendia annua*)

Jun–Aug

Taxonomy—Aster Family: Asteraceae.

Identification—Annual herb; stems prostrate or decumbent; herbage with short gray hairs; leaves oblanceolate, up to 3 cm long; heads terminal, sessile on the stems or on very short peduncles; ray florets pistillate, 12–30, fertile, white to pink; disk florets perfect, fertile, yellow, sometimes pink tipped.

Photographs: Jane Mygatt

Natural history—Annual Townsend aster grows on sandy flats, arroyo bottoms, and disturbed ground.

Status—Widespread and common.

Yellow Salsify   (*Tragopogon dubius*) [INT]

May–Sep

Taxonomy—Aster Family: Asteraceae.

Identification—Biennial or sometimes an annual herb
to 1 m; leaves long and grasslike; stems and leaves
with milky juice; peduncle inflated below the flower
head; flower heads large, composed of ligulate florets,
yellow; seed heads are similar to those of the dandelion but much larger and whitish tan in color.

Photographs: Jane Mygatt

Natural history—Yellow salsify grows in open or semishaded habitats with disturbed soils. There are 2 other
related species of salsify (*Tragopogon*). Peduncles of
meadow salsify (*Tragopogon pratensis*) are not swollen below the flower head; leek salsify (*Tragopogon
porrifolius*) is similar but has purple flowers. All were
introduced from Europe.

Status—Widespread and common.

Lacy Sleep-daisy   (*Xanthisma spinulosum*)

May–Sep

Taxonomy—Aster Family: Asteraceae;
Synonymy: *Machaeranthera pinnatifida,
Haplopappus spinulosus*.

Identification—Perennial herb to 60 cm tall with a woody
stem base; stems branched, with or without hairs; leaves
alternate, narrow, pinnate to bi-pinnately lobed to 6 cm
long, lobes bristle tipped; inflorescence terminal with
yellow ray and disk florets; ray florets 8–10 mm long.

Jane Mygatt

Natural history—Lacy sleep-daisy grows in dry, open
habitats in sandy soils. The species is highly variable and
contains a number of varieties.

Status—Widespread and common.

Rough Cocklebur   (*Xanthium strumarium*)

Jun–Aug

Taxonomy—Aster Family: Asteraceae;
Synonymy: *Xanthium strumarium* var. *canadense*.

Identification—Annual herb to 1 m tall; stems and leaves
hairy and rough; leaves alternate, broadly triangular; male
and female flower heads separate, male heads in terminal
clusters, female heads in axillary clusters, white or greenish; fruits oval with spreading and hooked prickles.

Robert Sivinski

Natural history—Rough cocklebur grows in deep, sandy
soils most commonly in the floodplain. This plant is easily
dispersed by animals as the heads have hooked bristles
and the fruits have 2 strong hooked beaks.

Status—Widespread and common.

Desert Willow   (*Chilopsis linearis*)

May–Sep

Taxonomy—Bignonia Family: Bignoniaceae.

Identification—Large deciduous shrub to small tree; leaves alternate, simple and entire, long and linear, willowlike; flowers showy and fragrant, somewhat 2-lipped, upper lips 3-toothed, lower lips 2-toothed, pink to lavender; fruits of long capsules with numerous winged seeds.

Natural history—Desert willow grows along washes or in arroyo bottoms but apparently was planted both at the Rio Grande Nature Center and near the visitor center at the Bosque del Apache NWR. Although the common name refers to it as a willow (owing to its linear leaves and habitat preference), it is not related to the willow but is in the same family as the catalpa tree. It is often planted as an ornamental in southwestern gardens, and the pleasantly scented flowers are visited by hawk moths in the evening.

Status—Widespread throughout the lower ⅔ of the state and infrequent in the Middle Rio Grande riparian floodplain.

Thick-sepal Cat's-eye   (*Cryptantha crassisepala*)

Apr–Jul

Taxonomy—Borage Family: Boraginaceae.

Identification—Annual herb to 10–15 cm tall; herbage coarsely hairy; leaves alternate, oblanceolate, 20–30 mm long; flowers small, in terminal scorpioid (coiled) arrays, white.

Natural history—Thick-sepal cat's-eye grows in highly disturbed soils in full sun along the tops of ditches and levees and along the dirt trails.

Status—Widespread and common.

Seaside Heliotrope   (*Heliotropium curassavicum*)

Apr–Oct

Taxonomy—Borage Family: Boraginaceae.

Identification—Perennial prostrate herb from stout creeping roots; stems branched, spreading; leaves fleshy, glabrous, linear-oblong; flowers inconspicuous, in terminal scorpioid (coiled) cymes, white.

Natural history—Seaside heliotrope grows in saline and alkaline soils, often in the beds of dried ponds. It is widespread throughout the world and grows on coastal beaches.

Status—Widespread and occasionally encountered.

Spiny Sheepbur (*Lappula occidentalis*)

Apr–Jun

Taxonomy—Borage Family: Boraginaceae.

Identification—Annual herb 20–60 cm tall; stems erect, branched; herbage hairy; leaves linear to oblong, 10–20 mm long; flowers on elongated flowering stems (racemes); racemes with leafy bracts; corolla funnelform, 5-lobed, 2–3 mm long, white to pale blue.

Natural history—Spiny sheepbur grows in highly disturbed soils in full sun along the tops of ditches and levees along the dirt trails. The hooked spines on the fruits readily attach to clothing and animal fur.

Status—Widespread and common.

Jane Mygatt

Western Tansymustard (*Descurainia pinnata*)

Apr–Jun

Taxonomy—Mustard Family: Brassicaceae.

Identification—Annual herbs to 70 cm tall; stems erect, branching; herbage densely hairy (some varieties glandular); leaves alternate, pinnate to deeply pinnatifid; inflorescence very compact in flower, elongating in fruit; flowers yellow; fruit a club-shaped silique, usually less than 12 mm long and 2 mm wide.

Natural history—Western tansymustard grows in dry, open, disturbed habitats, especially along the tops of ditches. The Mustard family can be recognized by the number and arrangement of petals and sepals: members of the family always have 4 petals, 4 sepals, and 6 stamens. The fruits of the Mustard family are either long and slender (siliques), as in *Descurainia*, or broader than long (silicles), as in *Dimorphocarpa*.

Status—Widespread and abundant.

Robert Sivinski

Flixweed (*Descurainia sophia*) [INT]

Apr–Jun

Taxonomy—Mustard Family: Brassicaceae.

Identification—Annual herb to 100 cm tall; stems with star-shaped hairs; leaves alternate, fernlike (bi-pinnately or tri-pinnately divided), the segments linear to 1 mm wide; petals yellow; fruit a silique (long and linear), 25 mm long, 1 mm wide.

Natural history—Flixweed grows in open areas, especially along the tops of ditches. Very weedy and similar to *Descurainia pinnata*, differing in fruit size and leaf characteristics. Introduced from Europe.

Status—Widespread and abundant.

Photographs: Patrick Alexander

Spectaclepod (*Dimorphocarpa wislizenii*)

Apr–Sep

Taxonomy—Mustard Family: Brassicaceae; Synonymy: *Dithyrea wislizenii.*

Identification—Annual herb to 50 cm tall; herbage with minute star-shaped hairs; leaves lanceolate, grayish; petals white, 5-8 mm long, borne in elongated racemes; fruit a silicle.

Natural history—Spectaclepod grows in sandy soils in disturbed habitats. The fruits are generally rounded, usually not more than 2 times as long as wide. The common name refers to the fruits' resemblance to a miniature pair of eyeglasses.

Status—Widespread and abundant.

Robert Sivinski

Broad-leaf Pepperweed (*Lepidium latifolium*) [INT]

Apr–Jun

Taxonomy—Mustard Family: Brassicaceae.

Identification—Perennial herb to 1 m tall; stems and leaves glaucous; flowers small, borne in dense clusters at the tops of the stems; petals 4, white; fruit a silicle to 2 mm long.

Natural history—Broad-leaf pepperweed tolerates a wide range of ecological sites in riparian zones but is most often found in ditch systems. It can tolerate soils with high salt concentrations. Introduced from Europe and western Asia, broad-leaf pepperweed is on the noxious weed list for New Mexico.

Status—Widespread and common.

Steve Shoup

Watercress (*Nasturtium officinale*) [INT]

Apr–Aug

Taxonomy—Mustard Family: Brassicaceae; Synonymy: *Rorippa nasturtium-aquaticum.*

Identification—Aquatic perennial herb; stems to 40 cm long, trailing and rooting at the nodes, usually ends of stems are held above the water; leaves mostly pinnately compound; leaflets with wavy margins, terminal lobe larger than lateral lobes; flowers small, petals 4, white; fruits cylindrical and slightly curved, 10–30 mm long and 2 mm wide.

Natural history—Watercress grows in clear water of slow-running ditches or along the margins of rivers. A favorite food of waterfowl and muskrats, it is widely used as a salad herb for its spicy, peppery flavor. Introduced from Europe.

Status—Widespread and occasionally encountered.

Gene Jercinovic

Tall Tumblemustard (*Sisymbrium altissimum*) [INT]

Apr–Jun

Taxonomy—Mustard Family: Brassicaceae.

Identification—Annual herb to 1 m tall; leaves of 2 distinct kinds, lower leaves deeply lobed, upper leaves smaller, pinnatifid, the segments linear; fruiting stalks (pedicels) spreading widely, 5–8 mm long × 1 mm thick; fruit of linear siliques, 5–10 cm long, 1 mm wide.

Natural history—Tall tumblemustard grows in dry, disturbed soils in sunny and semishaded areas. Closely related to but not as widespread as London rocket (*Sisymbrium irio*). Introduced from Europe.

Status—Widespread and frequently encountered.

Photographs: Patrick Alexander

London Rocket (*Sisymbrium irio*) [INT]

Feb–May

Taxonomy—Mustard Family: Brassicaceae.

Identification—Annual herb to 80 cm; stems without hairs; upper and lower leaves similar in shape, deeply divided; pedicels thread-like; flowers with 4 petals, 3–4 mm long, yellow, borne in racemes; fruit a slender silique, 2–4 cm long.

Natural history—London rocket is a weedy species growing in sandy soils in open areas of the levees, ditches, and riverbanks. London rocket is closely related to tall tumblemustard (*Sisymbrium altissimum*) and may be confused with flixweed (*Descurainia sophia*); see those entries. As with most Brassicaceae, the mature fruits are the diagnostic feature and essential for proper identification. Introduced from Europe.

Status—Widespread and abundant.

Jane Mygatt

Tree Cholla (*Cylindropuntia imbricata*)

Jun–Jul

Taxonomy—Cactus Family: Cactaceae; Synonymy: *Opuntia imbricata*.

Identification—Succulent shrub from 1.5–2.5 m tall; stems whorled, grayish green, cylindrical; spines variable, generally 8–15 per areole; flowers dark pink to magenta; fruits yellow, barrel shaped, fleshy.

Natural history—Tree cholla occurs in sandy, disturbed soil in open areas. Dense populations indicate massive disturbance, including overgrazing by livestock.

Status—Widespread and occasionally encountered in the bosque.

Robert Sivinski

Desert Christmas Cholla *(Cylindropuntia leptocaulis)*

May–Jun

Taxonomy—Cactus Family: Cactaceae; Synonymy: *Opuntia leptocaulis*.

Identification—Succulent shrub from 0.5-1.8 m tall; stem segments slender, 2-8 cm long, up to 5 mm wide; spines 0-1 per areole, gray to pink; flowers pale yellow to green-yellow; fruits fleshy, obovate, red when mature.

Natural history—Christmas cholla grows in dry, sandy flats and bottomlands. The fruits turn a bright red in the winter months, giving rise to the common name, Christmas cholla. The fruit of the Christmas cholla provides food for wildlife, and the spiny vegetation provides protection for nesting birds.

Status—Widespread in the Chihuahuan Desert grasslands in the lower half of the state; occasionally encountered in the bosque.

Club Cholla, Dagger-thorn Cholla *(Grusonia clavata)*

Jun

Taxonomy—Cactus Family: Cactaceae; Synonymy: *Opuntia clavata*.

Identification—Succulent shrub to 10 cm tall, forming low-sprawling clumps; stem segments 4-5 cm long × 2.5 cm wide; areoles with 10-20 spines; spines daggerlike, white; flowers 3-5 cm wide × 5 cm long, yellow-green; fruit to 4 cm long, yellow, fleshy.

Natural history—Club cholla grows in sandy soils.

Status—Widespread and frequently encountered in the Rio Grande Valley and drainages. Endemic to New Mexico.

Engelmann's Prickly-pear *(Opuntia engelmannii)*

May–Jun

Taxonomy—Cactus Family: Cactaceae.

Identification—Succulent shrub to 1 m tall, forming wide-spreading clumps; stems elliptic to round, 20-30 cm long, 18-22 cm wide, pale green; spines 25-50 mm long, 1-4 per areole, white to gray; flowers yellow to orange-yellow; fruit barrel shaped, fleshy, ripening to a wine red in late summer.

Natural history—Engelmann's prickly-pear grows in sandy soils in the bosque. The ripe fruits are called tunas and are eaten fresh or dried.

Status—Localized and occasionally encountered.

Plains Prickly-pear

(*Opuntia phaeacantha*)

May–Jun

Taxonomy—Cactus Family: Cactaceae.

Identification—Succulent shrub 0.3–1 m; stems low sprawling, fleshy, green to dark green, reddish when water stressed,
pads obovate to rounded, 12–25 cm long, 10–20 cm wide; areoles 5–7 per diagonal row across the pad, tan to brownish,
graying with age; spines 2–8 per areole, ranging anywhere
from the majority of areoles to the upper ¼ of stems or
absent, brown to white, straight, curved, or twisted; central
spines spreading or reflexed, color variable from brown to
reddish brown to gray or tan, 30–70 mm long, 1–3 per areole,
brown; inner petals yellow, basal portions red, 30–40 mm
long; stigma green to yellow-green; fruit barrel shaped,
fleshy, ripening to wine red or purple.

Natural history—Plains prickly-pear grows in sandy soils in
grassy or semishaded areas in the bosque.

Status—Widespread and common throughout the state.

Phil Tonne

Dave Ferguson

Starvation Prickly-pear

(*Opuntia polyacantha*)

May–Jun

Taxonomy—Cactus Family: Cactaceae;
Synonymy: *Opuntia polyacantha*
var. *juniperina, Opuntia hystricina*.

Identification—Shrub to 25 cm high; stems sprawling, fleshy, broadly ovate, 8–10 cm long × 5–8 cm
wide; spines variable in size but occur in most areoles; upper spines long, 2–6 per areole in upper ¼ of
pad, extending forward, downward, and upright to
8 cm long; smaller spines 4–5 per areole; flower color
yellow or magenta; stigma green; fruit spiny and dry
when mature.

Jane Mygatt

Natural history—Starvation prickly-pear grows in
sandy soils on open or semishaded river valley bottoms. Two varieties occur in the
Rio Grande Valley, *Opuntia polyacantha* var. *hystricina* and *Opuntia polyacantha*
var. *juniperiana*.

Status—Fairly widespread throughout the mid-northern portion of the state and
frequently encountered.

Pott's Prickly-pear (*Opuntia pottsii*)

May–Jun

Taxonomy—Cactus Family: Cactaceae; Synonymy: *Opuntia pottsii* var. *montana*, *O. macrorhiza* var. *montana*.

Identification—Shrub to 30 cm high; stems upright, fleshy, obovate to round, 5–13 cm long × 3–10 cm wide, waxy blue-green; spines 1–4 per areole in upper ⅓–¼ of the pad, erect to spreading, whitish to gray, often twisted; flower 5–9 cm long × 4–6 cm wide, color variable, yellow, orange, magenta, or pink; stigma white to cream colored; fruits fleshy, 2.5–5 cm long × 2 cm wide, pinkish purple.

Natural history—Pott's prickly-pear grows in sandy soils in grassy woodlands or semishaded river bottoms. In the Albuquerque area, flowers are usually yellow with red centers; other colors are more common southward.

Status—Fairly widespread throughout the mid-northern part of the state and frequently encountered.

Photographs: Jane Mygatt

Rocky Mountain Beeplant (*Cleome serrulata*)

Jun–Oct

Taxonomy—Caper Family: Capparaceae.

Identification—Annual herb to 1 m; stems erect, branched; leaves alternate, 3-foliate; leaflets lanceolate, entire to minutely toothed; flowers many flowered in dense, elongated racemes; petals 4, pinkish purple, rarely white; fruit of linear-cylindric capsules, drooping downward.

Natural history—Rocky Mountain beeplant grows in open, sunny areas near ditches and the river. The Caper family (Capparaceae) is closely related to the Mustard family (Brassicaceae) and has similarities in petal and sepal number and a superficial similarity in the fruit, which in *Cleome* and *Polanisia* is long and slender. The number of stamens in the Caper family can be 4-many, whereas the Mustard family always has 6 stamens (4 long, 2 short).

Status—Widespread and common.

Robert Sivinski

Clammyweed   (*Polanisia dodecandra* ssp. *trachysperma*)

May–Oct

Taxonomy—Caper Family: Capparaceae.

Identification—Annual herb to 1 m tall; herbage malodorous, with sticky hairs; leaves alternate, 3-foliate; leaflets elliptic, the leaf margins entire; bracts of the flowering stalk leaflike; petals 4, white, 8–12 mm long; stamens long, pink to purple; fruit with slightly hairy capsules, to 50 mm long, held erect to ascending.

Natural history—Clammyweed grows in sandy soils in clearings and disturbed ground around ditches and sandbars. The common name refers to the moist or sticky residue left on the hands after handling the plant. Clammyweed is attractive to insect pollinators.

Status—Widespread and frequently encountered.

Robert Sivinski

Japanese Honeysuckle   (*Lonicera japonica*) [INT]

Jun–Jul

Taxonomy—Honeysuckle Family: Caprifoliaceae.

Identification—Woody semi-evergreen vine; stems climbing to 5 m; leaves ovate, 2–8 cm long; flowers in pairs; corolla tubular, 2-lipped, reflexed, 15–35 mm long, white or yellow; fruit a round berry, black, 4–6 mm wide.

Natural history—Japanese honeysuckle grows in sandy soil in sunny or semishaded areas near the riverbanks. Flowers are highly scented and pollinated by moths. Escaped from cultivation, this honeysuckle is native to Asia.

Status—Localized and frequently encountered.

Jane Mygatt

Four-wing Saltbush   (*Atriplex canescens*)

May–Jun

Taxonomy—Goosefoot Family: Chenopodiaceae.

Identification—Shrub to 1.5 m tall; branches numerous; leaves grayish, linear-oblong to 5 cm long; pistillate inflorescence a panicle to 40 cm long; staminate inflorescence of dense spikes to 3 mm wide; fruit thin walled with a single seed (utricle) to 1 cm long, prominently 4-winged.

Natural history—Long lived and drought tolerant, four-wing saltbush is tolerant of saline and alkaline soils. Mature leaves concentrate and exude salts. Saltbush is used extensively for land reclamation, particularly in saline soils.

Status—Widespread and common.

Robert Sivinski

Mealy Goosefoot   (*Chenopodium incanum*)

May–Sep

Taxonomy—Goosefoot Family: Chenopodiaceae.

Identification—Annual herb to 35 cm tall; herbage powdery-mealy; leaf blades diamond shaped with arrow-shaped lobes, upper and lower surfaces powdery-mealy; flowers small, in clusters arranged in crowded spikelike arrays.

Natural history—Mealy goosefoot grows in sandy or gravelly soils in waste areas.

Status—Widespread and common.

Narrowleaf Goosefoot   (*Chenopodium leptophyllum*)

Jul–Oct

Taxonomy—Goosefoot Family: Chenopodiaceae.

Identification—Annual herb to 40 cm; stems generally erect and branching from the base; herbage powdery-mealy; leaves linear to oblong, somewhat fleshy, margins entire to arrow shaped toward the leaf base; lower leaf blade densely powdery-mealy; flowers small, in clusters arranged in terminal and axillary panicles.

Natural history—Narrowleaf goosefoot grows in sandy waste grounds and disturbed sites. The young shoots can be boiled and used for greens. The seeds were ground and used as mush by Apache and Hopi tribes.

Status—Widespread and common.

Winged Tumbleweed   (*Cycloloma atriplicifolia*)

May–Sep

Taxonomy—Goosefoot Family: Chenopodiaceae.

Identification—Annual taprooted herb to 60 cm tall; stems erect, much branched; leaves alternate, linear-oblong, tapering to the base, 4 cm long, 1 cm wide; leaf margins with 3–4 teeth per side; inflorescence in open panicles of flower clusters; flowers minute, subtended by a leaflike bract; fruit round, winged with irregular margin, to 4 mm wide.

Natural history—Winged tumbleweed grows in open areas of deep, sandy soils near the river.

Status—Widespread and frequently encountered.

Kochia, Summer Cypress   (*Kochia scoparia*) [INT]

Jul–Oct

Taxonomy—Goosefoot Family: Chenopodiaceae.

Identification—Annual herb to 2 m tall; stems upright, much branched, ascending, reddish when mature; leaves alternate, linear to linear-lanceolate, 10–40 mm long; flowers inconspicuous, found in clusters in the axils of leaves and in terminal spikes, greenish yellow.

Natural history—Kochia tolerates a wide range of soil types and forms dense populations. Plants are wind-pollinated and are an important hay fever plant. Introduced from Asia.

Status—Widespread and abundant.

Winterfat   (*Krascheninnikovia lanata*)

May–Oct

Taxonomy—Goosefoot Family: Chenopodiaceae; Synonymy: *Ceratoides lanata, Eurotia lanata*.

Identification—Perennial herb from woody crown; herbage woolly with simple and star-shaped hairs; leaves alternate, simple, linear to lanceolate, leaf margins rolled backward; flowers in dense spikelike clusters, petals lacking, calyx and floral bracts with dense soft hairs.

Natural history—Winterfat grows on dry soil in disturbed areas.

Status—Widespread and occasionally encountered.

Tumbleweed, Russian Thistle   (*Salsola tragus*) [INT]

Jul–Sep

Taxonomy—Goosefoot Family: Chenopodiaceae.

Identification—Annual herb to 1 m; stems densely branched, forming round bushy clumps; leaves alternate, linear, spine tipped; flowers in leaf axils, subtended by a pair of spine-tipped bracts.

Natural history—Tumbleweed grows in full sun or semishaded areas. Introduced from Eurasia, it is now a troublesome weed in disturbed areas and cultivated fields. As tumbleweed matures, the plants develop a spherical form that breaks at the soil line. Tumbleweed blows with the wind, scattering seeds as it tumbles. Mature tumbleweed contains nitrates and calcium oxalate that can be toxic to livestock.

Status—Widespread and abundant.

Field Bindweed

(*Convolvulus arvensis*) [INT]

May–Jul

Taxonomy—Morning Glory Family: Convolvulaceae.

Identification—Perennial vine to 1.5 m long; stems prostrate from deep-rooted rhizomes; leaves variable, mostly arrow shaped, to 6 cm long; corolla of 5 fused petals, 1.5–3 cm long, white to pale pink.

Natural history—Field bindweed tolerates a wide range of habitats, and its spread is facilitated by disturbance. Field bindweed is difficult to control due to its deep root system and its ability to spread vegetatively. Native to Eurasia, this species is a pest species throughout the U.S. and is a state-listed noxious weed in New Mexico.

Status—Widespread and common.

Jane Mygatt

Common Morning Glory

(*Ipomoea purpurea*) [INT]

Jul–Oct

Taxonomy—Morning Glory Family: Convolvulaceae.

Identification—Annual vine to 2–3 m; leaves hairy, heart shaped, often deeply lobed, to 12 cm long; flowers funnel shaped, blue to purple to white, 5–7 cm long, 3–6 cm wide.

Natural history—Morning glory grows in the moist soil of ditches and cultivated fields. Introduced from tropical America, it is poisonous to humans and livestock.

Status—Widespread and occasionally encountered.

Jane Mygatt

Buffalo Gourd

(*Cucurbita foetidissima*)

May–Aug

Taxonomy—Cucumber Family: Cucurbitaceae.

Identification—Perennial herbaceous vine; stems prostrate with tendrils; leaves triangular with rough, stiff hairs; flowers unisexual, staminate and pistillate on same plant, bell shaped, bright orange-yellow, to 15 cm long; fruit a round pepo to 10 cm in diameter.

Natural history—Buffalo gourd grows in sandy soils in full sun. The foliage is unpleasantly strong scented. The fruit of buffalo gourd is not edible, although it is related to the cultivated varieties of *Cucurbita pepo*, including pumpkins and squash.

Status—Widespread and common.

Robert Sivinski

Russian Olive

(*Elaeagnus angustifolia*) [INT]

May–Jun

Taxonomy—Oleaster Family: Elaeagnaceae.

Identification—Shrub or small tree to 8 m tall; branches thorny; leaves alternate, lanceolate to oblong lanceolate, green on upper surface, silvery on lower surface; flowers small, very fragrant; calyx 4-lobed, yellow; petals lacking; stamens 4; fruit in clusters of silvery drupelike achenes.

Natural history—Russian olive is one of the dominant understory shrubs in the cottonwood bosque. The lack of overbank flooding may contribute to its spread as Russian olives can outcompete native vegetation that require periodic flooding for renewal. Russian olive can fix nitrogen in its roots, allowing it to grow on nutrient-poor soils. Fruit are eaten and dispersed by birds. Native to southern Europe and central and western Asia.

Status—Widespread and abundant, especially in the northern half of the state.

Thyme-leaf Spurge

(*Chamaesyce serpyllifolia*)

Jun–Oct

Taxonomy—Spurge Family: Euphorbiaceae.

Identification—Annual herb with milky latex; stems low spreading to 30 cm long; herbage with or without hairs; leaves opposite, ovate to oblong, 3–14 mm long; leaf tip rounded, leaf margins finely toothed; inflorescence a cup-shaped cyathium (involucre) containing several minute stamens and a pistil, sepals and petals lacking; small oval glands at the base of small white petal-like appendages extend from the cyathium; fruit a round and lobed capsule 2 mm wide, with or without hairs.

Natural history—Thyme-leaf spurge grows on dry, disturbed soils in full sun.

Status—Widespread and common.

David's Spurge

(*Euphorbia davidii*)

Jul–Oct

Taxonomy—Spurge Family: Euphorbiaceae.

Identification—Annual herb 20–80 cm tall; stems erect, herbage hairy; leaves opposite, often lower ones alternate; leaf blade ovate-lanceolate, 60 mm long, 20 mm wide, toothed; flowers much reduced and subtended by a cup-shaped involucre (cyathium); one gland per cyathium; cyathia clustered at the ends of branches; fruit a capsule, 2–3 mm long, 4–5 mm wide.

Natural history—David's spurge grows in dry, disturbed habitats.

Status—Widespread and occasionally encountered.

False Indigo-bush   (*Amorpha fruticosa*)

May–Jul

Taxonomy—Bean Family: Fabaceae.

Identification—Shrub to 2 m tall; stems of young branches hairy; leaves glandular dotted on underside, pinnately compound with 9–25 leaflets; inflorescence of terminal or axillary spikes 6–15 cm long; calyx with glandular dots; corolla 5 mm long, purple, composed of 1 petal folded around stamens and style; stamens 10, anthers orange; fruit a legume 7–8 mm long, curved, glandular dotted.

Natural history—False indigo-bush is often associated with wetlands and grows on moist soils. Due to its spreading root system, it is useful for erosion control.

Status—Widespread and common.

Freckled Milkvetch   (*Astragalus lentiginosus*)

Mar–Jun, Sep–Oct

Taxonomy—Bean Family: Fabaceae.

Identification—Perennial herb to 40 cm long; stems with hairs; leaves pinnately compound with 15–21 leaflets; flowers in compact racemes; corolla papilionaceous, 15–20 mm long, pinkish purple with white; fruit an inflated ovoid legume, 15–30 mm long, yellowish tinged with red or purple blotches.

Natural history—Freckled milkvetch grows in open, dry, and disturbed areas.

Status—Widespread and common.

Foxtail Prairie Clover   (*Dalea leporina*)

Jun–Sep

Taxonomy—Bean Family: Fabaceae.

Identification—Annual herb to 60 cm tall; stems erect, branched, without hairs; leaves pinnately compound with 15–41 leaflets; leaflets linear-oblong, 3–10 mm long; flowers minute, papilionaceous, in dense, terminal, cylindrical spikes, 2–8 cm long, blue to whitish; fruit a small legume, hairy.

Natural history—Foxtail prairie clover is a weedy species found in disturbed soils in full sun or semishade.

Status—Widespread and common.

Albuquerque Prairie Clover   (*Dalea scariosa*)

Aug–Sep

Taxonomy—Bean Family: Fabaceae.

Identification—Perennial herb 20–70 cm long; stems pros-trate to spreading; leaves pinnately compound, 1–2.5 cm long; leaflets 5–9, 3–8 mm long; inflorescence a spike; flow-ers papilionaceous, petals pale pink to pink-purple, 7–8 mm long; fruit a legume, 3–4 mm long, glandular dotted.

Natural history—Albuquerque prairie clover grows on sandy soils and on cobblestone bluffs in open, sunny areas only in the Rio Grande Valley. It is an attractive spe-cies that deserves cultivation.

Status—Endemic to New Mexico and rare but found in sufficient numbers that it is not endangered.

Honey-locust   (*Gleditsia triacanthos*) [INT]

May–Jun

Taxonomy—Bean Family: Fabaceae.

Identification—Tree to 24 m tall with spreading crown; branches prominently zigzag, with reddish brown thorns; leaves alter-nate, pinnately compound to 20 cm long; flowers small, green-ish, to 8 cm long, fragrant; fruit a flattened, twisting legume to 20 cm long.

Natural history—Honey-locust is well established in the Albu-querque bosque along the riverbanks and in open burned areas where cottonwoods formerly grew. Native to the east-central United States.

Status—Localized and common.

American Licorice   (*Glycyrrhiza lepidota*)

Jun–Aug

Taxonomy—Bean Family: Fabaceae.

Identification—Perennial herb to 1 m tall from an extensive root system; leaves pinnately compound with 13–19 leaflets; inflores-cence of axillary racemes 3–8 cm long; flowers papilionaceous, 7–12 mm long, whitish; fruit of oblong legumes 8–18 mm long with numerous hooked prickles.

Natural history—American licorice forms extensive colonies in shady areas in sandy soils. Licorice has been used for medicinal purposes for centuries. The chief substance in licorice root is gly-cyrrhizin. Licorice candy is flavored mostly with anise (a different plant in the Carrot family, Apiaceae), which contains little glycyr-rhizin. Like many legumes, this species has a symbiotic relation-ship with certain soil bacteria, which form nodules on the roots and fix atmospheric nitrogen.

Status—Widespread and abundant.

Alfalfa (*Medicago sativa*) [INT]

May–Oct

Taxonomy—Bean Family: Fabaceae.

Identification—Perennial herb to 1 m; leaves trifoliate; leaflets oblong to ovate, 10–30 mm long, toothed toward the apex; flowers in oval clusters, 1–2.5 cm long × 1–2 cm wide, arising from leaf axils; flowers papilionaceous, purple-violet, 6–15 mm long.

Natural history—Due to its deep root system, alfalfa can tolerate a wide range of habitats and drought. An important forage crop for livestock, the roots of alfalfa can fix atmospheric nitrogen. Native to Iran, alfalfa was introduced to the U.S. around 1860.

Status—Widespread and frequently encountered.

Patrick Alexander

Gene Jercinovic

White Sweetclover (*Melilotus albus*) [INT]

May–Sep

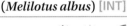

Taxonomy—Bean Family: Fabaceae.

Identification—Biennial herb to 2 m; stems branched; leaves alternate, trifoliate; leaflets narrowly oblong, toothed; flowers papilionaceous, small, +/–50, in elongate erect clusters, 4–12 cm long, white.

Natural history—White sweetclover is weedy in many disturbed habitats in full sun or semi-shade. The plants are edible and used medicinally. Coumarin, a blood-thinning medicine, is derived from this genus. Introduced from Europe and Asia.

Status—Widespread and abundant.

Jane Mygatt

Yellow Sweetclover (*Melilotus officinalis*) [INT]

May–Sep

Taxonomy—Bean Family: Fabaceae.

Identification—Biennial herb to 2 m; stems branched; leaves alternate, trifoliate; leaflets toothed, oblong; flowers papilionaceous, small, +/–50, in elongate erect clusters to 8 cm long, yellow.

Natural history—Yellow sweetclover is weedy in disturbed habitats in sandy soils. It grows in full sun or semishade. Introduced from Europe.

Status—Widespread and abundant.

Photographs: Jane Mygatt

Screwbean Mesquite   (*Prosopis pubescens*)

May–Jun

Taxonomy—Bean Family: Fabaceae.

Identification—Shrub or small tree to 5 m, bark sheds in long stringy sections; multibranched from the base; stems and branches with sharp spines; leaves pinnately compound with 6–18 leaflets; leaflets linear-oblong, 5–10 mm long; flowers in pendulous clusters, 5–8 cm long, yellow; fruit of tightly spiraling (corkscrew) bean pods.

Natural history—Screwbean mesquite grows in open or semi-shaded areas (and arroyo bottoms) of moist, desert riparian zones. It is easily recognized by the twisted pods and long spines. The young pods are edible, as are the mature seeds.

Status—Localized and frequently encountered.

Robert Sivinski

Broom Dalea   (*Psorothamnus scoparius*)

Jun–Sep

Taxonomy—Bean Family: Fabaceae;
Synonymy: *Dalea scoparia*.

Identification—Shrub to 1 m tall; stems many branched, gray-green; herbage glandular dotted; leaves small, linear, 8–10 mm long; flowers small, clustered at the tips of stems, papilionaceous, fragrant, dark purple.

Natural history—Broom dalea grows in open, sunny areas in dunes and sandy arroyo bottoms. It is a highly xerophytic shrub that is nearly leafless and covered in gray hairs.

Status—Widespread and frequently encountered.

Jane Mygatt

Black Locust   (*Robinia pseudoacacia*)

May–Jun

Taxonomy—Bean Family: Fabaceae.

Identification—Deciduous tree to 15 m tall; leaves pinnately compound with 9–19 oval leaflets, 20–50 mm long; flowers in drooping racemes; corolla papilionaceous, 14–25 mm long, white or pink; fruit a glabrous legume, 5–10 cm long.

Natural history—Black locust grows in sandy, well-drained soils in full sun to semishaded areas. The flowers are fragrant and pollinated by bees.

Status—Widespread and frequently encountered.

Patrick Alexander

Red Bladdervetch, Alkalai Swainsonpea   (*Sphaerophysa salsula*) [INT]

May–Jul

Taxonomy—Bean Family: Fabaceae.

Identification—Perennial herb 40–150 cm tall; leaves alternate, pinnately compound; leaflets 9–25, oblong to ovate with silvery hairs; flowers 4–8, clustered in leaf axils, reddish orange, papilionaceous; fruit an inflated legume, 14–24 mm long.

Natural history—Red bladdervetch grows in alkaline or sandy soils in open or semishaded areas. It is a noxious weed in several western states. Native to Asia.

Status—Patchy distribution and common.

Redstem Stork's Bill   (*Erodium cicutarium*) [INT]

Mar–Jul

Taxonomy—Geranium Family: Geraniaceae.

Identification—Annual herb to 50 cm long, spreading; herbage hairy and glandular; leaves pinnate, the leaflets toothed or lobed; corolla with 5 petals, 5–9 mm long, rose-purple; column of the style (the stork bill), 3–5 cm long.

Natural history—Redstem stork's bill grows in disturbed, sandy, well-drained soils but prefers moist soils and full sun. Flowers are pollinated by bees, butterflies and moths, and beetles. The common name, stork's bill, comes from the long stylar column, which resembles the bill of a stork. Introduced from Europe.

Status—Widespread and frequently encountered.

Golden Currant   (*Ribes aureum*)

May–Jun

Taxonomy—Currant Family: Grossulariaceae.

Identification—Deciduous shrub to 2 m tall; herbage spineless; leaves alternate, mostly 3-lobed, 15–50 mm wide; flowers yellow; fruit a round berry, greenish yellow, red, or black, 6–8 mm wide.

Natural history—Golden currant grows in sunny to semishaded areas in well-drained soils. The flowers are pollinated by insects, and the fruits are eaten by wildlife and birds.

Status—Localized and frequently encountered.

Parrot's Feather   (*Myriophyllum aquaticum*) [INT]

Jun–Sep

Taxonomy—Water Milfoil Family: Haloragaceae.

Identification—Perennial aquatic herb; leaves pinnately divided in a featherlike pattern with threadlike segments less than 1 mm wide; leaves whorled, 4–6 around the stem; flower small, inconspicuous, in leaf axils.

Natural history—Parrot's feather grows in slow-moving waters of ditches with permanent water. Plants are either anchored by roots or form a dense mat of intertwined stems in the water. Upper portions of stems emerge out of the water. Native to South America, now widely established in North America and considered an invasive weed in some parts of the country.

Status—Widespread and frequently encountered.

Jane Mygatt

Sandbells   (*Nama hispidum*)

Feb–Sep

Taxonomy—Waterleaf Family: Hydrophyllaceae.

Identification—Annual herb 5–15 cm long, trailing; herbage with rough hairs; leaves alternate, entire, linear to narrowly oblong, curled inward, 10–25 mm long, 1–4 mm wide; flowers solitary in the leaf axils; corolla funnelform, 10–12 mm long, reddish purple, the lobes reflexed.

Natural history—Sandbells grow in dry, gravelly, or sandy soils in full sun.

Status—Widespread and frequently encountered.

Robert Sivinski

Gypsum Scorpion-weed   (*Phacelia integrifolia*)

May–Sep

Taxonomy—Waterleaf Family: Hydrophyllaceae.

Identification—Annual herb, 20–50 cm tall; herbage hairy, glandular and sticky to the touch; leaves alternate, oblong; leaf margins with rounded teeth; inflorescence of scorpioid cymes (coiled); flowers mostly bluish purple, sometimes white.

Natural history—Gypsum scorpion-weed grows on dry soils in open areas and on sandbars.

Status—Widespread and common.

Robert Sivinski

American Water Horehound   (*Lycopus americanus*)

Jul–Sep

Taxonomy—Mint Family: Lamiaceae.

Identification—Perennial herb 20–60 cm tall; stems 4-angled; leaves opposite, oblong-lanceolate, to 10 cm long; leaf margins irregularly toothed and rounded; flowers small, clustered in the axils of the leaves; corolla nearly symmetric, white, 5 mm long.

Natural history—American water horehound spreads by above-ground stems (stolons) that grow along the surface in wet or moist soil on riverbanks, pond edges, and seepage areas.

Status—Widespread and occasionally encountered.

Robert H. Mohlenbrock @ USDA-NRCS PLANTS Database

Field Mint   (*Mentha arvensis*)

Jun–Sep

Taxonomy—Mint Family: Lamiaceae.

Identification—Perennial herb to 80 cm tall, aromatic; stems 4-angled, branching or simple; leaves opposite, ovate, toothed; flowers clustered in the axils of the leaves; corolla lavender, 2-lipped, 3–6 mm long; upper lip single lobed, lower lip 3-lobed.

Natural history—Grows on moist or wet, muddy soils in cattail marshes. The seeds are eaten by waterfowl.

Status—Widespread and frequently encountered.

Gene Jercinovic

Prairie Flax   (*Linum lewisii*)

May–Jun

Taxonomy—Flax Family: Linaceae.

Identification—Perennial herb to 60 cm; stems several, slender; herbage hairless, glaucous; leaves alternate, linear, 1–3 cm long; flowers in small open clusters; petals 5, blue, 10–23 mm, falling early; fruit a round capsule.

Natural history—Prairie flax grows in sandy, well-drained soils in full sun or semishaded areas. The showy petals drop off by early afternoon.

Status—Localized and occasionally encountered.

Jane Mygatt

Adonis Blazingstar

(Mentzelia multiflora)

May–Sep

Taxonomy—Loasa Family: Loasaceae.

Identification—Biennial or perennial herb to 60 cm; stems erect, branched at the base, whitish; herbage with rough barbed hairs; leaves alternate, deeply lobed; flowers in clusters at the ends of branches; petals 5, yellow, 15–20 mm long; stamens in several series, outer series petal-like, yellow; fruit a capsule, oblong, 15–20 mm long.

Natural history—Adonis blazingstar grows in gravelly, sandy, dry soils in full sun. The seeds are apparently edible, and the plant has been used medicinally.

Status—Widespread and common.

Patrick Alexander

Alkali Mallow

(Malvella leprosa)

May–Oct

Taxonomy—Mallow Family: Malvaceae; Synonymy: *Malva hederacea, Sida hederacea, Sida leprosa.*

Identification—Perennial herb 10–40 cm, erect to prostrate; herbage densely covered with minute star-shaped hairs; leaves alternate, triangular to 5 cm long, margins toothed; flowers in leaf axils, solitary or in clusters, 25–35 mm wide; petals 10–12 mm long, creamy white, fading to pink.

Natural history—Alkali mallow grows on the alkaline soils of drained wetlands in open areas.

Status—Sporadic and occasionally encountered.

Jane Mygatt

Copper Globemallow

(Sphaeralcea angustifolia)

May–Oct

Taxonomy—Mallow Family: Malvaceae.

Identification—Perennial herb to 1.5 m tall; stems spreading, erect; herbage densely covered with hairs; leaves alternate, oblong-lanceolate to linear-lanceolate; leaf blade somewhat arrow shaped; leaf margin with rounded teeth; flowers clustered in leaf axils, mostly orange-red to salmon, drying purplish.

Natural history—Copper globemallow grows in highly disturbed sites in full sun and semishaded areas. It is one of the most common flowers seen throughout the region. The leaves are covered with tiny star-shaped hairs visible with a hand lens.

Status—Widespread and abundant.

Robert Sivinski

White Mulberry

(***Morus alba***) [INT]

Fruiting Jun–Jul

Taxonomy—Mulberry Family: Moraceae.

Identification—Deciduous tree to 12 m; roots orange; leaves alternate, ovate, the margins variously lobed or entire, serrate; flowers white and fleshy; fruit composed of numerous, fleshy red (sometimes white) drupes.

Natural history—White mulberry is an ornamental escapee spreading through parts of the Albuquerque bosque. Birds eat the fruits and widely disperse the seeds. Native to China.

Status—Localized and common.

New Mexico Desert-olive

(***Forestiera pubescens***)

May–Jun

Taxonomy—Olive Family: Oleaceae.

Identification—Deciduous shrub to 4 m; leaves simple, opposite or grouped in clusters; flowers inconspicuous and clustered; fruit of elliptic drupes, green, maturing to purple, 5-7 mm long.

Natural history—New Mexico desert-olive grows in semishaded, sandy soils. Flowers appear before leaves develop and are an important food source for bees in spring. Generally a dioecious species, with male and female flowers on separate plants, but can also have male and female flowers on the same plant (polygamodioecious). Commonly used in xeriscape gardens.

Status—Widespread and common.

Scarlet Beeblossom

(***Gaura coccinea***)

May–Aug

Taxonomy—Evening Primrose Family: Onagraceae.

Identification—Perennial herb 20-60 cm tall; stems erect, branching from the base; leaves alternate, linear to lanceolate, grayish green to 6 cm long; inflorescence in elongated spikelike racemes; petals 4, initially white, fading to pink, 3-6 mm long; stamens 8; stigma 4-lobed.

Natural history—Scarlet beeblossom grows in disturbed, open, or semishaded sites in dry soil.

Status—Widespread and frequently encountered.

Velvetweed (*Gaura mollis*)

May–Sep

Taxonomy—Evening Primrose Family: Onagraceae; Synonymy: *Gaura parviflora*.

Identification—Annual herb to 2 m tall; stems and leaves densely glandular-hairy; leaves to 13 cm long, narrowly elliptic to ovate; inflorescence in elongated spikelike racemes, usually nodding; petals 4, pink, 2 mm long; stamens 8; stigma 4-lobed.

Natural history—Velvetweed grows in disturbed, open or semi-shaded sites in dry soil.

Status—Widespread and common.

Hooker's Evening Primrose (*Oenothera elata* ssp. *hirsutissima*)

Jun–Sep

Taxonomy—Evening Primrose Family: Onagraceae.

Identification—Biennial or short-lived perennial herb to 2 m; stems erect, reddish, with short hairs; leaf blade lanceolate, margins wavy; flowers showy; petals 4, yellow; stamens 8, stigma 4-lobed.

Natural history—Hooker's evening primrose grows in moist and wet soils along the slopes of ditches, riverbanks, and sandbars.

Status—Widespread and frequently encountered.

Pale Evening Primrose (*Oenothera pallida*)

May–Sep

Taxonomy—Evening Primrose Family: Onagraceae.

Identification—Perennial herb to 40 cm tall; stems branched; herbage with or without short hairs; leaves narrowly lanceolate to ovate, 2–4 cm long; leaf margins deeply wavy (sinuate-pinnatifid); petals 4, 10–25 mm long, white.

Natural history—Pale evening primrose grows in sandy, open, disturbed habitats. The flowers open around sunset and are pollinated by the white-lined sphinx moth. White petals fade to pink.

Status—Widespread and common.

English Plantain (*Plantago lanceolata*) [INT]

May–Oct

Taxonomy—Plantain Family: Plantaginaceae.

Identification—Perennial herb in basal rosettes; leaf blade narrowly lanceolate to 20 cm long, prominently veined; leaf margins entire to toothed; inflorescence spikelike, ovoid to cylindric; flowers small, white.

Natural history—English plantain grows in moist or wet soil in open and semishaded areas. Commonly seen at the Bosque del Apache NWR along the irrigation canal. Introduced from Europe.

Status—Widespread and common.

Jane Mygatt

Great Plantain (*Plantago major*) [INT]

Jun–Sep

Taxonomy—Plantain Family: Plantaginaceae.

Identification—Annual or biennial herb in basal rosettes; leaves oval, prominently veined, narrowing abruptly to the petiole, to 15 cm long; leaf margins often toothed; inflorescence spikelike, elongate; flowers small, white.

Natural history—Great plantain is tolerant of many soil types but requires moist soil and sunshine. Introduced from Europe.

Status—Widespread and frequently encountered.

Jane Mygatt

Woolly Plantain (*Plantago patagonica*)

Apr–Aug

Taxonomy—Plantain Family: Plantaginaceae; Synonymy: *Plantago purshii*.

Identification—Annual herb in basal rosettes; herbage with long soft hairs; leaves linear, gradually tapering to the base, to 10 cm long; inflorescence spikelike, long-cylindrical, 2–6 cm long.

Natural history—Woolly plantain grows in sandy or gravelly soils in full sun. It is used medicinally by Native Americans. The seeds become mucilaginous when wetted.

Status—Widespread and frequently encountered.

Robert Sivinski

Blue Trumpets

(*Ipomopsis longiflora*)

May–Oct

Taxonomy—Phlox Family: Polemoniaceae.

Identification—Annual herb, 15–30 cm tall; leaves pinnatifid, linear; flowers in open arrays; corolla trumpet shaped, the slender tube, 30–50 mm long, the lobes 8–10 mm long, pale blue or white.

Natural history—Blue trumpets grow in sandy soils in full sun or semishaded areas.

Status—Widespread and frequently encountered.

Pale Smartweed

(*Persicaria lapathifolia*) [INT]

May–Oct

Taxonomy—Buckwheat Family: Polygonaceae;
Synonymy: *Polygonum lapathifolium*.

Identification—Annual herb to 1 m tall; stems jointed at the nodes; leaves alternate, lanceolate, to 30 cm long and 6 cm wide; inflorescence spikelike, densely flowered to 8 cm long, nodding; flowers small, 2–3 mm long, white to pinkish.

Natural history—Pale smartweed grows in moist soils in disturbed sites often near the edges of rivers and ponds. Easily distinguished from spotted lady's-thumb (*Persicaria maculosa*) by the nodding racemes of the panicle. A dark spot is often in the center of the leaves, but it is not as obvious as in spotted lady's-thumb. Introduced from Europe.

Status—Widespread and common.

Spotted Lady's-thumb

(*Persicaria maculosa*) [INT]

Jul–Sep

Taxonomy—Buckwheat Family: Polygonaceae;
Synonymy: *Polygonum persicaria*.

Identification—Annual herb to 1 m tall; stems jointed at the nodes; leaves alternate, lanceolate to linear-lanceolate to 11 cm long and 2 cm wide, often with a purple splotch in middle of the blade; inflorescence spikelike, to 3 cm long, erect to ascending; flowers small, to 3.5 mm long, rose pink.

Natural history—Spotted lady's-thumb grows in marshes, seepage areas, and river and pond margins and is recognized by the characteristic purple spot in the center of the leaf. Introduced from Europe.

Status—Widespread and common.

Curly Dock   (*Rumex crispus*) [INT]

Apr–Sep

Taxonomy—Buckwheat Family: Polygonaceae.

Identification—Perennial herb to 1 m or more; stems much branched, erect, becoming red with age; leaves alternate, margins very wavy; inflorescence in narrow terminal panicles to 40 cm long; perianth consists of 2 series of sepals, inner and outer; outer series of 3 greenish yellow sepals, 3-angled.

Natural history—Curly dock is a wetland species growing in ditches, irrigated fields, and river margins. Introduced from Eurasia.

Status—Widespread and common.

Photographs: Jane Mygatt

Sand Dock   (*Rumex hymenosepalus*)

Jun–Sep

Taxonomy—Buckwheat Family: Polygonaceae.

Identification—Perennial herb, 60–100 cm tall, from tuberous roots; stems reddish green; leaves alternate, fleshy, oblong, 6–30 cm long, somewhat crisped along the margins; ochrea 1–3 cm long; flowers in elongated panicles, pinkish; perianth of 6 sepals, outer 3 herbaceous, 2 mm long, the inner 3 (the valves), 10–15 mm long in fruit, pinkish.

Natural history—Sand dock grows in sandy soils, often at the water's edge in full sun or semishade. A unique feature of many genera in the Polygonaceae is the modified stipule structure, called an *ochrea*. The ochrea is a translucent sheath at the base of the leaf that forms a tube around the stem.

Status—Widespread and common.

Photographs: Jane Mygatt

Garden Purslane   (*Portulaca oleracea*) [INT]

Jun–Sep

Taxonomy—Purslane Family: Portulacaceae.

Identification—Annual herb to 40 cm long, succulent; stems branched, prostrate to ascending; leaves alternate, flat, ovate, to 3 cm long; flowers terminal, solitary or in clusters; petals 5, 3–4 mm long, notched at the tip, yellow; fruit a circumscissile capsule (opening around the circumference), 5–8 mm long.

Natural history—Garden purslane grows on moist, disturbed soils and around ponds and flooded areas. Leaves and flowers are edible and used in salads. Introduced from Eurasia.

Status—Widespread and frequently encountered.

Gene Jercinovic

Kiss-me-quick   (*Portulaca pilosa*)

Jul–Sep

Taxonomy—Purslane Family: Portulacaceae; Synonymy: *Portulaca mundula.*

Identification—Annual herb to 20 cm long, succulent; stems branched, prostrate to spreading; leaves alternate, linear, rounded to 15 mm long, with obvious hairs at the leaf axils; flowers terminal, solitary or in small clusters; petals 5, 3–4 mm long, magenta; fruit a circumscissile capsule (opening around the circumference), 3 mm wide.

Natural history—Kiss-me-quick grows in dry to moist sandy soils in disturbed habitats. Plants growing on dry soils are more hairy than those found on moist soil.

Status—Widespread and occasionally encountered.

Patrick Alexander

Rio Grande Cottonwood   (*Populus deltoides* ssp. *wislizenii*)

Apr

Taxonomy—Willow Family: Salicaceae.

Identification—Large tree to 30 m tall, dioecious with separate male and female trees; winter buds with fine hairs; leaves triangular, usually wider than long, margin toothed, leaf blade 5–7 cm long, petioles flattened, 3–5 cm long; capsules ellipsoid, 4–10 mm long; fruiting pedicels as long or longer than the capsules; seeds each with an attached tuft of hairs (cotton).

Natural history—Rio Grande cottonwood is a phreatophyte, meaning its roots grow to the water table. At present Rio Grande cottonwood typically occurs in stands of mature to senescent trees and is the main habitat-defining tree species in the bosque. Cottonwoods require overbank flooding to create open, muddy flats, where germination and establishment of seedlings occur. Significant floods have not occurred since the 1940s; hence the increasingly senescent stands predominating in the bosque. Rio Grande cottonwood now competes against exotic saltcedar (*Tamarix chinensis*) during seedling establishment. Research has shown that Rio Grande cottonwood outcompetes saltcedar seedlings if overbank flooding occurs. Cottonwoods provide valuable sources of food and shelter for a variety of birds, mammals, and arthropods.

Status—Widespread and common.

Jane Mygatt

Peachleaf Willow   (*Salix amygdaloides*)

Apr–May

Taxonomy—Willow Family: Salicaceae.

Identification—Dioecious tree to 12 m tall; young twigs yellow to grayish yellow; leaves alternate, broadly lanceolate, upper leaf surface yellow-green, lower surface glaucous (whitish bluish waxy), 5–13 cm long and 22–36 mm wide; leaf margins finely glandular serrate, petioles 10–20 mm long; inflorescence spikelike with numerous unisexual flowers, emerging with the leaves.

Natural history—Peachleaf willow grows on alluvial soil along the banks of rivers, ponds, and wetlands.

Status—Widespread and common.

Photographs: Jane Mygatt

Coyote Willow   (*Salix exigua*)

Apr–May

Taxonomy—Willow Family: Salicaceae.

Identification—Dioecious (separate female and male trees) shrubs or small trees to 5 m tall; leaves with fine hairs on both surfaces, linear to linear-lanceolate, entire to minutely toothed, the blades 2–10 cm long and 3–10 mm wide, petioles 3–7 mm long; capsules 4–5 mm long; flowers unisexual, in separate terminal spikelike clusters; sepals and petals absent; flowers appear before or with emerging leaves.

Natural history—Coyote willow can form extensive stands where it becomes a habitat-defining plant. Willows help stabilize stream banks from erosion and provide food and shelter to wildlife. Native Americans use the stripped branches in basket making. Willows contain salicin, a chemical closely related to acetylsalicylic acid, commonly known as aspirin.

Status—Widespread and abundant.

Jane Mygatt

Goodding's Willow   (*Salix gooddingii*)

Mar–May

Taxonomy—Willow Family: Salicaceae.

Identification—Dioecious(separate female and male trees) tree to 15 m tall; young twigs yellowish, older branches dark gray; leaves alternate, green on both surfaces (lower surface may be a lighter shade of green but never bluish waxy), narrowly lanceolate, leaf margins finely toothed, the blades 6–13 cm long  and 9.5–15 mm wide, petioles 5–10 mm long; inflorescence spikelike with numerous unisexual flowers, emerging with the leaves.

Natural history—Goodding's willow grows on riverbanks and in marshy habitats, where it provides important wildlife habitat, especially as nesting sites for birds.

Status—Widespread and common.

Yerba Mansa   (*Anemopsis californica*)

Jun–Sep

Taxonomy—Lizard's Tail Family: Saururaceae.

Identification—Perennial herb to 10–50 cm tall; leaves large, leathery, entire, basal; sepals and petals absent, flowers inconspicuous, arranged in dense spikes, subtended by white, petal-like bracts 10–25 mm long.

Natural history—Yerba mansa grows in moist alkaline or saline soils in shady areas of the bosque under cottonwood trees. As the plant matures, reddish purple blotches appear on the leaves and stems. The roots of this plant have a variety of medicinal uses. Yerba mansa is increasingly being used as a bedding plant in southwestern gardens.

Status—Widespread and occasionally encountered.

Roundleaf Monkeyflower   (*Mimulus glabratus*)

May–Jul

Taxonomy—Figwort Family: Scrophulariaceae.

Identification—Perennial herb to 40 cm long, spreading and rooting at the nodes; stems fleshy, reddish; leaves opposite, broadly ovate to rounded, entire to toothed; flowers solitary from leaf axils; corolla slightly 2-lipped, 9–15 mm long, yellow.

Natural history—Roundleaf monkeyflower is a wetland species that can form thick mats in open areas in the mud.

Status—Widespread and common.

Moth Mullein (*Verbascum thapsus*) [INT]

Jun–Sep

Taxonomy—Figwort Family: Scrophulariaceae.

Identification—Biennial herb 1–2 m tall; herbage with dense woolly hairs; leaves alternate, (first-year leaves a basal rosette); leaf blade oblong, entire to somewhat toothed to 40 cm long; inflorescence a spikelike cluster to 30 cm tall or more; flowers 5-lobed, 15–25 mm wide, yellow; stamens 5, upper 3 with hairs; fruit a hairy capsule to 1 cm long.

Natural history—Moth mullein is a weedy species that grows in dry, disturbed ground. Sometimes used medicinally. Introduced from Eurasia.

Status—Widespread and common.

Photographs: Jane Mygatt

American Brooklime (*Veronica americana*)

May–Aug

Taxonomy—Figwort Family: Scrophulariaceae.

Identification—Perennial herb 10–60 cm long; stems erect to spreading; leaves opposite, ovate to lanceolate, 1–8 cm long, 6–30 mm wide, toothed; inflorescence in leaf axils, 10–25 flowered; flowers 5–10 mm wide, violet-blue; fruit a rounded capsule with a slight notch at the tip, 2.5–4 mm long.

Natural history—American brooklime grows in shallow water or along moist riverbanks and swampy areas.

Status—Widespread and frequently encountered.

Jane Mygatt

Tree of Heaven (*Ailanthus altissima*) [INT]

Jun–Jul

Taxonomy—Tree of Heaven Family: Simaroubaceae.

Identification—Deciduous and dioecious tree to 35 m tall; compound leaves pinnate, composed of 11–25 lanceolate leaflets; inflorescence in terminal panicles, yellow-green; fruit dry and winged (samara).

Natural history—Tree of heaven grows in disturbed, sandy soils and is a serious weed tree in many states. Reproducing both by seed and vegetatively by sprouting, it easily establishes in recently burned areas. The fruits mature from July to September. Introduced from central China.

Status—Widespread and common.

Jane Mygatt

Oak-leaf Thorn-apple   (*Datura quercifolia*)

Aug–Oct

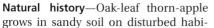

Taxonomy—Potato Family: Solanaceae.

Identification—Annual or perennial herb to 1.5 m tall; leaves alternate, 6–20 cm long; leaf margins wavy and lobed (oak-like), the lobes often toothed; flowers tubular-funnelform, 5-lobed, 4-6 cm long, lavender-purple; fruit a spiny round capsule.

Natural history—Oak-leaf thorn-apple grows in sandy soil on disturbed habitats. *Quercifolia* means "oak leaved." All parts of this plant are poisonous. Butterfly and moth larvae (Lepidoptera) feed on the leaves of *Datura*.

Status—Localized and occasionally encountered.

Sacred Thorn-apple   (*Datura wrightii*)

Jul–Oct

Taxonomy—Potato Family: Solanaceae; Synonymy: *Datura meteloides*.

Identification—Perennial herb to 1.5 m tall; herbage with short hairs, malodorous; leaves ovate, 5–20 cm long, gray-green; flowers axillary, solitary, trumpet shaped, 15–20 cm long, white with lavender tinges, fragrant; fruit a round, nodding, spiny capsule.

Natural history—Sacred thorn-apple grows in disturbed sandy soil. The large, white, fragrant flowers open at dusk and are pollinated by hawk moths. All parts of the plant contain toxic alkaloids.

Status—Widespread and common.

Pale Wolfberry   (*Lycium pallidum*)

May–Jun

Taxonomy—Potato Family: Solanaceae.

Identification—Shrub to 2 m tall; stems branched, spiny; leaves alternate, mostly in clusters (fascicles); leaf blade spatulate, 1–4 cm long × 5–15 mm wide; flowers funnel shaped, 2 cm long; petals 5-lobed, greenish white tinged with purple; fruit a berry, 8–10 mm wide, red at maturity.

Natural history—Pale wolfberry occurs in sandy soils of riparian woodlands but is more common in desert regions and can tolerate saline soils. The fruits are eaten by wildlife.

Status—Localized and frequently encountered.

Torrey's Wolfberry (*Lycium torreyi*)

May–Jun

Taxonomy—Potato Family: Solanaceae.

Identification—Shrub to 2 m tall; stems branched, may or may not have stout spines; leaves alternate, mostly in clusters (fascicles); leaf blade spatulate to linear, 1–5 cm long × 3–10 mm wide; flowers narrowly funnel shaped, greenish lavender or whitish; calyx 2.5–4.5 mm long, the lobes with small fine hairs; corolla 10–15 mm long, the lobes with small fine hairs; fruit a berry, 6–10 mm wide, red at maturity.

Photographs: Jane Mygatt

Natural history—Torrey's wolfberry grows in dry, sandy soils. Similar to pale wolfberry (*Lycium pallidum*) but differing in having smaller flowers and fine hairs on the lobes of the calyx and corolla (can be seen with a hand lens). *Lycium* berries provide food for birds and wildlife.

Status—Widespread and common.

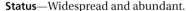

Silverleaf Nightshade (*Solanum elaeagnifolium*)

May–Oct

Taxonomy—Potato Family: Solanaceae.

Identification—Perennial herb from deep-rooted rhizomes to 1 m tall; herbage with rough hairs and sharp prickles; leaves oblong, the margins entire to wavy; flowers purple, occasionally white, 5-lobed, 20–30 mm wide; fruit a berry, yellow to orange, 8–15 mm wide.

Natural history—Silverleaf nightshade grows in highly disturbed sandy soils. A close relative of the potato, this plant is toxic to livestock. The underground roots can grow to a depth of 3 m. Silverleaf nightshade can outcompete many agricultural species and is difficult to control. It readily spreads by seed, by its extensive root system, and by root fragmentation due to digging or tilling. Although a native species, it is considered a noxious weed in many states.

Robert Sivinski

Status—Widespread and abundant.

Buffalobur (*Solanum rostratum*)

Jun–Sep

Taxonomy—Potato Family: Solanaceae.

Identification—Annual herb to 45 cm tall; herbage covered with hairs and numerous yellow prickles; leaves alternate, irregularly lobed, 4–12 cm long; flowers funnel shaped, 5-lobed, 2–3 cm wide, yellow; fruit a berry, surrounded by the prickly calyx.

Natural history—Buffalobur grows on disturbed soils in open habitats. Although native to New Mexico, this is a noxious weed in many states.

Robert Sivinski

Status—Widespread and frequently encountered.

Saltcedar
(*Tamarix chinensis*) [INT]

Apr–Jul

Taxonomy—Tamarix Family: Tamaricaceae; Synonymy: *Tamarix pentandra*.

Identification—Shrub to 6 m; branches slender, reddish or purplish; leaves alternate, minute, scalelike, blue-green; flowers spikelike, 2–5 cm long, pink.

Natural history—Saltcedar grows in sandy soils and is a facultative wetland species, usually growing in wet or moist soils. Smaller populations can also occur in dry openings and in the bosque. It hybridizes with *Tamarix ramosissima*, a closely related but separate species of saltcedar, and some of the bosque populations may be hybrids. Spreading rapidly, it forms dense thickets along the river and the ditch system. Saltcedar is listed as a noxious weed in New Mexico. Introduced from Asia and eastern Europe.

Status—Widespread and abundant.

Robert Sivinski

Siberian Elm
(*Ulmus pumila*) [INT]

Mar–Apr

Taxonomy—Elm Family: Ulmaceae.

Identification—Deciduous tree to 20 m tall; leaves alternate, ovate, 2–6 cm long, leaf margins toothed, leaf base unequal; flowers small, pale green, occurring in spring before the leaves; fruit a samara (dry and winged), round, notched at the tip, less than 15 mm wide.

Natural history—Siberian elm is particularly common in the Albuquerque bosque and grows in sandy soil in disturbed areas. The copious amounts of wind-dispersed samaras allow for rapid establishment and spread of these weedy trees. Siberian elm is listed as a noxious weed in New Mexico.

Status—Widespread and abundant.

Robert Sivinski

Jane Mygatt

Thicket Creeper   (*Parthenocissus vitacea*)

Fruiting Jul–Oct

Taxonomy—Grape Family: Vitaceae.

Identification—Perennial woody vine reaching 20 m; tendrils branched, without adhesive pads; leaves 5–7 lobed, coarsely toothed; flowers small, in flat-topped clusters (cymes), greenish; fruit a round berry, 8–10 mm wide, bluish black at maturity.

Natural history—Thicket creeper grows as an understory plant in shade and climbs by wrapping its tendrils around plants, fences, and posts. The berries are poisonous to mammals but provide valuable winter food for birds. The leaves turn brilliant colors in the autumn. Flowers in spring.

Status—Widespread and common.

Jane Mygatt

Warty Caltrop   (*Kallstroemia parviflora*)

Aug–Oct

Taxonomy—Creosote Bush Family: Zygophyllaceae.

Identification—Annual herb; stems prostrate to ascending, to 80 cm long; leaves pinnately compound, leaflets in 4–10 pairs; flowers solitary, axillary; petals 6–12 mm long, orange; fruit ovoid, 4–6 mm wide, with a column (beak) 4–6 mm long.

Natural history—Warty caltrop grows in open habitats in sandy soil. Somewhat resembles puncturevine (*Tribulus terrestris*) and often grows next to it.

Status—Widespread and common.

Patrick Alexander

Puncturevine   (*Tribulus terrestris*) [INT]

Apr–Sep

Taxonomy—Creosote Bush Family: Zygophyllaceae.

Identification—Annual spreading herb to 50+ cm long; leaves pinnately compound, leaflets in 3–6 pairs, oblong to elliptic, hairy; flowers solitary, axillary; petals 2–5 mm long, yellow; fruit 5-angled, 5–12 mm wide, separating at maturity into 5 nutlets, each with 2 very sharp spines.

Natural history—Puncturevine grows in open, sandy areas and tolerates drought. It is a nuisance weed that readily reproduces by seed. Another common name for puncturevine is goat head, referring to the spiny fruits that resemble a goat's head with horns. Introduced from the Mediterranean.

Status—Widespread and abundant.

Jane Mygatt

GLOSSARY OF BOTANICAL TERMS

Achene: A small, dry fruit with one seed that does not break open when mature.

Alternate: Referring to the leaf arrangement of one leaf per node.

Annual: A plant completing its life cycle (germination, flowering, fruiting, and dying) in one year.

Anther: Upper portion of the stamen where pollen is produced.

Areole: A leaf node reduced to a raised area on a cactus stem (pad) where the spines attach.

Ascending: Growing upward at an angle of 40 to 60 degrees.

Auricle (Auriculate): An ear-shaped lobe at the base of a leaf. In grasses and sedges, auricles occur at the junction of the leaf blade and leaf sheath.

Awn: A slender bristle found at the apex of a structure.

Axil: The upper angle between the leaf and attachment to the stem.

Axis: Pertaining to the stem or elongated supporting structure.

Berry: A fleshy fruit without a core or stone.

Biennial: A plant completing its life cycle in two years, generally flowering the second year.

Blade: The broad portion of the leaf.

Bract: A modified leaf below a flower or inflorescence.

Calyx: The outer series of the perianth, composed of sepals.

Capsule: A dry fruit that splits open at maturity at several points.

Collar: The area at the junction of the leaf blade and sheath.

Column: A group of united floral structures.

Corolla: The combination of petals of a single flower, usually colored.

Corona: A whorl of appendages between the stamens and corolla characteristic of the Milkweed family (Asclepiadaceae).

Culm: The stem of a grass, rush, or sedge.

Cyathium: A small cup-shaped structure that bears the separate male and female flowers; found in several members of the Spurge family (Euphorbiaceae).

Cyme (Cymose): A broad, flat-topped array of flowers where the central flowers mature first.

Deciduous: Having leaves that are shed in response to seasonal change or drought.

Decumbent: Lying flat on the ground with the stem ends ascending.

Dioecious: Flowers unisexual; male and female flowers separated on different plants.

Disarticulation: Parts separating at maturity, referring to the Grass family (Poaceae).

Discoid head: In the Aster family (Asteraceae), discoid heads have only disk florets, no ray (ligulate) florets.

Disk florets: In the Aster family (Asteraceae), the corollas of the disk florets are tubular and have four or five teeth at the apex.

Drupe: A fleshy fruit with the seed enclosed in a hard "stone."

Entire: Referring to margins of leaves or petals being without teeth or lobes.

Fertile: Referring to a flower or floret being capable of producing fruit and seeds.

Floret: A small flower in a dense cluster, as in the Aster family (Asteraceae), or the term for a grass or sedge flower that includes the lemma and palea.

Follicle: A dry fruit splitting along one side when mature.

Frond: A leaflike structure.

Glabrous: Smooth surface with no hairs.

Glandular: Possessing glands; an appendage that produce (or appear to produce) a secretion.

Glaucous: A whitish or bluish waxy covering.

Glume: In the Grass family (Poaceae), the lower bracts of a spikelet.

Glutinous: Sticky or gummy.

Head: A term used for the Aster family (Asteraceae) to indicate a dense cluster of flowers or florets attached to an enlarged tip of the peduncle.

Herbaceous: A plant composed of nonwoody tissue.

Herbage: A term used to collectively describe the stems and leaves.

Hispid: Stiff, bristlelike hairs.

Inflorescence: The flower cluster.

Involucre (involucral bract): Leaflike bracts subtending a flower or inflorescence.

Lanceolate: Lance shaped; broadest toward the base, tapering toward the apex.

Leaflet: A leaflike section of a compound leaf.

Legume: A fruit type characteristic of the Bean family (Fabaceae) that splits along two sides when mature.

Lemma: The lowermost of two bracts enclosing a grass flower above the glumes.

Ligulate florets: In the Aster family (Asteraceae), ligulate florets are strap shaped and have three or five teeth at the apex.

Ligulate heads: In the Aster family (Asteraceae), ligulate heads have only ligulate (strap-shaped) corollas. No disk (tubular) florets are in the inflorescence.

Ligule: A hairy or membranous projection on the inside junction of the leaf sheath and blade. Often a diagnostic feature in the Grass family (Poaceae).

Margins: Referring to the edges of the leaf blades.

Node: The place on a stem where leaves and branches originate.

Oblanceolate: Inversely lanceolate; wider toward the apex, narrowing toward the leaf base.

Oblong: Longer than wide, the sides nearly parallel.

Obovate: Inversely ovate; wider toward the apex, narrowing toward the base.

Ochrea: A translucent sheath at the base of the leaf that forms a tube around the stem. A unique feature found in some members of the Buckwheat family (Polygonaceae).

Opposite: Referring to the leaf arrangement of two leaves per node.

Palea: In the Grass family (Poaceae), the upper of the two bracts enclosing a grass floret.

Panicle: A branched inflorescence with younger flowers opening at the apex.

Papilionaceous: Pealike flowers typical of the Bean family (Fabaceae).

Pedicel (Pedicellate): The flowering stalk to a single flower of an inflorescence.

Peduncle: The flowering stalk of an inflorescence.

Pepo: A fleshy fruit with a hard, thickened rind, characteristic of the Cucumber family (Cucurbitaceae).

Perennial: A plant lasting three or more years.

Perfect: A flower or floret with functional pistil and stamens.

Perianth: The collective term for the outer parts of the flower including the calyx and corolla.

Petal: An individual part of the corolla, usually colored.

Petiole: The stalk of a leaf blade or compound leaf.

Phyllaries: In the Aster family (Asteraceae), the leaflike bracts subtending the heads.

Pinnate (Pinnately): A compound leaf with leaflets attached on two opposite sides of an elongated axis.

Pinnatifid: Pinnately lobed or parted at least part way to the midrib of the leaf.

Pistil (Pistillate): The seed-producing (female) structure, consisting of ovary, style, and stigma.

Prostrate: Lying flat on the ground.

Punctate: Pitted with minute depressions.

Raceme: An inflorescence with flowers on pedicels.

Radiate heads: In the Aster family (Asteraceae), *radiate heads* refers to an inflorescence that has both ray and disk florets. The strap-shaped ray florets are positioned around the margin of the inflorescence, and the disk florets are found in the center.

Ray floret: In the Aster family (Asteraceae), ray florets are strap shaped (ligulate) and have three or five teeth at the apex.

Reflexed: Bending backward or downward.

Rhizome: A horizontal underground stem.

Sepal: An individual part of the calyx, usually green.

Serrate: Referring to a toothed leaf margin, with the teeth angling upward.

Sessile: Without a stalk.

Sheath: The part of the leaf (especially in grasses and sedges) that wraps around the stem.

Silicle: A fruit type characteristic of the Mustard family (Brassicaceae) that is rounded, usually not more than twice as long as wide.

Silique: A fruit type characteristic of the Mustard family (Brassicaceae) that is linear and elongate, longer than wide.

Spatulate: Spatula shaped; broad and rounded at the apex, tapering toward the base.

Spike: An inflorescence of sessile flowers on an elongated axis.

Spikelet: In grasses and sedges, a secondary unit of the spike containing the florets. In the Grass family (Poaceae), the spikelet is almost always subtended by glumes.

Stamens: The male organs of the flowers that produce pollen.

Staminate: Flowers having stamens only, pistils absent.

Sterile: Infertile, a flower or floret without a pistil or a stamen without an anther.

Stolon: Horizontal stems growing at, or above, ground level.

Synonymy: An alternate name for the same species.

Woody: Perennial plants with hardened stems.

SCOPE FOR THIS GUIDE

Invertebrates are animals lacking a backbone and usually with an external skeleton; they include most of the species on earth. All living organisms are classified by their evolutionary relationships from broad to specific: phylum, class, order, family, genus, and species. In this guide invertebrates are represented by four major groups, or phyla: Arthropoda (insects, arachnids, centipedes, millipedes, crustaceans), Annelida (earthworms, leeches), Mollusca (snails, slugs), and Nematomorpha (horsehair worms). In the bosque the majority of macroinvertebrates are arthropods. We have organized species by phyllum, class, order, family, and genus. Because many invertebrates do not have common names and because common names often vary by region (a doodlebug to some is an ant lion to others), we have emphasized their scientific names. However, we use published common names when available for species and have coined our own common names when they are not.

Taxonomic Scope

As with all organisms, biologists place the arthropods in categories that reflect their evolutionary history and relationship to one another. The examples on the next page list the classification of a spider, a butterfly, and a moth, beginning with the broadest category (phylum) and ending with the narrowest (species) (Table 1). The only group membership that the spider shares with the butterfly and moth is at the level of phylum, showing that it is only distantly related to them. The butterfly and moth, which are more closely related, share membership in the same phylum, class, and order. However, their evolutionary lineages separated at this point, producing different families, genera, and species. Table 2 shows the classification of the invertebrate groups presented in this field guide to the class level. Classification below the class level is provided with each species account.

This guide includes 251 invertebrates, only a fraction of the 2000 to 5000 species that we estimate occur in the bosque. We chose species that are common and often observed (such as butterflies, dragonflies, wasps, beetles, and grasshoppers) or are representatives of broader groups such as large families, whose genera cannot be easily separated (such as caterpillar hunter wasps in the genus *Ammophila*).

Table 1. Examples of biological taxonomic classification ranks applied to three different arthropods from the phylum- to the species-level ranks.

Common name	Carolina Wolf spider	Variegated Fritillary	White Lined Sphinx moth
Phylum	Arthropoda	Arthropoda	Arthropoda
Class	Arachnida	Insecta	Insecta
Order	Araneae	Lepidoptera	Lepidoptera
Family	Lycosidae	Nymphalidae	Sphingidae
Genus	*Hogna*	*Euptoieta*	*Hyles*
Species	*carolinensis*	*claudia*	*lineata*

Table 2. Taxonomic classification of invertebrate groups presented in this guide from the phylum- to the class-level ranks.

Phylum Mollusca
    Class Gastropoda: snails and slugs

Phylum Annelida
    Class Hirudinea: leeches
    Class Oligochaeta: earthworms

Phylum Nematomorpha
    Class (= Superfamily) Gordioidea: horsehair worms

Phylum Arthropoda
    Subphylum Chelicerata: chelicerates
        Class Arachnida: spiders, mites, scorpions, wind scorpions, etc.
    Subphylum Crustacea: crustaceans
        Class Malocostraca: isopods
    Subphylum Atelocerata
        Class Diplopoda: millipedes
        Class Chilopoda: centipedes
        Class Hexapoda (or Insecta): insects

Environmental Scope

We have selected species that are primarily terrestrial, living all or a part of their lives on land (some partly aquatic species are also included, such as dragonflies and water striders) and that occur in bosque habitats. We also include some species that are only associated with human structures and activities, such as agriculture. Many species make use of both human-made and more natural environments.

ARTHROPOD DIVERSITY, ECOLOGY, AND LIFE HISTORY

The numbers and kinds of arthropods (and invertebrates in general) can be overwhelming, particularly for people accustomed to identifying birds or mammals. No field guide can encompass all the arthropod species that occur in an area, and because of their small size, many species cannot be identified in the field. All the same, we have highlighted some of the more obvious species and others that can be recognized at a more general level, such as family.

Arthropods perform many ecological functions, or "jobs," in the environment: ants aerate soil and disperse plant seeds; bees, flies, and wasps pollinate flowers; crickets and pill bugs recycle dead plant tissue; spiders and robber flies hunt other arthropods; grasshoppers and some beetles consume live plants; and vertebrate animals eat many kinds of arthropods.

ARTHROPOD BODY STRUCTURE

Arthropod body shape and behavior are extremely variable, reflecting the way species "make a living" in the environment. Some examples involving just the legs are the "baskets" on bees' legs that carry pollen, the long legs of hunting wasps that help them carry their prey, the short legs of dragonflies that enable them to perch easily on branches, the strong broad legs of Jerusalem crickets that facilitate digging, the strong hind legs of grasshoppers that allow them to hop, and the long thin legs of tiger beetles that make rapid running possible.

The supporting framework, or exoskeleton, of arthropods encases the body and must be shed in order for the animal to grow. In the summer it is common to find the shed casing of the last juvenile stage of new adult cicadas on trees and fence posts. Arthropods follow one of two paths to the adult stage. The first is gradual metamorphosis, where juvenile stages resemble small adults but without wings or reproductive function. An example of this is a cricket, whose juveniles look like small adults without wings. The second is complete metamorphosis, where the juvenile stages (larvae) look nothing like the adult and must pass through a pupal stage before becoming an adult. The best-known example of this is a caterpillar, chrysalis, and adult butterfly. Most arthropods lay eggs, but in a few cases they give birth to a juvenile stage (aphids, for example).

The main body sections of insects and spiders are illustrated opposite page. Insects have three main body sections: head, thorax, and abdomen; six legs; and often two pairs of wings. Spiders have two main body sections: the cephalothorax (head and thorax combined) and abdomen; eight legs; and no wings.

Other arthropods such as scorpions, centipedes, millipedes, and isopods have bodies with many segments and eight or more legs. Worms such as earthworms, leeches, and horsehair worms have long many-segmented bodies but no legs. Mollusks (snails and slugs) lack segmented bodies and are composed largely of a soft but muscular body that produces a mucus trail and with rasping mouthparts for scraping vegetation or algae. Snails are covered by a calcium carbonate shell, but slugs are not. These features are summarized in Table 3 on the next page.

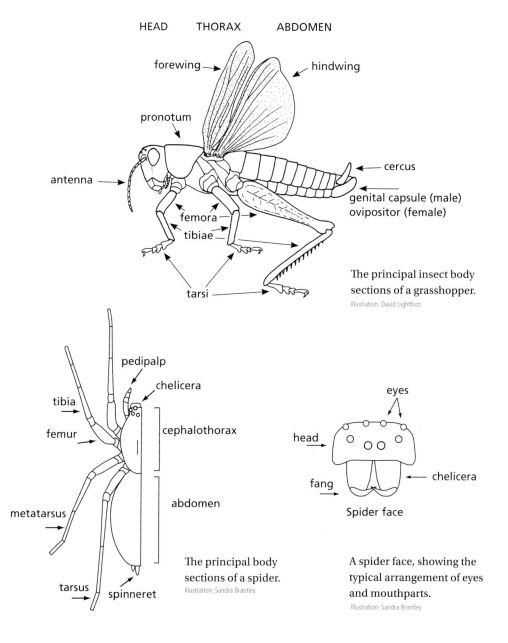

The principal insect body sections of a grasshopper.
Illustration: David Lightfoot

The principal body sections of a spider.
Illustration: Sandra Brantley

A spider face, showing the typical arrangement of eyes and mouthparts.
Illustration: Sandra Brantley

Table 3. Comparison of the basic structures of arthropods and other invertebrates.

Invertebrate group	Body segments	Antennae/ tentacles	Eye types	Mouthpart types	Legs	Wings
Snails (with shell)	1	4	Simple	Scraping	0	0
Slugs (without shell)	1	4	Simple	Scraping	0	0
Leeches	Many	0	Simple	Sucking	0	0
Earthworms	Many	0	0	Chewing	0	0
Horsehair worms	Many	0	0	0	0	0
Arachnids	1–2	0	Simple	Piercing	8	0
Centipedes	Many	2	Simple	Piercing	Many	0
Millipedes	Many	2	Simple	Chewing	Many	0
Isopods	Many	4	Compound	Chewing	14	0
Insects	3	2	Simple and compound	Piercing, chewing, sucking	6	2 or 4

Invertebrates have body parts that vertebrate animals do not have, and different invertebrate groups have different kinds of body parts. Anatomy is important for describing and identifying invertebrates. We use some of the more basic anatomical terms in this guide to describe and differentiate among invertebrates. Below is a list of those anatomical terms that we use for arthropod identification in this guide:

Elytron (plural, **elytra**)—In beetles, the thickened forewings that form the "shell" over the body; beetles use only the second pair of wings for flight.

Ovipositor—Structure at the end of the abdomen in female insects used for depositing eggs.

Palps—Fingerlike appendages near the mouth that are sensory and used in feeding.

Prolegs—On caterpillars, short abdominal appendages with tiny hooks that help the insect hold on to leaves and stems. The true legs are attached to the thorax as in all insects.

Pronotum—The part of the exoskeleton that covers the thorax on the top or dorsal side; often enlarged or modified in beetles, grasshoppers, and crickets.

Seta (plural, **setae**)—The hair covering the arthropod body; may be short or long, sparse or dense; used to detect vibrations and airborne chemicals and to help regulate body temperature.

Spinneret—Appendages at the end of the abdomen in spiders that release silk fibers for making webs and wrapping prey.

Stinger—Structure at the end of the abdomen in female Hymenoptera and both sexes in scorpions used to inject venom as a defense against predators or as the way to paralyze prey.

HOW TO FIND ARTHROPODS

Arthropods occur in conspicuous places such as on flowers or other plant parts, but many can be found by turning over logs, peeling away bark of dead trees, looking for appropriate perches or webs in shrubs, and walking along the shore of the river or along a ditch bank. In short, almost anyplace in the bosque will be home to arthropods; some are even active on sunny days in the winter.

OTHER RESOURCES

Internet

The Internet is home to many sites with information about arthropods; pages are written by government agencies, professional societies, universities, and individuals. As a result, the content varies widely from little more than an image to in-depth information on identification, life stages, and distribution.

Search by the common or scientific names given in this guide. Because the number of arthropods is so large, you may not find information for a particular species but will find more at the broader level of genus or family.

Field Guides

Many field guides to insects and other arthropods exist; we include a sample of some additional North American guides that readers may find useful.

General Arthropod Field Guides (see the bibliography for full citations)
Borror and White (1970), Milne and Milne (1980), Arnett and Jacques (1981), Eaton and Kaufman (2007), Evans (2007).

Field Guides to Selected Arthropod Groups
Caterpillars: Allen et al. (2005).
Dragonflies: Biggs (2004).
Butterflies: Brock and Kaufman (2003).
Spiders, scorpions, centipedes, millipedes, isopods: Levi (2002).

Suppliers for Insect-Collecting Supplies and Books
BioQuip Products
2321 Gladwick St.
Rancho Dominguez, CA 90220
www.bioquip.com

Carolina Biological Supply
2700 York Road
Burlington, NC 27215–3398
www.carolina.com

PHYLUM MOLLUSCA

Brown Gardensnail

(Cornu aspersum) ✳ ✳ [INT]

Sp, Su, F

Taxonomy—Class: Gastropoda; Order: Geophila; Family: Helicidae.

Identification—Most mollusks are aquatic in either freshwater or saltwater habitats, but many species of land snails can tolerate relatively dry conditions by withdrawing into the shell and closing it with a thick layer of mucus. The brown gardensnail adult shell is gray-brown with dark-colored bands interrupted by yellow streaks; shell 30 mm in diameter. No native land snails are known from the bosque, but they do occur in the surrounding mountains.

Natural history—Feed on living vegetation, active at night and after rains. Snails are hermaphrodites: each individual contains reproductive organs for both sexes but cross-fertilizes with other individuals; have elaborate courtship displays. Introduced from northwestern Europe, now established throughout the U.S.

Status—Widespread, common.

Tawny Garden Slug

(Limax flavus) ✳ ✳ [INT]

Sp, Su, F

Taxonomy—Class: Gastropoda; Order: Geophila; Family: Limacidae.

Identification—Slugs are a mollusk group without shells that live in damp terrestrial habitats. The tawny garden slug is brown with yellow spots, tentacles are bluish, mucus trail is yellow; body length 60 mm. No other slugs are known from the bosque.

Natural history—Feed on living vegetation; active at night and after rains. Slugs are hermaphrodites: each individual contains reproductive organs for both sexes but cross-fertilizes with other individuals; have elaborate courtship displays. Introduced from Europe.

Status—Widespread, common.

Pond Snails

(*Lymnea, Radix,* and others) * *

Sp, Su, F

Taxonomy—Class: Gastropoda; Order: Basommatophora; Family: Lymneidae.

Identification—Shells range from 1–7 cm in length and 2–3 cm in width. The coil of the shell is to the right, and the lung opening is also at the right side. The shell color is plain dark brown with a pale edge at the bottom and around the shell opening. The snails' tentacles are longer, darker, and more pointed than those of the gardensnail.

Natural history—Feed on living vegetation in ponds or other slow-moving water. Snails are hermaphrodites: each individual contains reproductive organs for both sexes but cross-fertilizes with other individuals.

Status—Widespread, common.

PHYLUM ANNELIDA

Freshwater Leech

(*Erpobdella punctata*) * *

Sp, Su, F

Taxonomy—Class: Hirudinea; Order: Arhynchobdellida; Family: Erpobdellidae.

Identification—Pale brown segmented worm with underlying blue or violet color, body length 70 mm; has sucker at the end of the abdomen but the mouth has no sucker or teeth. Probably the only leech in the bosque.

Natural history—Free-living predator on other invertebrates, including snails and small insects; it is not a blood feeder or parasite. Found in shallow quiet water near the shore, often concealed under leaves or wood, crawl on land during rains. Leeches are hermaphrodites: each individual contains reproductive organs of both sexes but cross-fertilizes with other individuals.

Status—Widespread, uncommon.

Earthworm (*Aporrectodea tuberculata*) ✳ ✳ [INT]

Sp, Su, F

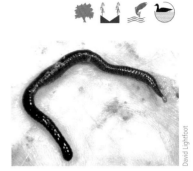

Taxonomy—Class: Oligochaeta; Order: Haplotaxida; Family: Lumbricidae.

Identification—Typical earthworm appearance, soft bodied, brown-gray, body length 75 mm.

Natural history—Found under wet leaf litter in forest and along the shore when river levels are low enough to leave exposed undisturbed shoreline. Consume dead and decaying organic matter, helping with the process of decomposition so that nutrients are returned to the soil for use again by plants. Earthworms are hermaphrodites: each individual contains reproductive organs of both sexes but cross-fertilizes with other individuals. An introduced species common throughout the U.S.

Status—Widespread, common.

PHYLUM NEMATOMORPHA

Horsehair Worm (*Gordius robustus*) ✳ ✳

Su, F

Taxonomy—Order: Gordioidea; Family: Gordiidae.

Identification—Nematomorph worms are internal parasites of insects, especially grasshoppers and crickets. When mature, the worm causes the insect to seek water; the worm breaks out through the insect's body and continues its life in freshwater. Very long and thin, found in shallow areas of streams and rivers, also stock ponds or tanks; difficult to tell head from tail and body is often coiled; dark brown in color; body length 20 cm. Probably the only horsehair worm species in the bosque.

Natural history—Adult female worms lay eggs in water, which are eaten by a variety of intermediate hosts, which are then eaten (probably as scavenged carcasses) by the final grasshopper or cricket host. It is unknown how the worm influences the behavior of the insect to seek out water.

Status—Widespread, uncommon.

PHYLUM ARTHROPODA

Pallid Wind Scorpion

(*Eremobates pallipes*)✳✳

Sp, Su, F

Taxonomy—Class: Arachnida; Order: Solifugae; Family: Eremobatidae.

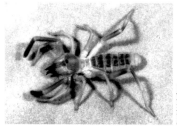

Identification—Arachnids are common arthropods that can be separated from insects by having 8 legs, 2–8 simple eyes, and sensory palps that are developed as pincers in scorpions and pseudoscorpions. Arachnids do not have antennae, wings, or compound eyes. Wind scorpions are not true scorpions because they lack pincers, tail, and stinger. The pallid wind scorpion is yellowish-reddish-tan, body hairy; 8 legs plus 2 blunt-tipped palps near face; 2 black eyes on top of the head. Body length 30 mm. Several similar-appearing species occur in the region.

Natural history—Gradual metamorphosis; live in burrows, active aboveground at night searching for insect and spider prey. Not venomous, use large jaws to crush prey. The name wind scorpion comes from the way they run rapidly like a leaf blowing in the wind; not harmful to people. Also called solifuges, sun spiders, and camel spiders.

Status—Widespread, uncommon.

David Lightfoot

Pseudoscorpion

(*Hysterochelifer urbanus*) ✳✳

Su, F

Taxonomy—Class: Arachnida; Order: Pseudoscorpiones; Family: Cheliferidae.

Identification—Tiny arachnids; body length 2 mm; resemble true scorpions in having pincers but unlike scorpions do not have a tail and are not venomous. Several similar species occur in the bosque.

Natural history—Gradual metamorphosis; inhabitants of damp leaf litter or at the bases of trees or grasses. Predators of small insects such as springtails and termites or early larval stages of other insects. Produce silk from glands in their pincers to wrap eggs in. Best collected by sifting through leaf litter; difficult to locate during dry seasons.

Status—Widespread, uncommon.

David Lightfoot

Coahuila Scorpion

(Vaejovis coahuilae) ✳ ✳

Su, F

Taxonomy—Class: Arachnida; Order: Scorpiones; Family: Vaejovidae.

Identification—Scorpions are arachnids that have lobsterlike bodies with pincers and a tail. The Coahuila scorpion is tan with small, thin pincers and the tail segments short and thick. Middle eyes look like black dots at the front of the head; lateral eyes on side of head are smaller. Body length 45 mm, including tail. Several similar-appearing scorpion species occur in the region.

Natural history—Gradual metamorphosis; prefers sandy soils with a cover of leaves, stones, or fallen branches under which it rests during the day, active at night. Eat small insects and other arthropods, including other members of its species. Exoskeletons are fluorescent under ultraviolet light, producing a yellow-green color.

Status—Widespread, uncommon.

Brown Dog Tick

(Rhipicephalus sanguineus) ✳ ✳

Sp, Su, F

Taxonomy—Class: Arachnida; Order: Acari; Family: Ixodidae.

Identification—Ticks are large mites that feed on blood, similar in appearance to small robust spiders, but the body is not divided into 2 parts. The brown dog tick is a dark reddish brown, broad, flat-bodied mite with short legs, adult body 3 mm (top photo). Females become enlarged with blood and become light gray and much larger (~10 mm) (bottom photo). Larval stage has 6 legs, other juvenile stages and all adults have 8. Few other ticks occur in the bosque and are specific to certain vertebrate hosts.

Natural history—Gradual metamorphosis; all life stages prefer to feed on dogs but rarely will feed on other mammals and humans. An unusual species that can complete its life cycle indoors: females lay eggs in protected areas where dogs are likely to pass. Life cycle can be completed in 2 months but can be extended in cold temperatures. The dog tick does not transmit Lyme disease.

Status—Widespread, common.

Velvet Mites

(*Trombidium* spp.) ✳ ✳

Sp, Su

Taxonomy—Class: Arachnida; Order: Acari; Family: Trombidiidae.

Identification—Bright red mites with a dense covering of short hair that gives them a velvety appearance; body length 4 mm. Several similar species and many other types of smaller mites occur in the bosque.

Natural history—Gradual metamorphosis; wander on the ground surface following summer rainfall, otherwise spend most of their time underground. Adults are predators on small insects and other invertebrates; juvenile stages are parasitic on other arthropods such as grasshoppers, crickets, and beetles but do not kill the hosts.

Status—Widespread, common.

David Lightfoot

Tarantula

(*Aphonopelma* sp.) ✳ ✳

Su, F

Taxonomy—Class: Arachnida; Order: Araneae; Family: Theraphosidae.

Identification—Spiders are similar to insects but have 2 main body parts, 8 legs, and mouthparts with piercing fangs. All have venom, but only a few species are dangerous to humans. Large, hairy dark spiders; body length 40–45 mm; yellow hair on the head and long reddish hairs on the abdomen; eyes in small group at the front of the carapace.

Natural history—Gradual metamorphosis; require about 7 years to mature; males generally die within a year after maturing, but females may live up to 25 years; females and juveniles live in burrows and stay close to them. Adult males wander in search of females in late summer. Their venom is not dangerous to humans.

Status—Widespread, uncommon.

Sharyn Davidson

Pill Bug Spider

(*Dysdera crocata*) ✳ ✳ [INT]

Sp, Su, F

David Lightfoot

Taxonomy—Class: Arachnida; Order: Araneae; Family: Dysderidae.

Identification—Legs and head red-brown, abdomen pale tan, fangs long and projecting forward; body length 8–12 mm. No other similar reddish spider with large fangs occurs in the bosque.

Natural history—Gradual metamorphosis. Feed mostly on pill bugs and sow bugs and were introduced with them from the Mediterranean region. Large fangs help the spiders hold prey; one fang rests on top of a pill bug or sow bug while the other fang pierces the underside. Spend most of their time in a silk retreat under decaying logs and in deep leaf litter.

Status—Widespread, uncommon.

Cellar Spider

(*Physocyclus enaulus*) [INT]

Sp, Su, F

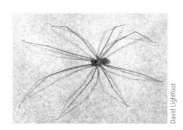

David Lightfoot

Taxonomy—Class: Arachnida; Order: Araneae; Family: Pholcidae.

Identification—Pale yellow with very long thin legs, abdomen round, sometimes has a mottled blue or gray appearance; body length 5–7 mm. Six eyes instead of the usual 8 (in 2 groups of 3); head with a dark Y-shaped marking. These are not recluse spiders. One other similar species occurs in the bosque.

Natural history—Gradual metamorphosis; very common in open grassy areas and in houses and garages; webs are minimal with the spiders hanging upside down from them; females wrap eggs in a few strands of silk and hold them with the fangs until they hatch. Often occur near black widows, which they eat. Another common name is the daddy longlegs spider.

Status—Widespread, common.

Black and Yellow Garden Spider

(*Argiope aurantia*) ✳ ✳

Sp, Su, F

David Lightfoot

Taxonomy—Class: Arachnida; Order: Araneae; Family: Araneidae.

Identification—Black spiders with bright yellow markings on the abdomen, head covered with silvery hair, legs black with some areas of red or yellow; body length female 19–28 mm, male 5–8 mm. Web is a round, vertical orb web with a zigzag line through the middle, made with silk, called the stabilimentum. Compare with banded garden spider.

Natural history—Gradual metamorphosis. Common spiders of roadsides and gardens as well as in trees and shrubs. Webs of adult females may be 50–60 cm in diameter and trap relatively large insects. Spiders usually found in the middle of the web during the day with the legs aligned with the stabilimentum and facing head down. They wrap prey in silk before biting and feeding on them. Sometimes called zipper spiders for the distinctive silk zigzag in their web.

Status—Widespread, common.

Banded Garden Spider

(*Argiope trifasciata*) ✳ ✳

Sp, Su, F

Andrea Campanella

Taxonomy—Class: Arachnida; Order: Araneae; Family: Araneidae.

Identification—Abdomen silvery white with thin bands of black and yellow, head covered with silvery hair. Body length female 19–25 mm, male 5–6 mm. Spin the typical spiderweb, or orb web, with an X shape or line through the middle, made with silk in a zigzag pattern (the stabilimentum). Compare with black and yellow garden spider.

Natural history—Gradual metamorphosis; common spiders of gardens as well as in trees and shrubs. Spiders usually found in the middle of the web during the day with its legs aligned with the stabilimentum and facing head down. They wrap prey in silk before biting and feeding on them.

Status—Widespread, common.

Pumpkin Spider

(Araneus illaudatus) ✳ ✳

Sp, Su, F

Taxonomy—Class: Arachnida; Order: Araneae; Family: Araneidae.

Identification—Abdomen oval or somewhat triangular, patterned tan or orange in color with light marks in a pattern like a cat's face, with "shoulder humps" on the anterior end; these features are the basis for the common names cat-faced spider or pumpkin spider. Body length adult female 15–20 mm, male 5–8 mm; spin a typical spiderweb, or orb web, up to 45 cm in diameter. Several other similar but smaller orb-web-building spiders occur in the bosque.

David Lightfoot

Natural history—Gradual metamorphosis; in spring and summer the small juvenile stages are rarely noticed, but in the fall large adult females are prominent. Tend to build webs around houses and yards in addition to trees and shrubs. Spiders spend the day in a retreat in a corner of the web but come to the center when an insect gets trapped in the web. They wrap prey in silk before biting and feeding on them.

Status—Widespread, common.

Long-jawed Orb Weaver

(Tetragnatha laboriosa) ✳ ✳

Sp, Su, F

Taxonomy—Class: Arachnida; Order: Araneae; Family: Tetragnathidae.

Identification—Slender, elongate body, abdomen varies from plain silver to having paired dark markings, legs tan, body length 8–10 mm. Males with greatly enlarged chelicerae (the fangs and their supporting bases). Make small orb webs with open centers and relatively few spiral threads; webs positioned in vegetation overhanging water. No similar spiders in the bosque.

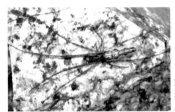

David Lightfoot

Natural history—Gradual metamorphosis. Prey are small flies from damp forest habitat or the shoreline of the river or ditches. The enlarged fangs of the males are used in fighting for access to females; they are not dangerous to humans.

Status—Widespread, uncommon.

Western Black Widow Spider

(*Latrodectus hesperus*) ✳ ✳

Sp, Su, F, W

Taxonomy—Class: Arachnida; Order: Araneae; Family: Theridiidae.

Identification—Females easily recognized by black body (sometimes with a few red or yellow marks), round abdomen with red "hourglass" shape on the underside (top photo). Body length female 10-13 mm, male 4-5 mm. Females hang upside down in the web. Juveniles and males are brown with red or white lines or spots, and the hourglass shape may be white or orange (bottom photo, male). Compare with the close relative, Steatoda spider, which is similar in shape and size but does not have the hourglass pattern on the abdomen.

Natural history—Gradual metamorphosis; the tangled webs are usually placed near the ground in low vegetation and are common in human structures too; spiders remain in retreats during the day, hanging in the web at night to catch prey. Egg sacs are hung in the web; the female does not always eat the male that mates with her. Black widow venom is dangerous to humans, but the spiders are not aggressive.

Status—Widespread, common.

Photographs: David Lightfoot

Steatoda Spider

(*Steatoda grandis*) ✳ ✳

Sp, Su, F

Taxonomy—Class: Arachnida; Order: Araneae; Family: Theridiidae.

Identification—Related to and resembling black widows but somewhat smaller; body length female 5-10 mm, male 3-7 mm. Head pale to red-brown; abdomen with a white stripe around the front and partway down the middle, while the rest is a dark purplish black; no hourglass mark on the underside of the abdomen (top photo). Males are also dark colored (bottom photo). Compare with black widow.

Natural history—Gradual metamorphosis; common in open grassy areas or where there are fallen tree branches or abandoned rodent burrows; the tangled webs are usually placed near the ground in low vegetation and are common in human structures too. Spiders remain in retreats during the day, hanging in the web at night to catch prey; venom is not considered as dangerous to humans as that of black widows.

Status—Widespread, common.

Photographs: David Lightfoot

Brown Wandering Spider   (*Meriola decepta*) ✴ ✴

Sp, Su, F

Taxonomy—Class: Arachnida; Order: Araneae; Family: Corinnidae.

Identification—Medium-size (5-6 mm) spider with dark reddish brown head and pale abdomen. Compare with pill bug spider.

Natural history—Gradual metamorphosis; these spiders do not live in webs but hunt for prey on the ground or in vegetation. They are active mostly at night.

Status—Widespread, common.

Running Spider   (*Thanatus coloradensis*) ✴ ✴

Sp, Su

Taxonomy—Class: Arachnida; Order: Araneae; Family: Philodromidae.

Identification—Yellowish to tan speckled spider, resembling a crab spider; body length 3-5 mm. Abdomen with a dark line down the middle of the anterior half; called the heart mark because a spider's heart is in the abdomen at about that position. Several similar running spiders occur in the bosque.

Natural history—Gradual metamorphosis; agile runners found in grasses and herbaceous plants; feed on small insects and spiders in vegetation.

Status—Widespread, common.

Apache Jumping Spider   (*Phidippus apacheanus*) ✴ ✴

Sp, Su

Taxonomy—Class: Arachnida; Order: Araneae; Family: Salticidae.

Identification—Very conspicuous with bright red abdomen and the rest of the body black; legs short and stout; body hairy; body length 9-11 mm. Two of the 8 eyes greatly enlarged; bases of the fangs metallic green. Movement is in short jerky bursts or the spider can jump; males usually more brightly colored than females. Many other species of jumping spiders occur in the bosque; most have different and distinctive markings and colors.

Natural history—Gradual metamorphosis; do not make webs but hunt prey by stealth in shrubs and trees; vision very good. Courtship displays elaborate; active during the day; frequently wander into buildings, where they readily climb walls and windows; alert and watchful, even of people.

Status—Widespread, common.

Flower Crab Spider

(*Mecaphesa* sp.) ✳ ✳

Su, F

Taxonomy—Class: Arachnida; Order: Araneae; Family: Thomisidae.

Identification—First 2 pairs of legs twice as long as the body and often held out to the side, resembling a crab; body length females 4–6 mm, males 3–4 mm. Body pale yellow or white with reddish marks, head pale green, body sparsely covered with short stiff hairs; males have first 2 pairs of legs with red bands.

Natural history—Gradual metamorphosis; coloring conceals these spiders well on the stems and flowers of herbaceous plants; do not make a web. Ambush hunters that feed on insects and other spiders, generally on flowers.

Status—Widespread, common.

David Lightfoot

Black Ground Spider

(*Zelotes anglo*) ✳ ✳

Sp, F

Taxonomy—Class: Arachnida; Order: Araneae; Family: Gnaphosidae.

Identification—Brownish gray to black without markings, abdomen may appear velvety; body length 4–8 mm. Middle pair of eyes on the back row appear pearly. Two of the 6 spinnerets (organs that spin silk) are large and may be seen protruding from the tip of the abdomen. Several similar ground spiders occur in the bosque.

Natural history—Gradual metamorphosis; nocturnal wandering spiders that do not make webs, although they use silk for egg sacs, retreats, and draglines ("safety lines") while walking. Found under bark or rocks during the day; prey consist of small insects and spiders living in grasses or under leaves and bark.

Status—Widespread, common.

David Lightfoot

Funnel-web Spider

(*Agelenopsis longistylus*) ✳ ✳

Sp, Su, F

Taxonomy—Class: Arachnida; Order: Araneae; Family: Agelenidae.

Identification—The funnel-web spider is brown and gray with 2 dark bands on the carapace, abdomen patterned with lines or dots, legs dull yellow-orange and may have dark bands; body length 6–8 mm. Resemble wolf spiders but live in webs (wolf spiders do not).

Natural history—Gradual metamorphosis; build webs usually close to the ground in grasses or in shrubs; web consists of a sheet or platform with a funnel-shaped retreat at the back. Webs are easy to see when sunlight angles are low, such as early morning or dusk. A common house spider (*Tegenaria domestica*) is a member of this family. Not related to the dangerous Australian funnel-web spider.

Status—Widespread, common.

Brown Lynx Spider

(*Oxyopes salticus*) ✳ ✳

Sp, Su

Taxonomy—Class: Arachnida; Order: Araneae; Family: Oxyopidae.

Identification—Head yellow with gray bands; abdomen tan to black and may have iridescent scales, legs with very long spines; body length 4–7 mm. Wandering spiders with eyes in a hexagonal pattern on top of the head. Compare with thin-legged wolf spider, which also has long spines on the legs. Several other lynx spiders occur in the bosque.

Natural history—Gradual metamorphosis; found in shrubs or larger herbaceous plants, where they hunt for insect prey coming to flowers or leaves; can jump short distances between twigs. Courtship is partly visual, with males pursuing females up and down plant stems; females attach egg sacs to leaves and guard them until they hatch.

Status—Widespread, common.

Thin-legged Wolf Spider

(Pardosa sternalis) ✳ ✳

Sp, Su, F

Taxonomy—Class: Arachnida; Order: Araneae; Family: Lycosidae.

Identification—Small spiders with long thin legs that have long spines; body length 4-6 mm. Body dark in coloration, head with thin yellow midline stripe, 2 of the 8 eyes are enlarged; wandering spiders that do not spin webs. Compare with lynx spider, which also has long spines on the legs. Similar to other wolf spiders in the bosque.

David Lightfoot

Natural history—Gradual metamorphosis; found along shorelines of rivers and ditches, run quickly on sand and walk on water surface of still pools; take cover in rocks or vegetation. Males perform dances during courtship; females carry egg sacs attached to the spinnerets at the tip of the abdomen (see photo); juveniles ride on the mother's back for a week or so.

Status—Widespread, common.

Carolina Wolf Spider

(Hogna carolinensis) ✳ ✳

Sp, Su, F

Taxonomy—Class: Arachnida; Order: Araneae; Family: Lycosidae.

Identification—Large, heavy-bodied spiders, brownish in color and covered with gray hairs (top photo); body length female 22-35 mm, male 18-20 mm. Head and abdomen black underneath; 2 of the 8 eyes enlarged. Wandering spiders that do not spin webs but may occasionally dig burrows. Several similar wolf spiders occur in the bosque.

Natural history—Gradual metamorphosis; fast runners and visual hunters that overcome their prey with strength as well as venom. Males perform dances during courtship; females carry egg sacs attached to the spinnerets at the tip of the abdomen; juveniles ride on the mother's back for a week or so (bottom photo).

Status—Widespread, common.

Photographs: David Lightfoot

Desert Centipede   (*Scolopendra polymorpha*) ✳ ✳

Su, F

Taxonomy—Class: Chilopoda; Order: Scolopendromorpha; Family: Scolopendridae.

Identification—Centipedes are long wormlike arthropods with many body segments and 1 pair of legs per segment; the last pair of legs are used as sensory organs. The head has antennae and clusters of small eyes on the side of the head. The forelegs are modified as fangs under the head. In the desert centipede, the head is red or tan, body segments yellowish with blue band; curved venomous fangs under head; 1 pair of legs per segment, 21 pairs of legs, last pair modified for sensory functions and can pinch; body length 112 mm, body shape flattened. The most common large centipede of the bosque.

Natural history—Gradual metamorphosis. Found under logs, stones, dead leaves; active at night or after rains. Voracious predator of arthropods either by ambush or active hunting. Life span may extend several years. Females lay eggs and wrap their bodies around them for protection. Venom not dangerous to people, but bite is painful.

Status—Widespread, uncommon.

Stone Centipede   (*Taiyubius harrietae*) ✳ ✳

Sp, Su, F

Taxonomy—Class: Chilopoda; Order: Lithobiomorpha; Family: Lithobiidae.

Identification—Stone centipedes are reddish tan or brown with 15 pairs of legs. Body length 20-25 mm, body shape flattened. Compare with desert centipede, which is larger and lighter in color and has 21 pairs of legs.

Natural history—Gradual metamorphosis; prefer places that are damp and offer concealment. Found by turning over leaf litter or stones or by examining decaying logs. Predators of small insects and spiders. Females protect their eggs until they hatch by wrapping their bodies around them. Venom not dangerous to people.

Status—Widespread, uncommon.

Desert Millipede   (*Orthoporus ornatus*) ✳ ✳

Su, F

David Lightfoot

Taxonomy—Class: Diplopoda; Order: Spirostreptida; Family: Spirostreptidae.

Identification—Millipedes are wormlike arthropods with many legs and a cylindrical shape. Their exoskeletons contain calcium and in dead individuals turn white over time. The desert millipede is large (body length 12.5 cm) and brown. Desert millipedes occur in rocky areas upslope from the bosque. Tiny duff millipedes do occur in the bosque but are seldom observed.

Natural history—Gradual metamorphosis; these millipedes spend most of their time underground feeding on decaying plant matter. During the summer rainy season they come to the surface, sometimes in large numbers in localized places. When handled, they release a bad-smelling fluid and coil up their bodies. They need several years to reach maturity.

Status—Widespread, uncommon.

Pill Bug or Roly-poly   (*Armadillidium vulgare*) ✳ ✳ [INT]

Sp, Su, F

David Lightfoot

Taxonomy—Subphylum: Crustacea; Order: Isopoda; Family: Armadilliidae.

Identification—Isopods are among the few land crustaceans and are more closely related to crayfish and crabs than to insects and spiders. The pill bug is gray (sometimes with light spots), convex shape, with several body segments, 7 pairs of legs; body length 12–15 mm. When disturbed, it rolls into a ball to protect the soft underside. Compare with sow bug and millipedes.

Natural history—Gradual metamorphosis. Introduced into the U.S. from the Mediterranean region in the 19th century. Prefers areas with thick damp leaf litter, feeds on decaying wood and leaves; commonly seen in the bosque. Pill bugs' decomposer role is important in returning nutrients to the soil.

Status—Widespread, common.

Sow Bug   (*Porcellio laevis*) ✳ ✳ [INT]

Sp, Su, F

Taxonomy—Subphylum: Crustacea; Order: Isopoda; Family: Porcellionidae.

Identification—Uniform gray, relatively flattened shape, body with several segments, 7 pairs of legs, body length 12–15 mm. When disturbed cannot roll into a ball. Compare with pill bug and millipedes.

Natural history—Gradual metamorphosis. Introduced into the U.S. from the Mediterranean region in the 19th century. Prefers areas with thick damp leaf litter, feeds on decaying leaves, leaving only the veins in a lacy pattern; commonly seen in the bosque. Sow bugs' decomposer role is important in returning nutrients to the soil.

Status—Widespread, common.

Entomobryid Springtails   ✳ ✳

Sp, Su, F, W

Taxonomy—Class: Hexapoda; Order: Collembola; Family: Entomobryidae.

Identification—Springtails are very small wingless insects that jump with a flexible, springlike appendage under the abdomen; soft bodied and most are gray in color. Entomobryids are pale with blue or purple markings; body length 3–5 mm. Many species in several families are common in the bosque.

Natural history—Found in moist habitats with dense vegetation or deep plant litter; feed on fungi and decaying plants; can occur in large numbers; can be active in winter.

Status—Widespread, common.

Silverfish   (*Lepisma* sp.) ✳ ✳

Sp, F

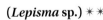

Taxonomy—Class: Hexapoda; Order: Thysanura; Family: Lepismatidae.

Identification—Soft bodied, wingless, silver-gray, eyes widely separated; 3 filaments extend from the end of the body; length 10–12 mm. An additional species occurs under leaf litter on the ground in the bosque; body is dark gray-blue with pale legs and antennae.

Natural history—Gradual metamorphosis. Live in cool damp areas with plant litter; feed on dead plants. Found on tree trunks and logs.

Status—Widespread, common.

Mayfly   (*Caenis simulans*) ✳ ✳

Su, F

Taxonomy—Class: Hexapoda; Order: Ephemeroptera; Family: Caenidae.

Identification—Fragile insects with clear wings held over the body at rest; 2 long filaments (cerci) extending from the end of the abdomen; elongated forelegs. Usually mottled gray in color, body length 13–15 mm.

Natural history—Gradual metamorphosis; juveniles aquatic, living on the bottoms of ponds, streams, and rivers; feed on algae. Adults emerge from water in large numbers to mate, live only a few days but fly and may be found far from water.

Status—Widespread, uncommon.

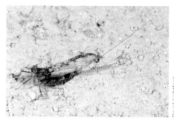

David Lightfoot

Blue-eyed Darner Dragonfly   (*Aeshna multicolor*) ✳ ✳

Sp, Su, F

Taxonomy—Class: Hexapoda; Order: Odonata; Family: Aeshnidae.

Identification—Dragonflies are large, long-bodied insects with long wings and are powerful fliers. Their large eyes cover most of their heads. They are larger than related damselflies and hold the wings outspread at rest. The immature states look very different and live in water (see flame skimmer photos). Blue-eyed darner male, eyes bright blue and body blue with dark brown markings (top photo); female, eyes brownish and body greenish blue with brown markings, wings clear (right side of bottom photo; male on left), body length 70–75 mm. Compare with common green darner.

Natural history—Gradual metamorphosis. Juvenile stages are aquatic predators and require several years to mature. Adults breed in ponds and lakes but may be found far from water; perch on twigs and branches. Adults are predators of small flying insects such as mosquitoes. Males patrol (fly back and forth) their territories, looking for females.

Status—Widespread, uncommon.

Photographs: Gordon Warrick

Common Green Darner Dragonfly   (*Anax junius*) ✳✳

Sp, Su, F

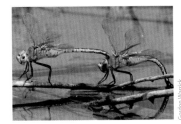

Taxonomy—Class: Hexapoda; Order: Odonata; Family: Aeshnidae.

Identification—Green darner is large, with green eyes and thorax, male, abdomen blue with brown dorsal streak, female, abdomen green with brown dorsal streak; body length 70–80 mm; wings clear, sometimes with yellowish tint (photo: male on left, female on right). Compare with blue-eyed darner.

Natural history—Gradual metamorphosis. Juvenile stages are aquatic predators and may require several years to mature. Adults breed in ponds and lakes but may be found far from water; perch on twigs and branches. Adults are predators of small flying insects such as mosquitoes. Males patrol (fly back and forth) along their shoreline territories, looking for females.

Status—Widespread, common.

Blue Dasher Dragonfly   (*Pachydiplax longipennis*) ✳✳

Sp, Su, F

Taxonomy—Class: Hexapoda; Order: Odonata; Family: Libellulidae.

Identification—Stout small dragonfly with clear wings; body length 35–40 mm. Male pale whitish blue with striped thorax, bright green-blue eyes, white face (top photo). Wings clear but may have yellowish tinge and a brownish stripe at the base in males. Female striped with brown, yellow, and white, with greenish brown eyes and white face (bottom photo). Compare with western pondhawk.

Natural history—Gradual metamorphosis. Juveniles are aquatic predators. Adults breed in ponds with emergent vegetation and are predators of small flying insects. Adults are usually found near ponds, where they rest on vegetation.

Status—Widespread, common.

Eight-spotted Skimmer Dragonfly

(*Libellula forensis*) ✳ ✳

Su, F

Taxonomy—Class: Hexapoda; Order: Odonata; Family: Libellulidae.

Identification—Wings with 2 large black blotches and 2 large white blotches; body length 40 mm. Males are pale chalky whitish blue with a black thorax and eyes like male twelve-spotted skimmer but without black wing tips; females are black, yellow, and white with dark gray eyes (photo). Compare with twelve-spotted skimmer, widow skimmer, and common whitetail. Several other black and white skimmers occur in the bosque.

Natural history—Gradual metamorphosis; juveniles are aquatic predators; adults breed in ponds and slow ditches. Adults are predators of small flying insects and found near ponds, where they perch on emergent vegetation.

Status—Widespread, common.

Widow Skimmer Dragonfly

(*Libellula luctuosa*) ✳ ✳

Su, F

Taxonomy—Class: Hexapoda; Order: Odonata; Family: Libellulidae.

Identification—Males pale chalky whitish blue with a black thorax and eyes, wings black at base and white on outer half (top photo). Females are black, yellow, and white with dark gray eyes, wings black at base and clear on outer half except for black tips (bottom photo). Body length 40–50 mm. Compare with twelve-spotted skimmer and common whitetail. Several other black and white skimmers occur in the bosque.

Natural history—Gradual metamorphosis; juveniles are aquatic predators. Adults breed in ponds and slow ditches. Adults are predators of small flying insects and usually found near ponds, where they perch on emergent vegetation.

Status—Widespread, common.

Twelve-spotted Skimmer Dragonfly

(*Libellula pulchella*) ✳ ✳

Sp, Su, F

Taxonomy—Class: Hexapoda; Order: Odonata; Family: Libellulidae.

Identification—Forewings with 3 large black blotches alternating with 2 large white blotches, hind wings with 3 large black blotches alternating with 3 large white blotches; body length 50–55 mm. Males have whitish bodies (photo), and females have brown bodies like the female eight-spotted skimmer. Compare with eight-spotted skimmer, widow skimmer, and common white-tail. Several other black and white skimmers occur in the bosque.

Gordon Warrick

Natural history—Gradual metamorphosis; juveniles are aquatic predators; adults breed in ponds and slow streams. Adults are predators of small flying insects and are often found near ponds, where they perch on emergent vegetation.

Status—Widespread, common.

Flame Skimmer Dragonfly

(*Libellula saturata*) ✳ ✳

Sp, Su, F

Taxonomy—Class: Hexapoda; Order: Odonata; Family: Libellulidae.

Identification—Male with light red body, wings red on basal half, eyes red; pale stripe along top of the body (top photo). Female pale red with pronounced dorsal white stripe, red eyes, wings clear with red tinge. Body length 50–60 mm. Compare with variegated meadowhawk.

Tom Kennedy

Natural history—Gradual metamorphosis; juveniles are aquatic predators (bottom photo). Adults breed in ponds and slow ditches and are predators of small flying insects. Adults sometimes range far from water.

Status—Widespread, common.

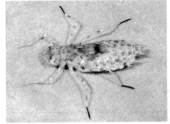

David Lightfoot

Western Pondhawk Dragonfly (*Erythemis collocata*) ✳ ✳

Su, F

Taxonomy—Class: Hexapoda; Order: Odonata; Family: Libellulidae.

Identification—Clear wings; body length 40 mm. Males pale chalky whitish blue (top photo), females and young males bright green with black stripes (bottom photo, female). Both genders have greenish blue eyes and a green face. The similar eastern pondhawk dragonfly is rare in the bosque. Compare with blue dasher dragonfly.

Natural history—Gradual metamorphosis; juveniles are aquatic predators. Adults breed in ponds and slow ditches and are predators of small flying insects. Usually found near ponds, where they perch on emergent vegetation or on bare ground.

Status—Widespread, common.

Photographs: Gordon Warrick

Desert Whitetail Dragonfly (*Plathemis subornata*) ✳ ✳

Sp, Su, F

Taxonomy—Class: Hexapoda; Order: Odonata; Family: Libellulidae.

Identification—Males pale chalky whitish blue with a black thorax and eyes, wings with broad black bands on outer half but clear at tips, white at the base (top photo). Females are black, yellow, and white with dark gray eyes, wings with narrow black bands on outer half and at tip plus black marks at base (bottom photo). Body length 40–45 mm. Compare with twelve-spotted skimmer and widow skimmer. Several other black and white skimmers occur in the bosque.

Natural history—Gradual metamorphosis; juveniles are aquatic predators. Adults breed in ponds and slow ditches. Adults are predators of small flying insects and usually found near ponds, where they perch on emergent vegetation.

Status—Widespread, common.

Photographs: Gordon Warrick

Variegated Meadowhawk Dragonfly   (*Sympetrum corruptum*) ✳ ✳

Sp, Su, F

Taxonomy—Class: Hexapoda; Order: Odonata; Family: Libellulidae.

Identification—Clear wings; body length 35–45 mm. Males with variable pattern of red, brown, yellow, gray, and white on the body and reddish eyes (top photo). Female less red, more yellow, with grayish blue eyes (under red male in bottom photo). Most common reddish skimmer in the bosque.

Natural history—Gradual metamorphosis. Juveniles are aquatic predators. Adults breed in ponds and slow ditches and are predators of small flying insects. Adults range far from water and are thought to be migratory.

Status—Widespread, common.

Tom Kennedy

Gordon Warrick

Black Saddlebags Dragonfly   (*Tramea lacerata*) ✳ ✳

Sp, Su, F

Taxonomy—Class: Hexapoda; Order: Odonata; Family: Libellulidae.

Identification—Males and females with black bodies (females also with yellow dots), clear forewings, hind wings broad and black at base, clear to tip. Body length 45–55 mm. Compare with other black and white species: widow skimmer, twelve-spotted skimmer, and common whitetail.

Gordon Warrick

Natural history—Gradual metamorphosis; juveniles are aquatic predators. Adults breed in ponds and slow ditches and are predators of small flying insects. Adults range far from water and are thought to be migratory. Common name comes from the position of the black markings on the hind wings, resembling a horse's saddlebags.

Status—Widespread, common.

American Rubyspot Damselfly

(*Hetaerina americana*) ✳ ✳

Su, F

Taxonomy—Class: Hexapoda; Order: Odonata; Family: Calopterygidae.

Identification—Damselflies are generally smaller and more delicate than dragonflies, with threadlike abdomens. The American rubyspot has a metallic bronze-red abdomen and red thorax, body length 35-50 mm. Wings of males bright red on basal half clear to tip (top photo), wings of females pale red throughout (bottom photo). No other metallic red damselflies occur in the bosque.

Natural history—Gradual metamorphosis; juveniles are aquatic predators. Adults breed in flowing water only, including the Rio Grande and ditches. Adults fly above flowing water and perch on streamside vegetation. Males often "flash" their brightly colored wings at each other when establishing shoreline territories.

Photographs: Gordon Warrick

Status—Widespread, common.

Powdered Dancer Damselfly

(*Argia moesta*) ✳ ✳

Su, F

Taxonomy—Class: Hexapoda; Order: Odonata; Family: Coenagrionidae.

Identification—Females are tan and black (top photo), males are blue and black (bottom photo); wings clear; body length 35-40 mm. Dancers rest on the ground and in vegetation with their wings folded over their bodies. Several similar dancers occur in the bosque and may be difficult to identify in the field.

Natural history—Gradual metamorphosis. Juveniles are aquatic predators. Adults breed in slow streams and shallow ponds; feed on small flying insects and fly close to plant foliage, plucking small insects from plants. Usually found close to water.

Status—Widespread, common.

Photographs: David Lightfoot

Bluet Damselfly

(*Enallagma* spp.) ✳ ✳

Sp, Su, F

Taxonomy—Class: Hexapoda; Order: Odonata; Family: Coenagrionidae.

Identification—Females are tan and black (top photo), males are blue and black (bottom photo); wings clear; body length 30–40 mm. Bluets rest on vegetation with their wings folded vertically over their bodies (compare with dragonflies). Several similar bluet damselflies occur in the bosque and are very difficult to identify to species in the field.

Natural history—Gradual metamorphosis. Juveniles are aquatic predators. Adults breed in shallow ponds and lakes; feed on small flying insects and fly close to plant foliage, plucking insects from plants. Usually found close to water.

Status—Widespread, common.

Photographs: David Lightfoot

Western Forktail Damselfly

(*Ischnura perparva*) ✳ ✳

Sp, Su, F

Taxonomy—Class: Hexapoda; Order: Odonata; Family: Coenagrionidae.

Identification—Females are orange-tan and black, males are blue, green, and black (photo); wings clear; body length 20–30 mm. Forktails have pale bands around the bases of each abdominal segment. Several similar forktail damselflies occur in the bosque and are very difficult to identify to species in the field.

Natural history—Gradual metamorphosis. Juveniles are aquatic predators. Adults breed in shallow ponds and lakes; feed on small flying insects and fly close to plant foliage, plucking insects from plants. Usually found close to water.

Status—Widespread, common.

David Lightfoot

Green Bird Grasshopper (*Schistocerca shoshone*) ✳ ✳

Su, F

Taxonomy—Class: Hexapoda; Order: Orthoptera; Family: Acrididae.

Identification—Grasshoppers are medium-size to large insects with enlarged hind legs for jumping. The fore-wings are thick and serve to protect the folding hind wings that are used for flight. Most are brown, green, or gray. Green bird grasshoppers are bright green with a longitudinal yellow dorsal stripe on the thorax, body length 60 mm. Hind wings clear, hind tibiae red; eyes with blue bands. The very similar spotted green bird grasshopper (*Schistocerca lineata*) also occurs in the bosque (bottom photo) and has black spots on the abdomen, which *S. shoshone* lacks.

Natural history—Gradual metamorphosis. Live and feed on green leafy vegetation, including shrubs and low trees. Especially common along the river and ditches.

Status—Widespread, common.

Photographs: David Lightfoot

Narrow-winged Grasshopper (*Melanoplus angustipennis*) ✳ ✳

Su, F

Taxonomy—Class: Hexapoda; Order: Orthoptera; Family: Acrididae.

Identification—Body mottled brownish gray with clear hind wings and blue hind tibiae, body length 25 mm. The spur-throat grasshoppers have a small bump on the underside of the thorax; many species occur in the bosque and are difficult to identify to species.

Natural history—Gradual metamorphosis. Feed on grasses and forbs; prefer areas with low herbaceous vegetation near trees.

Status—Widespread, common.

David Lightfoot

Differential Grasshopper (*Melanoplus differentialis*) ✳ ✳

Su, F

Taxonomy—Class: Hexapoda; Order: Orthoptera; Family: Acrididae.

Identification—Pale brown and yellowish with black markings on the sides of the hind femurs; hind wings clear and hind tibiae yellow. Body length 40 mm, the larg-est species of *Melanoplus* in the bosque.

Natural history—Gradual metamorphosis. Feed on green leafy herbaceous vegetation; especially common along ditch banks.

Status—Widespread, common.

David Lightfoot

Red-legged Grasshopper   (*Melanoplus femurrubrum*) ✳ ✳

Su, F

Taxonomy—Class: Hexapoda; Order: Orthoptera; Family: Acrididae.

Identification—Dark brownish gray and olive green with clear hind wings and red hind tibiae; body length 25 mm. Differ from other *Melanoplus* species of the bosque by the more uniform dull body color.

Natural history—Gradual metamorphosis. Feed on grasses and herbaceous plants; prefer dense vegetation along the river and ditches.

Status—Widespread, uncommon.

David Lightfoot

Red-winged Grasshopper   (*Arphia pseudonietana*) ✳ ✳

Su, F

Taxonomy—Class: Hexapoda; Order: Orthoptera; Family: Acrididae.

Identification—The red-winged grasshopper is a uniform black to very dark brown grasshopper (top photo) with bright red hind wings (bottom photo), body length 30 mm. Red hind wings and a loud crackling sound are displayed in flight. No other grasshoppers of the bosque are black with red wings.

Natural history—Gradual metamorphosis. Grasshoppers feed mostly on plant foliage; some are specific to certain plants, others are generalists. All hop and most fly when disturbed. Red-winged grasshoppers prefer open grassy habitats. The flight display is used to attract mates.

Status—Widespread, common.

Photographs: David Lightfoot

Mudflat Grasshopper   (*Encoptolophus subgracilis*) ✳ ✳

Su, F

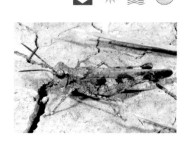

Taxonomy—Class: Hexapoda; Order: Orthoptera; Family: Acrididae.

Identification—Body pale brownish gray with 2 dark marks on forewings (top photo). Hind wings pale amber, dark brown near margins (bottom photo); body length 30 mm. Compare with the green-striped grasshopper, which includes individuals that have more brown than green on the body.

Natural history—Gradual metamorphosis. Feed on scattered grasses and forbs of damp open mudflats; body colors match the soil to provide camouflage from predators. Males actively fly short distances to attract females and produce a crackling sound.

Status—Widespread, uncommon.

Photographs: David Lightfoot

Carolina Grasshopper   (*Dissosteira carolina*) ✳ ✳

Su, F

Taxonomy—Class: Hexapoda; Order: Orthoptera; Family: Acrididae.

Identification—Gray, brown, or reddish brown, uniform color (top photo), body length 45 mm. Hind wings black with pale yellow margins (bottom photo), hind tibiae yellow to gray.

Natural history—Gradual metamorphosis. Prefer areas of bare open dry soil, especially along dirt roads and open sandy areas. Body color provides camouflage protection from predators. Feed on herbaceous plants near the soil surface. Adults do not produce sound in flight.

Status—Widespread, common.

Photographs: David Lightfoot

Mottled Sand Grasshopper (*Sphargemon collare*) ✳ ✳

Su, F

Taxonomy—Class: Hexapoda; Order: Orthoptera; Family: Acrididae.

Identification—Gray-brown with dark and light mottling, 3 mottled bands on forewings (top photo), body length 35 mm. Hind wings deep yellow at base, black band midway, and clear toward tip (bottom photo), hind tibia red. High ridge along top of thorax. Compare with the maritime grasshopper, which lacks the ridge.

Natural history—Gradual metamorphosis. Prefer open dry sandy areas near the river or ditches; well camouflaged on sandy soil. Feed on herbaceous plants near the soil surface. Adults produce a loud buzzing sound when they fly to attract mates. Several other similar species occur in the bosque.

Status—Widespread, uncommon.

Photographs: David Lightfoot

Maritime Grasshopper (*Trimerotropis maritima*) ✳ ✳

Su, F

Taxonomy—Class: Hexapoda; Order: Orthoptera; Family: Acrididae.

Identification—Gray-brown with dark and light mottling, 3 mottled bands on forewings, body length 35 mm. Hind wings deep yellow at base, black band midway, and clear toward tip, hind tibia red. Compare with pallid-winged and mottled sand grasshoppers.

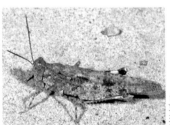

David Lightfoot

Natural history—Gradual metamorphosis. Prefer open dry sandy areas near the river or ditches; well camouflaged on sandy soil. Feed on herbaceous plants near the soil surface. Adults produce a loud buzzing sound when they fly to attract mates. Several other similar species occur in the bosque.

Status—Widespread, uncommon.

Pallid-winged Grasshopper

(*Trimerotropis pallidipennis*) ✳ ✳

Sp, Su, F

Taxonomy—Class: Hexapoda; Order: Orthoptera; Family: Acrididae.

Identification—Gray-brown with dark and light mottling, 3 dark bands on forewings (top photo), body length 35 mm. Hind wings pale yellow at base, black band midway, and clear toward tip (bottom photo), hind tibiae yellow. Compare with maritime grasshopper.

Natural history—Gradual metamorphosis. Prefer areas of bare open dry soil, especially along dirt roads and open sandy areas. Body color provides camouflage protection from predators. Feed on herbaceous plants near the soil surface. Adults produce a crackling sound in flight to attract mates.

Status—Widespread, common.

Photographs: David Lightfoot

Green-striped Grasshopper

(*Chortophaga viridifasciata*) ✳ ✳

Sp, Su, F

Taxonomy—Class: Hexapoda; Order: Orthoptera; Family: Acrididae.

Identification—Green, gray, or tan with hind wing yellowish at base and brownish near tip (brown form in photo). Body length 30 mm. Soft crackling sound produced in flight. Compare with mudflat grasshopper, which has dark cross-bands on forewings.

Natural history—Gradual metamorphosis. Feed on grasses and forbs near the ground and prefer damp grassy areas near water, especially associated with saltgrass (*Distichlis*). Body colors match both live and dead grass to provide camouflage from predators. Males actively fly short distances to attract females.

Status—Widespread, uncommon.

David Lightfoot

Two-striped Grasshopper

(*Mermiria bivittata*) ✳ ✳

Su, F

Taxonomy—Class: Hexapoda; Order: Orthoptera; Family: Acrididae.

Identification—Pale yellow or green with a black stripe on both sides of the head and thorax, body length 50 mm. Face slanted down and backward. Two black stripes on the forewings, hind wings clear, hind tibiae red. Compare with the toothpick grasshopper, which is much smaller and lacks black stripes.

Natural history—Gradual metamorphosis. Live and feed in tall perennial grasses such as sacaton (dropseed, *Sporobolus*) species. Slender body shape and coloration camouflage the grasshoppers from predators. Produce rasping sounds by rubbing their hind legs against the forewings.

Status—Widespread, common.

Toothpick Grasshopper

(*Paropomala pallida*) ✳ ✳

Su, F

Taxonomy—Class: Hexapoda; Order: Orthoptera; Family: Acrididae.

Identification—Pale yellow, gray, or green grasshoppers with face strongly slanting down and backward and a white stripe on the side of the head and thorax; body length 25 mm. Hind wings clear, hind tibiae pale yellow. Compare with the two-striped grasshopper, a larger slant-faced species.

Natural history—Gradual metamorphosis. Live and feed on perennial grasses. Slender body shape and coloration camouflage the grasshoppers from predators. Produce rasping sounds by rubbing their hind legs against the forewings.

Status—Widespread, common.

Brown-winged Slant-faced Grasshopper

(*Syrbula admirabilis*) ✳ ✳

Su, F

Taxonomy—Class: Hexapoda; Order: Orthoptera; Family: Acrididae.

Identification—Green and/or brown grasshoppers with face slanted forward, large wavy dark brown mark along top margin of forewings; hind wings and hind tibiae brown; body length 35 mm. Most similar to the toothpick grasshoppers, but more robust in body shape.

Natural history—Gradual metamorphosis. Live and feed on tall green perennial grasses. Body shape and color provide camouflage from predators. Males produce loud rasping sounds by rubbing their hind legs on their forewings.

Status—Widespread, common.

Awl-shaped Pygmy Grasshopper
(*Tettrix subulata*) ✳ ✳

Su, F

Taxonomy—Class: Hexapoda; Order: Orthoptera; Family: Tettrigidae.

Identification—Pygmy grasshoppers are mottled brown-gray; body length 10 mm. Pronotum (plate over thorax) extends back over the entire abdomen; forewings very small. Individuals with short robust body forms (top photo) occur along with more elongate forms (bottom photo). Several other species of pygmy grasshoppers probably occur in the bosque. No other grasshoppers resemble pygmy grasshoppers.

Natural history—Gradual metamorphosis. Live on damp sand and mud of riverbanks and ditch banks; feed on the algae that grow there. Very well camouflaged on the ground; body colors and patterns are highly variable.

Status—Widespread, common.

Photographs: David Lightfoot

Jerusalem Cricket
(*Stenopelmatus fuscus*) ✳ ✳

Sp, Su, F

Taxonomy—Class: Hexapoda; Order: Orthoptera; Family: Stenopelmatidae.

Identification—Robust wingless, tan crickets with large round yellow-orange heads and small dark brown eyes; abdomen with black bands; body length 50 mm. Legs robust, yellow-orange with large spines at the tips of the tibiae. No similar crickets in the bosque; somewhat similar in appearance to wind scorpions (Arachnida, Solifugae).

David Lightfoot

Natural history—Gradual metamorphosis. Burrow in sandy dry soil but wander the ground surface at night. Feed on dead plants and insects, occasionally taking live insects as well. These crickets have large powerful jaws and can bite, but have no venom and are not dangerous to humans. Also called "child of the earth" or "niña de la tierra." Adults and juveniles communicate by drumming on the ground with their bodies. They have no wings and do not chirp like true crickets.

Status—Widespread, common.

Pallid Camel Cricket   (*Ceuthophilus pallidus*) ✳ ✳

Sp, Su, F

Taxonomy—Class: Hexapoda; Order: Orthoptera;
Family: Rhaphidophoridae.

Identification—Wingless, pale tan crickets with darker
brown markings and humpbacked appearance; body
length 15 mm. Legs and antennae long and slender.
Females with flat, blunt, toothed ovipositor. The Rio
Grande sand treader camel cricket (*Ammobaenetes
phrixocnemoides*) may occur in the bosque and can be
recognized by a series of long spines at the apex of the
hind tibiae.

Natural history—Gradual metamorphosis. Live in rodent burrows,
other holes in the ground, and under logs. Feed on dead plants and
insects. Do not produce chirping sounds like other crickets.

Status—Widespread, uncommon.

Greater Angle-winged Katydid   (*Microcentrum rhombifolium*) ✳ ✳

Su, F

Taxonomy—Class: Hexapoda; Order: Orthoptera;
Family: Tettigoniidae.

Identification—Katydids are similar to crickets but usually green and winged. Green with broad leaflike
forewings; body length 60 mm. Adult females have a
blunt-tipped, flat upturned ovipositor. No other large
leaflike katydid in the bosque.

Natural history—Gradual metamorphosis. Katydids are
named for one species in the eastern U.S. whose call
sounds like "Katy did." Live in broad-leaved trees and
feed on leaves. At night, adult males produce a rapid series of 5–10 loud
ticks from high in trees, with long pauses between the series.

Status—Widespread, common.

Mexican Bush Katydid   (*Scudderia mexicana*) ✳ ✳

Su, F

Taxonomy—Class: Hexapoda; Order: Orthoptera;
Family: Tettigoniidae.

Identification—Green with narrow leaflike forewings;
body length 55 mm. Adult females have a blunt-tipped,
flat upturned ovipositor. Smaller and more narrow than
the angle-winged leaf katydid.

Natural history—Gradual metamorphosis. Live in broad-
leaved trees and shrubs and feed on leaves. At night, adult
males produce a slow series of zicking sounds from trees
and shrubs, with long pauses between the series.

Status—Widespread, common.

Delicate Meadow Katydid (*Orchelium delicatulum*) ✳ ✳

Su, F

Taxonomy—Class: Hexapoda; Order: Orthoptera; Family: Tettigoniidae.

Identification—The delicate meadow katydid is slender, green, with tan-green forewings; body length 35 mm. Adult females have a long, narrow, flat ovipositor. Another similar species also occurs in the bosque.

Natural history—Gradual metamorphosis. Delicate meadow katydids live and feed on dense, green grasses, sedges, and rushes along the river and ditches. Adult males produce a soft, high-pitched, intermittent series of buzzing trills, broken by ticking sounds. The much larger but similar-looking cone-headed katydid is less common on marsh grasses and makes a very loud continuous buzzing sound.

Status—Widespread, common.

Southwestern Riparian Field Cricket (*Gryllus alogus*) ✳ ✳

Sp, Su

Taxonomy—Class: Hexapoda; Order: Orthoptera; Family: Gryllidae.

Identification—Light brown crickets with short wings; body length 25 mm. Females have long, slender, cylindrical ovipositor. Compare with mud crack cricket. Photo of male.

Natural history—Gradual metamorphosis. Crickets are small to medium insects with flattened bodies and enlarged hind legs for jumping. Females have a cylindrical ovipositor extending from the tip of the abdomen. Males have a file and scraper on the base of their forewings used to produce sound. Live in leaf litter under the canopy of trees near the river; feed on dead plants and insects. Adult males call day and night by producing a repeated series of short chirps by rubbing their forewings together.

Status—Widespread, common.

Mud Crack Cricket (*Gryllus integer*) ✳ ✳

Sp, Su

Taxonomy—Class: Hexapoda; Order: Orthoptera; Family: Gryllidae.

Identification—Black crickets with long wings; body length ~25 mm. Forewings light brown. Compare with southwestern riparian cricket. Photo of male.

Natural history—Gradual metamorphosis. Live in cracks in mud, usually in open areas with sparse plant cover. Feed on dead plants and insects. Adult males produce series of variable-length trilling chirps by rubbing their forewings together. Adults fly to lights at night.

Status—Widespread, common.

Carolina Ground Cricket (*Eunemobius carolinus*) ✳✳

Su, F

David Lightfoot

Taxonomy—Class: Hexapoda; Order: Orthoptera; Family: Gryllidae.

Identification—Carolina ground cricket is shiny dark brown; adults may have short or long wings (photo); body length 10 mm. No other small shiny dark crickets occur in the bosque. May be confused with juvenile field crickets but have wings.

Natural history—Gradual metamorphosis. Crickets tend to be scavengers, but some also eat live plants. Most live on the ground except for tree crickets. Carolina ground cricket lives in cracks and crevices in muddy river and ditch banks, often under vegetation. Males produce a high-pitched trilling call both day and night. Long-winged adults fly to lights at night.

Status—Widespread, common.

Tree Cricket (*Oecanthus* spp.) ✳✳

Su, F

David Lightfoot

Taxonomy—Class: Hexapoda; Order: Orthoptera; Family: Gryllidae.

Identification—Slender, pale yellowish green; body length 15 mm. Adult males with a very broad file and scraper area on the forewings (photo: male *O. quadripuctatus*), females have narrow wings. Several similar tree crickets occur in the bosque and can be identified by markings on the base of the antennae and their songs.

Natural history—Gradual metamorphosis. Live and feed on tall grasses, herbaceous plants, shrubs, and low trees. Males produce loud, high-pitched, continuous trilling calls from vegetation, generally at night.

Status—Widespread, common.

Mesquite Walkingstick   (*Diapheromera velii*) ✳ ✳

Su, F

Taxonomy—Class: Hexapoda; Order: Phasmatodea; Family: Heteronemiidae.

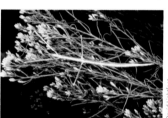

Identification—Stick insects have long thin bodies and legs. The mesquite walkingstick is greenish yellow; body length 100 mm; antennae longer than 50% of the body length; females are much broader and heavier than males. The Colorado short-horned walkingstick is similar but smaller, with antennae length less than 50% of body length.

Natural history—Gradual metamorphosis. Live and feed in shrubs and small trees, especially mesquite (*Prosopis*) and indigo bush (*Psorothamnus*). Generally sit still in the foliage during the day, where they are well camouflaged, and move about and feed at night.

Status—Southern part of the bosque, common.

Colorado Short-horned Walkingstick   (*Parabacillus coloradus*) ✳ ✳

Su, F

Taxonomy—Class: Hexapoda; Order: Phasmatodea; Family: Heteronemiidae.

Identification—Gray to yellow; body length 90 mm; length of antennae less than 20% of body length. Compare with mesquite walkingstick.

Natural history—Live and feed in plants and small shrubs of the mallow (Malvaceae) and sunflower (Asteraceae) families. Generally sit still in the foliage during the day, where they are well camouflaged, and move about and feed at night.

Status—Widespread, uncommon.

Ring-legged Earwig   (*Euborellia annulipes*) ✳ ✳ [INT]

Sp, Su, F

Taxonomy—Class: Hexapoda; Order: Dermaptera; Family: Carcinophoridae.

Identification—Earwigs are shiny, slender, dark brown insects; tip of the abdomen with pinching forceps. Adults wingless and lacking inner spine on the pincers (forceps); legs ringed with dark bands. Body length ~15 mm. Compare with brown-winged earwig.

Natural history—Gradual metamorphosis; adults and juveniles live in damp, dark places and feed on dead plant material; usually restricted to habitats around human settlements; gregarious, often occurring in groups of adults and young. The pinching forceps are used in defense against predators.

Status—Widespread, uncommon.

Arid-land Subterranean Termite

(*Reticulitermes tibialis*) ✳✳

Sp, Su, F

Taxonomy—Class: Hexapoda; Order: Isoptera; Family: Rhinotermitidae.

Identification—Social insects with king, queen, workers, and soldiers. Workers are wingless, white with yellow heads and resemble ants; body length 5 mm. Soldiers have brown heads and very large mandibles; queen and king termites are dark brown or black and have long dark brown wings, which are removed after mating (photo shows workers and winged queens and kings). The much larger southwestern damp-wood termite (*Zootermopsis laticeps*) occurs in dead cottonwood trees in the bosque.

David Lightfoot

Natural history—Gradual metamorphosis; live in large colonies underground in moist soil. Feed on dead wood in the soil or on the soil surface, especially dead tree roots. Not present in areas that flood frequently. Reproductive kings and queens have swarming flights in the spring after rains. Each colony has one fertile queen; workers cannot reproduce.

Status—Widespread, uncommon.

Bordered Mantis

(*Stagmomantis limbata*) ✳✳

Su, F

Taxonomy—Class: Hexapoda; Order: Mantodea; Family: Mantidae.

Identification—Large; green, yellow, or brown; females with wings shorter than the abdomen (top photo); males smaller and slender, with wings longer than the abdomen (bottom photo). Body length 55 mm. The California mantis, also in the bosque, is very similar but smaller and with black bands on top of the first 4 abdominal segments. Several non-native species such as the European mantis are being introduced across the country and may become naturalized in the bosque.

Natural history—Gradual metamorphosis; predators of insects and spiders, which they grab with their powerful spiny forearms. Females cannot fly; males can. Both spread their colored wings when threatened as a defense display. Usually found near flowers where insects are common; males fly to lights at night. Tan egg cases seen on vegetation during the winter. Prefer dense herbaceous vegetation, generally along woodland margins.

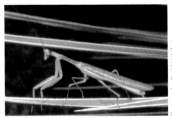

Photographs: David Lightfoot

Status—Widespread, common.

Desert Sand Cockroach

(*Arenivaga erratica*) ✳ ✳

Sp, Su, F

Taxonomy—Class: Hexapoda; Order: Blattodea; Family: Polyphagidae.

Identification—Cockroaches are best known from the few species that are found in houses, but most species live outside in plant litter. They are oval, flattened insects, with or without wings and with long legs; heads are often covered by the large thorax. Desert sand cockroach females and juveniles are dull copper brown and lack wings (top photo); adult males are elongate with whitish wings (bottom photo). Bodies are covered with short hair, and legs have stiff spines. Body length ~15 mm. The hairy desert sand cockroach (*Eremoblatta subdiaphana*) is similar but covered with more hair.

Natural history—Gradual metamorphosis. Live in sandy soil, where they burrow and feed on dead plant litter. Females and juveniles spend the day underground but wander on the surface at night; males fly to lights at night. Not pests in houses.

Photographs: David Lightfoot

Status—Widespread, common.

Field Cockroach

(*Blatella vaga*) ✳ ✳ [INT]

Su, F

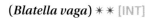

Taxonomy—Class: Hexapoda; Order: Blattodea; Family: Blatellidae.

Identification—The field cockroach is yellowish brown with 2 longitudinal dark stripes on the top of the thorax; adults have wings; body length 15 mm. Very similar to the German cockroach, not found in the bosque. Other locally occurring introduced species, such as the American, Turkistan, and Oriental cockroaches, are larger and shiny dark brown.

David Lightfoot

Natural history—Gradual metamorphosis. Live in low dense grass and deep leaf litter in damp habitats near the river; feed on dead plant litter. Spend the day under litter but wander on the surface at night; adults fly to lights at night. Thought to be introduced from southern Asia but not known to be a pest in houses.

Status—Southern parts of bosque, uncommon.

Water Strider Bug

(*Gerris remigis*) ✳ ✳

Su, F

Taxonomy—Class: Hexapoda; Order: Hemiptera; Family: Gerridae.

Identification—True bugs (Hemiptera) are similar in appearance to beetles, but the mouthparts are a piercing tube, or "beak," rather than mandibles. There are two subgroups: one with forewings that are thickened on the anterior half and membranous on the posterior half; the other with completely membranous forewings. Water striders are narrow, elongate, dark bugs with very long middle and hind legs. Forelegs are short and used for grasping. Wings are present or absent. Found on the surface of water; body length 12 mm. Several similar species occur in the bosque.

Tom Kennedy

Natural history—Gradual metamorphosis; predators and scavengers of insects floating on the surfaces of still and slow open waters. Body covered with dense velvety waterproof hair, and long waterproof hair on the tarsi allows these insects to walk and skate across the water surface. Often observed on ponds and slow river and ditch waters adjacent to the bosque.

Status—Widespread, common.

Toad Bug

(*Gelastocoris oculatus*) ✳ ✳

Su, F

Taxonomy—Class: Hexapoda; Order: Hemiptera; Family: Gelastocoridae.

Identification—Broad-bodied, toadlike insects with a rough, well-camouflaged body that is the same mottled color as the background soil; large, protruding eyes; body length 7.5–9 mm. One similar species occurs in the bosque.

Sharyn Davidson

Natural history—Gradual metamorphosis; predators of small insects and spiders along damp shorelines of the river, ditches, and ponds. Resemble and behave like small toads; hop with enlarged hind jumping legs.

Status—Widespread, common.

Bee Assassin Bug   (*Apiomerus spissipes*) ✳ ✳

Su, F

Taxonomy—Class: Hexapoda; Order: Hemiptera; Family: Reduviidae.

Identification—Assassin bugs are relatively elongate bugs with long middle and hind legs and grasping forelegs; large piercing mouthparts usually obvious. Black with red to yellow borders around the edges of the body, stout body, short legs; body length 14–19 mm. One other similar species in the bosque.

Natural history—Gradual metamorphosis; predators of other arthropods; generally occur on green plant foliage, often near flowers, where they attack bees and flies.

Status—Widespread, common.

Wheel Bug   (*Arilus cristatus*) ✳ ✳

Su, F

Taxonomy—Class: Hexapoda; Order: Hemiptera; Family: Reduviidae.

Identification—Gray-brown, legs and antennae reddish, thorax with a serrated crest that resembles a cogwheel; body length 28–36 mm.

Natural history—Gradual metamorphosis. Wheel bugs are predators that grasp arthropod prey in manner similar to that described for damsel bugs. Wheel bugs will bite humans if held, so be cautious about handling these insects. Wheel bugs are found on branches of trees and shrubs.

Status—Widespread, uncommon.

Zelus Assassin Bug   (*Zelus exsanguis*) ✳ ✳

Su, F

Taxonomy—Class: Hexapoda; Order: Hemiptera; Family: Reduviidae.

Identification—Slender, light green, small spines on the thorax, antennae long; body length 15–17 mm. Several similar species in the bosque.

Natural history—Gradual metamorphosis; predators of other arthropods; generally occur on green plant foliage, often near flowers.

Status—Widespread, uncommon.

Lygus Plant Bug   (*Lygus* sp.) ✳ ✳

Su, F

Taxonomy—Class: Hexapoda; Order: Hemiptera; Family: Miridae.

Identification—Robust, yellowish, green, or brown; body length 6 mm. Many similar species of plant bugs, including other species of *Lygus*, occur in the bosque; difficult to identify to species.

Natural history—Gradual metamorphosis; adults and juveniles feed on plant sap, many species feed on only one or a few species of plants; some species are predators of small arthropods.

Status—Widespread, common.

Yellow Plant Bug   (*Phytocoris laevis*) ✳ ✳

F

Taxonomy—Class: Hexapoda; Order: Hemiptera; Family: Miridae.

Identification—Body yellow, antennae long, body elongate, length 10 mm, large for plant bugs.

Natural history—Gradual metamorphosis; juveniles and adults live and feed mostly on plants in the sunflower family (Asteraceae).

Status—Widespread, uncommon.

White Lace Bug   (*Corythucha marmorata*) ✳ ✳

Su, F

Taxonomy—Class: Hexapoda; Order: Hemiptera; Family: Tingidae.

Identification—Lace bugs are small and flat, with the thorax and wings enlarged and lacelike. The white lace bug is pale; body length 3–4 mm. Several other species of lace bugs occur in the bosque but are darker in color.

Natural history—Gradual metamorphosis. Lace bugs feed on plant sap; often seen in clusters on leaves and can cause leaf discoloration and dead spots. In some species, the adults live with and protect the young nymphs from predators. The white lace bug prefers plants in the sunflower family (Asteraceae).

Status—Widespread, common.

Damsel Bug

(*Nabis alternatus*) ✳ ✳

Su, F

Taxonomy—Class: Hexapoda; Order: Hemiptera; Family: Nabidae.

Identification—Slender, light brownish gray; body length 6–9 mm. Similar in appearance to many other true bugs, especially plant bugs (Miridae).

Natural history—Gradual metamorphosis; predators, much like assassin bugs. All life stages feed on other small arthropods by grasping them with their forelegs, injecting prey with enzymes through their piercing mouthparts, and drinking the body fluids.

Status—Widespread, common.

David Lightfoot

Burrower Bug

(*Dallasiellus discrepans*) ✳ ✳

Sp, Su, F

Taxonomy—Class: Hexapoda; Order: Hemiptera; Family: Cydnidae.

Identification—Shiny black, broad bodied, resembling beetles; legs with many stout spines; body length 6–8 mm. Several similar species occur in the bosque.

Natural history—Gradual metamorphosis; burrow in the soil and feed mostly on the sap of grass roots. Adults wander on the soil surface at night.

Status—Widespread, common.

David Lightfoot

Tree Bark Stink Bug

(*Brochymena sulcata*) ✳ ✳

Sp, Su, F

Taxonomy—Class: Hexapoda; Order: Hemiptera; Family: Pentatomidae.

Identification—Body flat, oval; mottled light gray and brown; body length 10–12 mm; well camouflaged on the bark of trees; compare with Say's stink bug. Many species of stink bugs occur in the bosque.

Natural history—Gradual metamorphosis; feed on plant sap and prey on other smaller arthropods; give off a strong odor when disturbed or handled.

Status—Widespread, common.

David Lightfoot

Say's Stink Bug   (*Chlorochroa sayi*) ✳ ✳

Su, F

Taxonomy—Class: Hexapoda; Order: Hemiptera; Family: Pentatomidae.

Identification—Broad bodied, green with small white spots on the top side; body length 12 mm. Several other green stink bugs occur in the bosque.

Natural history—Gradual metamorphosis; adults and juveniles feed on plant sap, fruits, seeds, and flowers of many different plant species. Give off a strong odor when disturbed or handled.

Status—Widespread, common.

Harlequin Bug   (*Murgantia histrionica*) ✳ ✳

Su, F

Taxonomy—Class: Hexapoda; Order: Hemiptera; Family: Pentatomidae.

Identification—Boldly marked black and orange stink bugs, body length 10 mm. No other stink bugs in the bosque have this color pattern.

Natural history—Gradual metamorphosis; adults and juveniles feed on sap and fruits of plants in the Mustard family (Brassicaceae). Give off a strong odor when disturbed or handled.

Status—Widespread, uncommon.

Blue Stink Bug   (*Zirconia caerulea*) ✳ ✳

Su, F

Taxonomy—Class: Hexapoda; Order: Hemiptera; Family: Pentatomidae.

Identification—Dark, metallic blue stink bugs; body length 5 mm. No other stink bugs in the bosque are uniform blue.

Natural history—Gradual metamorphosis; adults and juveniles are predators, mostly of leaf beetles and their larvae. Give off a strong odor when disturbed or handled.

Status—Widespread, uncommon.

Small Milkweed Bug

(*Lygaeus kalmi*) ✶ ✶

Su, F

Taxonomy—Class: Hexapoda; Order: Hemiptera; Family: Lygaeidae.

Identification—Elongate, red and black, wing membranes with bright white dot; body length 15 mm. Another larger milkweed bug and several other black and red true bugs occur in the bosque.

Natural history—Gradual metamorphosis; adults and juveniles live and feed on milkweed plants (Asclepiadaceae). Conspicuous because they are unpalatable; incorporate milkweed poisons into their bodies.

Status—Widespread, uncommon.

False Chinch Bug

(*Nysius* sp.) ✶ ✶

Sp

Taxonomy—Class: Hexapoda; Order: Hemiptera; Family: Lygaeidae.

Identification—Gray-brown, legs pale with dark speckles, piercing mouthparts, body length 5 mm. Many other similar species occur in the bosque, and they are difficult to identify to species.

Natural history—Gradual metamorphosis; adults and juveniles feed on seeds and plant sap. Especially prefer seeds of wild mustard plants, which are numerous in the late spring.

Status—Widespread, common.

Squash Bug

(*Anasa tristis*) ✶ ✶

Su, F

Taxonomy—Class: Hexapoda; Order: Hemiptera; Family: Coreidae.

Identification—Robust shape, dull yellow-brown, head brown with 3 yellow stripes, body length 13–18 mm. Compare with stink bugs and assassin bugs. Several other coreid bugs occur in the bosque.

Natural history—Gradual metamorphosis; adults and juveniles feed on plant sap and prefer plants in the squash family (Cucurbitaceae), including coyote gourd. Juveniles and adults may be found together. They have scent glands and emit a foul odor when disturbed.

Status—Widespread, uncommon.

Red Bug
(*Dysdercus* sp.) ✳ ✳

Su, F

Taxonomy—Class: Hexapoda; Order: Hemiptera; Family: Pyrrhocoridae.

Identification—Slender, orange-red, body length 10 mm. Similar in appearance to many other true bugs, especially seed bugs (Lygaeidae).

Natural history—Gradual metamorphosis; feed on the sap of plants. Usually gregarious, found in large numbers locally but absent from other areas.

Status—Widespread, common.

Yellow Scentless Plant Bug
(*Arhyssus lateralis*) ✳ ✳

Su, F

Taxonomy—Class: Hexapoda; Order: Hemiptera; Family: Rhopalidae.

Identification—True bugs in this family lack the scent gland that is present in other members of the true bugs (Hemiptera). Yellow scentless plant bugs are yellow to reddish brown, variable in color even within a single location; body length 5-7 mm. Several other similar species occur in the bosque.

Natural history—Gradual metamorphosis; adults and juveniles feed on plant sap. The red and black box elder bug (*Leptocoris trivittatus*) is another rhopalid but mimics some species of seed bugs (Lygaeidae).

Status—Widespread, common.

Giant Cicada
(*Tibicen marginatus*) ✳ ✳

Su, F

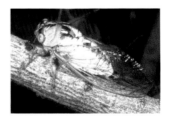

Taxonomy—Class: Hexapoda; Order: Hemiptera; Family: Cicadidae.

Identification—The only tan and white cicada associated with deciduous trees in the region; body length 35 mm. Widely separated eyes, antennae short, bristlelike, sucking mouthparts short, wings clear and held rooflike over the body (top photo). A related species (*Tibicen townsendi*) occurs in adjacent desert habitats.

Natural history—Gradual metamorphosis; juveniles feed on tree roots for 5-10 years, emerge at night and climb tree trunks to become adults, leaving behind cast skins (bottom photo). Adult males produce loud buzzing calls high in trees during summer to attract mates. Adults feed on plant sap. In the bosque the species is restricted to cottonwood bosque. These cicadas belong to a different genus from the periodical cicadas from the eastern U.S. (genus *Magicicada*).

Status—Widespread, common.

Spittle Bugs   ✳ ✳

Su, F

Sharyn Davidson

Taxonomy—Class: Hexapoda; Order: Hemiptera; Family: Cercopidae.

Identification—Small, jumping insects with broad body shape and short legs; body length 6–8 mm (top photo). Compare with leafhoppers. The juveniles produce a frothy white mass on plant stems (bottom photo).

Natural history—Gradual metamorphosis; adults and juveniles feed on plant sap through their piercing mouthparts and are found on many different plants. Foam produced by juveniles protects them from drying out and from predators.

David Lightfoot

Status—Widespread, uncommon.

Three-cornered Treehopper   (*Spissistilus festinus*) ✳ ✳

Su, F

Taxonomy—Class: Hexapoda; Order: Hemiptera; Family: Membracidae.

Identification—Treehoppers are similar in form to leafhoppers and cicadas but have stout bodies often resembling thorns. Three-cornered treehoppers are bright green with humpbacked thorax; body length 4–6 mm. Several other similar treehoppers also occur in the bosque.

David Lightfoot

Natural history—Gradual metamorphosis. Adults and juveniles feed on plant sap through their piercing mouthparts; many are host-specific to certain trees or shrubs. Three-cornered treehoppers feed on many types of herbaceous plants, especially in the pea family (Fabaceae); hop and fly when disturbed.

Status—Widespread, common.

Brown Leafhopper   (*Graphocephala* sp.) ✳ ✳

Sp, Su, F

Taxonomy—Class: Hexapoda; Order: Hemiptera; Family: Cicadellidae.

Identification—Leafhoppers look much like small cicadas; most are less than 5 mm long; usually green, brown, and/or gray, many with patterns on the wings and head. The brown leafhopper has an elongate shape (body size 5 mm), pale brown color, sometimes with black markings on the head.

David Lightfoot

Natural history—Gradual metamorphosis; adults and juveniles feed on plant sap through their piercing mouthparts; found on many different plants; hop and fly when disturbed. The brown leafhopper is often found on willows.

Status—Widespread, common.

Saltcedar Leafhopper

(*Opsius stactogalus*) ✳ ✳ [INT]

Su, F

David Lightfoot

Taxonomy—Class: Hexapoda; Order: Hemiptera; Family: Cicadellidae.

Identification—The saltcedar leafhopper is green with brown markings; body length 4-6 mm. Many species of leafhoppers occur in the bosque and are difficult to identify to species.

Natural history—Gradual metamorphosis; adults and juveniles feed on plant sap through their piercing mouthparts; found on many different plants; hop and fly when disturbed. Some species are specific to certain host plants; saltcedar leafhopper was accidentally introduced to North America with saltcedar; not known to feed on any other plant species.

Status—Widespread, common.

White Plant Hopper

(*Anormenis* sp.) ✳ ✳

Su, F

David Lightfoot

Taxonomy—Class: Hexapoda; Order: Hemiptera; Family: Flatidae.

Identification—Similar in form to leafhoppers (Cicadellidae) and cicadas (Cicadidae) but have broader wings and bodies. The white plant hopper is bright white; body length 4-5 mm. Several other types of plant hoppers (other families too) occur in the bosque, but none are white.

Natural history—Gradual metamorphosis. Plant hoppers in the flatid family feed on plant sap through their piercing mouthparts. The white plant hoppers feed on many types of plants; hop and fly when disturbed.

Status—Widespread, common.

Aphids

✳✳

Sp, Su, F

Taxonomy—Class: Hexapoda; Order: Hemiptera; Family: Aphidae.

Identification—Aphids are small soft insects that live in colonies of adults and juveniles on plant foliage; colors range from green to gray-black to orange. Green aphids are bright green; body length 2 mm (top photo). Several other similar species of green aphids occur in the bosque; aphids may also resemble leafhoppers and jumping plant lice (Psyllidae). Some aphids produce galls on plants, such as the cottonwood leaf stem gall (bottom photo).

Natural history—Gradual metamorphosis. Many aphids are specific to certain types of plants, but others such as the green aphid occur on many different host plants. Feed on plant sap through their piercing mouthparts. Ants often protect aphids and feed on sugar they excrete. Aphids have complex life histories with alternating winged, non-winged, and female-only populations.

Photographs: David Lightfoot

Status—Widespread, common.

Western Flower Thrips

(*Frankliniella occidentalis*) ✳✳

Sp, Su

Taxonomy—Class: Hexapoda; Order: Thysanoptera; Family: Thripidae.

Identification—Yellow, slender; body length 1–2 mm; wings are edged with fringe of hairs, not strong fliers. Many other species of thrips occur in the bosque.

Natural history—Complete metamorphosis. Adults and larvae can be found in large numbers feeding on flowers and new leaves, leaving white spots or causing wilting.

David Lightfoot

Status—Widespread, common.

Fiery Searcher Ground Beetle

(Calosoma scrutator) ✷✷

Su

Taxonomy—Class: Hexapoda; Order: Coleoptera; Family: Carabidae.

Identification—Beetles are easily recognized by the modified front wings, which form a protective "shell" over the body. Only the hind wings are used for flight, and many species are flightless. Ground beetles are agile hunters of insect prey. Many species can fly but spend most of their time running on the ground and are most active at night. Generally found in moist environments, many are black with metallic green and bronze coloring. The fiery searcher ground beetles have metallic green wing covers, thorax much smaller than abdomen and with metallic red/yellow margins. Body length 35 mm. Several other metallic green ground beetles occur in the bosque but are much smaller than the fiery searcher.

Natural history—Complete metamorphosis; predator that actively hunts for caterpillars so may be found on the ground or in trees. Larvae are predators of small insects and spiders on the ground. In bosque this species is restricted to cottonwood bosque.

Status—Widespread, uncommon.

Pan-American Big-headed Tiger Beetle

(Tetracha carolina) ✷✷

Sp, Su, F

Taxonomy—Class: Hexapoda; Order: Coleoptera; Family: Carabidae.

Identification—Tiger beetles are a group of ground beetles known for their swift running, large eyes, and sharp mandibles for piercing prey. They are common in areas of open bare soil. Metallic green with reddish sheen, cream-colored markings on the wing covers only at the posterior end, eyes large, legs yellow. Body length 18 mm. The only bosque tiger beetle with yellow legs.

Natural history—Complete metamorphosis; common name comes from their swift, active hunting style. Found in damp areas along shorelines and ditch banks. Unlike most other tiger beetles, they are nocturnal and do not fly. The larvae are also predacious, living in burrows with their heads at ground level to catch unwary prey that pass by.

Status—Southern part of bosque, uncommon.

Western Tiger Beetle
(*Cicindela oregona*) ✳ ✳

Sp, Su, F

Taxonomy—Class: Hexapoda; Order: Coleoptera; Family: Carabidae.

Identification—Metallic green and red with cream-colored markings on the wing covers, eyes large, legs long and thin. Body length 12 mm. Compare with bronzed tiger beetle. Several other species of similar-appearing tiger beetles occur along the bosque.

Natural history—Complete metamorphosis; common name comes from their swift, active hunting style. Found in open sandy areas, along shorelines and ditch banks, where they have a good view of their surroundings. Capture many kinds of insects. The larvae are also predacious, living in burrows with their heads at ground level to catch unwary prey that pass by.

Status—Widespread, common.

Tom Kennedy

Bronzed Tiger Beetle
(*Cicindela repanda*) ✳ ✳

Sp, Su, F

Taxonomy—Class: Hexapoda; Order: Coleoptera; Family: Carabidae.

Identification—Metallic red or green with cream-colored markings on the wing covers, eyes large, legs long and thin. Body length 12 mm. Compare with western tiger beetle. Several other species of similar-appearing tiger beetles occur along the bosque.

Natural history—Complete metamorphosis; common name comes from their swift, active hunting style. Found in open sandy areas, along shorelines and ditch banks. The larvae are also predacious, living in burrows with their heads at ground level to catch unwary prey that pass by.

Status—Widespread, common.

David Lightfoot

Pasimachus Ground Beetle
(*Pasimachus* spp.) ✳ ✳

Su, F

Taxonomy—Class: Hexapoda; Order: Coleoptera; Family: Carabidae.

Identification—Large (20–25 mm), solid black broad-bodied beetle with a "waist" between the thorax and abdomen. In some individuals the edge of the body may have a blue-purple sheen. Mandibles are large and pincer shaped. Several species occur in New Mexico, and all have the same appearance.

Natural history—Complete metamorphosis. These beetles are predators on caterpillars and other soft-bodied insects. They occur in open grassy habitats.

Status—Widespread, common.

David Lightfoot

Shoreline Ground Beetles

(*Bembidion* spp.) ✳ ✳

Sp, Su, F

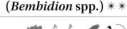

Taxonomy—Class: Hexapoda; Order: Coleoptera; Family: Carabidae.

Identification—Small (2–5 mm) beetles, sometimes with a metallic sheen; eyes large; fast running.

Natural history—Complete metamorphosis. These ground beetles are active predators on small insects and are common along open shorelines of rivers and ponds; restricted to damp shorelines.

Status—Widespread, common.

Metallic Ground Beetle

(*Poecilus chalcites*) ✳ ✳

Sp, Su

Taxonomy—Class: Hexapoda; Order: Coleoptera; Family: Carabidae.

Identification—Body straight sided, black; wing covers bright metallic green, may also be reddish or bronze. Body length 12 mm. Compare with shoreline ground beetle.

Natural history—Complete metamorphosis; predator on soft-bodied insects. Found in fields and open woods near water.

Status—Widespread, common.

Harpalus Ground Beetle

(*Harpalus pennsylvanicus*) ✳ ✳

Su, F

Taxonomy—Class: Hexapoda; Order: Coleoptera; Family: Carabidae.

Identification—Broad bodied, dark brown to black, wing covers with fine lines (striations), threadlike antennae. Body length 10–12 mm. Several similar ground beetles in the bosque.

Natural history—Complete metamorphosis; unlike most carabids, species in the genus *Harpalus* feed on seeds and roots of grasses and wildflowers. Active at night.

Status—Widespread, common.

Galerita Ground Beetle

(*Galerita janus*) ✳ ✳

Su, F

Taxonomy—Class: Hexapoda; Order: Coleoptera; Family: Carabidae.

Identification—Black body with red thorax and blue-black wing covers; legs and antennae red-brown. Body length 20 mm. No other bosque ground beetles have a red thorax.

Natural history—Complete metamorphosis; predator on soft-bodied insects. Found under leaf litter in cottonwood forest; active at night.

Status—Widespread, uncommon.

David Lightfoot

Burying Beetle

(*Nicrophorus guttulus*) ✳ ✳

Sp, Su, F

Taxonomy—Class: Hexapoda; Order: Coleoptera; Family: Silphidae.

Identification—Large (12–20 mm) black beetle with red tips on the antennae and large red patches on the wing covers. The wing covers are short, exposing some of the abdominal segments. The mandibles are pincerlike.

Natural history—Complete metamorphosis. These beetles are important decomposers of carcasses of small animals. Another common name for them is burying beetles, because a male and female dig out the ground under the carcass and then cover it with soil. Within this underground chamber the female lays eggs on the carcass, and both parents care for the larvae and keep the carcass free from fungi and bacteria. By the time the larvae are ready to pupate, they have consumed the carcass except for the bones. The parents open the chamber and leave; the larvae pupate in the soil nearby. Carrion beetles are a rare example of parental care in beetles. The American burying beetle in the midwestern U.S. is an endangered species.

David Lightfoot

Status—Widespread, common.

Carrion Beetle

(*Heterosilpha ramosa*) ✳ ✳

Sp, Su, F

Taxonomy—Class: Hexapoda; Order: Coleoptera; Family: Silphidae.

Identification—Large (11–16.5 mm) black beetles with netlike sculpturing on the wing covers. The thorax is smooth and shiny. Compare with pasimachus ground beetle and some darkling beetles. Very different in form from the burying beetle, which is also in the silphid family.

Natural history—These relatives of the burying beetles do not bury a carcass but lay their eggs under it, and the larvae feed on the carcass along with other arthropods, such as flies, that also help in decomposition. The species is common in much of the Midwest and western North America.

David Lightfoot

Status—Widespread, common.

Rove Beetles ✳✳

Sp, Su, F

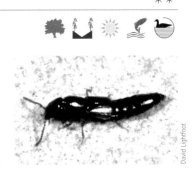

David Lightfoot

Taxonomy—Class: Hexapoda; Order: Coleoptera; Family: Staphylinidae.

Identification—Rove beetles are slender, black or brown, with most of the abdomen exposed; full-size wings folded under very short wing covers; large antlike head, piercing mandibles. Body size of most species is less than 5 mm. Many similar rove beetles of various sizes occur in the bosque. Also compare with the sap beetle.

Natural history—Complete metamorphosis; predator in moist habitats in cottonwood forest. When disturbed, run with the back of the abdomen curled over the body or take flight.

Status—Widespread, common.

Ten-lined June Beetle   (*Polyphylla decimlineata*) ✳✳

Su

Photographs: David Lightfoot

Taxonomy—Class: Hexapoda; Order: Coleoptera; Family: Scarabaeidae.

Identification—Scarab beetles are a large family, including dung beetles, leaf chafers, and June beetles. They are generally heavy bodied, small to large in size, with distinctive fan-shaped antennae and long legs. Ten-lined June beetle wing covers are orangish brown and marked by faint to bright white lines; ends of antennae are fanlike; eyes large and black (top photo). Body length 25–28 mm. One other large June beetle, *P. hammondi*, is similar but lacks pronounced white lines. Many other smaller, plain brown June beetles also occur in the bosque.

Natural history—Complete metamorphosis; adults feed on leaves of many kinds of plants, larvae are white, C-shaped grubs that feed on grass roots (bottom photo); adults are strongly attracted to lights at night.

Status—Widespread, common.

Southwestern Masked Chafer Beetle (*Cyclocephala pasadenae*) ✳ ✳

Su

Taxonomy—Class: Hexapoda; Order: Coleoptera; Family: Scarabaeidae.

Identification—Body light brown, sometimes with a few dark lines along the sides of the wing covers. Body length 10-12 mm. Similar to several other small May or June beetles.

Natural history—Complete metamorphosis; adults do not feed, larvae are white, C-shaped grubs that feed on grass roots; adults active at night and fly to lights in great numbers.

Status—Widespread, common.

David Lightfoot

Southwestern Fig Beetle (*Cotinus mutabilis*) ✳ ✳

Su, F

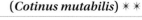

Taxonomy—Class: Hexapoda; Order: Coleoptera; Family: Scarabaeidae.

Identification—The southwestern fig beetle has green wing covers with tan margins, wings are dark; underside is bright metallic green. Body length 24-28 mm. Compare with fiery searcher ground beetle. No other nonmetallic large greenish beetle in the bosque.

Natural history—Complete metamorphosis; adults feed on ripe or decaying fruit and fly with a noisy buzz. Larvae feed on decomposing organic material.

Status—Widespread, common.

David Lightfoot

Bumble Flower Beetle (*Euphoria inda*) ✳ ✳

Su, F

Taxonomy—Class: Hexapoda; Order: Coleoptera; Family: Scarabaeidae.

Identification—Stout, square body, golden brown speckled with black; underside hairy. Body length 15 mm. No similar beetles in the bosque.

Natural history—Complete metamorphosis; adults feed on flowers and decaying fruit and buzz when they fly. Larvae feed on roots and are often found in compost piles. Found in open sunny areas.

Status—Widespread, common.

David Lightfoot

Bee-mimic Wood-boring Beetle
(*Acmaeodera* spp.) ✳ ✳

Sp, Su

David Lightfoot

Taxonomy—Class: Hexapoda; Order: Coleoptera; Family: Buprestidae.

Identification—Bee-mimic wood-boring beetles are bronze colored, bullet shaped (tapering) at the end with wing covers speckled bronze or yellow and black, large eyes; body length 8–10 mm. Several species of similar appearance occur in the bosque.

Natural history—Complete metamorphosis; adults feed on flowers and are often dusted with pollen, very active in sunlit areas on trunks, leaves, and flowers. Larvae are called flat-headed borers, which bore into and feed on many kinds of trees, shrubs, and even cacti and need several years to mature.

Status—Widespread, common.

Blue Metallic Wood-boring Beetle
(*Psiloptera drummondi*) ✳ ✳

Sp, Su

David Lightfoot

Taxonomy—Class: Hexapoda; Order: Coleoptera; Family: Buprestidae.

Identification—Blue body, bullet shaped (tapering) at the end, wing covers metallic blue with yellow spots; large eyes; body length 16–20 mm. Compare with desert blister beetle and fiery searcher ground beetle. No other large blue metallic wood-boring beetle species occur in the bosque.

Natural history—Complete metamorphosis; adults feed on flowers and are often dusted with pollen, very active in sunlit areas on trunks, leaves, and flowers. Larvae are called flat-headed borers, which bore into trees of the legume (Fabaceae) and willow (Salicaceae) families; need several years to mature.

Status—Widespread, common.

Click Beetle

(*Melanotus* sp.) ✳ ✳

Sp, Su

Taxonomy—Class: Hexapoda; Order: Coleoptera; Family: Elateridae.

Identification—The click beetles are generally dark colored and straight sided with sharp extensions on the posterior end of the thorax; a few species are brightly colored. The click beetle from the bosque is plain brown, elongate; body length 10–12 mm. Many other similar click beetles in the bosque.

Natural history—Complete metamorphosis; larvae feed on roots of grasses and garden crops and take several years to mature; adults feed on flowers and buds. On the underside these beetles have a click mechanism that allows them to arch the body and flip over in mid-air; also fly to lights at night. Prefer open grassy areas and agricultural fields near the river.

Status—Widespread, common.

Desert Firefly Beetle

(*Microphotus* sp.) ✳ ✳

Su

Taxonomy—Class: Hexapoda; Order: Coleoptera; Family: Lampyridae.

Identification—Females retain larval features and never develop wings; males develop full wings, which loosely cover the body; body length 8 mm; eyes very large. No other firefly beetles in the bosque.

Natural history—Complete metamorphosis; females produce a green glow at the tip of the abdomen to attract males, but males of these fireflies do not produce light. Prefers damp grassy habitats near water.

Status—Widespread, uncommon.

Soldier Beetle

(*Chauliognathus* sp.) ✳ ✳

Su, F

Taxonomy—Class: Hexapoda; Order: Coleoptera; Family: Cantharidae.

Identification—Long slender beetles with straight sides and soft wing covers. Thorax and wing covers yellow or orange with black markings. Body length 8–14 mm. Several similar but mostly black species occur in the bosque.

Natural history—Complete metamorphosis; adults often aggregate on flowers in open sunny areas. Feed mostly on nectar and pollen but also are predators on aphids. Larvae are predators on insect eggs or soft-bodied insects such as aphids.

Status—Widespread, common.

Red Checkered Beetle

(*Enoclerus* sp.) ✳ ✳

Su, F

Taxonomy—Class: Hexapoda; Order: Coleoptera; Family: Cleridae.

Identification—Checkered beetles have elongate bodies (12–14 mm) covered with bristly hairs; head and eyes large, thorax long and collarlike. Many species are brightly colored. Several species of checkered beetles occur in the bosque.

Natural history—Complete metamorphosis; found on flower stalks, where they hunt insects coming to flowers.

Status—Widespread, uncommon.

Soft-winged Flower Beetle

(*Attalus* spp.) ✳ ✳

Su, F

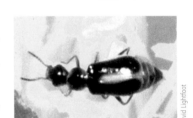

Taxonomy—Class: Hexapoda; Order: Coleoptera; Family: Melyridae.

Identification—Soft-winged flower beetles are small and pear shaped with wing covers that are often brightly colored and only loosely cover the body. Species in the genus *Attalus* have the head and legs dark, wing covers yellow-orange with broad dark blue stripes; body length 4–6 mm. Several similar soft-winged flower beetles occur in the bosque.

Natural history—Complete metamorphosis; larvae are predators of soft-bodied insects; adults feed on pollen, nectar, and soft-bodied insects. Prefer open sunny areas.

Status—Widespread, common.

Pallid-winged Sap Beetle

(*Carpophilus pallipennis*) ✳ ✳

Su, F

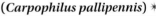

Taxonomy—Class: Hexapoda; Order: Coleoptera; Family: Nitidulidae.

Identification—Sap beetles are small, dark or tan with flattened body shape, wing covers that cover only the front half of the abdomen, and antennae with large round clubs at the ends. The pallid-winged sap beetle is dark brown with wing covers short and pale tan; body length 4–5 mm. No similar beetles in the bosque.

Natural history—Complete metamorphosis; adults and larvae feed on decaying fruits, the sap from tree wounds, and the fungi in rotting vegetation. Prefer forest habitats with well-developed litter layer.

Status—Widespread, common.

Twice-stabbed Ladybird Beetle

(*Chilocoris stigma*) ✳ ✳

Sp, Su, F

Taxonomy—Class: Hexapoda; Order: Coleoptera; Family: Coccinellidae.

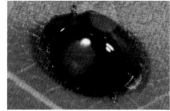

Identification—The ladybird beetles are often red with black spots but can be all or mostly black, blue, large and shiny, or small and hairy. The twice-stabbed ladybird beetle is broadly oval, shiny black, with 2 red spots on the middle of the wing covers; body length 4-6 mm. No other similar beetle in the bosque.

Natural history—Complete metamorphosis; predators of scale insects on trees and shrubs. Prefer open, sunny habitats, including open areas within forests.

Status—Widespread, uncommon.

Spotted Ladybird Beetle

(*Coleomegilla maculata*) ✳ ✳

Sp, Su, F

Taxonomy—Class: Hexapoda; Order: Coleoptera; Family: Coccinellidae.

Identification—Head, thorax, and wing covers red to pink with black markings; underside black; body length 4–8 mm. More slender and less convex than the convergent ladybird beetle.

Natural history—Complete metamorphosis; adults feed equally on aphids and pollen. Larvae are predators on aphids. Prefer open, sunny habitats, including open areas within forests.

Status—Widespread, common.

Convergent Ladybird Beetle

(*Hippodamia convergens*) ✳ ✳

Sp, Su, F

Taxonomy—Class: Hexapoda; Order: Coleoptera; Family: Coccinellidae.

Identification—Head and thorax black with tan markings; 2 converging white lines on the thorax; wing covers red with small black spots, number of spots varies greatly from none to about 12; underside black (top photo). Body length 6–8 mm. Several other similar ladybird beetles in the bosque, but spot patterns differ. Compare with spotted ladybird beetle.

Natural history—Complete metamorphosis; the familiar "ladybug" used by many gardeners to control aphids; both adults and larvae are aphid predators. Larvae are small, elongate, and black with red spots (bottom photo); found on shrubs and flowers with the adults. Prefer open, sunny habitats, including open areas within forests.

Status—Widespread, common.

Blue Ladybird Beetle

(*Neoharmonia venusta*) ✳ ✳

Sp, Su, F

Taxonomy—Class: Hexapoda; Order: Coleoptera; Family: Coccinellidae.

Identification—Head and thorax pale, wing covers convex, metallic blue. Body length 5–7 mm. No similar ladybird beetle in the bosque.

Natural history—Complete metamorphosis; predators of aphids and perhaps of scale insects and some leaf beetles. Found primarily on cottonwood in the bosque.

Status—Widespread, uncommon.

Tumbling Flower Beetle

(*Mordellistena* sp.) ✳ ✳

Sp, Su

Taxonomy—Class: Hexapoda; Order: Coleoptera; Family: Mordellidae.

Identification—The tumbling flower beetles are black, humpbacked, or wedge shaped with short antennae; hind legs longest. Body length 4–8 mm. Distinct body shape; unlike any other beetles in the bosque.

Natural history—Complete metamorphosis; adults jump and tumble when disturbed, feed on flowers and foliage; larvae feed on decomposing plant material; prefer open, sunny habitats.

Status—Widespread, uncommon.

Sand Darkling Beetle

(*Eusattus reticulatus*) ✳ ✳

Sp, Su, F, W

Taxonomy—Class: Hexapoda; Order: Coleoptera; Family: Tenebrionidae.

Identification—The darkling beetles are common and conspicuous members of arid habitats around the world. The large species are usually flightless, but the smaller species often fly. Sand darkling beetles are black, flightless, thorax broad, body convex with black patterns. Body length 10 mm. No similar round darkling beetle occurs in the bosque.

Natural history—Complete metamorphosis; specialist in sandy habitats found on sandbars in the river as well as open, sandy areas in the forest. Food sources, seasonality, and life span as for tailed darkling beetle.

Status—Widespread, common.

Stenomorpha Darkling Beetle

(*Stenomorpha rimata*) ✳ ✳

Su, F, W

Taxonomy—Class: Hexapoda; Order: Coleoptera; Family: Tenebrionidae.

Identification—Black, flightless, with convex thorax and pear-shaped body. Body length 20–25 mm. Similar in appearance to other darkling beetles in the bosque.

Natural history—Complete metamorphosis; food sources, seasonality, and life span as for tailed darkling beetle. Slow moving, play dead when handled.

Status—Widespread, common.

Tailed Darkling Beetle

(*Eleodes caudiferus*) ✳ ✳

Sp, Su, F, W

Taxonomy—Class: Hexapoda; Order: Coleoptera; Family: Tenebrionidae.

Identification—Species in the genus *Eleodes* are black, flightless, and slow moving. The tailed darkling beetle has extensions of the wing covers at the tip of the abdomen that extend for a few mm, forming a small "tail." Body length 20 mm. Several similar darkling beetles in the bosque but none with the "tail."

Natural history—Complete metamorphosis. In New Mexico these beetles are also called stink bugs or pinacate beetles. When disturbed, these beetles turn and raise their abdomen at an attacker and spray a bad-smelling defensive chemical. Larvae feed on plant roots; adults feed on decaying plant matter and sometimes live vegetation. Adult life span can be as long as 5 years. Generally active at dusk and at night during warm weather but seen even in winter on sunny days.

Status—Widespread, common.

Obsolete Darkling Beetle

(*Eleodes obsoletus*) ✳ ✳

Sp, Su, F, W

Taxonomy—Class: Hexapoda; Order: Coleoptera; Family: Tenebrionidae.

Identification—Black, broad bodied, wing covers not as flat as those of other *Eleodes* beetles. Lines on the wing covers are faint, or "obsolete"; body length 18–20 mm.

Natural history—Complete metamorphosis. Habitat preferences, food sources, seasonality, and life span as in tailed darkling beetle.

Status—Widespread, common.

Red-lined Darkling Beetle   (*Eleodes suturalis*) ✳ ✳

Sp, Su, F, W

Taxonomy—Class: Hexapoda; Order: Coleoptera; Family: Tenebrionidae.

Identification—Black, flightless with a broad thorax and wing covers, often with a red stripe down the middle. Body length 25-30 mm. Compare with other *Eleodes* species.

Natural history—Complete metamorphosis; seasonality, activity, and food sources as for tailed darkling beetle. Prefers areas of the bosque near water.

Status—Widespread, common.

Flanged Darkling Beetle   (*Embaphion contusum*) ✳ ✳

Sp, Su, F, W

Taxonomy—Class: Hexapoda; Order: Coleoptera; Family: Tenebrionidae.

Identification—Black; thorax distinctive with sides expanded and curved upward; back of wing covers flat. Body length 10-15 mm. Only bosque darkling beetle with flanges along the side of the pronotum.

Natural history—Complete metamorphosis; habitat preferences, food sources, seasonality similar to those for red-lined darkling beetle.

Status—Widespread, common.

Fire Blister Beetle   (*Pyrota punctata*) ✳ ✳

Sp, Su

Taxonomy—Class: Hexapoda; Order: Coleoptera; Family: Meloidae.

Identification—The blister beetle family contains several species with strange body shapes and bright colors. The fire blister beetle has an elongate body with red head and thorax, wing covers tan with wide black bands in the middle and several dots at the anterior end; underside and legs mostly red. Body length 10–15 mm. No similar beetle in the bosque.

Natural history—Complete metamorphosis; larvae are nest parasites of ground-dwelling bees; adults feed on flowers or aggregate on flowering shrubs for mating.

Status—Widespread, uncommon.

Red-banded Blister Beetle   (*Megetra cancellatus*) ✴ ✴

Su

Sharyn Davidson

Taxonomy—Class: Hexapoda; Order: Coleoptera; Family: Meloidae.

Identification—Black flightless beetles with very short wing covers that do not cover the abdomen and have a netlike red pattern; abdominal segments outlined in red; body length 25 mm. Another similar but smaller species occurs in the bosque.

Natural history—Complete metamorphosis; larvae are nest parasites of ground-dwelling bees; adults feed on flowers or aggregate on flowering shrubs for mating. Adults contain a defensive chemical, cantharidin (also known as Spanish fly), which is released through the leg joints and causes blisters on human skin. Horses may become poisoned if they ingest the beetles, which are sometimes baled with alfalfa.

Status—Widespread, uncommon.

Desert Blister Beetle   (*Cysteodemus wislizenii*) ✴ ✴

Sp, Su

David Lightfoot

Taxonomy—Class: Hexapoda; Order: Coleoptera; Family: Meloidae.

Identification—The desert blister beetle is metallic blue or green, round, and patterned with many small depressions. Body length 10–15 mm. Compare with the blue metallic wood boring beetle. No other similar round, blue or green beetle in the bosque.

Natural history—Complete metamorphosis; this unmistakable beetle is usually found on the ground, in open, sunny areas, even during midday, when many other insects are resting in shade. Larvae are nest parasites of ground-dwelling bees; adults feed on flowers or aggregate on flowering shrubs for mating.

Status—Widespread, uncommon.

Giant Root-boring Longhorn Beetle   (*Prionus heroicus*) ✳ ✳

Sp, Su

David Lightfoot

Taxonomy—Class: Hexapoda; Order: Coleoptera; Family: Cerambycidae.

Identification—The family of longhorn beetles are also known as round-headed borers for the shape and habits of the larvae. Adults may be large or small, but most have antennae longer than the body, especially in the males. Giant root-boring longhorn beetles are plain brown to black beetles with spines on the sides of the thorax; antennae long and saw toothed, eyes large, mandibles large. Body length 40–50 mm. Two other similar large brown longhorn beetles occur in the area.

Natural history—Complete metamorphosis; females deposit eggs at the bases of deciduous trees such as cottonwood or fruit trees; larvae feed on and bore into the large roots, requiring 3–4 years to mature. Adults are active at night.

Status—Widespread, uncommon.

Snakeweed Longhorned Beetle   (*Crossidius pulchellus*) ✳ ✳

Su, F

David Lightfoot

Taxonomy—Class: Hexapoda; Order: Coleoptera; Family: Cerambycidae.

Identification—Golden brown beetle 12–15 mm in length; antennae very long and dark. Compare with soldier beetle.

Natural history—Adults feed on flowers, often aggregating in large numbers; larvae feed on the roots of snakeweed plants, occasionally killing them.

Status—Widespread, common.

Spotted Tylosis Longhorn Beetle   (*Tylosis maculatus*) ✳ ✳

Su, F

David Lightfoot

Taxonomy—Class: Hexapoda; Order: Coleoptera; Family: Cerambycidae.

Identification—Distinctive appearance; black head and antennae (much longer than the body), red thorax with black dots, red wing covers with black markings; markings range from weak to strong. Body length 17–20 mm. Several other bosque longhorn beetles also are orange but have different black patterns.

Natural history—Complete metamorphosis; prefer open habitats with mallows (Malvaceae), which are the larval food plant. Adults are active during the day.

Status—Widespread, common.

Cottonwood Longhorn Beetle

(*Plectrodera scalator*) ✳ ✳

Su

Taxonomy—Class: Hexapoda; Order: Coleoptera; Family: Cerambycidae.

Identification—The cottonwood borer is large and boldly marked in black and white; body length 30 mm. No similar-appearing beetle in the bosque, but many other species of longhorn beetles do occur there.

Natural history—Complete metamorphosis; adults found on or near cottonwood or willow trees. Eggs are deposited in dead cottonwoods; larvae feed on and bore into wood. Adults are active during the day.

Status—Widespread, uncommon.

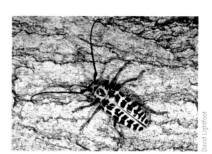

David Lightfoot

Wasp-mimic Longhorn Beetle

(*Stenelytrana gigas*) ✳ ✳

Sp, Su

Taxonomy—Class: Hexapoda; Order: Coleoptera; Family: Cerambycidae.

Identification—Black body with orange wing covers, resembling tarantula hawk wasps (Pompilidae) in flight. Body length 28 mm. No other similar beetle in the bosque.

Natural history—Complete metamorphosis; adults are active during the day and feed on flowers, larvae bore into hardwood trees.

Status—Widespread, uncommon.

David Lightfoot

Three-lined Potato Beetle

(*Lema trilinea*) ✳ ✳

Su, F

Taxonomy—Class: Hexapoda; Order: Coleoptera; Family: Chrysomelidae.

Identification—Yellow beetle with 3 black stripes on the wing covers, head and thorax reddish, body length 5-6 mm.

Natural history—Complete metamorphosis. Larvae and adults feed on plants in the nightshade family (Solanaceae). In the bosque the beetles are found on datura (also called moonflower or jimson weed).

Status—Widespread, common.

David Lightfoot

Cottonwood Leaf Beetle   (*Chrysomela scripta*) ✳ ✳

Sp, Su

Taxonomy—Class: Hexapoda; Order: Coleoptera; Family: Chrysomelidae.

Identification—Species in the leaf beetle family are often restricted to feeding on one or a few species of plants. Many leaf beetles are unpalatable to predators and are often brightly colored to advertise this. The cottonwood leaf beetle has the head black, thorax edged in reddish tan, wing covers yellowish gray with black lines and dots, underside black. Body length 8 mm. Many other species of leaf beetles in the bosque, but none with the same types of markings.

Natural history—Complete metamorphosis; adults and larvae feed on cottonwood leaves. Larvae feed in groups and can cause extensive leaf damage.

Status—Widespread, common.

Twelve-spotted Cucumber Leaf Beetle   (*Diabrotica undecimpunctata*) ✳ ✳

Sp, Su, F

Taxonomy—Class: Hexapoda; Order: Coleoptera; Family: Chrysomelidae.

Identification—Body straight sided, yellow-green with 12 black spots. Body length 6–7 mm. No other similar beetle in the bosque.

Natural history—Complete metamorphosis; adults feed on flowers, leaves, and young fruits of many kinds of plants; larvae feed on roots.

Status—Widespread, common.

Flea Leaf Beetles   ✳ ✳

Sp, Su, F

Taxonomy—Class: Hexapoda; Order: Coleoptera; Family: Chrysomelidae.

Identification—Dark with metallic sheen or with stripes; jump when disturbed but also fly. Body length 2–5 mm. Many similar genera and species in the bosque.

Natural history—Complete metamorphosis; adults chew small round holes in the upper surface of leaves, larvae feed on roots. Various species specialize on plant families, such as crucifers (Brassicaceae), the tomato family (Solanaceae), evening primrose (Onagraceae), and others. Prefer open, sunny habitats in the bosque.

Status—Widespread, common.

Sunflowerhead-clipping Weevil

(*Haplorhynchites aeneus*) ✳ ✳

Su, F

Taxonomy—Class: Hexapoda; Order: Coleoptera; Family: Curculionidae.

Identification—The weevils, or snout beetles, are the largest family of beetles in the world. They feed on plants and are often very specific about which plant species or plant part (seed, stem, root, etc.) they feed on. The front of the face is elongate, forming a snout that may be short and thick or very long and thin. The mandibles are at the end of the snout, and the antennae may be found partway down the snout rather than close to the eyes. The sunflowerhead-clipping weevils are plain black shiny beetles with long snouts; body length 8 mm. Many similar weevils occur in the bosque.

Natural history—Complete metamorphosis; females cut through a sunflower stem just below the head, and after the flower falls to the ground, she lays eggs in it. Adults feed on pollen and prefer open, sunny areas.

Status—Widespread, uncommon.

Broad-nosed Weevil

(*Ophryastes* spp.) ✳ ✳

Sp, Su, F

Taxonomy—Class: Hexapoda; Order: Coleoptera; Family: Curculionidae.

Identification—Convex body shape, striped gray to silver; body length 12-18 mm. Snout is short and thick. Several other similar weevils in the bosque.

Natural history—Complete metamorphosis; adults and larvae feed on trees, shrubs, grasses, and other plants; often found on the ground.

Status—Widespread, common.

Green Lacewing

(*Chrysopa* sp.) ✳ ✳

Sp, Su, F

Taxonomy—Class: Hexapoda; Order: Neuroptera; Family: Chrysopidae.

Identification—Neuroptera are a group of insects related to beetles but have 2 pairs of membranous wings with no hard wing covers like beetles. The green lacewing has a green body with pale green rounded wings, large golden eyes, body length 7-8 mm. Larvae resemble ant lions (Myrmeleontidae) but are found on vegetation. Eggs are small white ovals suspended from vegetation by slender stalks. Several similar species occur in the bosque.

Natural history—Complete metamorphosis. Adults and larvae feed on aphids in many kinds of trees and shrubs; also known as aphid lions. Adults come to lights at night.

Status—Widespread, common.

Ant Lions   ✳ ✳

Su, F

Taxonomy—Class: Hexapoda;
Order: Neuroptera;
Family: Myrmeleontidae.

Identification—Slender, fragile,
brown, resembling a damsel-
fly but have noticeable antennae (compare with damselflies)
(top right photo); body length
20–30 mm. Larvae are brown
and robust with large piercing
mandibles (top left photo); make pit traps in sandy areas
to catch ants (bottom photo). Many similar-appearing species in the bosque.

Natural history—Complete metamorphosis. Larvae make
cone-shaped pit traps in sand to capture ants and other
small arthropods; rest with their mandibles open at the bottom of the traps. When uncovered, quickly dig themselves
back into the sand. Also known as doodlebugs. Adults weak
flyers and active at night, often come to lights.

Status—Widespread, common.

Photographs: David Lightfoot

Horntail Wasp   (*Urocerus californicus*) ✳ ✳

Su, F

Taxonomy—Class: Hexapoda; Order: Hymenoptera;
Family: Siricidae.

Identification—The Hymenoptera is a very large group of
insects whose members include bees, wasps, and ants.
They range from tiny to large, predators to plant feeders,
solitary or colonial, extreme specialists to broad generalists
in habitats and prey. Many species are hunting wasps that
parasitize other insects: female wasps sting and paralyze
insect "hosts" with venom and then lay eggs in the bodies, which serve as food for the developing wasp larvae.
Adults of these species are generally nectar feeders. Many
Hymenoptera have the ovipositor (tube through which

David Lightfoot

eggs are laid) modified into a stinger; therefore the males cannot sting. The bees
are familiar for their important role as pollinators of many flowering plant species.
Most are solitary, with modifications to the legs and abdomen for carrying pollen.
Horntail wasps have an elongated brown, yellow, and black body; orange-amber
wings; body length 35 mm, lacking the typical narrow "wasp waist." Females have
2 blunt, stout, sharp projections (for depositing eggs) at the end of the abdomen. No
other similar wasps in the bosque.

Natural history—Complete metamorphosis; solitary wasps; females lay eggs in
wood of newly dead trees. Larvae bore into the wood, which they consume as they
develop. Females do not sting or have venom.

Status—Widespread, uncommon.

Ichneumon Wasps ✳✳

Sp, Su, F

David Lightfoot

Taxonomy—Class: Hexapoda; Order: Hymenoptera; Family: Ichneumonidae.

Identification—Red and black, orange or yellowish, females with long ovipositor extending beyond end of abdomen. Similar in appearance to digger wasps but smaller and more slender. Many similar species in the bosque.

Natural history—Complete metamorphosis. Parasitic on other arthropods (explained at the beginning of the Hymenoptera section). Adults feed on nectar. Females may have ovipositors (tube through which eggs are deposited) longer than their bodies, but they do not sting. Most are specialists on one or a few species of arthropods.

Status—Widespread, common.

Parasitic Microwasps ✳✳

Sp, Su, F

David Lightfoot

Taxonomy—Class: Hexapoda; Order: Hymenoptera; Superfamily: Chalcidoidea.

Identification—These tiny wasps include several families and many genera and species. Most are black and shiny, with greatly enlarged hind femurs; body length 2–7 mm; tube or spine for laying eggs may be visible at the end of the abdomen, but these wasps do not sting. Many families, genera, and species of very small parasitic wasps occur in the bosque.

Natural history—Complete metamorphosis. Solitary wasps that parasitize many kinds of insects, especially caterpillars; a single wasp egg can divide several times to produce several adults from a single host. Some are parasites of insect eggs. Adults feed on nectar. Important in biological control of insect pests in agricultural crops. Compare with Ichneumonidae.

Status—Widespread, common.

Cuckoo Wasp   (*Holopyga* sp.) ✳✳

Sp, Su

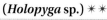

David Lightfoot

Taxonomy—Class: Hexapoda; Order: Hymenoptera; Family: Chrysididae.

Identification—Metallic blue-green wasp with a coarse-textured pattern all over the body; wings dark, body size 7–10 mm. Compare with the metallic green bee in the family Halictidae. Several cuckoo wasp species occur in the bosque.

Natural history—Complete metamorphosis. Females lay their eggs in the nests of solitary sand wasps that burrow in soil. The larvae hatch and feed on the resident larvae or food that was intended for them. The adults can curl into a ball when disturbed, protected by their hard exoskeleton.

Status—Widespread, uncommon.

Cricket Wasp

(*Chlorion aerarium*) ✳ ✳

Su

David Lightfoot

Taxonomy—Class: Hexapoda; Order: Hymenoptera; Family: Sphecidae.

Identification—Hunting wasps (Sphecidae) are solitary predators of other insects. Solitary females hunt for and paralyze insect and spider prey with a sting and deposit the prey in a nest with an egg for the larvae to feed on. Most wasp species specialize on particular types of prey. The cricket wasp is a metallic blue-black wasp with blue-black wings, body length 30–35 mm, with thin "wasp waist." Several species of blue-black spider wasps are similar but of heavier build and without the narrow "waist."

Natural history—Complete metamorphosis; females search for field crickets such as the southwestern riparian field cricket, which they paralyze with a sting and carry back to a burrow dug in the soil. Females and males visit flowers to feed on nectar.

Status—Widespread, common.

Black and Yellow Mud Dauber Wasp

(*Sceliphron caementarium*) ✳ ✳

Su

David Lightfoot

Taxonomy—Class: Hexapoda; Order: Hymenoptera; Family: Sphecidae.

Identification—Slender black body with yellow markings, dark amber wings, body length 25 mm. No other black and yellow slender thread-waisted wasp occurs in the bosque.

Natural history—Complete metamorphosis; females build mud nests high on vertical surfaces such as tree trunks and under bridges. They search for spiders, which they paralyze with a sting, and carry back to the mud nest and place in cells.

Status—Widespread, common.

Golden Digger Wasp

(*Sphex ichneumoneus*) ✳ ✳

Su

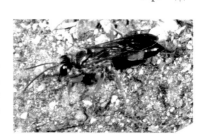

Taxonomy—Class: Hexapoda; Order: Hymenoptera; Family: Sphecidae.

Identification—Black and orange wasp with short, dense, golden hair; wings dark amber (top photo); body length 25 mm. First abdominal segments are long and thin, or "thread waisted." Other digger wasps are similar, including the caterpillar hunter and the grasshopper hunter, but are not as large and robust as the golden digger wasp.

Natural history—Complete metamorphosis; females search for katydids, which they paralyze with a sting and carry back to burrows (bottom photo). Females and males visit flowers to feed on nectar.

Status—Widespread, common.

Photographs: David Lightfoot

Grasshopper Wasp

(*Prionyx* spp.) ✳ ✳

Su, F

Taxonomy—Class: Hexapoda; Order: Hymenoptera; Family: Sphecidae.

Identification—Black with red abdomen, constricted waist short, dark brown wings (top photo), body length 20 mm. Compare with caterpillar wasp (*Ammophila* spp.), which is similar but has a longer "waist." Several species of black and red digger wasps also are similar.

Natural history—Complete metamorphosis; females search for grasshoppers, usually juvenile stages, which they paralyze with a sting and carry back to a burrow dug in the soil (bottom photo). Females and males visit flowers to feed on nectar.

Status—Widespread, common.

Photographs: David Lightfoot

Black Digger Wasp   (*Podalonia* spp.) ✳ ✳

Sp, Su

Taxonomy—Class: Hexapoda; Order: Hymenoptera; Family: Sphecidae.

Identification—Black with blue-black wings, body length 20 mm. Males of some species are red and black. Several species of blue-black digger wasps and spider wasps (Pompilidae) also are similar.

Natural history—Complete metamorphosis; females search for caterpillars, especially cutworms and armyworms (Noctuidae), which they paralyze with a sting and carry back to a burrow dug in the soil. Females and males visit flowers to feed on nectar.

Status—Widespread, common.

Caterpillar Wasp   (*Ammophila* spp.) ✳ ✳

Su

Taxonomy—Class: Hexapoda; Order: Hymenoptera; Family: Sphecidae.

Identification—Slender black body with red and black abdomen, wings clear, body length 20 mm. Several similar species of caterpillar wasps occur in the bosque. Compare with grasshopper wasp, which is similar but not as slender and with a shorter "wasp waist." Several species occur in the bosque.

Natural history—Complete metamorphosis. Adult females search for caterpillars, which they paralyze with a sting and carry back to a burrow dug in the soil. Females and males visit flowers to feed on nectar.

Status—Widespread, common.

Eastern Cicada Killer Wasp   (*Sphecius speciosus*) ✳ ✳

Su

Taxonomy—Class: Hexapoda; Order: Hymenoptera; Family: Sphecidae.

Identification—Very large black and yellow wasp with amber wings, body length ~40 mm. Body black with yellow markings on the abdomen, thorax with dense but very short reddish brown hairs (top photo). Two other species of cicada killer wasps are rare along the bosque; neither have black bodies.

Natural history—Complete metamorphosis; cicada killer wasps prey on giant cicadas, which females locate in trees, paralyze with a sting, and carry to a burrow dug in the soil (bottom photo). Cicada killer wasps are solitary and nest alone, but sometimes several will nest in the same area.

Status—Widespread, uncommon.

Little Sand Wasp

(*Microbembix* sp.) ✳ ✳

Su

Taxonomy—Class: Hexapoda; Order: Hymenoptera; Family: Sphecidae.

Identification—Compact; black and white (female) or black and yellow (male), wings clear; body length 10 mm. Similar to the sand wasps and several other black and yellow wasps but much smaller. Rows of long spines form brushes on the forefeet, which are used to dig in sand.

Natural history—Complete metamorphosis; females search for all kinds of small, recently dead or dying insects, which they carry back to a burrow dug in the soil. Females and males visit flowers to feed on nectar. Often gregarious with several females nesting in the same area but not social as honeybees are.

Status—Widespread, common.

David Lightfoot

Western Sand Wasp

(*Bembix occidentalis*) ✳ ✳

Su

Taxonomy—Class: Hexapoda; Order: Hymenoptera; Family: Sphecidae.

Identification—Black with yellow markings on thorax, legs yellow; abdomen with black and yellow bands, wings clear; body length 20 mm. Several similar species of sand wasps occur in the bosque; also similar to the yellow jacket hornet but have row of long spines forming a brush on the forefeet, which are used to dig in sand.

Natural history—Complete metamorphosis; females search for flies, which they paralyze with a sting and carry back to a burrow dug in the soil. Females and males visit flowers to feed on nectar. Often gregarious, with several females nesting in the same area, but not social as honeybees are. These and other soil nesting wasps dig with their forelegs as shown in the photograph.

Status—Widespread, common.

David Lightfoot

Metallic Green Bee

(*Agapostemon* spp.) ✳ ✳

Sp, Su, F

Taxonomy—Class: Hexapoda; Order: Hymenoptera; Family: Halictidae.

Identification—Females shiny metallic green (top photo), males with green head and thorax and black and yellow banded abdomen (bottom photo); body length 6–8 mm. Many species of halictid bees occur in the bosque.

Natural history—Complete metamorphosis. Nest in the ground, often near one another, but these bees are not social. Visit many kinds of flowers for pollen and nectar. Other species in the family are small and black, called sweat bees because they are attracted to the salt in human sweat.

Status—Widespread, common.

Photographs: David Lightfoot

Leaf-cutter Bee

(*Megachile* spp.) ✳ ✳

Sp, Su, F

Taxonomy—Class: Hexapoda; Order: Hymenoptera; Family: Megachilidae.

Identification—Broad bodied, hairy, dark with light-colored bands on the abdomen; body length 10–20 mm. Several similar species in the bosque.

Natural history—Complete metamorphosis. Do not have pollen baskets on the hind legs (compare with the honeybee and digger bees) but store pollen on the underside of the abdomen. Construct cells in wood, stone, or other natural cavities. Bees cut semicircular pieces from leaves or flower petals, which they use to line the nest and make partitions between cells containing larvae provisioned with pollen and nectar. Blue orchard bees (*Osmia* spp.) are members of this family and are commonly used by gardeners for pollination of vegetables and flowers.

Status—Widespread, common.

David Lightfoot

California Carpenter Bee

(*Xylocopa californica*) ✳ ✳

Sp, Su

Taxonomy—Class: Hexapoda; Order: Hymenoptera; Family: Apidae.

Identification—Large body (length 20–25 mm) metallic bluish black; heavy bodied; hairy; wings bluish black. Similar in appearance to a large bluish black bumblebee except bumblebees have no blue and are black and yellow.

Natural history—Complete metamorphosis. These solitary bees tunnel into weathered wood (they do not eat wood) to make nest cells for their eggs and young. They gather pollen and nectar from many kinds of flowers. Active during the day into early evening. Their flight is rapid, and they are often seen around flowers.

Status—Widespread, uncommon.

California Digger Bee

(*Anthophora californica*) ✳ ✳

Sp, Su

Taxonomy—Class: Hexapoda; Order: Hymenoptera; Family: Apidae.

Identification—Digger bees are robust, hairy; body length 12–18 mm; male abdomen with white bands of hair, face yellow, eyes light colored; female larger and less strongly banded.

Natural history—Complete metamorphosis; solitary bees that make burrows in the ground, provision the burrow with pollen and nectar for the larvae. Adults have rapid, erratic, hovering flight.

Status—Widespread, common.

Large Digger Bee

(*Svastra* sp.) ✳ ✳

Su, F

Taxonomy—Class: Hexapoda; Order: Hymenoptera; Family: Apidae.

Identification—Robust shape, hairy, body length 12 mm; hind legs with very large pollen baskets (note pollen on baskets in photo). Several similar species occur in the bosque.

Natural history—Complete metamorphosis; solitary bees that make burrows in soil, provision the burrow with pollen and nectar for the larvae. Adults have rapid, hovering flight; most are specialists on one or only a few plant families, such as the Aster family (Asteraceae).

Status—Widespread, common.

Bumblebee

(*Bombus* spp.) ✳ ✳

Sp, Su, F

Taxonomy—Class: Hexapoda; Order: Hymenoptera; Family: Apidae.

Identification—Heavy-bodied, hairy, black and yellow bees, body length 20–25 mm; make a humming sound as they visit flowers; agile in flight despite their size. Several species occur in the bosque.

Natural history—Complete metamorphosis. Live in small colonies (queen, workers, drones), usually in the ground or in abandoned mouse nests. Workers gather pollen and nectar from many kinds of flowers. Active early morning until early evening. Important pollinators for native and agricultural plants.

Status—Widespread, common.

David Lightfoot

European Honeybee

(*Apis mellifera*) ✳ ✳ [INT]

Sp, Su, F

Taxonomy—Class: Hexapoda; Order: Hymenoptera; Family: Apidae.

Identification—Brown-orange with black bands at the tip of the abdomen; body length 8 mm; pollen baskets on the hind legs. No similar bees in the bosque.

Natural history—Complete metamorphosis. Social bees (with castes of queens, workers, and drones) living in human-constructed hives or cavities in trees or rocks. Workers pollinate many kinds of flowers, including agricultural crops, and are of great economic importance. This introduced species competes with native bee species. Appearance alone will not distinguish European honeybees from the closely related African honeybees (present in southern New Mexico).

Status—Widespread, common.

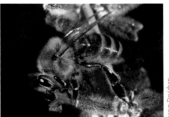

Sharyn Davidson

Velvet Ant Wasp (*Dasymutilla* sp.) ✳ ✳

Su, F

Taxonomy—Class: Hexapoda; Order: Hymenoptera; Family: Mutillidae.

Identification—Orange-red hairy antlike wasps, medium size (6–20 mm); females wingless, resembling large hairy ants (top photo), males with black wings (bottom photo). Legs and underside black, top bright or rusty red. Several similar-appearing species in the bosque, varying from yellowish to grayish in color.

Natural history—Complete metamorphosis; wasps, not ants; females lay eggs in the nests of ground-dwelling bees, wasp larvae feed on the host larvae. Sting of the female is very painful; males do not sting. Females make a squeaking noise when disturbed.

Status—Widespread, common.

Photographs: David Lightfoot

Tarantula Hawk Wasp (*Pepsis formosa*) ✳ ✳

Su, F

Taxonomy—Class: Hexapoda; Order: Hymenoptera; Family: Pompilidae.

Identification—Spider wasps are solitary hunting wasps like the sphecid wasps. The females search for and capture spiders, which they paralyze with a sting and deposit in a burrow. Different species specialize on different types of spiders. Black with metallic blue iridescence, orange wings, and long legs; body length 35–40 mm. Females are larger and heavier than males. Compare with green tarantula hawk wasp.

David Lightfoot

Natural history—Complete metamorphosis. Adults visit flowers, especially milkweed, for nectar. Females search for, sting, and paralyze tarantulas, burying them in burrows in the soil as food for their young.

Status—Mostly in the southern parts of the bosque, common. The official New Mexico state insect.

Green Tarantula Hawk Wasp

(*Pepsis pallidolimbata*) ✳ ✳

Su, F

Taxonomy—Class: Hexapoda; Order: Hymenoptera; Family: Pompilidae.

Identification—Black with greenish blue iridescence, orange wings, long legs; body length 25–30 mm. Females are larger and heavier than males. Compare with tarantula hawk wasp.

Natural history—Complete metamorphosis. Adults visit flowers, especially milkweeds, for nectar. Females hunt for tarantulas as food for their young.

Status—Widespread, common.

David Lightfoot

Spider Wasp

(*Pompilus scelestus*) ✳ ✳

Su, F

Taxonomy—Class: Hexapoda; Order: Hymenoptera; Family: Pompilidae.

Identification—Bluish black body and wings, body length 20–22 mm (top photo). In the bosque are many species of medium to small spider wasps in colors ranging from bluish black to greenish black to black to red-orange and black.

Natural history—Complete metamorphosis. Adults visit flowers, especially milkweeds, for nectar. Female spider wasps hunt for and paralyze spiders as food for their young (bottom photo another species of spider wasp with wolf spider prey).

Status—Widespread, common.

Photographs: David Lightfoot

Yellow Scarab Hunter Wasp

(*Campsomeris pilipes*) ✳ ✳

Su, F

Taxonomy—Class: Hexapoda; Order: Hymenoptera; Family: Scoliidae.

Identification—Black wasp with a yellow-banded abdomen, body length 30 mm, dark brown wings. Other smaller black and yellow scarab-hunting wasp species occur in the bosque. Compare with red scarab hunter wasp. Also resemble some digger wasps, especially the cicada killer wasp.

Natural history—Complete metamorphosis; females parasitize the larvae of scarab beetles (also known as white grubs) as food for their young.

Status—Widespread, common.

Red Scarab Hunter Wasp

(*Triscolia ardens*) ✳ ✳

Su, F

Taxonomy—Class: Hexapoda; Order: Hymenoptera; Family: Scoliidae.

Identification—Blue-black body with red-orange abdomen, hairy; wings blue-black; body length 30 mm. Other similar blue-black scarab-hunting wasp species occur in the bosque but are about ½ the body size and have yellow markings on the abdomen. Compare with yellow scarab hunter wasp. Also resemble velvet ants and digger wasps.

Natural history—Complete metamorphosis; females parasitize tarantulas as food for their young.

Status—Mostly the southern half of the bosque, common.

Yellow Potter Wasp

(*Eumenes* sp.) ✳ ✳

Su, F

Taxonomy—Class: Hexapoda; Order: Hymenoptera; Family: Vespidae.

Identification—Robust yellow and brown body, brown wings; abdomen round; mandibles elongate and sharp; body length 18 mm. Several similar species of potter wasps occur in the bosque; many are smaller and black with yellow or white markings.

Natural history—Complete metamorphosis; solitary wasps that construct small pot-shaped nests of mud made from soil and saliva and shaped with the mandibles. The wasp places paralyzed insect larvae and a wasp egg in the nest and caps it with mud. Adults visit flowers for nectar.

Status—Widespread, common.

Yellowjacket Hornet (*Dolichovespula arenaria*) ✶✶

Su, F

Taxonomy—Class: Hexapoda; Order: Hymenoptera; Family: Vespidae.

Identification—Black robust body with yellow legs and markings on head and thorax, yellow bands on abdomen, wings clear or amber, body length 20 mm. No other species of hornets are known from the bosque. Many other wasps are similar in appearance, especially sand wasps (*Bembix* spp.).

Natural history—Complete metamorphosis. Hornets and paper wasps (Vespidae) are social wasps and live in small to large colonies composed of one queen and many female workers. Yellowjacket hornets are aggressive and hunt or scavenge other insects to feed their larvae. Each colony generally lives one year and constructs large paper nests made from wood and saliva in cavities in trees or in the ground.

Status—Widespread, common.

David Lightfoot

Apache Paper Wasp (*Polistes apachus*) ✶✶

Su, F

Taxonomy—Class: Hexapoda; Order: Hymenoptera; Family: Vespidae.

Identification—Slender brown and yellow body, brown wings, body length 25 mm. Several other paper wasp species occur in the bosque that are also similar in appearance to some digger wasps (Sphecidae). One other similar paper wasp occurs in the bosque.

Natural history—Complete metamorphosis; social wasps with queen and workers; construct small paper nests that hang from a stalk under tree branches or in cavities. Nests are open at the bottom, exposing the larval cells. Workers hunt for insects to feed the larvae in the nest. Adults visit flowers for nectar.

Status—Widespread, common.

David Lightfoot

Acrobat Ant

(*Crematogaster cerasi*) ✳ ✳

Su, F

Taxonomy—Class: Hexapoda; Order: Hymenoptera; Family: Formicidae.

Identification—Ants live in colonies and have caste members like the social bees and wasps. The workers, which are wingless, are the ones most often encountered; winged queens and males are seen only in mating swarms once or twice a year. Only the queens can produce eggs; workers are sterile. The acrobat ants are dark brown or black, shiny, body length 3–4 mm; abdomen is heart shaped when viewed from above, end of thorax with sharp spines.

David Lightfoot

Natural history—Complete metamorphosis. Nest at the bases of plants, under stones, or under decaying wood. Workers usually found on vegetation tending aphids and scale insects for their sugary excretions; also feed on nectar. When workers are disturbed, they raise their abdomens vertically and wave them back and forth. This arboreal species retreats up trees during floods.

Status—Widespread, common.

Little Black Ant

(*Monomorium cyaneum*) ✳ ✳

Sp, Su, F

Taxonomy—Class: Hexapoda; Order: Hymenoptera; Family: Formicidae.

Identification—Very small (body length 3 mm), black, shiny ant.

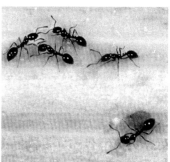

David Lightfoot

Natural history—Complete metamorphosis; nests under stones or logs or in the open, where the entrance is surrounded by a small mound. In New Mexico found from riparian areas to pine forests and in urban areas.

Status—Widespread, common.

Western Harvester Ant   (*Pogonomyrmex occidentalis*) ✱ ✱

Su, F

David Lightfoot

Taxonomy—Class: Hexapoda; Order: Hymenoptera; Family: Formicidae.

Identification—Red to reddish brown, head large and square with large mandibles, end of thorax without spines (compare with the black and red harvester ant); long hairs under the head used as basket for carrying sand grains; body length 5-6 mm. The Maricopa harvester ant is another common species occurring in the bosque.

Natural history—Complete metamorphosis; nest in well-drained soils, mounds tall and pyramid shaped with bare soil about 1 m around it. Workers harvest seeds; not active at night. Reproductives (new queens and males) fly June–August, colonies form July–October. Sting is painful.

Status—Widespread, common.

Black and Red Harvester Ant   (*Pogonomyrmex rugosus*) ✱ ✱

Sp, Su, F

David Lightfoot

Taxonomy—Class: Hexapoda; Order: Hymenoptera; Family: Formicidae.

Identification—Black head and thorax with reddish abdomen, head large and square with large mandibles; end of thorax with large spines; body length 6-8 mm (photo shows a worker carrying a plant seed).

Natural history—Complete metamorphosis; nest in sandy to gravelly soils, entrance surrounded by large disk (up to 1 m diameter) of small pieces of gravel. Feed on seeds and dead insects; during the hottest part of a summer day workers return to the nest, re-emerge in late afternoon, although they are not active at night. Reproductives (new queens and males) fly June–August, colonies form July–October. Sting is painful.

Status—Widespread, common.

Crazy Ant · (*Dorymyrmex insanus*) ✳ ✳

Sp, Su, F

Taxonomy—Class: Hexapoda; Order: Hymenoptera; Family: Formicidae.

Identification—Brown, eyes large, body length 3–4 mm; thorax with prominent pyramid-shaped spine.

Natural history—Complete metamorphosis. Colony entrances marked by a small crater or mound of fine sand; feed on living and dead insects and gather sugary excretions from aphids. Do not sting but have an unpleasant odor. Generally fast moving, but when the nest is disturbed, the workers race over and around it. Sometimes nest near a colony of harvester ants, which ignore them.

Status—Widespread, abundant.

Carpenter Ant · (*Camponotus vicinus*) ✳ ✳

Su, F

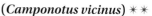

Taxonomy—Class: Hexapoda; Order: Hymenoptera; Family: Formicidae.

Identification—*Camponotus vicinus* has a red head and thorax and black abdomen; members of the same colony are of different sizes; body length 4–12 mm. Thorax strongly arched, heads large. Many species of carpenter ants occur in the bosque.

Natural history—Complete metamorphosis. Nest in rotting wood or in the ground under stones; active at night and during the day. Feed on sugary excretions of aphids and scavenge on dead insects. Do not sting but bite and spray the wound with formic acid.

Status—Widespread, common.

Field Ant · (*Lasius pallitarsus*) ✳ ✳

Sp, Su, F

Taxonomy—Class: Hexapoda; Order: Hymenoptera; Family: Formicidae.

Identification—Small brown ants with large eyes, body length 4 mm.

Natural history—Complete metamorphosis. Nest at the base of plants or under stones or dead leaves; colonies may contain thousands of individuals. Feed on live and dead insects, nectar, and tend aphids for their sugary excretions. Workers do not sting but spray formic acid.

Status—Widespread, common.

Clear-winged Moths   ✳ ✳

Sp, Su

Taxonomy—Class: Hexapoda; Order: Lepidoptera;
Family: Sesiidae.

Identification—Butterflies and moths and their caterpillars are among the most familiar of insects. Adults drink nectar from a variety of flowers, but the caterpillars chew plant foliage and are often restricted to certain species of host plants. The pupal stages are often called cocoons for moths and chrysalises for butterflies. Clear-winged moths are black and yellow banded moths that mimic wasps; body 15 mm, wingspan 20 mm. Several similar species occur in the bosque.

Natural history—Complete metamorphosis. Active during the day. Larvae bore into roots and stems of many kinds of plants.

Status—Widespread, uncommon.

David Lightfoot

Fruit-tree Leaf Roller Moth   (*Archips purpurana*) ✳ ✳

Sp, Su

Taxonomy—Class: Hexapoda; Order: Lepidoptera;
Family: Tortricidae.

Identification—Top side forewings pale brown with cream-colored markings on the edges of the wings, hind wings light brown with fringe of pale hairs. Wingspan 14–23 mm. Caterpillar smooth pale green with dark head and dark thorax.

Natural history—Complete metamorphosis. Caterpillar food plants: in the bosque the caterpillars feed on cottonwood leaves, which they fold over and tie with silk to give them protection (or tie 2 leaves together flat); when disturbed, they writhe violently. Adults active at night and fly to lights.

Status—Widespread, common.

David Lightfoot

Plume Moths   ✳ ✳

Sp, Su, F

Taxonomy—Class: Hexapoda; Order: Lepidoptera;
Family: Pterophoridae.

Identification—Brown or gray, very slender long-legged moths with long narrow wings; adults rest with their narrow wings held at right angles to the body in a T shape; body length 8 mm. Only a few species occur in the bosque.

Natural history—Complete metamorphosis. Caterpillars feed on leaves or bore into plant stems. Habitat preferences are forest canopy trees and shrubby undergrowth.

Status—Widespread, uncommon.

David Lightfoot

Pyralid Moths

Sp, Su, F

Taxonomy—Class: Hexapoda; Order: Lepidoptera; Family: Pyralidae.

Identification—Gold to brown moths, some with patterns or lines on the wings; body length 5–6 mm. Many species occur in the bosque.

Natural history—Complete metamorphosis. Larvae feed on leaves, bore into plant stems, or feed on grass roots. Habitats include forests and open grassy areas.

Status—Widespread, common.

Funereal Duskywing Skipper   (*Erynnis funeralis*) ✳✳

Sp, Su, F

Taxonomy—Class: Hexapoda; Order: Lepidoptera; Family: Hesperiidae.

Identification—Top side dark brown to black with a light patch on the forewing; hind wing black with fringe of white hairs, also visible on the underside. Antennal clubs hooked as in all skippers. Wingspan 40 mm. Caterpillar pale green with fine yellow stripes along the sides; head prominent, dark brown with small orange patches on the sides; top of the head with 2 points, or "ears." Several similar hesperiid butterflies in the bosque but none as uniformly dark brown.

Natural history—Complete metamorphosis. Caterpillar food plants: several species in the pea family (Fabaceae). Found mostly in dry areas but also along forest edges.

Status—Widespread, common.

Common Checkered Skipper   (*Pyrgus communis*) ✳✳

Sp, Su, F

Taxonomy—Class: Hexapoda; Order: Lepidoptera; Family: Hesperiidae.

Identification—Top side checkered black and white, males brighter than females. Underside hind wing mostly white with tan or olive spots and bands. Antennal clubs hooked as in all skippers. Wingspan 25 mm. Caterpillar pale green, covered with fine white hair, head black with red collar. Only small black and white butterfly of the bosque.

Natural history—Complete metamorphosis. Caterpillar food plants: mallows (Malvaceae). Found in many habitats, including disturbed areas such as roadsides and ditches.

Status—Common and widespread.

Pipevine Swallowtail Butterfly (*Battus philenor*)

Sp, Su, F

Taxonomy—Class: Hexapoda; Order: Lepidoptera; Family: Papilionidae.

Identification—Top side male forewing black with iridescent blue, hind wing iridescent blue-green (photo), female all black with rows of white dots on wing edges. Underside hind wing iridescent blue with a row of orange spots. Wingspan 100 mm. Compare with black swallowtail. Caterpillar body black and red, head with a pair of long fleshy tubercles, posterior with 3 pairs of long fleshy tubercles.

Natural history—Complete metamorphosis. Caterpillar food plants: pipevines (Aristolochiaceae). Caterpillars and adults retain the poisons of their host plants. Adult flight pattern rapid with fluttering wing beats, at low heights. Prefers open areas or woodland edges, and males patrol territory for finding females.

Status—Mostly the southern part of the bosque, uncommon.

Sharyn Davidson

Two-tailed Swallowtail Butterfly (*Papilio multicaudata*) ✷ ✷

Sp, Su, F

Taxonomy—Class: Hexapoda; Order: Lepidoptera; Family: Papilionidae.

Identification—Top side yellow with thin black stripes and black borders on wing edges, only swallowtail species with 2 tails. Underside also yellow with black stripes and with dark blue near the edge of the hind wing; 2 red spots on hind wing edge. Wingspan 105 mm. Caterpillar early stages resemble bird droppings; later stages green with yellow eyespot blue in the center and thinly ringed in black; "neck" with white and black bands. The similar western tiger swallowtail occurs in the nearby mountains.

Natural history—Complete metamorphosis. Caterpillar food plants: leaves of ash and cherry trees. Largest of the western butterflies. Adult flight pattern is high and soaring. Found along woodland edges. Males fly slowly along watercourses looking for females.

Status—Common and widespread.

Collin Leslie

Black Swallowtail Butterfly

(*Papilio polyxenes*) ✳ ✳

Sp, Su, F

Taxonomy—Class: Hexapoda; Order: Lepidoptera; Family: Papilionidae.

David Lightfoot

Identification—Top side of male is black with yellow spots along the wing edges and a yellow band near the edge of the wing; on females the band is reduced to a few yellow spots on the forewing and the hind wings have patches of iridescent blue (photo), resembling the pipevine swallowtail. Red spots at edge of hind wing have black centers. Underside with white spots, a median blue band edged with row of orange spots. Wingspan 90 mm. Caterpillar early stages are black with white and green bands and yellow or orange dots. Later stages resemble bird droppings.

Natural history—Complete metamorphosis. Caterpillar food plants: many species in the parsley family (Apiaceae), both cultivated and native species.

Status—Common and widespread.

Cabbage White Butterfly

(*Pieris rapae*) ✳ ✳ [INT]

Sp, Su, F

Taxonomy—Class: Hexapoda; Order: Lepidoptera; Family: Pieridae.

Identification—Top side white with black on wingtip and 1 black dot (male; top photo) or 2 black dots (female) on forewing, hind wing plain white. Underside white with or without black dot. Wingspan 56 mm. Compare with checkered white butterfly. Caterpillar green with yellow dashes along the lateral margin (bottom photo).

Natural history—Complete metamorphosis. Caterpillar food plants: native and exotic plants in the Mustard family (Brassicaceae). Introduced from Europe in the 19th century and now found all across North America. Flight pattern is erratic, may be high or low; one of the first species seen in the spring. Seen with checkered whites.

Photographs: David Lightfoot

Status—Widespread, common, especially near urban areas.

Checkered White Butterfly

(*Pontia protodice*) ✳ ✳

Sp, Su, F

Taxonomy—Class: Hexapoda; Order: Lepidoptera; Family: Pieridae.

Identification—Top side white marked with gray patches, more gray on females. Underside white with veins outlined in yellow-brown, not as pronounced in lightly marked males. Wingspan 64 mm. Compare with cabbage white butterfly. Caterpillar with short hair, body sprinkled with small black spots, alternating stripes of yellow and grayish purple.

Natural history—Complete metamorphosis. Caterpillar food plants: native and introduced species in the Mustard family (Brassicaceae). Found in open habitats, including roadsides and other disturbed areas where mustards colonize. Flight pattern low and erratic. Occur with cabbage whites.

Status—Widespread, common.

Southern Dogface Butterfly

(*Colias cesonia*) ✳ ✳

Sp, Su, F

Taxonomy—Class: Hexapoda; Order: Lepidoptera; Family: Pieridae.

Identification—Top side of male strongly contrasting black and yellow, pattern on forewing resembles a dog in profile (photo), female also black and yellow but much paler. Underside plain yellow with a few white spots, those on the forewing ringed in black. Wingspan 50 mm. Compare with orange sulphur butterfly. Caterpillar green with white lateral stripe, may or may not have yellow bands edged in black.

Natural history—Complete metamorphosis. Caterpillar food plants: indigo bush, clover, and other legumes (Fabaceae). Perch with wings closed; fluttering flight, frequent flower visitors.

Status—Widespread, common.

Orange Sulphur Butterfly

(*Colias eurytheme*) ✳ ✳

Sp, Su, F

Taxonomy—Class: Hexapoda; Order: Lepidoptera; Family: Pieridae.

Identification—Top side of male bright yellow and black (top photo), female paler with more black on the wings and with black spot on forewing and red spot on hind wing (middle photo). Underside of male yellow with white spot, female paler with 1 white spot and a few darker ones. Color variation ranges from orange-yellow to yellow to occasional white. The very similar clouded sulphur (*Colias philodice*) also occurs in the region but is considered by some not to be a distinct species from the orange sulphur. Compare with southern dogface and cloudless sulphur butterflies. Caterpillar green with white lateral stripe and thin yellowish stripe near midline of back (bottom photo).

Natural history—Complete metamorphosis. Caterpillar food plants: white clover, alfalfa, and other legumes (Fabaceae). Found in many open habitats, including alfalfa fields and roadsides. Perch with wings closed; fluttering flight, frequent flower visitors.

Status—Widespread, common.

Photographs: David Lightfoot

Cloudless Sulphur Butterfly

(*Phoebis sennae*) ✳ ✳

Su, F

Taxonomy—Class: Hexapoda; Order: Lepidoptera; Family: Pieridae.

Identification—Top side of male conspicuous bright yellow with no markings ("cloudless") (photo), female yellow to greenish with dark edging on wings and dark spot on forewing. Underside yellow to greenish with 2 spots on both wings. Wingspan 78 mm. Compare with orange sulphur and southern dogface butterflies. Caterpillar has 2 forms, green with yellow lateral stripe topped with blue dashes or yellow with purplish black bands.

David Lightfoot

Natural history—Complete metamorphosis. Caterpillar food plants: senna (family Fabaceae). Flight is strong and fast; migrates southward in the fall.

Status—Widespread but mostly in the southern bosque, uncommon.

Dainty Sulphur Butterfly

(Nathalis iole) ✴ ✴

Sp, Su, F

Taxonomy—Class: Hexapoda; Order: Lepidoptera; Family: Pieridae.

Identification—Top side forewing yellow with black tips and black patch near hind edge, hind wing yellow. Some males have a dark bar on the forewing rather like the barred yellow (*Eurema daira*), which does not occur in bosque. Underside pale yellow to pale green, black spot near hind edge of forewing. No similar small yellowish bosque butterflies. Wingspan 23 mm, smallest sulphur in North America. Caterpillar green with 2 red bumps above the head, may or may not have purplish stripes along the sides and back of body.

Natural history—Complete metamorphosis. Caterpillar food plants: species in the sunflower family (Asteraceae). Fluttering flight very near the ground. Found in open habitats.

Status—Widespread, common.

Western Pygmy Blue Butterfly

(Brephidium exilis) ✴ ✴

Sp, Su, F

Taxonomy—Class: Hexapoda; Order: Lepidoptera; Family: Lycaenidae.

Identification—Very small butterfly, wingspan 12 mm. Top side coppery with blue at the base; underside pale except forewing edges tan and hind wing edges marked with black spots. Caterpillar sluglike, greenish, with pinkish stripe down the middle back and often outlined with white chevrons; body has grainy texture.

Natural history—Complete metamorphosis. Caterpillar food plants: saltbush, tumbleweed, lambsquarters, and others. Caterpillars may be tended by ants for their sugary excretions or "honeydew"; well camouflaged, look for them on buds or flowers of their food plants where there are ants.

Status—Widespread, common.

Acmon Blue Butterfly

(Plebejus acmon) ✳ ✳

Sp, Su, F

Taxonomy—Class: Hexapoda; Order: Lepidoptera; Family: Lycaenidae.

Identification—Top side of male bluish lilac with a pinkish orange band across the edge of the hind wing (photo), female brown with orange hind wing band. Underside whitish with black spots, orange band on hind wing edged with metallic blue spots. Wingspan 16 mm. Caterpillar sluglike, green with short white hair and faint chevron markings. Several similar lycaenid butterflies in the bosque.

Natural history—Complete metamorphosis. Caterpillar food plants: buckwheats and legumes, particularly vetches (Fabaceae). Found in many habitats, including disturbed areas such as roadsides and ditches. Caterpillars may be tended by ants for their sugary excretions or "honeydew"; well camouflaged, look for them on buds or flowers of their food plants where there are ants.

Status—Common and widespread.

Palmer's Metalmark Butterfly

(Apodemia palmeri) ✳ ✳

Sp, Su, F

Taxonomy—Class: Hexapoda; Order: Lepidoptera; Family: Riodinidae.

Identification—Top side orange-brown with orange margins, fore- and hind wings scattered with white spots; underside paler, also with white spots. Wingspan 28–30 mm. Compare with sagebrush checkerspot, field crescent, and bordered patch butterflies. Caterpillars gray-green with white stripes down the back, covered with fine hair.

Natural history—Complete metamorphosis. Caterpillar food plants: mesquites (*Prosopis* spp.); caterpillars tie mesquite leaves together with silk to form a retreat. Adults are frequent flower visitors, often aggregate.

Status—Widespread in southern bosque, uncommon.

Variegated Fritillary Butterfly

(*Euptoieta claudia*) ✳ ✳

Sp, Su, F

Taxonomy—Class: Hexapoda; Order: Lepidoptera; Family: Nymphalidae.

Identification—Top side brownish orange with black marks and a pale spot outlined in black on the edge of the forewing; underside brown with paler patches, pale spot from forewing visible, no silver coloring as the greater fritillaries have (top photo). Wingspan 35–40 mm. Compare with the similar queen, monarch, and viceroy. Caterpillars red with white longitudinal stripes edged in black, black branched spines, and a pair of clubbed spines on the head (bottom photo).

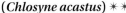

Natural history—Complete metamorphosis. Caterpillar food plants: flax, violets, and many other plants. Frequent flower visitors, and flight height is often low.

Status—Widespread, common.

Photographs: David Lightfoot

Sagebrush Checkerspot Butterfly

(*Chlosyne acastus*) ✳ ✳

Sp, Su

Taxonomy—Class: Hexapoda; Order: Lepidoptera; Family: Nymphalidae.

Identification—Top side bright to brownish orange with dark marks at the trailing edge of the forewing (top photo); underside with bright white areas that strongly contrast with the orange bands and spots. Wingspan 40 mm. Compare with the similar field crescent and bordered patch butterflies. Caterpillars black with black branched spines; small white dots on body and orange dashes along the midline (bottom photo).

Natural history—Complete metamorphosis. Caterpillar food plants: rabbitbrush (*Ericameria nauseosus*) and other members of the Aster family. Males patrol territory looking for females.

Status—Widespread, common.

Photographs: David Lightfoot

Bordered Patch Butterfly

(*Chlosyne lacinia*) ✳ ✳

Sp, Su, F

Taxonomy—Class: Hexapoda; Order: Lepidoptera; Family: Nymphalidae.

Identification—Top side forewing black with rows of white or orange spots, hind wing black with orange band across the middle (width may vary). Underside hind wing black with a cream band across the middle and cream spots along the edge. Wingspan 35 mm. Compare with the similar sagebrush checkerspot and field crescent butterflies. Caterpillar with variable amounts of orange and black, black branched spines, head usually black, sometimes orange. Early caterpillar stages feed together.

Natural history—Complete metamorphosis. Caterpillar food plants: sunflowers, cockleburs, ragweed, and other plants in the aster family.

Status—Common and widespread.

Field Crescent Butterfly

(*Phyciodes campestris*) ✳ ✳

Sp, Su, F

Taxonomy—Class: Hexapoda; Order: Lepidoptera; Family: Nymphalidae.

Identification—Top side mostly orange with black lines near the edges of the wings; wing area near the body marked with irregular darker orange spots. Underside dark yellow on the forewing, hind wing paler with several white patches. Antennal clubs orange. Wingspan 33 mm. Compare with sagebrush checkerspot and bordered patch. Caterpillar is black, mottled with white spots and with black branched spines, wide lateral brown stripe with orange spines.

Natural history—Complete metamorphosis. Caterpillar food plants: thistles. Adults found in wetter habitats and in disturbed areas such as ditches. Males patrol territory to find females.

Status—Widespread, common.

Mourning Cloak Butterfly

(Nymphalis antiopa) ✳ ✳

Sp, Su, F

Taxonomy—Class: Hexapoda; Order: Lepidoptera; Family: Nymphalidae.

Identification—Top side dark brown with yellow borders and blue spots; underside dark brown with whitish borders (top photo). Wingspan 85 mm. No similar butterflies in the bosque. Caterpillars black with small white dots and black branched spines, a line of red dots down the middle of the back, prolegs are red (bottom photo).

Natural history—Complete metamorphosis. Caterpillar food plants: willows, cottonwoods, elms, hackberries. Overwintering adults appear at the beginning of spring; unusual for adult butterflies to spend the winter in the adult stage. Found in many habitats (forest, along streams, open areas) but not in great numbers. Caterpillars feed in groups.

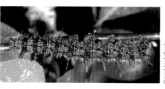

Tom Kennedy

David Lightfoot

Status—Widespread, uncommon.

Painted Lady Butterfly

(Vanessa cardui) ✳ ✳

Sp, Su, F

Taxonomy—Class: Hexapoda; Order: Lepidoptera; Family: Nymphalidae.

Identification—Top side orange to pinkish with black forewing tips with white spots; other black lines on the forewing but veins not outlined (top photo). Underside hind wing brown with 4 blue eyespots ringed in yellow. Wingspan 65 mm. Compare with variegated fritillary. Caterpillar brown with a thin yellow lateral stripe and double yellow stripes down the middle of the back, spines and hair are gray or whitish (bottom photo).

Natural history—Complete metamorphosis. Caterpillar food plants: thistles, mallows, and many others. Adults migrate to Mexico for the winter. Fast, erratic flyers. May occur in large numbers some years, especially when migrating through a local area.

Photographs: David Lightfoot

Status—Common and widespread.

Common Buckeye Butterfly

(*Junonia coenia*) ✳ ✳

Su, F

Taxonomy—Class: Hexapoda; Order: Lepidoptera; Family: Nymphalidae.

Identification—Top side brown with contrasting eyespots on fore- and hind wings, forewing with white bar that extends to ring eyespot, also 2 orange bars near forewing edge. Underside brown with orange and white bars showing through from the top side. Wingspan 50 mm. No similar bosque butterflies with eyespots on wings. Caterpillar black with blue dashes down the middle of the back and white lateral stripes, head with 2 short black spines.

Natural history—Complete metamorphosis. Caterpillar food plants: snapdragons, plantains, and others. Prefer open areas with flowers and some bare ground. Males patrol territory usually from ground level to find females.

Status—Common and widespread.

Viceroy Butterfly

(*Limenitis archippus*) ✳ ✳

Sp, Su, F

Taxonomy—Class: Hexapoda; Order: Lepidoptera; Family: Nymphalidae.

Identification—The well-known mimic of the monarch butterfly. Top side brownish orange with black borders; single row of white spots in the border. Veins outlined in black; hind wings crossed midway by black line that is absent in the monarch. Viceroy smaller than monarch. Wingspan 50 mm. Compare with the similar monarch, queen, and variegated fritillary. The Arizona viceroy subspecies occurs in the southern part of the bosque and is more brownish, less orange, with reduced black on the wing veins, perhaps mimicking the queen butterfly. Caterpillar brown to green with short knobs on head, body with a white saddle-shaped patch and raised humps resembling a bird dropping.

Natural history—Complete metamorphosis. Caterpillar food plants: willows. Adults prefer edges of streams, rivers, and woods. Flight less gliding than that of monarch.

Status—Widespread and uncommon; viceroy in the northern bosque, Arizona viceroy in the southern bosque (both occur in the Isleta region).

Queen Butterfly

(Danaus gilippus) ✳✳

Sp, Su, F

Taxonomy—Class: Hexapoda; Order: Lepidoptera; Family: Nymphalidae.

Identification—Top side mahogany brown-orange with black edging and scattered white spots near wingtips. A relative of the monarch butterfly but lacking the black lines outlining the wing veins; underside dark brown with veins outlined on the hind wing. Wingspan 85 mm. Also compare with the similar viceroy and variegated fritillary. Caterpillars banded black, white, and yellow but with more black than the monarch caterpillar and with 3 pairs of fleshy sensory filaments on the back.

Natural history—Complete metamorphosis. Caterpillar food plants: milkweeds (Asclepiadaceae). Adults roost in groups at night; may be migratory like the monarch. Their bright contrasting colors are a warning to birds that the butterflies are poisonous because they contain the toxins of their food plants.

Status—Widespread, uncommon.

Monarch Butterfly

(Danaus plexippus) ✳✳

Sp, Su, F

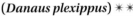

Taxonomy—Class: Hexapoda; Order: Lepidoptera; Family: Nymphalidae.

Identification—Top side brownish orange with black veins and wing borders; white dots on the wing borders and on the body (top photo). Underside paler yellow with black veins. Wing borders black with bright white dots. Wingspan 85–90 mm. Compare with the similar queen, viceroy, and variegated fritillary. Caterpillar banded evenly with black, white, and yellow; 2 pairs of fleshy sensory filaments on the back (bottom photo).

Natural history—Complete metamorphosis. Caterpillar food plants: milkweeds (Asclepiadaceae). This species is well known for its annual migration between Canada and the U.S. to Mexico (there are many websites about their life history). Their bright contrasting colors are a warning to birds that the butterflies are poisonous because they contain the toxins of their food plants.

Status—Widespread, common, although pesticide use in the U.S. and winter habitat destruction in Mexico are negatively impacting the species.

Geometrid Moths   ✳ ✳

Sp, Su, F

Taxonomy—Class: Hexapoda; Order: Lepidoptera; Family: Geometridae.

Identification—Gray and brown mottled moths with broad wings folded at rest in a characteristic triangular shape (top photo). Color and pattern match tree bark. Medium size, body length 12 mm, wingspan 30 mm. Caterpillars pale yellowish brown, gray, or green; very slender and lack legs throughout the middle portion of their body; crawl in an arching and stretching forward manner, often called inchworms (bottom photo). Several similar species in the bosque. Similar to noctuid moths but more delicate and triangular.

Natural history—Complete metamorphosis. Caterpillars feed on a variety of plants, especially in the Aster family. Most species specialize on certain food plants. Caterpillars and adults are active at night, and adults often fly to lights at night.

Status—Widespread, uncommon.

Photographs: David Lightfoot

Southwestern Tent Caterpillar   (*Malacosoma incurvum*) ✳ ✳

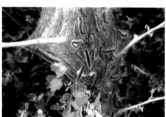

Su, F

Taxonomy—Class: Hexapoda; Order: Lepidoptera; Family: Lasiocampidae.

Identification—Caterpillars pale orange-brown on top, blue stripes on sides of body, long thin whitish hairs throughout, about 40 mm in length (photo). Many individuals live together in a large silk tent that they produce from silk glands in their mouthparts. The tents look like large spiderwebs and are usually in upper branches of trees. Leaves within and surrounding the tent are eaten by the caterpillars. The adults are brownish yellow medium-size moths similar in appearance to noctuid moths. Robust and hairy; body length 15 mm; wingspan 30 mm.

Natural history—Complete metamorphosis. Caterpillars feed on a variety of broad-leaved trees and shrubs, especially cottonwood. Adults are active at night and often fly to lights at night.

Status—Widespread, uncommon.

Sharyn Davidson

Mesquite Buck Moth   (*Hemileuca juno*) ✳ ✳

Su

Taxonomy—Class: Hexapoda; Order: Lepidoptera; Family: Saturniidae.

Identification—Top side of males black and white forewing, black hind wing, top side of abdomen red, females with forewing and hind wing black and white, top side of abdomen black (photo); wingspan 50–55 mm. No similar moths in the bosque. Caterpillar dark gray with 3 lateral lines and black-tipped red spines.

David Lightfoot

Natural history—Complete metamorphosis. Caterpillar food plants: honey mesquite (*Prosopis glandulosa*) and screwbean mesquite (*P. pubescens*). Caterpillars feed in groups in early stages. Adults fly during the day and may come to lights at night. Another saturniid moth, the large tan polyphemus moth (*Antheraea polyphemus*), occurs more frequently at higher elevations in New Mexico but may be seen occasionally in the bosque.

Status—Widespread in the southern part of the bosque, uncommon.

White-lined Sphinx Moth   (*Hyles lineata*) ✳ ✳

Sp, Su

Taxonomy—Class: Hexapoda; Order: Lepidoptera; Family: Sphingidae.

Identification—Heavy-bodied moth; forewing narrow and elongate, brownish with white line crossing it from tip to base, hind wing small and mostly pink (top photo). Wingspan 65–90 mm. Rapid hummingbird-like flight. Caterpillars have 2 color phases, a typical green form with pink stripes (middle photo) and a black and yellow striped form (bottom photo) during years when population densities are high. The caterpillars are called hornworms because they have a small back-curved spine at the posterior tip of the body. Several similar sphinx moths, including the tomato hornworm moth, occur in the bosque.

Sharyn Davidson

Natural history—Complete metamorphosis. Caterpillar food plants: many kinds of plants, including four o'clocks (*Mirabilis*), evening primrose (*Oenothera*), vetch (*Astragalus*), and tomatoes (*Lycopersicon*). Adults are important pollinators of night-blooming flowers, particularly jimsonweed (*Datura wrightii*). Also called hawk moths or hummingbird moths because of their large size and hovering flight in front of flowers.

David Lightfoot

Status—Widespread, common.

David Lightfoot

Underwing Moth

(*Catacola* spp.) ✳ ✳

Su, F

Taxonomy—Class: Hexapoda; Order: Lepidoptera; Family: Noctuidae.

Identification—Top side forewings mottled dark brown, patterned like tree bark, hind wings orange with curved black bands. Underside strongly banded white with orange or dark brown. Wingspan 70–80 mm. Caterpillars gray-brown, strongly resembling twigs or branches; 2 bumps near the end of the abdomen. The largest noctuid moth in the bosque, and no others have bright red underwings.

Natural history—Complete metamorphosis. Caterpillar food plants: cottonwood, willow, fruit trees. Caterpillars feed at night, during the day are well camouflaged on twigs and branches (compare with Geometridae). Adults resting on trees are difficult to see but if disturbed will display the bright hind wings to startle predators.

Status—Widespread, uncommon.

Army Cutworm Moth

(*Euxoa auxiliaris*) ✳ ✳

Sp, Su, F

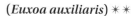

Taxonomy—Class: Hexapoda; Order: Lepidoptera; Family: Noctuidae.

Identification—Gray-brown medium-size moths (20–25 mm), hairy bodies, wings with various dark and light marks. Caterpillars are gray and mottled, common on the ground and low plants in the spring. Many similar-appearing species of cutworm and other noctuid moths occur in the bosque.

Natural history—Complete metamorphosis.

Status—Widespread, common.

Sticktight Flea

(*Echidnophaga gallinacea*) ✳ ✳ [INT]

David Lightfoot

Taxonomy—Class: Hexapoda; Order: Siphonaptera; Family: Pulicidae.

Identification—Dark brown, body length 2 mm; most strongly associated with poultry although can also be found on dogs, cats, horses, and occasionally humans; females feed on blood by burying head into the host's body; difficult to remove. Several other free-living flea species occur in the bosque associated with rodent nests.

Natural history—Complete metamorphosis. Females remain embedded in host, produce eggs that drop to the ground; larvae feed on dead organic material, pupate in the ground, and as adults move on to a passing host. Do not transmit diseases. Depending on environmental conditions, the life cycle can be completed within days or months.

Status—Widespread, common.

Crane Flies

✳ ✳

David Lightfoot

Taxonomy—Class: Hexapoda; Order: Diptera; Family: Tipulidae.

Identification—Slender bodied, resembling giant mosquitoes but not related to them. Legs very long and thin; wings thin and elongate in shape. Head usually has an elongated rostrum, or "nose." Body length 2–60 mm. Compare with mosquito.

Natural history—Complete metamorphosis. Habitats for larvae range from freshwater to decaying wood to fungi to grasslands. Adults usually found in low vegetation in damp habitats. Life cycles range from 6 weeks to several years depending on the species and environmental temperatures. They do not bite.

Status—Widespread, common.

Biting Midges   ✳✳

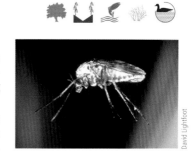

Taxonomy—Class: Hexapoda; Order: Diptera; Family: Ceratopogonidae.

Identification—Dark colored, robust body shape; males with feathery antennae; body length 1–6 mm. Several similar species occur in the bosque. Compare with nonbiting midges (Chironomidae) and mosquito.

Natural history—Complete metamorphosis; found in moist habitats; larvae are scavengers on decaying organic matter; adults most active at dusk; both sexes visit flowers, but like mosquitoes, the females require a blood meal to produce eggs. Adults form mating swarms over a landmark, such as a shrub. Bites of the females are painful and irritating. Another common name for them is punkies.

Status—Widespread, common.

David Lightfoot

Chironomid Midges   ✳✳

Taxonomy—Class: Hexapoda; Order: Diptera; Family: Chironomidae.

Identification—Slender, wings narrow, legs long and thin, mosquito-like but without proboscis, front legs longer than back legs; males with feathery antennae. Body length 1–10 mm. Compare with mosquito. Many species occur in the bosque.

Natural history—Complete metamorphosis; adults live only a few weeks, forming mating swarms over landmarks. Larvae are aquatic or in other wet habitats. Some species have many generations per year. Many species used as indicators of water quality because of their sensitivity to water temperature and oxygen levels. Larvae that live in stagnant water are called bloodworms because they contain hemoglobin, the same oxygen-carrying pigment that humans use.

Status—Widespread, common.

David Lightfoot

Southern House Mosquito

(*Culex quinquefasciatus*) ✳✳

Sp, Su

Taxonomy—Class: Hexapoda; Order: Diptera; Family: Culicidae.

Identification—Slender body, with back legs longer than front legs and frequently held raised when the fly is at rest; proboscis longer than the head; body length 3–9 mm. The body and wing veins are covered with scales; males have feathery antennae. Compare with nonbiting midges (Chironomidae). Many species of mosquito occur in the bosque, all similar in appearance.

David Lightfoot

Natural history—Complete metamorphosis; the familiar annoying flies found around areas with standing water; larvae are aquatic and an important food source for fish. Depending on the species, adults may be active during the day, at night, or at dusk and dawn. Females require a blood meal for egg production and are very good at detecting human body heat, sweat, and exhaled carbon dioxide. Species in the bosque do transmit West Nile virus but no other important diseases to humans.

Status—Widespread, common.

Dark-winged Fungus Gnats

✳✳

Sp, Su, F

Taxonomy—Class: Hexapoda; Order: Diptera; Family: Sciaridae.

Identification—Body form slender to robust; color brown or black; wings dark; legs long; body length 2–6 mm. Compare with mosquito, biting midges (Ceratopogonidae), and nonbiting midges (Chironomidae).

David Lightfoot

Natural history—Complete metamorphosis. Larvae feed on fungi on decaying vegetation; adults feed on nectar or aphid honeydew on leaves. Found in woodlands, where large numbers collect in shady areas near riverbanks or decaying logs. Active at dusk in low vegetation. They do not bite.

Status—Widespread, common.

Gall Midges

✳ ✳

Taxonomy—Class: Hexapoda; Order: Diptera; Family: Cecidomyiidae.

Identification—Small, delicate, with long beaded antennae and long legs; plump or cylindrical abdomen; eyes wrap around antennal bases and meet at the top of the head. Body length 1–5 mm. The galls produced on plant stems and leaves are generally observed more often than the flies (top photo: saltbush stem gall). Many species occur in the bosque; most are specific to certain plants.

Natural history—Complete metamorphosis. Larvae induce the formation of a gall on stems, leaves, or twigs. A gall is similar to scar tissue produced by the plant to surround the invading larva; the gall provides plant tissue for food and protection for the larva. The shape of a gall may be rounded, rough and irregular, large or small. Many other insects cause galls on plants, including sawflies and aphids.

Status—Widespread, common.

March Flies

(*Bibio* sp.) ✳ ✳

Taxonomy—Class: Hexapoda; Order: Diptera; Family: Bibionidae.

Identification—Dark, moderately hairy flies with a distinctive narrow or elongated head, antennae short with 7–10 rounded compact segments. Abdomen and legs long and slender, body length 5–9 mm. Two species occur in the bosque.

Natural history—Complete metamorphosis; very abundant for a few weeks in the spring (March–April). Larvae are scavengers on decaying organic matter and are found in grasses or forest litter. Males perform mating dances in swarms to attract females. Adults often seen mating end to end; hence another common name for them is lovebugs.

Status—Widespread, common.

Black Soldier Fly

(Hermetia illucens) ✳ ✳

Sp, Su, F

Taxonomy—Class: Hexapoda; Order: Diptera; Family: Stratiomyidae.

Identification—Body slender to broad in shape without bristles, thorax may appear velvety. Antennae moderately long and held in a Y shape. Body black with clear areas on top of the abdomen, other species are usually brightly colored or patterned or with metallic sheen, some resembling wasps; body length 12–18 mm.

Natural history—Complete metamorphosis; adults feed on flowers, and some have hovering flight like flower flies. Larvae feed on decaying organic matter or dung or are predators on other insect larvae in rotting wood.

Status—Widespread, uncommon.

Deer Fly

(Chrysops sp.) ✳ ✳

Sp, Su, F

Taxonomy—Class: Hexapoda; Order: Diptera; Family: Tabanidae.

Identification—Body without bristles but may have short hair covering the thorax; eyes large, often green or striped and taking up most of the head. Antennae moderately long and thick, abruptly tapering to points. Proboscis short and thick. Abdomen often patterned; body length 5–10 mm.

Natural history—Complete metamorphosis. Blood-feeding insects that attack livestock and horses, wild mammals, and people. Bite is painful. Larvae prefer damp soils and wetlands or the edges of streams and are predators of other insects and earthworms.

Status—Widespread, common.

Horse Fly

(Tabanus punctifer) ✳ ✳

Sp, Su, F

Taxonomy—Class: Hexapoda; Order: Diptera; Family: Tabanidae.

Identification—Large black fly with yellowish thorax and large eyes with green and red bands. Antennae moderately long and thick, abruptly tapering to points. Proboscis short and thick. Body length 16–20 mm. Several other smaller and gray horse flies are in the bosque.

Natural history—Complete metamorphosis. Blood-feeding insects that attack livestock and horses, wild mammals, and people. Bite is painful. Larvae prefer damp soils and wetlands or the edges of streams and are predators of other insects and earthworms. Populations in the bosque are supported by farming and ranching near the river.

Status—Widespread, common.

Efferia Robber Fly

(*Efferia albibarbis*) ✳ ✳

Su, F

Taxonomy—Class: Hexapoda; Order: Diptera; Family: Asilidae.

Identification—Robber flies vary in shape from elongate to short and robust, length 4-40 mm; colors vary from grays and browns to black or reddish. Large eyes widely separated; antennae short and thick; face often covered with hair giving many species a bearded look; mouthparts are short and tubular. Legs stout and usually spiny to help hold prey. The efferia robber fly is gray to tan; abdomen long and tapered; body length 15-30 mm. Males have large black genital capsules at the end of the abdomen (photo). Compare with other robber flies.

Natural history—Complete metamorphosis. Robber flies prefer open sunny habitats, including open areas within woodlands; frequently perch on tips of shrub branches, on top of stones, or on another local high point so that flying prey can be readily seen and attacked. Prey include grasshoppers, flies, bees, and spiders. Flies stab prey with their mouthparts and suck out the fluids and soft tissue. Larvae live in the soil and are predators on other invertebrates. Efferia adults prefer open areas with bare soil and perch on the ground or low vegetation.

Status—Widespread, uncommon.

Woodland Robber Fly

(*Proctacanthella cacopiloga*) ✳ ✳

Sp, Su, F

Taxonomy—Class: Hexapoda; Order: Diptera; Family: Asilidae.

Identification—Robust flies with tapering abdomen; legs stout and spiny; tarsal claws sharp. Body length 17-40 mm. Compare with efferia robber fly.

Natural history—Complete metamorphosis; predators of many kinds of insects, particularly juvenile grasshoppers. Prefer open bare soil and perch on the ground or low vegetation.

Status—Widespread, uncommon.

Sand Robber Fly

(*Stichopogon catulus*) ✳ ✳

Sp, Su, F

Taxonomy—Class: Hexapoda; Order: Diptera; Family: Asilidae.

Identification—Body mottled gray or tan that matches background sand or mud; body with silver hairs, eyes large; body length 5 mm. Compare with the larger species efferia robber fly and woodland robber fly.

Natural history—Complete metamorphosis; prefer open areas along shoreline or ditches or bare sandy areas in forest, where they perch on the ground. Eat small flying insects.

Status—Widespread, uncommon.

Bee-mimic Robber Fly   (*Mallophora fautrix*) ✳ ✳

Sp, Su, F

Taxonomy—Class: Hexapoda; Order: Diptera;
Family: Asilidae.

Identification—Mimics a bumblebee, stout bodied, hairy, black and yellow. Antennae shorter and face hairier than in real bees. Body length 15–18 mm. Compare with bumblebee. The only large bee-mimicking robber fly in the bosque.

Natural history—Complete metamorphosis. Looks like a bumblebee but does not collect pollen; perches on branch tips, usually near flowers; prefers bees and wasps as prey.

Status—Widespread, uncommon.

David Lightfoot

Pale Bee Fly   (*Phthiria* sp.) ✳ ✳

Su, F

Taxonomy—Class: Hexapoda; Order: Diptera;
Family: Bombyliidae.

Identification—Bee flies are small to large, dark to brightly colored; wings often with brown or black patterns; proboscis short to very long; eyes large; body sometimes very hairy; some species mimic bees. Pale bee flies are light colored with darker stripes or spots on body or face; proboscis very long; body length 1.5–5.0 mm. Many species of bee flies occur in the bosque.

Natural history—Complete metamorphosis; larvae are parasites of other insects, especially moths, beetles, or flies, or feed on the eggs of grasshoppers. Adults visit flowers and are pollinators (they do not bite); hovering flight; prefer open sunny areas.

Status—Widespread, common.

David Lightfoot

Dark Bee Fly   (*Thyridanthrax* sp.) ✳ ✳

Su, F

Taxonomy—Class: Hexapoda; Order: Diptera;
Family: Bombyliidae.

Identification—Brownish fly with dark coloring on the front half of the wings; short proboscis; body length 10–12 mm. Many species of bee flies occur in the bosque.

Natural history—Complete metamorphosis; often seen on the ground with the wings held out to the side; larvae attack grasshopper eggs and larvae of other flies; adults feed on flowers, especially in the sunflower family (Asteraceae).

Status—Widespread, common.

David Lightfoot

Mydas Fly

(*Mydas* sp.) ✳ ✳

Sp, Su, F

Taxonomy—Class: Hexapoda; Order: Diptera; Family: Mydidae.

Identification—Bluish black body, length 20-25 mm; wings orange; wasp mimic; antennae elbowed, stout, close together on the head and form a Y shape.

Natural history—Complete metamorphosis. Adults are predators on many kinds of arthropods; larvae feed on beetle larvae associated with rotting logs. Adults mimic wasps, especially the spider wasps (Pompilidae). In the bosque the larvae are found in cottonwood forest, while the adults are found in sunny open areas, often on flowers.

Status—Widespread, uncommon.

David Lightfoot

Long-legged Flies

✳ ✳

Sp, Su, F

Taxonomy—Class: Hexapoda; Order: Diptera; Family: Dolichopodidae.

Identification—Slender body with long legs (especially the middle and hind ones), body usually shining metallic green or bronze. Body length 5-9 mm. Several similar species occur in the bosque.

Natural history—Complete metamorphosis; predators on small insects as adults and larvae (which feed on mosquito larvae); found near water as well as in fields or open grassy areas. Often seen running about on leaves in sunlight.

Status—Widespread, common.

David Lightfoot

Flower Fly

(*Chamaesyrphus* sp.) ✳ ✳

Sp, Su, F

Taxonomy—Class: Hexapoda; Order: Diptera; Family: Syrphidae.

Identification—Body slender, black and yellow. Thorax without bristles; body length 4-6 mm. Many similar species occur in the bosque.

Natural history—Complete metamorphosis. Adults feed at flowers, have hovering flight, and can change directions quickly; important pollinators for many plants; among the best mimics of bees and wasps among the flies. Larvae are predators on other insect larvae or aphids or are scavengers in decaying organic matter.

Status—Widespread, common.

David Lightfoot

Green Bottle Flies

(*Lucilia* spp.) ✳ ✳

Sp, Su, F

Taxonomy—Class: Hexapoda; Order: Diptera; Family: Calliphoridae.

Identification—Robust bright iridescent green to coppery flies with bright red eyes; body length 4–16 mm. Several similar species occur in the bosque.

Natural history—Complete metamorphosis; larvae feed on carcasses and dung. Adults visit flowers and low vegetation in open sunny areas; when flying, their buzzing is loud and constant. Among the first insects to arrive at carrion and important in the breakdown of organic matter.

Status—Widespread, common.

David Lightfoot

Blue Bottle Flies

(*Calliphora* spp.) ✳ ✳

Sp, Su, F

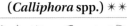

Taxonomy—Class: Hexapoda; Order: Diptera; Family: Calliphoridae.

Identification—Robust dark iridescent blue to blackish flies with bright red eyes; body length 4–18 mm. Several similar-appearing species occur in the bosque.

Natural history—Complete metamorphosis; larvae feed on carcasses and dung. Adults visit flowers and low vegetation in open sunny areas; when flying, their buzzing is loud and constant. Among the first insects to arrive at carrion and important in the breakdown of organic matter.

Status—Widespread, common.

David Lightfoot

House Fly

(*Musca domestica*) ✳ ✳

Sp, Su, F

Taxonomy—Class: Hexapoda; Order: Diptera; Family: Muscidae.

Identification—Muscid flies are broad-bodied flies ranging from large to small in size, most resembling house flies in coloration. The house fly has a black thorax with gray stripes and numerous bristles, sponging mouthparts, abdomen with brown patterns and large clear yellow patches; body length 7–8 mm. Compare with tachina flies (family Tachinidae). Several other flies are similar in appearance but lack the clear yellow patches on the abdomen.

David Lightfoot

Natural history—Complete metamorphosis; adults and larvae found in wet or dry habitats on rotting vegetation, dung, flowers, carrion. Life cycle can be completed in 30 days in warm weather. Abundances in the bosque are supported by human agriculture and ranching nearby.

Status—Widespread, common.

Stable Fly

(*Stomoxys calcitrans*) ✳ ✳

Sp, Su

Taxonomy—Class: Hexapoda; Order: Diptera; Family: Muscidae.

Identification—Resembles a large house fly but with a short black proboscis and more pronounced brown spotting on the abdomen; body length 10 mm.

Natural history—Complete metamorphosis; adults are blood-feeding insects, using the proboscis to stab horses, cattle, and humans. The bite is painful. They take several blood meals over their lifetime. Larvae feed on decaying vegetation or dung. Abundance is supported by human use of the area near the bosque for agriculture and ranching.

Status—Widespread, common.

David Lightfoot

Rabbit Bot Fly

(*Cuterebra austeni*) ✳ ✳

Sp, Su, F

Taxonomy—Class: Hexapoda; Order: Diptera; Family: Oestridae.

Identification—Large heavy-bodied flies covered with velvety short hair that is black on most of the body but whitish on the thorax; large eyes black and red; red markings on the legs; body length 20–25 mm.

Natural history—Complete metamorphosis. Adults lay eggs on vegetation and the larvae crawl onto passing rabbits and burrow beneath the skin, leaving a small opening at the surface through which they breathe. Larvae feed on host fluids and tissue and are very difficult to remove. Larvae leave the host to pupate in soil.

Status—Widespread, uncommon.

David Lightfoot

Flesh Flies

(*Sarcophaga* spp.) ✳ ✳

Sp, Su, F

Taxonomy—Class: Hexapoda; Order: Diptera; Family: Sarcophagidae.

Identification—Stout bodied; gray with stripes on the thorax and spots or other patterns on the abdomen; bright red eyes; compare with the house fly; body length 2.5–10 mm. Many similar species occur in the bosque.

Natural history—Complete metamorphosis; adults feed on nectar or plant sap; larvae are often scavengers on dead animals or are parasitic on a wide range of insects and spiders.

Status—Widespread, common.

David Lightfoot

Tachina Flies

Sp, Su, F

Taxonomy—Class: Hexapoda; Order: Diptera; Family: Tachinidae.

Identification—Body usually black or dark gray with many long black bristles; some species are red, orange, or yellow and resemble bees, others resemble the house fly; body length 5-20 mm.

Natural history—Complete metamorphosis; adults feed on flowers, especially those in the sunflower family (Asteraceae). Males look for females by gathering in small groups at local high spots or places with a landmark. Larvae are parasites of many kinds of insects, including grasshoppers, bees, crickets, and beetles.

Status—Widespread, common.

Tom Kennedy

Fruit Flies

Sp, Su, F

Taxonomy—Class: Hexapoda; Order: Diptera; Family: Tephritidae.

Identification—Body brightly colored, wings with dark bands, spots, or other patterns. Compare with vinegar flies, which are often called fruit flies. Body length 4-8 mm. Many similar species with different wing patterns occur in the bosque.

Natural history—Complete metamorphosis. Adults feed on flowers; larvae feed on living plant tissue with a preference for members of the sunflower family (Asteraceae), although larvae of some species attack fruit, such as apples. Most are specific to certain plants. The Mediterranean fruit fly belongs to this family but is not present in the bosque.

Status—Widespread, common.

David Lightfoot

Vinegar Flies

(*Drosophila* sp.)

Sp, Su, F

Taxonomy—Class: Hexapoda; Order: Diptera; Family: Drosophilidae.

Identification—Yellow, brown, or black body with bright red eyes; body length 3-5 mm; often called fruit flies, but compare with true fruit flies (Tephritidae) above. Several similar-appearing species occur in the bosque.

Natural history—Complete metamorphosis; the famous "fruit flies" used in genetics research, but many species occur in nature, feeding on decaying fruits, fungi, and sap of tree wounds. In the bosque they may also be found on rotting cactus pads.

Status—Widespread, common.

David Lightfoot

SCOPE FOR THIS GUIDE

Vertebrates are bilaterally symmetrical (the left and right sides of the body look identical) with a distinctly shaped head and typically two pairs of limbs. They have a bony or cartilaginous internal skeleton, or endoskeleton, to which muscles are attached. Part of the endoskeleton is jaws with or without teeth (except in lampreys) and a set of vertebrae, making up a vertebral column that runs along the dorsal side of the body from head to tail. The skin of vertebrates consists of two tissues, the outer epidermis and the inner dermis. It is often modified to produce scales, plates, feathers, or hairs. Protected by the rib cage, the heart has a ventral position and consists of two to four chambers. Vertebrates have blood that circulates throughout the body in specialized hollow organs, the blood vessels. Their body also contains paired kidneys and a liver and a pancreas, two large digestive glands. The male and the female have paired gonads, specialized glands producing reproductive cells.

Vertebrates evolved more than 500 million years ago, during the Cambrian Period of the Paleozoic Era. Since then they have become dominant on land and in the oceans. All belong to the subphylum Vertebrata, represented by approximately 57,400 living species, among them 28,000 fish, 6,000 amphibians, 8,000 reptiles, 10,000 birds, and 5,400 mammals. Each of the five classes is further divided into orders, families, and genera. This taxonomic arrangement reflects evolutionary history as best as science can re-create. Taxonomy is always in flux, however. Species are sometimes reassigned to new genera, a species may be split into two new species, or two species may be lumped into one. Several of the vertebrates described in the field guide have had their taxonomic status changed recently.

Featured in the field guide are 9 amphibians, 29 reptiles, 181 birds, and 35 mammals. These 254 species represent a large proportion, but not all, of the terrestrial vertebrates recorded in the bosque. Among them are all the most common species and several rare but charismatic, emblematic, or conservation-sensitive taxa. In the latter category is the northern leopard frog (*Rana pipiens*), once widespread along the Middle Rio Grande but now on the verge of extirpation. Rare but high-profile species include the mountain lion (*Felis concolor*) and the black bear (*Ursus americanus*). Due to space constraints, some rare or occasional vertebrate species had to be excluded from our coverage. Most of them are birds, and we recommend that local bird checklists be used to complement the field guide.

VERTEBRATE ECOLOGY AND LIFE HISTORY

Vertebrates exhibit extreme variation not only in body size and appearance, but also regarding their ecology and natural history. Besides fish (not included in the field guide), amphibians and reptiles are ectotherms, whereas birds and mammals are homeotherms, capable of regulating their body temperature internally. Most amphibians begin their life in water before undergoing metamorphosis. Some lizard species are parthenogenetic, with no males and no fertilization of the female's eggs. Amphibians, birds, and most reptiles lay eggs, but some lizards and snakes and nearly all mammals give birth to live young. Many mammals and birds form pair bonds and provide parental care. Birds and bats have evolved the ability to fly. Some of them are migratory, flying over large distances back and forth between breeding and wintering grounds.

As much as possible, natural history information provided in the following species accounts is specific to the bosque. However, local natural history information is sparse for many amphibians, reptiles, and mammals and some of the more secretive or uncommon bird species. In such cases as these, we have included information collected outside the bosque but generally applying to the entire geographic range of a species.

HOW TO FIND VERTEBRATES

All you may need in the bosque are binoculars, essential for observing and identifying birds in particular. A spotting scope is another valuable tool where viewing distances can be great. If you visit the Bosque del Apache NWR or the Rio Grande Nature Center, you may want to stop by the visitor center and inquire about unusual species reported recently by staff or other visitors. Experience the bosque on a warm summer night after rain or near a pond and listen for frog or toad choruses. Learn to recognize the calls and songs of birds. You will find it an immensely rewarding effort.

As you use this field guide, keep in mind that a common species of the bosque is not always frequently encountered by the visitor. Among vertebrates, only the birds tend to be highly detectable during the day. A common bird can be defined as one seen or heard on most or all visits to the bosque at the appropriate season and in areas with proper habitat. The same cannot be said of many other vertebrate animals, which give the impression of being rare in the bosque when they are not. To detect some of these animals may require finding their tracks on the ground (see the mammal section) or specialized techniques and tools used by researchers.

Amphibians

Amphibians evolved from fish about 370 million years ago, during the Devonian Period. They were the first vertebrates to crawl out of the water and onto land. In order to reproduce, they have retained a close association to aquatic environments. Their eggs, which in most species are fertilized externally, lack a waterproof shell and will dry out unless deposited in water or in very moist soils. All amphibians are also ectotherms, meaning that they regulate their body temperature largely by exchanging heat with their external environment. Their skin is moist and thin and lacks scales. They have no claws and no external ear opening. The heart consists of three chambers. The life cycle typically involves a larval stage spent in water and an adult stage partly or completely on land. The larvae (called tadpoles in frogs) have gills and a tail. During metamorphosis, they usually lose their gills and their tail while growing legs and developing lungs. Contrary to toads and frogs, salamanders retain their tail in the adult stage.

Of the three orders of amphibians, two are represented in the bosque, the urodeles (salamanders) and the anurans (toads and frogs). The nine species occurring regularly in the bosque account for nearly one-third of all the amphibians found in New Mexico. Most of these nine species spend a large part of their adult lives buried underground. They emerge after rains during the spring and summer and congregate toward ponds or seasonal pools. The male toads and frogs sing, forming choruses. The two amphibians most likely to be encountered during the day are the American bullfrog (*Rana catesbeiana*) and the Woodhouse's toad (*Bufo woodhousii*). The American bullfrog is easily recognized by its deep and resonant call. It is not native to the Middle Rio Grande Valley and, as a ravenous predator, has contributed to the local decline of the northern leopard frog (*Rana pipiens*). The Woodhouse's toad is the amphibian most likely to be encountered in the leaf litter on the floor of the cottonwood woodland, especially the young, newly metamorphosed adults. Many of the other amphibians of the bosque are strictly nocturnal. As you listen for choruses at night look for the eyes of toads and frogs reflecting the beam of your flashlight.

Tiger Salamander (*Ambystoma tigrinum*) ✳ ✳

Jan–Mar, APR–OCT, Nov–Dec

Taxonomy—Class: Amphibia; Order: Caudata; Family: Ambystomatidae.

Identification—Large salamander with broad head, rounded snout, and well-developed legs. Typical adult (top) has black body with yellow blotches and bands, but some individuals may be uniformly light brown. Larva (bottom) has plumose (featherlike) external gills and fully develops 4 legs soon after hatching.

Natural history—Adults spend most of the year in rodent burrows, typically emerging after rain events and migrating to nearby seasonal pools or permanent ponds for reproduction (may be active aboveground during warm winter days). Larvae (often called water dogs and used as fish bait) are aquatic and likely suffer high mortality from many potential predators (crayfish, fish, turtles, grebes, ducks, herons, raccoons, bullfrogs).

Status—Widespread and locally common.

Photographs: Bill Gorum

Couch's Spadefoot

(Scaphiopus couchii) ✳ ✳

APR–OCT

Taxonomy—Class: Amphibia; Order: Anura; Family: Pelobatidae.

Identification—Small toadlike frog with smooth skin and horny, sickle-shaped spade (metatarsal tubercle) on hind feet. No bony protuberance between eyes. Adults tend to be larger than those of other spadefoot species. Greenish back has dark, irregular mottling; belly is light colored. Call resembles bleat of goat or sheep.

Natural history—Nocturnal and well adapted to arid conditions, this frog spends much of its time buried underground, emerging aboveground after spring or summer rains. "Explosive" breeder in temporary ponds formed by summer monsoon rains; tadpoles with rapid development to metamorphosis. Eats arthropods. Skin secretions toxic to people and pets.

Status—Widespread and uncommon.

Plains Spadefoot

(Spea bombifrons) ✳ ✳

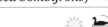

APR–OCT

Taxonomy—Class: Amphibia; Order: Anura; Family: Pelobatidae.

Identification—Distinguished from other spadefoots by presence of bony bump (or "boss") between eyes. Spade on hind feet is wedge shaped. Greenish gray to greenish brown with darker markings and often yellowish tubercles (small, rounded protuberances) dorsally. Call, a short, repeated, rasping bleat.

Natural history—Found in open grassy areas. Nocturnal, remaining in burrows during the day. Breeds in temporary ponds formed after heavy rains.

Status—Widespread. Common at night during the summer rainy season at the Bosque del Apache NWR.

New Mexico Spadefoot
(Spea multiplicata) ✳ ✳

APR–OCT

Taxonomy—Class: Amphibia; Order: Anura; Family: Pelobatidae.

Identification—Much like Couch's spadefoot but spade is short and wedge shaped. No bony protuberance between eyes (unlike in adults of plains spadefoot). Back brown or gray with dark spots and smaller, scattered red dots. Call, short and snorelike.

Natural history—Nocturnal. Spends much of the year in underground burrow. "Explosive" breeder in temporary pools formed by summer monsoon rains; tadpoles rapidly develop to metamorphosis. Emerges after rain to feed. Eats arthropods. Skin secretion is an irritant.

Status—Widespread and uncommon. Known to hybridize with plains spadefoot.

Robert Sivinski

Great Plains Toad
(Bufo cognatus) ✳ ✳

APR–OCT

Taxonomy—Class: Amphibia; Order: Anura; Family: Bufonidae.

Identification—Dorsal coloration variable, locally often brown in juvenile toads. Conspicuous cranial crests; elongate parotoid glands. Males have dark throat and vocal sac that is sausage shaped. Call is a very loud, metallic trill that is repeated fast and can last 20 seconds.

Natural history—Mostly along river channel and in open wooded habitats. Adults largely nocturnal, hiding in burrows and under surface debris during the day; juveniles often seen during day. Breeds after rainfall, congregating at pools of water or ponds and forming choruses. Diet consists of insects. Parotoid glands of Great Plains and other toads secrete a poison that acts as a deterrent against predation.

Status—Widespread and common (but not as numerous as Woodhouse's toad).

Bill Gorum

Woodhouse's Toad

(*Bufo woodhousii*) ✳✳

APR–OCT

Jean-Luc Cartron

Taxonomy—Class: Amphibia; Order: Anura; Family: Bufonidae.

Identification—Large gray-brown toad with numerous warts all over, prominent bony ridges behind the eyes, oblong parotoid glands, and conspicuous whitish mid-dorsal stripe. Female larger than male. Metamorphs typically show large dark blotches and smaller red spots both within and outside the blotches, together with light mid-dorsal stripe that is indistinct and does not extend to head. Tadpoles distinctive with ventral tail fin unpigmented. Call of chorusing male is sheep-like bleat.

Natural history—Adults are active mostly at night. During the day, they are usually hidden in cool, shallow burrows. In April, males begin to concentrate near water and call to attract females, often forming large choruses. Gravid females deposit long strings of eggs in the water. Young metamorphosed toads are visible during the day. All individuals hibernate underground during winter. A wide variety of arthropod prey are taken. Natural enemies include ravens, raccoons, skunks, and snakes.

Status—Widespread and common to abundant.

Western Chorus Frog

(*Pseudacris triseriata*) ✳✳

Feb–Mar, APR–OCT

Taxonomy—Class: Amphibia; Order: Anura; Family: Hylidae.

Identification—Small frog with variable coloration, most often with 3 dark stripes along length of back and 1 additional dark stripe along each side from nostril through eye to groin. White stripe along upper lip. Webbing reduced on hind feet. Adult males have mottled throat. Call resembles sound made by fingers running through teeth of small comb.

Bill Gorum

Natural history—Occurs at small ephemeral pools within cottonwood woodland and at ponds, where it often sits upright on floating vegetation. Early breeding species, with choruses as early as late February in some years. Active during the day except during hot part of spring and in summer, when it becomes strictly nocturnal.

Status—Western chorus frog population in the Middle Rio Grande Valley may be isolated, with a distribution that extends from about Albuquerque south to Bernardo. Locally common in moist habitats.

American Bullfrog

(***Rana catesbeiana***) ✳ ✳ [INT]

Jan–Mar, APR–OCT, Nov–Dec

Taxonomy—Class: Amphibia; Order: Anura; Family: Ranidae.

Identification—Large frog identified by glandular fold extending from eye around back of eardrum to just above forearm. Yellowish green or brown back may be mottled with dark brown. Hind legs often show dark bands or blotches. Adults are often yellowish below. Tadpoles large, typically greenish, speckled black on back and on tail fin. Call, a loud, low-pitched, resonant "jug-o-rum."

Natural history—Predatory frog whose prey include numerous invertebrates and vertebrates, such as crayfish, frogs (even tadpoles and metamorphosed juveniles of its own species!), tiger salamanders, snakes, bats, and small rodents. Protracted reproductive season with females becoming receptive to males asynchronously. Males are territorial. Leaps into water with a loud squeak when threatened.

Status—Widespread and common and may be seen during warm winter periods. Introduced into the Rio Grande Valley as a food source in the early 20th century. Once protected in New Mexico, the species is no longer considered a game species. Species is a threat to other ranid frogs, including northern leopard frog.

Northern Leopard Frog

(***Rana pipiens***) ✳ ✳

Mar, APR–OCT

Taxonomy—Class: Amphibia; Order: Anura; Family: Ranidae.

Identification—Light green or brown above, whitish below. Dark spots on body and legs, nearly always surrounded by light halo. Dorsolateral folds are continuous and not inset posteriorly. Tadpoles have coarsely mottled tails and yellow irises. Call a mix of snores, grunts, and moans.

Natural history—Highly aquatic in ponds and wetlands. Reproductive season probably begins in late March or in April. Diet not studied in New Mexico but elsewhere includes wide variety of invertebrates.

Status—Once distributed along the entire Middle Rio Grande but apparently now found only between Isleta and Los Lunas and south of San Marcial. Local decline of this species caused by habitat alteration, disease, and spread of bullfrogs, which are predators of the northern leopard frog.

Reptiles

Reptiles evolved from amphibians about 300 million years ago, during the Carboniferous Period. They were the first amniotes, vertebrates that produce eggs with specialized internal membranes keeping the developing embryo within an aquatic environment. As a result they are better suited than amphibians to live in dry environments. Modern reptiles are divided into four orders, Crocodilia (crocodiles and allies), Sphenodontia (tuataras), Squamata (lizards, snakes, and worm-lizards), and Testudines (turtles and tortoises). Like amphibians, nearly all reptiles are ectotherms and they have a three-chambered heart. Unlike amphibians, their skin is thick and typically covered with scales that help the body retain water and prevent dehydration. Breeding occurs on land. Fertilization is internal. Some snakes and lizards give birth to live young. Most reptiles have two pairs of limbs, but the ancestors of snakes lost their legs. To move, snakes contract their muscles in waves running the length of their body while also adhering to the ground with specialized scales on their belly. Also modified is the body plan of turtles and tortoises. They have protective shells consisting of a ventral plastron and a dorsal carapace enclosing the limb girdles and covered with scales modified into plates called scutes.

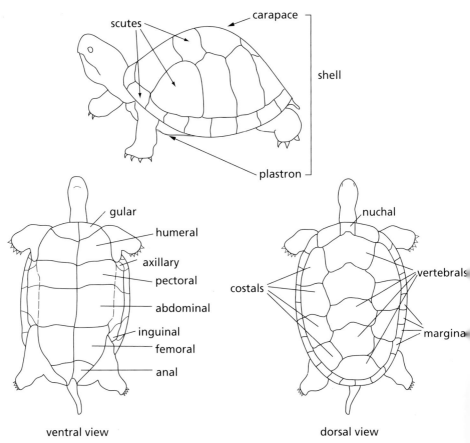

ventral view   dorsal view

Illustration: Jane Mygatt

The 29 species described in the field guide represent nearly one-third of all the reptiles known to occur in New Mexico. Thirteen of the 29 species are snakes, 10 are lizards, and 6 are turtles or tortoises. Lizards as a whole are ubiquitous and easily seen throughout the bosque. Some of the turtles are a familiar sight at ponds. Snakes are more difficult to see, but be sure to watch them only at a distance. Rattlesnakes typically bite only when left no room to retreat. Remember also that rattlesnakes are interesting and ecologically important species.

Snapping Turtle

(*Chelydra serpentina*) ✳ ✳ [INT]

Apr–Oct

Taxonomy—Class: Reptilia; Order: Testudines; Family: Chelydridae.

Identification—Large, stout, and somewhat cryptically colored (brown or nearly black) turtle. Large head with powerful jaws. Plastron has 3 rows of prominent keels in young turtles and some adults. Tail is long for a turtle and saw toothed.

Natural history—Active during day and night; rarely on land except to nest. Lives mostly underwater, often buried in mud or debris. Omnivorous, with a diet that includes aquatic plants, live animals (frogs, tadpoles, fish, and ducklings), and carrion. Slow on land but prone to defend itself by biting and capable of releasing foul odor from gland on underside of body. Hibernates underwater.

Charlie Painter

Status—Uncommon; spotty distribution in Middle Rio Grande drainage but recorded at Rio Grande Nature Center, La Joya, and Bosque del Apache NWR. Middle Rio Grande population introduced through liberated or escaped pets.

Painted Turtle

(*Chrysemys picta*) ✳ ✳

Jan–Mar, APR–OCT, Nov–Dec

Taxonomy—Class: Reptilia; Order: Testudines; Family: Emydidae.

Identification—Skin olive, lined with yellow. Carapace olive to brownish, smooth and flattened oval; dorsal scutes have red edges (marginal scutes also have white vertical lines). Plastron yellow or reddish with dark figure branching along sutures. Males have elongated claws on forefeet and a longer and thicker tail than females. Females typically larger.

Natural history—Mainly in ponds or along ditches; occasionally in river channel, including on flooded riverbanks and on sandbars. Active during day, basking in sun on logs. Submerged at night. Omnivorous.

Bill Gorum

Status—Widespread and common.

Ornate Box Turtle   (*Terrapene ornata*) ✳ ✳

APR–OCT

Taxonomy—Class: Reptilia; Order: Testudines; Family: Emydidae. The desert ornate box turtle, *T. ornata luteola*, is native; the eastern race, *T. ornata ornata*, is introduced.

Identification—Carapace is thick and high domed with slightly flat top. Typically each scute has radiating pattern of yellow lines on brown background. With age, carapace of western ornate box turtles (photo) becomes yellowish brown with no conspicuous barring pattern. Plastron is broad with single front hinge.

Natural history—Likely most abundant in open areas with sandy soils. Also occurs or likely occurs in dry cottonwood woodland, along ditches, and at ponds and wetlands. Diet includes plant material, invertebrates, some vertebrates, and carrion. Active from April to October, especially during summer rains. Hibernates in underground burrow.

Status—Uncommon and widespread; eastern box turtles present as escaped or liberated pets where bosque borders urban or semi-urban areas.

Big Bend Slider   (*Trachemys gaigeae*) ✳ ✳

Jan–Mar, APR–OCT, Nov–Dec

Taxonomy—Class: Reptilia; Order: Testudines; Family: Emydidae.

Identification—Medium-size turtle. Skin olive to olive-brown with yellow or orange stripes. Identified by presence of 1 or 2 black-bordered yellow, orange, or red spots on side of head, one large and always present, the other small (if present) and right behind eye (compare with red-eared slider). Also important are orange curved lines that may form eyelike spots on olive, weakly keeled carapace. Plastron yellow with dark patch along midline. Markings may become less discernable in older turtles. Webbed feet for swimming.

Natural history—May be seen basking in the sun on ditch banks, logs, and mudflats. Active in winter during spells of warm weather. Primarily herbivorous but diet also includes carrion; easily trapped with sardines as bait.

Status—Common at Bosque del Apache NWR; common to abundant in marshy areas south of San Marcial. Restricted distribution in New Mexico makes this a conservation-sensitive species. Hybridization with introduced red-eared slider is a threat to local persistence of Big Bend slider.

Red-eared Slider

(*Trachemys scripta*) ✳ ✳ [INT]

Jan–Mar, APR–OCT, Nov–Dec

Taxonomy—Class: Reptilia; Order: Testudines; Family: Emydidae.

Identification—Skin green (especially young hatchlings) to olive-brown with yellow stripes. Most diagnostic characteristic is red or orange stripe extending often continuously (may be broken up into segments) behind eye along side of head. Oval, flattened carapace is olive to brown and has weak mid-dorsal keel. Plastron yellow with dark markings at center of each scute. Webbed feet for swimming. Male smaller and often darker than female.

Natural history—Typical habitat is ponds and permanent wetlands although occurs also along ditches. Often seen on logs, basking in sun. Omnivorous species whose diet includes carrion. In winter enters torpor, presumably buried in sludge at bottom of ponds, but may be seen at the surface again during spells of warm weather.

Status—Largely restricted to ponds and permanent wetlands, where it may be common to abundant. Hybridization with Big Bend slider is a serious conservation concern.

Bill Garum

Spiny Softshell

(*Apalone spinifera*) ✳ ✳

APR–OCT

Taxonomy—Class: Reptilia; Order: Testudines; Family: Trionychidae.

Identification—Distinguished from other turtles of the bosque by its leathery and flat, olive, or tan carapace that has no cornified scutes and by its long neck and snorkel-like nose. Feet are webbed and clawed with only 3 claws on each foot. Edges of carapace flexible. Stripe present behind eye. Females larger than males and may reach 36 cm (14 in) in carapace length. Carapace of males and juveniles distinctly spotted with white; pattern of mature female is camouflage-like coloration. Males have a longer, thicker tail.

Charlie Painter

Natural history—Highly aquatic turtle found in and along the river channel, including on sandbars. Also occurs at some ponds and in ditches. Requires soft, shallow river bottoms, where it may bury itself. Prefers moderate to strong currents. May bask in the sun on riverbanks or ditch banks or on logs in middle of ponds. Nests on land near water. Carnivorous species known to eat fish, frogs, tadpoles, and invertebrates such as crayfish. Will bite in self-defense.

Status—Widespread (occurs north to Cochiti) and uncommon to locally common.

Desert Spiny Lizard

(*Sceloporus magister*) ✳ ✳

Mar, APR–OCT, Nov

Taxonomy—Class: Reptilia; Order: Squamata; Family: Phrynosomatidae.

Identification—Large, sexually dimorphic lizard most readily identified by black wedge-shaped mark above shoulder, distinctive head scalation (including 5 enlarged supra-ocular scales), and presence of 5–7 long and pointed scales extending backward over ear opening. Large keeled dorsal scales give it its spiny appearance. Male (top) has black, blue, or blue-green throat and belly patches. Female (bottom), smaller and duller. Hatchlings have a black collar with white specks.

Natural history—Active from late March through October (or even to mid-November). Eats insects. May bite if held.

Status—Found in southern half of bosque, where fairly common.

Photographs: Charlie Painter

Prairie Lizard

(*Sceloporus cowlesi*) ✳ ✳

APR–OCT

Taxonomy—Class: Reptilia; Order: Squamata; Family: Phrynosomatidae. Previously assigned to *Sceloporus undulatus*.

Identification—Gray brown above with keeled dorsal scales giving it its spiny appearance. Auricular scales project partially over ear opening. Males (photo) typically have conspicuous blue patches on sides of throat and belly, often rimmed along midline by dark to black blotches (blue of throat may also become black as it extends into shoulder area). Females may have blue on throat but usually not on belly.

Bill Gorum

Natural history—Habitat generalist but prefers open wooded areas of the bosque with some bare ground, sandy soils, and a sparse understory. May bask in sun on logs; climbs tree trunks when threatened. Eats insects and spiders.

Status—Widespread and one of the most abundant lizards in bosque.

Side-blotched Lizard   (*Uta stansburiana*) ✳ ✳

APR–OCT

Taxonomy—Class: Reptilia; Order: Squamata; Family: Phrynosomatidae.

Identification—Small lizard, to 6.3 cm (2.5 in) body length, with small granular dorsal scales, gular fold on throat, and distinct black blotch along flanks just behind front legs. Male very colorful: rows of blue and dark brown blotches on back, converging toward tail; sides a mix of dark and light brown blotches, some of them washed with yellow; pale below with some blue along sides of belly; scattered blue scales on tail; blue and orange on throat. Female duller.

Natural history—Occurs in less dense, less woody areas of cottonwood woodland and in open, sandy saltcedar associations. Generally associated with herbaceous ground cover. Bulk of diet consists of insects.

Status—Widespread and uncommon.

Chihuahuan Spotted Whiptail   (*Aspidoscelis exsanguis*) ✳ ✳

APR–OCT

Taxonomy—Class: Reptilia; Order: Squamata; Family: Teiidae. Recently reassigned from genus *Cnemidophorus* to genus *Aspidoscelis*. The species arose as a result of hybridization between at least 2 species.

Identification—Dark brown above, with 6 longitudinal stripes overlaid with light spots. In younger individuals, the stripes are conspicuous and yellow and white, the spots small and white or red. Older individuals have fainter white and tan stripes and very distinct white spots that extend down onto hind legs. Ventral aspect of the body is whitish. Tail, whiplike and longer than the body.

Natural history—Found mainly in cottonwood woodland, especially along edges and where understory is sparse and woody debris is abundant. Also occurs readily along ditches, where it digs small burrows for shelter. Diet consists of invertebrates (spiders, grasshoppers, termites, beetles, lepidopteran larvae). Not as shy as other whiptail lizards. Predators in bosque include roadrunners, various smaller raptors, snakes, and skunks. Parthenogenetic species: the eggs are not fertilized and all individuals are females.

Status—Widespread and common to abundant.

Checkered Whiptail (*Aspidoscelis tesselata*) ✳ ✳

APR–OCT

Taxonomy—Class: Reptilia; Order: Squamata; Family: Teiidae. Recently reassigned from genus *Cnemidophorus* to genus *Aspidoscelis* and previously described by some as *C. grahamii* (species has complex taxonomic and evolutionary history).

Identification—Large whiptail with long tail. In adults, background color of back and hind limbs is a distinctive yellowish orange, with conspicuous reticulate bold markings on sides, back, and legs. Similar markings also found on sides (but not as conspicuous on back) in close relative, the western whiptail (*A. tigris*). Belly cream and nearly immaculate except for scattered dark flecks. Juveniles have 6 to 10 cream to yellow longitudinal stripes on dark background.

Natural history—Parthenogenetic diploid species. Hatchlings become active before adults and remain so until later (October). Unwary; hunts for insect prey by digging.

Status—Spotty distribution. Uncommon at Bosque del Apache NWR; recorded as far north as Cochiti Lake. Western whiptail, one of the parent species of the checkered whiptail, also occurs in south but in smaller numbers.

New Mexico Whiptail (*Aspidoscelis neomexicana*) ✳ ✳

APR–OCT

Taxonomy—Class: Reptilia; Order: Squamata; Family: Teiidae. Arose as the product of hybridization between two other whiptail lizards (*Aspidoscelis inornata* and *A. marmorata*).

Identification—Striped and spotted lizard with a blue tail; wavy mid-dorsal stripe.

Natural history—Found in heavily disturbed areas and along edges (along ditches and levee roads; also on open, sandy riverbanks). Parthenogenetic species: the eggs develop without fertilization and all individuals are females. Hibernation occurs in narrow, shallow burrows. Documented diet consists of adult and larval insects (beetles, grasshoppers, ants, lepidopterans).

Status—Widespread and abundant.

Western Whiptail
(Aspidoscelis tigris) ✳ ✳

APR–OCT

Taxonomy—Class: Reptilia; Order: Squamata; Family: Teiidae.

Identification—Large whiptail, somewhat similar to checkered whiptail but smaller and with less conspicuous reticulate dorsal pattern (some dorsal markings more like bold stripes).

Natural history—Digs burrows. Wary, relying on its speed to escape potential predators. Eats insects.

Status—Restricted to the southern part of the Middle Rio Grande bosque. Uncommon.

Desert Grassland Whiptail
(Aspidoscelis uniparens) ✳ ✳

APR–OCT

Taxonomy—Class: Reptilia; Order: Squamata; Family: Teiidae. Arose from one or more hybridization events.

Identification—Small whiptail, brown to blackish above and with 6 conspicuous longitudinal stripes, 4 on the back and cream-colored or yellow and 1 along each lower side and white. No spots, light and unmarked below. Bluish tail. Hatchlings have bright blue tails.

Natural history—Prefers open grassy areas. Also found in cottonwood woodland. Parthenogenetic and insectivorous species.

Status—Widespread and common to abundant.

Many-lined Skink
(Eumeces multivirgatus) ✳ ✳

APR–OCT

Taxonomy—Class: Reptilia; Order: Squamata; Family: Scincidae.

Identification—Smaller than Great Plains skink. Occurs in 2 color morphs: adult striped morph (photo) is olive-gray with dark longitudinal stripes, adult stripeless morph is light tan to olive-brown with 1 indistinct dorsolateral streak on each side of the head and body. Juveniles are darker with bright blue tail.

Natural history—Secretive species found in cottonwood woodland, where it burrows under logs and under leaf litter.

Status—Not nearly as common and widespread as Great Plains skink but found at the Bosque del Apache NWR.

Great Plains Skink

(Eumeces obsoletus) ✳ ✳

APR–OCT

Taxonomy—Class: Reptilia; Order: Squamata; Family: Scincidae.

Identification—Large lizard with long body, short legs, and smooth, shiny scales; lateral scales arranged in oblique and uneven rows that trend downward and forward (unlike many-lined skink). Adult (top), beige or light gray, with black edges of scales resulting in indistinct stripes or speckled coloration. Juveniles (bottom), black with blue tails and white or cream-colored dots around mouth.

Natural history—Found in mesic and well-vegetated sites, for example along ditch sides with thick cover of annual plants and at cattail marshes; also in cotton-wood woodland with extensive herbaceous ground cover or understory shrubs. Lives mainly under-ground (where the eggs are laid) and eats invertebrates. Birds of prey among predators of Great Plains skink in bosque.

Status—Widespread and uncommon to locally common.

Photographs: Charlie Painter

Glossy Snake

(Arizona elegans) ✳ ✳

Feb–Mar, APR–SEP, Oct–Nov

Taxonomy—Class: Reptilia; Order: Squamata; Family: Colubridae.

Identification—Medium-size snake with smooth scales. Younger snakes have dark-edged mid-dorsal blotches, but that pattern is faded in adults. Belly white to cream. Dark line between eye and rear of jaw often present. Only 2 prefrontal scales and 1 pre-ocular scale.

Natural history—Mainly nocturnal; typically spends the day in underground burrow. Bulk of diet consists of lizards and small rodents, including kangaroo rats, killed by constriction. Female lays eggs. Known predators include kingsnakes and milk snakes.

Status—Widespread and rare to uncommon.

Charlie Painter

Racer *(Coluber constrictor)* ✳ ✳

Apr, MAY–OCT

Taxonomy—Class: Reptilia; Order: Squamata; Family: Colubridae.

Identification—Medium to large snake with smooth scales; adult body coloration not patterned, usually with a green, blue, or brown tinge dorsally and whitish to yellow ventrally. Young ground colored dorsally with a row of dark blotches or crossbands along the middle.

Natural history—Diurnal snake, found mainly on wetter soils of the bosque, including along ditches. Relies on speed to escape predators and to catch prey (does not constrict prey but instead swallows it alive). Not venomous but aggressive if handled. Hibernates underground.

Status—Widespread.

Charlie Painter

Western Hognose Snake *(Heterodon nasicus)* ✳ ✳

MAY–OCT

Taxonomy—Class: Reptilia; Order: Squamata; Family: Colubridae.

Identification—Medium-size, heavy-bodied snake with an upturned and pointed, plow-shaped snout. Background color pale with distinct dark blotches, large on back and smaller along sides. Belly largely black.

Natural history—Adept burrower generally associated with sandy or gravelly soils. Amphibians, reptiles and their eggs, and small rodents probably make up most of diet in bosque. When cornered may hide its head under its coils, strike with mouth closed, spread head and neck, puff up body, and hiss like cobra or turn over onto its back and feign death with mouth open and tongue out. Spends winter in underground burrow.

Status—Widespread and uncommon.

Heather Bateman

Common Kingsnake

(Lampropeltis getula) ✳ ✳

APR–OCT

Bill Gorum

Taxonomy—Class: Reptilia; Order: Squamata; Family: Colubridae.

Identification—Total body length typically 1.2 m (4 ft) or less. Background dorsal color is dark brown or black with highly variable yellow or white markings forming chains or consisting of single light-colored spots on each dorsal scale. Overall black (or brown), yellow, and white speckled appearance. Slender head often solid black. Smooth scales.

Natural history—Habitat generalist throughout its range but locally seems to occur primarily in cottonwood woodland, where it can be abundant. Gentle and not venomous but can defend itself by smearing attacker with feces (also hisses and vibrates its tail). Apparently immune to venom of rattlesnakes, which common kingsnakes kill by constriction. In bosque, documented diet includes lizards. Female lays eggs. No parental care after hatching.

Status—Widespread; fairly common from Los Lunas southward.

Coachwhip

(Masticophis flagellum) ✳ ✳

MAR–NOV

Charlie Painter

Taxonomy—Class: Reptilia; Order: Squamata; Family: Colubridae.

Identification—Long, slender snake, to near 1.8 m (6 ft), with variable, dorsal coloration (pink, tan, gray, or reddish brown). Dark crossbars conspicuous in juveniles, faint or absent in adults.

Natural history—Occurs in moist and dry bosque habitats alike. Often on ground along levee road but may be seen also along grassy riverbanks, in cottonwood woodland, or swimming in ditches. Prey generalist.

Status—Widespread and common.

Gophersnake
(Pituophis catenifer) ✳ ✳

Mar, APR–OCT, Nov

Taxonomy—Class: Reptilia; Order: Squamata; Family: Colubridae. Also called bullsnake.

Identification—Typical mid-dorsal markings are brown square blotches (saddles) on yellow background with smaller blotches along sides. Head light colored, usually with dark band from eye to angle of jaw. Reaches up to 1.8 m (6 ft) in length. Glossy snake has similar coloration pattern but is smaller and has smooth scales.

Natural history—Occurs in most habitat types but prefers dry areas and is most frequently seen along levee roads. Hunts for small vertebrates (especially rodents), which it kills by constriction. Sound of tail vibrating in leaves resembles rattle of rattlesnake. Hisses when cornered. Offspring hatch from eggs, presumably in late summer or early fall. Spends winter underground.

Status—Widespread and common.

Tom Kennedy

Plains Black-headed Snake
(Tantilla nigriceps) ✳ ✳

Mar, APR–SEP, Oct

Taxonomy—Class: Reptilia; Order: Squamata; Family: Colubridae.

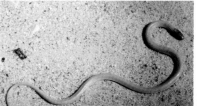

Identification—Small snake, 18–38 cm (7–15 in) long, uniformly tan or sand colored with black cap on head. Upper scales smooth; anal scale divided. Enlarged teeth on back of maxilla. Broad pink stripe along length of belly.

Natural history—Nocturnal and fossorial. Female lays eggs that hatch in late summer. Diet typically includes millipedes, centipedes, spiders, insects, and insect larvae. Species mildly venomous but not harmful to people and very docile. Probably spends winter in underground hibernaculum.

Status—Patchy distribution. Uncommon.

Heather Bateman

Blackneck Gartersnake   (*Thamnophis cyrtopsis*) ✳ ✳

MAR–OCT

Taxonomy—Class: Reptilia; Order: Squamata; Family: Colubridae.

Identification—Gray headed with 2 large black blotches on neck. Back, olive-gray to olive-brown with white dorsolateral stripes and 1 yellow or white mid-dorsal stripe becoming orange anteriorly where it separates the 2 black blotches. Two rows of alternating dark spots distinct anteriorly between the stripes.

Natural history—Largely aquatic; occurs in wetlands, where it likely preys on toads, frogs, and tadpoles. Hibernates.

Status—Recorded at the Bosque del Apache NWR, where uncommon.

Western Terrestrial Gartersnake   (*Thamnophis elegans*) ✳ ✳

Feb, MAR–OCT, Nov

Taxonomy—Class: Reptilia; Order: Squamata; Family: Colubridae.

Identification—Dorsal coloration highly variable. Two white dorsolateral stripes (1 on each side, on scale rows 3 and 4) and 1 white to yellow mid-dorsal stripe. Dark round spots along both sides of each stripe, distinct anteriorly but less so posteriorly (compare with other gartersnakes).

Natural history—Generally associated with water but found in New Mexico to be more terrestrial than other gartersnakes and with more generalized diet.

Status—Recorded at the Bosque del Apache NWR and in Bernalillo and Sandoval counties.

Checkered Gartersnake   (*Thamnophis marcianus*) ✳ ✳

MAR–OCT

Taxonomy—Class: Reptilia; Order: Squamata; Family: Colubridae.

Identification—Brown or olive-brown above with 3 light stripes, 1 along midback and 1 along each side. Large black spots invade stripes and form very distinct checkered pattern. Side of head shows light crescent followed by dark blotch on neck (similar-looking blackneck gartersnake has darker dorsal background coloration with less distinct spots).

Natural history—Generally found near water. Eats invertebrates and small vertebrates.

Status—Widespread and rare.

Charlie Painter

Common Gartersnake   (*Thamnophis sirtalis*) ✳ ✳

MAR–OCT

Taxonomy—Class: Reptilia; Order: Squamata; Family: Colubridae.

Identification—Largest gartersnake in the bosque (and in New Mexico). Has 1 vertebral stripe and 2 lateral stripes (on scale rows 2 and 3), all of them often yellow or tan. Dorsally, skin between stripes is typically red with black spots.

Natural history—Largely restricted to moist habitats such as ditch sides, grassy riverbanks, sandbars, and edges of ponds and wetlands. Occasionally along levee road and in dry cottonwood woodland. In bosque, prey consists largely of earthworms, tadpoles, frogs, and toads.

Status—Widespread and common.

Tom Kennedy

Western Diamondback Rattlesnake   (*Crotalus atrox*) ✳ ✳

Mar, APR–SEP, Oct–Dec

Taxonomy—Class: Reptilia; Order: Squamata; Family: Viperidae.

Identification—Broad triangular head, vertical pupils, and pale stripes extending from back of eye to corner of mouth; dark diamond-shaped blotches down back typically more distinct in younger snakes; tail ringed with alternating black and white bands (much like raccoon) above rattles. May reach a length of 1.8 m (6 ft), although most are 0.9 m (3 ft) or less.

Natural history—Like all other rattlesnakes has heat-sensing pit organs under nostrils for detecting prey (small to medium-size vertebrates and some invertebrates). Aggressive if cornered (raises its head and neck, coils, and rattles as warning before striking), and its bite is venomous and potentially lethal. Adult females give birth to live young in summer; limited parental care may exist in some cases. Species known to hibernate in large communal dens.

Status—Widespread and common.

Western Rattlesnake   (*Crotalus viridis*) ✳ ✳

Jan–Feb, MAR–NOV, Dec

Taxonomy—Class: Reptilia; Order: Squamata; Family: Viperidae.

Identification—Reaches less than 1.5 m (5 ft) in length. Dorsal coloration tan or light brown with darker blotches down midline (shaped as diamonds, squares, or ovals) thinly edged with white and narrowing into crossbands toward tail. Two rows of smaller blotches along each side. Lacks western diamondback's alternating black and white bands on tail. Large triangular head with vertical pupils. Two white lines on each side of face, extending obliquely from front and back of eye. Scales keeled. Before first shedding of skin, young have button rather than well-developed rattle.

Natural history—Found in cottonwood woodland but also observed along levee roads. Senses heat emanating from prey (small vertebrates). Venomous and aggressive if disturbed. Female bears live young. Species known to hibernate in large communal dens but activity aboveground possible during winter.

Status—Widespread and common.

Birds

Birds evolved from theropod dinosaurs approximately 150 to 200 million years ago, during the Jurassic Period. They are grouped in the class Aves, with more than half of all living birds belonging to the order Passeriformes. The distinguishing characteristics of modern birds include feathers, toothless beaks, and forelimbs modified for flight. Their hearts are divided into four chambers. Like mammals, they are homeotherms. Fertilization is internal, and the female lays hard-shelled eggs. In most species, one or both parents build a nest and incubate the eggs. Although some birds are sedentary, many others migrate. After the breeding season they fly toward warmer climates for the winter, returning in the spring to breed again. Birds tend to be social and rely extensively on vocal displays to communicate. In many passerine species, the males sing. Their songs are complex, often repeated musical phrases serving to advertise a territory and attract a mate. Most birds also give alarm, distress, flight, begging, feeding, and other calls.

The 181 bird species described in the field guide can be roughly divided into year-round bosque residents, summer breeding residents, winter residents, and spring and fall migrants. During the breeding season, the most abundant birds—summer and year-round residents—in mature stands of cottonwoods are the black-chinned hummingbird (*Archilochus alexandri*) and the mourning dove (*Zenaida macroura*), followed by a variety of other species such as the downy woodpecker (*Picoides pubescens*), Bewick's wren (*Thryomanes bewickii*), black-headed grosbeak (*Pheucticus melanocephalus*), summer tanager (*Piranga rubra*), and western wood-pewee (*Contopus sordidulus*). In open areas, typical nesting species include the western kingbird (*Tyrannus verticalis*) and the northern mockingbird (*Mimus polyglottos*). The red-winged blackbird (*Agelaius phoeniceus*) is abundant during the breeding season at ponds and wetlands. In winter, snow geese (*Chen caerulescens*), Canada geese (*Branta canadensis*), and sandhill cranes (*Grus canadensis*) occur in high numbers at ponds and wetlands, in the river channel, and/or in fields adjacent to the bosque; white-crowned sparrows (*Zonotrichia leucophrys*), song sparrows (*Melospiza melodia*), and dark-eyed juncos (*Junco hyemalis*) are abundant in cottonwood stands or along their edges. Spring and fall migrants are dominated in terms of numbers by the Wilson's warbler (*Wilsonia pusilla*), chipping sparrow (*Spizella passerina*), pine siskin (*Carduelis pinus*), white-crowned sparrow, MacGillivray's warbler (*Oporornis tolmiei*), yellow-rumped warbler (*Dendroica coronata*), dark-eyed junco, orange-crowned warbler (*Vermivora celata*), and ruby-crowned warbler (*Regulus calendula*). Among some of the most common year-round residents are the mallard (*Anas platyrhynchos*), American coot (*Fulica americana*), mourning dove, northern flicker (*Colaptes auratus*), and house finch (*Carpodacus mexicanus*).

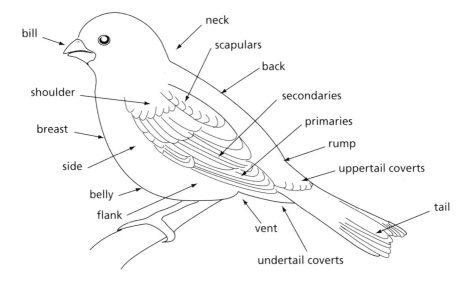

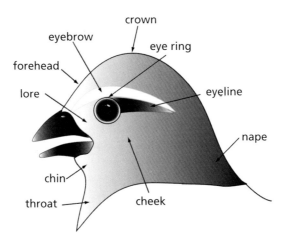

Snow Goose

(*Chen caerulescens*)

JAN–MAY, Jun–Jul, OCT–DEC

Taxonomy—Class: Aves; Order: Anseriformes; Family: Anatidae.

Identification—Adults of white form (photo) are nearly pure white with black primaries and pink legs and bill. Can be distinguished from Ross's geese by their larger size and their black "lips." Immatures are pale gray with black bill and legs. Adults of blue form have white head and upper neck contrasting with mostly dark gray body (belly may be white). Gray wings are black tipped. Immatures are gray-brown with dark legs and feet and dark bill. Flies in V formation and utters loud honks in chorus.

Natural history—Most birds found at ponds and wetlands and, during the day, feeding on corn stubble in adjacent fields, returning to water at dusk. Typically occurs in large flocks (not as closely knit as Ross's goose's). Bald eagles and coyotes are among the predators of snow geese.

Status—Patchily distributed. Abundant from mid-October through February at Bosque del Apache NWR. Uncommon in spring, and a few birds may rarely remain into the summer. In winter also abundant at Bernardo and La Joya, while only uncommon at the Rio Grande Nature Center ponds.

Ross's Goose

(*Chen rossii*)

JAN–MAR, Apr, OCT–DEC

Taxonomy—Class: Aves; Order: Anseriformes; Family: Anatidae.

Identification—Similar to snow goose but smaller and with shorter neck. Bill stubbier and shaped more like an equilateral triangle; lacks snow goose's black "lips" and bill instead has warty light bluish base. Calls higher pitched than those of snow goose.

Natural history—Found at ponds and wetlands and in adjacent fields, where it tends to forage in close-knit and continually moving flocks, unlike the more abundant snow geese. The two species also frequently occur in large mixed flocks. Feeds on corn stubble.

Status—Widespread but found most easily at the Bosque del Apache NWR, where common from mid-October through March with a few remaining into April.

Canada Goose (*Branta canadensis*) ✳ ✳

JAN–DEC

Taxonomy—Class: Aves; Order: Anseriformes; Family: Anatidae. Smaller forms of the Canada goose are now considered a distinct species, the cackling goose (*Branta hutchinsii*).

Identification—Males and females similar with black bill, head, and neck and white "chin strap"; upper parts brown with white rump and short black tail (but undertail coverts are white); breast white to dull brown; belly and wing coverts white. Often flies in V formation. Call is a 2-syllable honk ("aa-honk"). Cackling goose also present in bosque but is smaller (mallard size) with shorter, stubbier bill.

Gordon French

Natural history—Forages on river islands and sand-bars, in ponds, in shallow river waters near the shoreline, and along open ditch banks; also in fields adjacent to bosque. Species' diet includes shoots, roots, seeds, aquatic invertebrates, and grain (winter). Nesting begins in March. The nest is on the ground near water (often on a small island in a pond) and lined with gray down. Some pairs are with goslings (up to 10) by late April or early May.

Status—Widespread and common (spring, summer) to abundant (fall, winter). Known to have bred in New Mexico in mid-19th century. Later found in the state only during winter but breeding reported again since about 1970. Cackling goose found mainly at Rio Grande Nature Center, where large flocks possible, and in fields adjacent to bosque in Albuquerque South Valley.

Wood Duck (*Aix sponsa*) ✳ ✳

JAN–DEC

Taxonomy—Class: Aves; Order: Anseriformes; Family: Anatidae.

Identification—Male (right) has bright red eyes and strikingly beautiful plumage: iridescent green, purple, and black head striped with white; swept-back droopy crest, cinnamon breast dotted with white; dark iridescent back and white belly. Female (left) has a very pronounced white eye patch but is otherwise dull brownish gray and with a crest not as prominent as that of the male. Calls include an odd, high, whistling "hweeeee."

Jean-Luc Cartron

Natural history—Nests in large natural tree cavities and in nest boxes. Incubation of the eggs is by the female, guarded by the male until shortly before hatching. Some females are with ducklings by early May. Species' diet consists mainly of aquatic vegetation (including seeds), invertebrates, grain, and berries. Found locally at bird feeders.

Status—Widespread but primarily in the Albuquerque bosque, where uncommon to common in spring and summer, common to locally abundant in fall and winter. Much less common elsewhere.

Gadwall
(Anas strepera) ✳

JAN–DEC

Taxonomy—Class: Aves; Order: Anseriformes; Family: Anatidae.

Identification—Male (photo) dull for a duck but black rump stands out next to gray of body. Reddish brown on forewings and white wing patch (mostly visible during flight) also help with identification. Head light brown. Female brown, its bill black with orange edge; white wing patch as in male. Female utters a series of quacks similar to those of female mallard but higher pitched.

Natural history—Dabbling duck (tips its head below the surface to feed with tail uppermost); eats mostly plant material.

Status—Widespread. Common to locally abundant from November through April; rare to locally common in summer. Breeding recorded at the Bosque del Apache NWR. See also section on Elephant Butte Reservoir.

American Wigeon
(Anas americana)

JAN–MAY, Jun–Aug, SEP–DEC

Taxonomy—Class: Aves; Order: Anseriformes; Family: Anatidae.

Identification—Male (photo) easily identified by combination of light blue bill, white forehead, and deep green patch behind eye; also black and white vent. Female brown and less easily recognizable (may be mistaken for a female pintail or gadwall) but has blue bill and, together with male, shows a white patch on forewing when in flight (patch on forewing of northern shoveler is blue but may also appear white). Calls reminiscent of a rubber duck being squeezed!

Natural history—Species' diet includes small aquatic invertebrates, aquatic plants, seeds, and grass. Like other ducks often forages by tipping over in the water. Males and females typically observed together.

Status—Uncommon to common in all seasons except during summer, when it is only occasional. See also section on Elephant Butte Reservoir.

Blue-winged Teal
(*Anas discors*) ✳ ✳

Jan–Feb, MAR–OCT, Nov–Dec

Taxonomy—Class: Aves; Order: Anseriformes; Family: Anatidae.

Identification—Small duck. Male (photo) identified by white crescent in front of eye, extending from fore-head down to chin. Head blue-gray or gray-brown, contrasting with brownish, spotted body. Small white patch along sides. Female duller, mottled grayish brown with white eye ring and white spot at base of bill. Both sexes have pale blue shoulder patches revealed in flight. Male utters high-pitched peeps, female high-pitched quacks.

Natural history—Dabbling duck but rarely tips up and mostly skims water with bill in search of seeds and other plant material. Also eats mollusks.

Status—Widespread and uncommon to common in spring, summer, and fall. One of the latest ducks to arrive in New Mexico, generally recording highest abundance in April and early May and again in fall in September. Breeds at Bosque del Apache NWR. Quite rare in winter.

Cinnamon Teal
(*Anas cyanoptera*) ✳ ✳

Jan, FEB–SEP, Oct–Dec

Taxonomy—Class: Aves; Order: Anseriformes; Family: Anatidae.

Identification—Small duck. Male (photo) mostly cin-namon red with red eye and brown back. Blue-gray patch on forewing conspicuous in flight (when largely similar to blue-winged teal). Female mottled brown; resembles female blue-winged teal but is darker and browner. Cinnamon teal has more spatulate bill than blue-winged teal.

Natural history—Dabbling duck but rarely tips up and mostly skims water with bill in search of seeds and other plant material. Also eats mollusks.

Status—Widespread but found mostly at ponds. Uncommon in late winter, becoming common in March and especially April. Fewer seen after mid-May and through summer; rare to occasional during most of fall and in early winter. Uncommon during summer at Bosque del Apache NWR, where fairly regular breeder.

Mallard

(Anas platyrhynchos) ✴ ✴

JAN–DEC

Taxonomy—Class: Aves; Order: Anseriformes; Family: Anatidae. The Mexican duck (*A. p. diazi*) is generally considered a subspecies of the mallard but may instead be a valid, separate species.

Identification—Male (top photo, right) is unmistakable with green head and neck and yellow bill (compare with northern shoveler). Female (top photo, left) is typically accompanied by male in all months and has orange bill with dark "saddle" and mottled brown body. Deep blue secondaries of male and female revealed in flight. Both sexes of the Mexican duck are similar to female mallard but with overall darker appearance. Male (bottom photo) has prominent yellow to green bill and variable mottling; male mallard-Mexican duck hybrid may show some iridescent green on the head. The mallard's familiar quacks, loud and descending, are produced only by the female.

Natural history—Found in the river; on riverbanks, sandbars, and islands; in ponds and wetlands; and during nesting also in cottonwood woodland. The nest is usually a small depressed area, lined with down, in grassy overgrowth, in downed branches, or among dead leaves not far from water, rarely an old hawk nest up in a tree. The female incubates the eggs, guarded by the male. Hatching may be as early as May. Mallards forage in the water and on land, including under bird feeders.

Status—Widespread and common to locally abundant. Most Mexican ducks along the Middle Rio Grande are mallard hybrids.

Photographs: Doug Brown

Northern Shoveler

(Anas clypeata) ✴

JAN–MAY, Jun–Aug, SEP–DEC

Taxonomy—Class: Aves; Order: Anseriformes; Family: Anatidae.

Identification—Duck readily identified by long spatulate bill and in flight by large pale blue forewing patch. Male (photo) has green head, black bill, yellow iris, white breast, chestnut sides and belly, and white patch just before black tail. Female is duller, mostly mottled brown with orangish bill. Most common vocalization is a "whkuck."

Natural history—Typically seen at ponds, less often along ditches and in river. Mainly a surface-feeding duck.

Robert Sivinski

Status—Overall, most common during migration while only uncommon during winter. Observed year-round at Bosque del Apache NWR, where common to abundant from September to May and where breeding recorded.

Northern Pintail

(Anas acuta) ✳

JAN–APR, May–Aug, SEP–DEC

Taxonomy—Class: Aves; Order: Anseriformes; Family: Anatidae.

Identification—An elegant long-necked, long-tailed duck. Male (photo) easily identified by white stripe extending up from white foreneck onto side of brown head near nape. Hind neck brown; breast and belly white; sides, wings, and back gray; tail pointed. Female mottled brown with shorter tail. Vocalizations include a high-pitched "peep."

Natural history—Occurs only in areas with ponds and wetlands. Like other dabbling ducks, forages by tipping over in the water, its tail sticking out and its neck reaching below for aquatic plants and their seeds and for aquatic invertebrates.

Status—Widespread. Common to abundant from late September through April; occasional to rare from midspring through summer, although breeding has been recorded at Bosque del Apache NWR.

Green-winged Teal

(Anas crecca) ✳

JAN–MAY, Jun–Sep, OCT–DEC

Taxonomy—Class: Aves; Order: Anseriformes; Family: Anatidae.

Identification—Smallest dabbling duck in North America. Male (photo) recognized by glossy green patch over eye and across side of chestnut brown head (compare with American wigeon), vertical white stripe behind breast and extending down side, and buffy yellow vent patch. Body is gray. Female speckled brown. Both male and female have green speculum. Male utters a whistled "crick-et."

Natural history—Bulk of diet consists of seeds of sedges and other aquatic plants, with also aquatic invertebrates and tadpoles. Adept at walking on land.

Status—Widespread. Locally common during fall, winter, and spring; occasional during summer. Breeding recorded at Bosque del Apache NWR. See also section on Elephant Butte Reservoir.

Canvasback

(Aythya vasilineria) ✳

JAN–APR, May–Sep, OCT–DEC

Taxonomy—Class: Aves; Order: Anseriformes; Family: Anatidae.

Identification—Male (photo) has chestnut head and neck; red eyes; long bill and sloping forehead that form near straight line; black breast and tail; and white back, wings, and sides. (Redhead is smaller, lacks long bill and profile, has a round head and gray back and sides, and its bill is bluish with a black tip.) Female canvasback has grayish back, wings, and sides; dark brown breast; reddish tinge on neck and head; and white eye ring. Female utters soft "ker-ker."

Doug Brown

Natural history—Strongly associated with ponds and wetlands, where it eats aquatic plants and invertebrates. Travels in V-shaped flocks.

Status—Widespread. Uncommon in fall, winter, and spring; very rare in summer at Bosque del Apache NWR (where breeding has been recorded).

Redhead

(Aythya americana) ✳

JAN–JUL, Aug–Sep, OCT–DEC

Taxonomy—Class: Aves; Order: Anseriformes; Family: Anatidae.

Identification—Male (photo) similar to male canvasback with reddish brown head and black breast and tail but round rather than sloping forehead, shorter blue-gray bill with black tip, yellow eyes, and gray back and sides. Female brown with whitish eye ring and same bill pattern as male's. In flight, both sexes show a light gray wing stripe. Male very vocal during pairing, uttering several calls, including a "weow."

Doug Brown

Natural history—Nest not described locally but elsewhere is placed on mat of aquatic vegetation at edge of water. Bulk of diet consists of plant material. Foraging conducted through dabbling or diving.

Status—Widespread. Uncommon to locally common except in August and September, when more occasional. Breeding recorded at Bosque del Apache NWR.

Ring-necked Duck   *(Aythya collaris)*

JAN–APR, May, Aug, SEP–DEC

Taxonomy—Class: Aves; Order: Anseriformes; Family: Anatidae.

Identification—Male (photo) has dark head, neck, breast, and back (head is glossed with purple); white belly and shoulder stripe; and gray sides. Brownish red ring at base of neck is difficult to see. Gray bill has 2 white rings (species was once also and perhaps more appropriately named ring-billed duck). Female mostly brown with whitish ring around bill, white eye ring, and indistinct whitish streak extending back from eye. Both sexes have gray wing stripes. Typically silent.

Doug Brown

Natural history—Diving duck feeding mainly on aquatic vegetation. Male and female pair up by early spring.

Status—Widespread, uncommon to common winter resident.

Lesser Scaup   *(Aythya affinis)* ✳

JAN–APR, May, Sep, OCT–DEC

Taxonomy—Class: Aves; Order: Anseriformes; Family: Anatidae.

Identification—Male (photo) similar to ring-necked duck with dark head (sometimes a dark purple gloss appears at a distance, occasionally green) and black breast and tail. However, back is gray instead of black and bill is blue-gray and tipped with black without any ring. Female is brown with conspicuous white patch surrounding bill base. In flight, both sexes have broad white stripe along trailing edge of wing secondaries. Usually silent along the Middle Rio Grande.

Doug Brown

Natural history—Diet includes seeds and aquatic invertebrates. Adept diver capable of feeding at depths of 4.5–6 m (15–20 ft).

Status—Species has been declining in North America for several decades. Remains widespread and uncommon from October to early May. No recent summer records but old breeding records from Bosque del Apache NWR. See also section on Elephant Butte Reservoir.

Bufflehead   (*Bucephala albeola*)

JAN–APR, May, Oct, NOV–DEC

Taxonomy—Class: Aves; Order: Anseriformes; Family: Anatidae.

Identification—Small diving duck with short bill. Male (photo) readily identified by white patch on rear half of head down to cheek (compare with hooded merganser). Forehead and lower cheek dark with green and purple gloss. Breast and underparts white; back, black. Female brown above with white patch behind eye. Both sexes have white wing patches (larger in male). Usually silent along Middle Rio Grande.

Doug Brown

Natural history—Dives to feed on aquatic plant material and on invertebrates.

Status—Widespread and uncommon to locally common. Most birds from mid-November through early April but can be found into late May in spring and as early as October in fall.

Common Goldeneye   (*Bucephala clangula*)

JAN–FEB, Mar, NOV–DEC

Taxonomy—Class: Aves; Order: Anseriformes; Family: Anatidae.

Identification—Male mainly black above (head glossed with dark green) with white round patch near base of bill. Neck, breast, and underparts white. Female has gray back and sides, brown head, white collar, and usually a dark bill with light yellow or orange patch near tip. Both sexes have yellow eyes and white wing patches. Generally silent, though may give a nasal "beep" during early spring courtship displays. Wings make loud whistling sound in flight.

Mike Yip

Natural history—Often in small flocks. Prefers areas of river with rocky bottoms and swift currents. Occasionally seen in ditches or ponds. Diving bird; diet includes aquatic invertebrates and seeds and other plant material.

Status—Uncommon at Cochiti Dam spillway. Rare elsewhere.

Hooded Merganser
(*Lophodytes cucullatus*) ✳

JAN–MAR, Apr–Oct, NOV–DEC

Patrick O'Brien

Taxonomy—Class: Aves; Order: Anseriformes; Family: Anatidae.

Identification—Male (photo) readily identified by fan-shaped white patch on otherwise black hooded head. Crest with white patch may be completely raised (as in photo) or completely lowered showing very little white. Neck, back, and tail mostly black; sides chestnut; breast and underparts white with 2 black stripes extending down each side from fore-wing to belly. Female much like female common merganser but smaller, all dark. Both sexes have a thin, dark bill. Silent when not breeding.

Natural history—Breeds in tree cavities and nest boxes. Dives to feed on aquatic invertebrates, fish, frogs, tadpoles, and seeds and roots of aquatic plants.

Status—Widespread and uncommon from November through March. Rare in summer in Socorro County, where breeding has been recorded.

Common Merganser
(*Mergus merganser*)

JAN–APR, May, Oct, NOV–DEC

Doug Brown

Taxonomy—Class: Aves; Order: Anseriformes; Family: Anatidae.

Identification—Male (photo) has dark green head with no conspicuous crest, black back, white secondaries with 1 black bar, and whitish breast and sides. Female has rusty crested head, rusty neck, white contrasting chin and breast, gray back and sides, and white speculum. Both sexes have a long, thick-based red bill. Usually silent.

Natural history—Diving duck feeding on fishes, frogs, aquatic invertebrates, and plant material. Often found in small concentrations.

Status—May be observed anywhere along Middle Rio Grande, where uncommon to common in late fall, winter, and early spring (and can reach very high numbers at Cochiti Lake and Elephant Butte Reservoir).

Ruddy Duck
(Oxyura jamaicensis) ✳ ✳

JAN–DEC

Taxonomy—Class: Aves; Order: Anseriformes; Family: Anatidae.

Identification—Breeding male (photo) unmistakable; has black cap and hind neck, white cheek, bright blue bill, rusty body, and black tail. Winter male has gray or dull blue bill, white cheek, slaty brown cap and back. Female similar to winter male but cheek is buff crossed by dark line. Usually silent.

Natural history—Diving duck typically occurring singly or in pairs. Eats mostly plant food along with some aquatic invertebrates. Nest concealed under cover of wetland vegetation. Does not walk on land.

Status—Found only in areas with ponds and wetlands (e.g., Bosque del Apache NWR, Isleta Marsh, Rio Grande Nature Center), where uncommon to common in fall, winter, and spring. Uncommon breeding summer resident at the Bosque del Apache NWR and elsewhere, including Isleta Marsh. See also section on Elephant Butte Reservoir.

Doug Brown

Ring-necked Pheasant
(Phasianus colchicus) ✳ ✳ [INT]

JAN–DEC

Taxonomy—Class: Aves; Order: Galliformes; Family: Phasianidae. Two subspecies are represented in the bosque: the Chinese race, *P. c. torquatus*, and the Afghan white-winged race, *P. c. bianchii* (photo). The 2 subspecies hybridize.

Identification—More often heard than seen (the call is an explosive, hoarse "kaw kawk"). Sexes different but both easily recognizable by large size, long pointed tail, and chickenlike bill. Male (photo) has bare red skin around the eyes, green neck, iridescent multicolored body, and often (but not always) a white "necklace." Female and immature are smaller with buffy plumage mottled and spotted with darker brown. In flight, rapid wing beats are followed by a glide.

Matias J. Vega

Natural history—Found in cottonwood woodland, in open, weedy areas, along the banks of the river, and along ditches; also in fields adjacent to bosque. Tall weeds and riverbank vegetation are important for cover. Local diet likely includes grains, leafy vegetation, and insects. Nests on the ground under cover of weedy vegetation or in thickets.

Status—Widespread and common year-round.

Wild Turkey

(*Meleagris gallopavo*) ✳ ✳

JAN–DEC

Gordon French

Taxonomy—Class: Aves; Order: Galliformes; Family: Phasianidae. Subspecies in bosque is the Rio Grande turkey (*M. g. intermedia*).

Identification—Unmistakable: very large and tall with unfeathered red or blue head and upper neck. Neck long. Wings rounded, broad, and short. Tail fan shaped. Rump and tail feather tips tan. Flight feathers dark, banded white. Male (also called tom; photo) stands at a height of up to 1 m (40 in) with dark iridescent body, conspicuous red wattle, caruncle (wartlike projection from forehead), and tuft of hairlike fibers (called beard) hanging from midline of breast. Females are similar but smaller and paler, wattle less conspicuous, beard often absent. Call by toms is a repeated loud gobble.

Natural history—Most likely to be seen in open areas with herbaceous cover, less often in mature woodland. In winter, congregate in flocks of up to 50 or more and relies on corn as food. Proximity to water is key as are presence of tall trees for roosting at night and mesic, grassy areas providing a diet of insects for young turkeys (poults). Numerous potential predators of adult turkeys, poults, and eggs include bobcats, coyotes, raccoons, foxes, great horned owls, and snakes.

Status—Uncommon to common at Bosque del Apache NWR (existing population began as transplant from Texas but species historically present along Middle Rio Grande). Elsewhere locally uncommon north to at least Albuquerque.

Gambel's Quail

(*Callipepla gambelii*) ✳ ✳

JAN–DEC

Taxonomy—Class: Aves; Order: Galliformes; Family: Odontophoridae.

Identification—Male (photo) has chestnut crown, black face and throat rimmed posteriorly with white, and forward-tilting, comma-shaped black plume. Female duller with shorter brown plume. Both sexes have red-brown sides striped with white. Utters whines, chuckles, and grunts; also a 4-note "chi-ca-go-go."

Robert Sivinski

Natural history—Found mainly in open areas with some ground cover, less often in cottonwood woodland and along its edges and along ditches. In the fall, families congregate to form coveys, or groups of 12 or more individuals. Eats seeds and green plants.

Status—Common year-round in the south; less common farther north.

Pied-billed Grebe

(*Podilymbus podiceps*) ✶ ✶

JAN–DEC

Taxonomy—Class: Aves; Order: Podicipediformes; Family: Podicipedidae.

Identification—Small, crestless grebe with a thick bill and no white wing patch (other grebes have thinner bills and wing patches). Sexes similar. Summer birds (photo) have black throat and forehead and a black ring around grayish bill (thus a "pied" bill). Body mostly brownish with darker back and white undertail coverts, often visible on swimming bird. Winter birds have whitish throat and yellowish bill with no ring.

Doug Brown

Natural history—Breeds in ponds, building a floating nest with aquatic vegetation. The incubating bird covers the eggs before leaving the nest. The young are precocial and may be carried on the parents' backs. The species' diet consists mainly of invertebrates, fish, and amphibians (including tiger salamander along the Middle Rio Grande) with some aquatic vegetation.

Status—Widespread and common.

Eared Grebe

(*Podiceps nigricollis*)

Jan–Feb, MAR–MAY, AUG–DEC

Taxonomy—Class: Aves; Order: Podicipediformes; Family: Podicipedidae.

Identification—Easily identified during summer by black crested head, yellow ear tufts along sides of head, red eyes (year-round), black neck and upper parts, and rusty flanks; thin, slightly upturned dark bill. In winter plumage (photo) duller, with less sharply contrasting features. Black above and white to gray below. White patch behind ears stands out. Young birds have a yellowish eye in fall, which turns to red by early winter.

Doug Brown

Natural history—Occurs in small groups during migration. Eats mainly aquatic invertebrates and their larvae.

Status—Widespread and uncommon during spring and fall migration, some birds lingering through late fall. Rare to occasional through most of winter.

Western Grebe
(Aechmophorus occidentalis) ✳ ✳

Feb–Mar, APR–MAY, Jun–Jul, AUG–OCT, Nov

Taxonomy—Class: Aves; Order: Podicipediformes; Family: Podicipedidae.

Identification—Large black and white grebe with swanlike neck. Sexes largely alike (male is larger). Black on crown (going down to enclose eye), back of neck, and back; underparts white. Bill is long, pointed, and olive-yellow; iris is red. Call, a loud "keek kreet." Bill color and whether black surrounds or goes above the eye are the best ways to distinguish species from Clark's grebe.

Natural history—As with all other grebes remains on water at all times (except when in flight). Often occurs in mixed flocks with Clark's grebes and common mergansers. Builds a floating nest. Species' diet consists of fish and invertebrates. Known to hybridize with Clark's grebe.

Status—Uncommon in spring and fall at Bosque del Apache NWR, where it has begun to breed in recent years. Rare elsewhere. See also section on Elephant Butte Reservoir.

Gordon French

Clark's Grebe
(Aechmophorus clarkii) ✳ ✳

Feb–Mar, APR–OCT, Nov

Taxonomy—Class: Aves; Order: Podicipediformes; Family: Podicipedidae.

Identification—Nearly identical to western grebe but black of crown does not encircle eye and bill is yellow-orange (bill color alone is generally the easiest field mark to discern species at a distance). Back is also generally a lighter shade than on western grebe, and black on nape is not as wide. Utters a single call note "kreet" instead of the doubled note call of the western grebe.

Natural history—Often occurs in mixed flocks with western grebes and common mergansers. Builds a floating nest. Species' diet consists of fish and invertebrates. Hybridizes with western grebe.

Status—Uncommon to common in spring, summer, and fall at the Bosque del Apache NWR, where small numbers breed annually. See also section on Elephant Butte Reservoir.

Doug Brown

American White Pelican   (*Pelecanus erythrorhynchos*)

Jan, **FEB–APR**, Jun–Jul, **AUG–OCT**, Nov–Dec

Taxonomy—Class: Aves; Order: Pelecaniformes; Family: Pelecanidae.

Identification—Large white bird with long flat bill and extendable throat pouch. Sexes alike, adults unmistakable: black outer wing feathers and orange legs and (webbed) feet. Immatures have dark crown and dusky bill. In flight, head is drawn back; alternates several wing flaps with glides. Flocks fly in undulating ribbons.

Natural history—Unlike brown pelican does not dive from the air to catch fish but submerges head into the water while swimming. Fishing often conducted cooperatively, with all birds herding fish into shallow water and then synchronously dipping heads into the water.

Status—Mainly a spring and fall migrant found at the Bosque del Apache NWR (where common). Occasionally seen flying up or down river elsewhere or during summer and recently winter. See also section on Elephant Butte Reservoir.

Gordon French

Neotropic Cormorant   (*Phalacrocorax brasilianum*) ✳ ✳

JAN–DEC

Taxonomy—Class: Aves; Order: Pelecaniformes; Family: Phalacrocoracidae.

Identification—Large black waterbird with hook-tipped bill. Adults can be distinguished from double-crested cormorants by smaller size, head and neck measuring about the same length as tail, and throat patch in the shape of a V pointing toward back of head, orange-yellow in summer but duller in winter and outlined in white. Immature gray-brown above, pale below. Swims with bill uptilted.

Natural history—Typically seen in ponds, where spends large amounts of time sitting on floating logs and half-submerged stumps. Rarely seen in the river. Nests in mixed rookeries with other species such as double-crested cormorant and black-crowned night-heron. Nests are in partially submerged snags or half-dead trees. Species' diet consists mainly of fish.

Status—Common at Bosque del Apache NWR. Rarely encountered farther north, mainly in spring.

Robert Shantz

Double-crested Cormorant   (*Phalacrocorax auritus*) ✳ ✳

JAN–DEC

Taxonomy—Class: Aves; Order: Pelecaniformes; Family: Phalacrocoracidae.

Identification—Large black waterbird with hook-tipped bill. Head and neck significantly longer than tail. Adult has green eyes; crest rarely conspicuous; can be differentiated from neotropic cormorant mainly by orange-yellow throat patch, which is larger and rounded toward back of head, not V shaped. Immature grayish brown with contrasting ivory throat and breast. Swims with head tilted up. Utters croaks around nest.

Robert Shantz

Natural history—Spends much of its time on floating logs or emerging stumps in middle of ponds. Also found in the river (much more frequently than neotropic cormorant). Nests in wetlands and shallow ponds in mixed rookeries with other species such as neotropic cormorant and great egret. Nests are at heights of up to 9 m (30 ft) in partly submerged snags (including dead saltcedars) and half-dead cottonwoods. Eggs recorded in May. Eats fish.

Status—Uncommon year-round. In contrast to neotropic cormorant is found along the entire length of the Middle Rio Grande.

American Bittern   (*Botaurus lentiginosus*) ✳ ✳

Jan–Dec

Taxonomy—Class: Aves; Order: Ciconiiformes; Family: Ardeidae.

Identification—About the size of a snowy egret, with heavy body and relatively short legs. Dark brown above; yellow-buff below with heavy rufous brown streaking. Look for thin white eyebrow and, in adults only, black stripe along side of upper neck. Sides of chin and throat white, dark primaries. When walking points its bill upward at an angle. Call, a loud "uunk-ka-lunk" (accent on second syllable), typically heard at dusk and at night.

Gordon French

Natural history—Secretive species found in wetlands, where it blends in with surrounding vegetation. Nest may be in cattails or rushes. Diet not described in bosque; generally includes frogs, fish, gartersnakes, and aquatic invertebrates.

Status—Occasional year-round at Bosque del Apache NWR, where breeding occurs. Also recorded at Isleta Marsh.

Least Bittern
(*Ixobrychus exilis*) ✳ ✳

APR–AUG

Taxonomy—Class: Aves; Order: Ciconiiformes; Family: Ardeidae.

Identification—Very small member of heron family. Best identified by large buff and chestnut wing patches visible in flight and at rest. Otherwise similar to green heron: male (photo) has dark cap, back, and flight feathers; white chin; orange-brown and white streaking along foreneck and breast; orange-brown sides of neck. Female has more brownish cap and back. Immature similar to female but with broader brown streaks on throat and breast. Song is a fast, muted "coo-coo-coo."

Natural history—Very secretive species that relies on concealment under cover of marshy vegetation; when flushed may fly but rarely more than a short distance before hiding again. Nests among cattails in ponds and wetlands.

Status—Found in the south (recorded nesting north almost to Belen), where uncommon during spring and summer.

Greg W. Lasley

Great Blue Heron
(*Ardea herodias*) ✳ ✳

JAN–DEC

Taxonomy—Class: Aves; Order: Ciconiiformes; Family: Ardeidae.

Identification—Stands about 1.2 m (4 ft) tall, with long legs and long, pointed bill. Back and wings blue-gray; neck mostly gray with some white; head largely white with black line over eye and white crown; trail of 2 black feathers extending from back of head (in breeding plumage). In flight, long neck is folded, drawing head back to shoulders; slow wing beats (compare with sandhill crane). Call is a deep, rough squawk.

Natural history—Found in river channel, along ditches, and at ponds. Builds its stick nest in dead trees, singly or in rookeries. Stands motionless in shallow water or on a low perch, shooting out its long neck and seizing prey with daggerlike bill. Eats mostly aquatic invertebrates and vertebrates.

Status—Widespread and common year-round.

Robert Shantz

Great Egret
(*Ardea alba*) ✳ ✳

Jan–Feb, **MAR–NOV**, Dec

Taxonomy—Class: Aves; Order: Ciconiiformes; Family: Ardeidae.

Identification—All white and nearly as tall as great blue heron (all other white heron species are notably smaller). Bill yellow; legs all black (compare bill and leg color with cattle and snowy egrets'). Usually silent.

Natural history—Found near water. Nests in mixed rookeries with other species, including the double-crested cormorant. Eggs observed in May. Species' diet includes fish, frogs, crayfish, and insects.

Status—Found mostly in the south, including at the Bosque del Apache NWR, where common in summer, uncommon in spring and fall, and occasional in winter. Occasional to rare elsewhere.

Robert Sivinski

Snowy Egret
(*Egretta thula*) ✳ ✳

Jan–Feb, **MAR–OCT**, Nov–Dec

Taxonomy—Class: Aves; Order: Ciconiiformes; Family: Ardeidae.

Identification—Medium-size white heron with black legs and yellow feet. Bill slender and black. During breeding season, back of head and lower back have very conspicuous, long white plumes. Sexes alike. Immature bird with back of legs yellow-green. Compare with great and cattle egrets.

Natural history—Nests communally with other species, such as the black-crowned night-heron and the cattle egret. Rookeries observed in dense cottonwood, willow, and Russian olive vegetation along river channel. Also nests in stands of dead saltcedar in wetlands. Diet includes fish, crayfish, and frogs.

Status—Widespread. Common in spring, summer, and early fall; rare in winter.

Doug Brown

Cattle Egret
(*Bubulcus ibis*) ✳ ✳ [INT]

Jan–Feb, MAR–NOV, Dec

Taxonomy—Class: Aves; Order: Ciconiiformes; Family: Ardeidae.

Identification—White heron with yellow or orange bill; much smaller than great egret. Adults have yellow legs and feet, turning orange during breeding (but immatures have greenish to black legs). Breeding adults have buffy to orange plumes on crown, nape, back, and breast.

Natural history—Forages in inundated open areas of bosque and in adjacent fields, often in small flocks and near livestock. Nests in mixed rookeries with snowy egrets and black-crowned night-herons. Diet mainly includes insects.

Status—Widespread. Uncommon to locally common from spring to fall; rare to occasional during winter. Originally from Old World and now established in the New World.

Green Heron
(*Butorides virescens*) ✳ ✳

APR–SEP, Oct

Taxonomy—Class: Aves; Order: Ciconiiformes; Family: Ardeidae.

Identification—Small heron. Adult (photo) has dark blue cap, back, and wings all with greenish gloss, white chin and throat with brown streaks, rufous sides of neck, and grayish belly. No buff wing patches (unlike similar-looking but smaller least bittern). Legs are yellow to bright orange. Immature bird is brown and dark green with heavy brown streaking on whitish neck and breast. When alarmed utters a loud and startling "skeow." Another call is a softer "kuk kuk kuk . . ."

Natural history—May nest singly or communally with other species. Some nests are in tall Russian olives in dense streamside vegetation. Diet includes fish, crayfish, and frogs.

Status—Mostly in south, where common in spring and summer. Very rare in winter.

Black-crowned Night-heron

(Nycticorax nycticorax) * *

JAN–DEC

Taxonomy—Class: Aves; Order: Ciconiiformes; Family: Ardeidae.

Identification—Adult (top) has black crown and back, gray wings, and pale underparts. Eyes red; bill dark and stout; legs generally yellowish green and short for a heron. Immature (bottom) is brown above with some white spots; white underparts are heavily streaked with brown. Call is a low "kwock."

Natural history—Nests in mixed rookeries mainly with snowy egrets. Species' diet varies based on seasonal opportunities and includes fish, aquatic invertebrates, small rodents, and even nestlings of other colonial birds. Typically eats at night but can be seen during the day.

Status—Widespread and common in spring, summer, and fall. In winter, occasional to locally uncommon.

Robert Shantz

Gordon French

White-faced Ibis

(Plegadis chihi) *

Jan–Feb, MAR–NOV, Dec

Taxonomy—Class: Aves; Order: Ciconiiformes; Family: Threskiornithidae.

Identification—Most of body plumage is glossy chestnut (may appear black at a distance) with metallic bronzy green wings. Red eyes encircled by white; patch of bare red skin at base of long, down-curved bill. Long legs mostly dusky greenish with red "knees" in spring. Flies with neck extended outward. Immatures and nonbreeding adults are same shape but with dull brownish body and many small white streaks. Utters grunts.

Natural history—Occurs in flocks of up to 500 birds. Forages along river channel, at ponds and wetlands, and in fields adjacent to bosque. Species' diet includes insects, snails, crustaceans, frogs, and fishes.

Status—Widespread and generally common during spring and fall migration. Breeding recorded once or twice at Bosque del Apache NWR.

Doug Brown

Turkey Vulture

(Cathartes aura)

MAR–OCT

 in air above

Taxonomy—Class: Aves; Order: Ciconiiformes; Family: Cathartidae.

Identification—Highly recognizable. Sexes alike: head is small, bare, and red (blackish and fuzzy in juveniles); beak is red with a yellow hook at tip; body blackish brown; 2-toned underwings with silvery primaries and secondaries contrasting with dark brown wing coverts. In flight, wings are held in a shallow V. Usually silent; utters a hiss when alarmed.

Natural history—Usually seen soaring overhead. Also frequently found roosting on snags in burned areas in flocks of up to 50; more occasionally in live trees. Warms up in early morning by stretching out wings as in photo. Feeds on carrion often located by smell first (this is one of the few birds with a good sense of smell).

Status—Widespread and common in spring, summer, and fall but does not breed in bosque.

Osprey

(Pandion haliaetus) ✳

Mar, APR–MAY, Jun, Aug, SEP–OCT

Taxonomy—Class: Aves; Order: Falconiformes; Family: Accipitridae.

Identification—Large bird of prey, dark brown above, mostly white below. Distinctive brown eye stripe on white head. In flight, readily identified by narrow wings bent at wrist, black wrist patches, and fine dark bands on underwings (flight feathers only) and undertail. Females have speckled breasts reminiscent of necklaces. Call includes a series of sharp whistles, "cheep cheep cheep . . ."

Natural history—May be observed flying overhead or perched in a tree or a snag along the river, at a pond, or along a ditch. Bulk of diet consists of fish. Hovers over water and dives with head and feet projected first.

Status—Widespread and rare to uncommon during spring and fall migration. One pair nested below Cochiti Dam from 1997 through 2004 (not in the bosque proper but on a utility pole along the road to the dam). See also Elephant Butte Reservoir section.

Mississippi Kite   (*Ictinia mississippiensis*) ✳ ✳

May–Aug

Taxonomy—Class: Aves; Order: Falconiformes; Family: Accipitridae.

Identification—Sexes similar. Mostly light to medium gray below with slate gray back and wing coverts, black primaries, and pale secondaries. Head is pale gray with red eyes edged by black feathers. Tail is black with no bars; feet are yellow to orange. Immatures are streaked with brown, with black tail showing 3 white bars on underside. Utters a high-pitched, whistled "phee-phew."

Natural history—Found in cottonwood woodland and along ditches (but mainly forages outside bosque in adjacent fields). Diet consists mainly of insects, often consumed in midair.

Status—Overall rare and local, with breeding reported only in the Corrales bosque and at Los Lunas River Park. Apparently in New Mexico since only the 1950s.

Larry Brock

Bald Eagle   (*Haliaeetus leucocephalus*)

JAN–MAR, Apr, NOV–DEC

Taxonomy—Class: Aves; Order: Falconiformes; Family: Accipitridae.

Identification—Large bird of prey holding its wings flat in flight. Adults (photo) easily recognized by their snow white head and tail. Hatch-year birds uniformly dark brown with a black beak. Older, immature bald eagles usually show white (or mottled white) belly contrasting with dark breast, upside-down white triangle on back, dark eye line, and white mottling of otherwise dark body. Subadults have dirty white tail and head. Risk of confusion is with young golden eagle (both may have base of tail white), but only immature bald eagles show white axillary spots (wing pits) in flight. Utters loud, high-pitched cackle, very unseemly for an eagle, and as a result often misrepresented on TV commercials by a red-tailed hawk scream!

Natural history—Typically found in a live cottonwood or snag facing open water near concentrations of waterfowl, its apparent staple diet along the Middle Rio Grande. The species is both a predator and a scavenger.

Status—Widespread and found mainly from November through mid-March, when occasional to locally common. Once endangered, the bald eagle has been making a steady comeback. Has nested in the Rio Grande Valley near Caballo Lake but no nesting record along the Middle Rio Grande.

Robert Shantz

Northern Harrier

(Circus cyaneus) ✳

JAN–APR, May–Aug, SEP–DEC

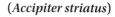

Taxonomy—Class: Aves; Order: Falconiformes; Family: Accipitridae. Also called marsh hawk.

Identification—Easily identified. Flies low above ground, alternating soaring and flapping, its wings held in a V and its rump showing a conspicuous white patch. Owl-like face with frontal eyes also diagnostic. Three distinct plumages: adult male is medium gray above, mostly whitish below with dark gray face and tips of flight feathers black; adult female (photo) has brown upper parts, buffy breast and belly both streaked with dark brown, and barred tail; immature similar to female but has underparts more rufous and with less streaking.

Natural history—Typically perches on the ground rather than in trees. Flies low in search of small vertebrates. Predation on wood ducks observed at Rio Grande Nature Center ponds. Nest is on the ground.

Status—Widespread but highest numbers at Bosque del Apache NWR, where common in spring and fall and abundant in winter and where breeds irregularly. Elsewhere uncommon in fall, winter, and spring and absent in summer.

Sharp-shinned Hawk

(Accipiter striatus)

JAN–APR, Aug, SEP–DEC

Taxonomy—Class: Aves; Order: Falconiformes; Family: Accipitridae.

Identification—Smaller than Cooper's hawk; tail more square tipped and with thinner terminal white band. Otherwise generally similar with barred tail that is relatively long and short, rounded wings. Adults dark blue-gray (males) to gray-brown (females) above and with rufous barring across chest. Female larger than male. Juveniles (photo) are brown above and with streaked underparts. In flight, alternates flapping of wings with gliding (like Cooper's hawk).

Natural history—Mainly found in cottonwood woodland. Species' diet consists mostly of small birds.

Status—Widely distributed; uncommon as winter resident and during spring and fall migration.

Cooper's Hawk   (*Accipiter cooperii*) ✳ ✳

JAN–DEC

Taxonomy—Class: Aves; Order: Falconiformes; Family: Accipitridae.

Photographs: Doug Brown

Identification—Adults (right) have bluish gray (males) to brownish gray (females) upperparts and white underparts barred crosswise with rufous. Wings short; tail long with 4 or more black transverse bars and a white terminal band that is often noticeably wide. Iris orange, turning to red in older individuals. Females noticeably larger than male. Juveniles (left) brown above and white below with brown longitudinal streaking; yellow irises. Compared to similar sharp-shinned hawk, Cooper's hawk is much more common; also larger, with tail more rounded at tip and with head that projects in front of wrists in flight. Utters a noisy alarm call around nest, "cac cac cac."

Natural history—Primarily found in cottonwood woodland (dense stands of mature cottonwoods are preferred for nesting) but hunts also in wooded vegetation along ditches, along riverbanks, and at ponds and wetlands. The large nest is typically high up in the crotch of a mature cottonwood tree, and up to 5 nestlings are raised to fledging. Male hunts for female and for young. Much of diet consists of small birds.

Status—Widely distributed and common year-round.

Swainson's Hawk   (*Buteo swainsoni*) ✳ ✳

MAR–OCT

Taxonomy—Class: Aves; Order: Falconiformes; Family: Accipitridae.

Identification—Typical adult plumage (light morph; photo): upper parts uniformly brown, underparts largely white but with dark (gray or brown) face and "bib" that contrast with white throat, 2-tone underwings with dark flight feathers and white wing coverts, small dark bands across whitish tail. Immature light morph blackish brown above with variable white markings; buffy underparts are spotted and streaked with brown. Adult and immature dark morph all brown. In flight holds its wings in a shallow V. Vocal around its nest; utters a shrill, descending scream, "kreeeeeer."

Robert Shantz

Natural history—Nests in cottonwood woodland at the top of tall cottonwoods, often very well hidden by surrounding foliage. Diet includes small mammals, birds, lizards, and amphibians. Often seen soaring over fields adjacent to bosque but also hunts over river channel and cottonwood woodland.

Status—Widespread, uncommon to locally common.

Red-tailed Hawk

(Buteo jamaicensis) ✳

JAN–MAY, Jun–Aug, SEP–DEC

Taxonomy—Class: Aves; Order: Falconiformes; Family: Accipitridae.

Identification—Large hawk with variable plumage. Most adult red-tailed hawks in bosque are dark brown above with conspicuous red tail. Light-colored scapulars form a V-shaped patch in back of perched birds. Underparts mostly white to light buff with dark leading edge of wings and crescent-shaped patch beyond wrists (patagial mark). Dark belly band often pronounced but may be absent; undertail pale orange. Head appears hooded with throat variably white or dark. Immatures have barred brown tail and are more heavily marked below.

Robert Shantz

Natural history—Prefers more open areas of bosque. Also found in nearby agricultural areas. Species' diet is diverse but consists largely of small to medium-size mammals.

Status—Widespread and common in fall, winter, and spring, rare to occasional in summer. Nesting in bosque is rare.

American Kestrel

(Falco sparverius) ✳ ✳

JAN–DEC

Taxonomy—Class: Aves; Order: Falconiformes; Family: Falconidae.

Identification—Small, sexually dimorphic falcon with double mustache. Male (left) has rufous back, blue-gray wings, and rufous tail with conspicuous black subterminal band; rusty wash on whitish underparts. Female (right) has rufous upper parts with black cross-bars; rusty streaks on whitish underparts. When excited or alarmed utters a loud "klee klee klee."

Natural history—Found mostly in open (including postfire) areas of the bosque and along its agricultural edges. Nesting is in a tree cavity, beginning in early May. Prior to egg laying, during courtship, the male is often seen bringing food to the female. The diet consists of invertebrates and small vertebrates.

Jean-Luc Cartron

Status—Widespread and common.

Peregrine Falcon (*Falco peregrinus*)

Jan–Mar, **APR–MAY**, Jun–Jul, **AUG–OCT**, Nov–Dec

Taxonomy—Class: Aves; Order: Falconiformes; Family: Falconidae.

Identification—Crow size with long, pointed wings. Sexes alike in plumage but female notably larger. Blue-gray above with dark hood and wide black mustache giving it a hooded appearance. Pale below (often with salmon-colored wash) with clear white breast and barred belly and underwings. Yellow ceres and legs stand out. Immatures are dark brown above, buffy below with dark streaking. Usually silent in bosque.

Natural history—Typically associated with ponds and wetlands, where it often occurs perched on snags. Bulk of diet consists of birds, including wild ducks, shorebirds, and doves. Possibly the fastest of all birds, kills its prey by overtaking it or swooping down on it.

Status—Widespread. Rare to occasional except during spring and fall migration, when uncommon.

Robert Shantz

Virginia Rail (*Rallus limicola*) ✳ ✳

Jan–Mar, **APR–SEP**, Oct–Dec

Taxonomy—Class: Aves; Order: Gruiformes; Family: Rallidae.

Identification—Medium size and colorful. Bill long, down curved, and red; eyes red; crown black; face gray; chin, throat, breast, and sides rufous; back brown, streaked with black; flanks barred black and white. Immatures similar but bill is black and underparts are mottled. Downy young are all black. Calls include a repeated "kidik," squeaks, and grunts.

Natural history—Mainly found at ponds and wetlands, less often along ditches. Secretive. Diet consists mainly of invertebrates.

Status—Locally uncommon in spring, summer, and fall. Locally occasional in winter. Year-round resident at Bosque del Apache NWR, where the species breeds. Also breeds south of San Marcial.

Robert Shantz

Sora
Mar, APR–OCT, Nov

(*Porzana carolina*) ✳ ✳

Taxonomy—Class: Aves; Order: Gruiformes; Family: Rallidae.

Identification—Medium size. Upper parts brown with black streaks and thin white lines on back and wings. Underparts gray with white, brown, and black barring on sides and belly. Bill chickenlike and yellow. Black patch between bill and eye extends down onto throat. Tail short and often held cocked. Utters a descending whinny.

Natural history—Secretive and strongly associated with rank aquatic vegetation of ponds and wetlands. Peak of breeding season in bosque is in May. Eats aquatic plants and their seeds and aquatic invertebrates.

Status—Widespread and uncommon to fairly common during spring and fall migration. Locally common breeding summer resident, including at Bosque del Apache NWR.

American Coot
JAN–DEC

(*Fulica americana*) ✳ ✳

Taxonomy—Class: Aves; Order: Gruiformes; Family: Rallidae.

Identification—Unmistakable ducklike waterbird. Sexes alike. Mostly slaty gray with black head and neck, short thick white bill, and red eyes. White patches along sides of undertail. Small chicks are reddish, turning darker as they mature. Call, "kuk kuk kuk kuk."

Natural history—Strongly associated with ponds and wetlands although also occurs occasionally in ditches and in river. Builds floating nest attached to standing plants amid or at edge of cattail marsh. Mixed diet of aquatic plants, invertebrates, tadpoles, and small fish. May forage by diving or by tipping over. Also known for occasional food piracy behavior (steals plants from ducks). Skitters on takeoff.

Status—Widespread and common to abundant year-round.

Sandhill Crane   (*Grus canadensis*)

JAN–MAR, Apr–May, OCT–DEC

Taxonomy—Class: Aves; Order: Gruiformes; Family: Gruidae.

Identification—1.2–1.5 m (4–5 ft) tall with long neck and long legs. The plumage is ash gray with white cheeks and red forehead. In flight can be distinguished from great blue heron by rapid upstroke and outstretched neck (herons fly with slow, steady wing beats, their heads and necks tucked into their shoulders, forming an S). Utters a loud, rattling "kar-rrrooo."

Natural history—Feeds chiefly on waste corn in fields of the Middle Rio Grande Valley as well as chufa nuts (nut sedge). Also forages in shallow waters of the river and on sandbars. Individuals fly over cottonwood woodland as they move back and forth between fields and the river channel. Natural enemies include coyotes and golden eagles, the latter known to attack migrating flocks.

Status—Widespread but found mostly from Albuquerque south. Time of occurrence is mainly from October to March as winter resident and also spring and fall migrant (some individuals follow the Middle Rio Grande to and from wintering grounds in southwestern New Mexico and northern Mexico). Common to abundant with large flocks of several thousand individuals at the Bosque del Apache NWR and other areas with extensive (seasonal) wetlands or agricultural fields.

Jean-Luc Cartron

Killdeer   (*Charadrius vociferus*) ✳ ✳

JAN–DEC

Taxonomy—Class: Aves; Order: Charadriiformes; Family: Charadriidae.

Identification—Sexes alike. Easily identified by its 2 black breast bands (immature has only 1). Note also the red eyes, white eyebrow, orange rump (revealed especially in flight), white wing stripe, and white underparts. Utters a very distinctive, loud "kill-deeah" and a plaintive "dee-ee."

Natural history—Found mainly on sandy or muddy beaches and on sandbars of the river channel. Nests on the ground, typically along the river, less often in open areas away from water. Both adults care for the brood. The killdeer's diet consists mostly of small aquatic invertebrates. In winter killdeers are often in fields adjacent to the bosque.

Status—Widely distributed. Uncommon in winter; common the rest of the year.

Robert Svinski

Black-necked Stilt

(*Himantopus mexicanus*) ✳ ✳

MAR–AUG, Sep

Taxonomy—Class: Aves; Order: Charadriiformes; Family: Recurvirostridae.

Identification—Unmistakable shorebird. Black above and white below; slender, long, pointed black bill; red stiltlike legs. Conspicuous white spot between black crown and black stripe through eye. Utters a sharp "yip yip yip."

Natural history—Hunts for aquatic invertebrates in shallow waters of river or ponds. Species typically nests in small colonies on ground near water.

Status—Widespread. Common at the Bosque del Apache NWR, uncommon elsewhere; most birds observed in March and April during spring migration. Breeding recorded at Bosque del Apache NWR, La Joya, and Belen.

American Avocet

(*Recurvirostra americana*) ✳

FEB–JUN, Jul–Aug, SEP–OCT

Taxonomy—Class: Aves; Order: Charadriiformes; Family: Recurvirostridae.

Identification—Graceful shorebird with long legs and long, thin, upturned bill. Lower back and wings pied black and white. Upper back and underparts white. Head and neck in breeding plumage (photo) are cinnamon; in nonbreeding plumage grayish. Utters loud "wheep."

Natural history—Occurs at ponds and wetlands and on sandbars of river channel; also found in flooded fields adjacent to bosque. Nests on the ground near water. Mixed diet of aquatic invertebrates and seeds of aquatic plants.

Status—Widespread and rare to locally common during spring and fall migration. Recorded breeding at Bosque del Apache NWR and Bernardo.

Greater Yellowlegs
(Tringa melanoleuca)

Jan–Feb, MAR–MAY, Jun–Jul, AUG–OCT, Nov–Dec

Taxonomy—Class: Aves; Order: Charadriiformes; Family: Scolopacidae.

Identification—Slim, tall shorebird with long, bright yellow legs and long, slightly upturned bill that is black except for gray base (lesser yellowlegs' is smaller and has notably shorter, straight, all-black bill). Back gray-brown and dotted or streaked with black and white. Underparts mostly white with variable amount of speckling on neck and breast. In flight, white rump and tail contrast with dark wings (no wing stripe) and legs extend beyond tail. Call, a loud, clear, whistled "tew-tew-tew."

Natural history—Occurs at ponds and wetlands and along ditches. Also found in inundated fields adjacent to bosque. Wades through water in search of aquatic invertebrates, fish, and tadpoles.

Status—Widespread and uncommon to common during spring and fall migration (the first fall migrants may arrive in July). Rare to occasional transient in winter.

Lesser Yellowlegs
(Tringa flavipes)

Jan–Mar, APR–MAY, Jul, AUG–SEP, Oct–Dec

Taxonomy—Class: Aves; Order: Charadriiformes; Family: Scolopacidae.

Identification—Resembles greater yellowlegs closely but smaller, with shorter bill that is all black and straight, not slightly upturned. Call is shorter and flatter than that of greater yellowlegs, often just a "tew-tew."

Natural history—Found along ponds, wetlands, and drains; also in inundated fields adjacent to bosque. Often solitary but up to 5 individuals may be seen together. Bulk of diet consists of aquatic invertebrates.

Status—Widespread. Uncommon during fall migration, arriving as early as July; rare to uncommon in spring migration. Rare to occasional transient in winter.

Solitary Sandpiper

(*Tringa solitaria*)

APR–MAY, JUL–AUG, Sep

Taxonomy—Class: Aves; Order: Charadriiformes; Family: Scolopacidae.

Identification—Larger and darker than spotted sandpiper with shape similar to a yellowlegs'. Back and wings dark brown or gray with white flecks. Conspicuous white eye ring. Rump dark (greater and lesser yellowlegs have white rump, otherwise they are similarly marked in fall); sides of tail white, barred with black. Bobs head and tail. Call, "peet-weet," reminiscent of spotted sandpiper.

Natural history—Usually solitary but also recorded in groups of up to 5 individuals in bosque. Often in shallow water at ponds and wetlands and in drains. Diet includes mainly aquatic invertebrates and frogs.

Status—Widespread and uncommon spring and fall migrant. Does not nest in New Mexico even though fall migrants begin appearing in July.

Lisa Spray

Spotted Sandpiper

(*Actitis macularius*) ✳ ✳

Jan–Mar, APR–SEP, Oct–Dec

Taxonomy—Class: Aves; Order: Charadriiformes; Family: Scolopacidae.

Identification—Readily recognizable in breeding plumage (photo): brown above, white below with conspicuous, large, round dark spots; white line over eye. Immatures and adults in nonbreeding plumage: gray-brown above, white below without spots, white line over eye fainter; look for white wedge-shaped patch enclosed by dusky smudge at shoulder. In flight, wings are down curved and show white stripe. Wing beats narrow, giving appearance of stiff flight. Utters a loud whistled "peet-wheet!"

Natural history—Occurs on sandbars of river channel and along ditches, ponds, and wetlands. Searches for invertebrates along edge of water; wades into shallow water, where may also catch small fish. Ground nester.

Status—Widespread and uncommon to locally common during spring and fall migration. Breeds at Bosque del Apache NWR, where common in summer. Rare in winter in south.

Gordon French

Willet   (*Catoptrophorus semipalmatus*)

Apr–May, Jul–Oct

Taxonomy—Class: Aves; Order: Charadriiformes; Family: Scolopacidae.

Identification—Large, long-legged sandpiper. Bill long and straight, dark toward tip but with thick gray base; legs blue-gray. In flight, distinctive white central stripe on largely black wings both above and below. Adults in winter plumage (photo) solid gray above, white below; in breeding plumage spotted, streaked, and barred with brown. Juveniles similar to adults, grayish above but with flecks of buff and brown. Calls include a whistled "pill-will-willet."

Gordon French

Natural history—Usually in small flocks. Forages in shallow waters and on mudflats, searching for invertebrates by sight or probing for them with its bill.

Status—Widespread and occasional during spring and fall migration. Most likely to be seen in April, May, and July.

Long-billed Curlew   (*Numenius americanus*)

Mar–May, Jul–Sep

Taxonomy—Class: Aves; Order: Charadriiformes; Family: Scolopacidae.

Identification—Large shorebird with small head and long neck. Adults (photo) unmistakable with very long (longer in female), down-curved bill. Back and upper wings mottled with brown and buff. Underparts largely buff. Legs long and grayish. In flight, shows cinnamon underwing linings. Tail barred. No pronounced striped head pattern (contrary to whimbrel, which is rare but possible along Middle Rio Grande). Juvenile has relatively short bill into first winter and could be confused with whimbrel; has bold cinnamon feather edges. Utters a clear, whistled "cur-lee," rising on second note.

Robert Shantz

Natural history—Typically seen in small flocks (but flocks of up to 80 birds seen) foraging on mudflats and in shallow waters; also in fields along agricultural edges of bosque. Diet during nonbreeding season consists of invertebrates, seeds, and berries.

Status—Occasional during spring and fall migration.

Marbled Godwit (*Limosa fedoa*)

Mar–May, Jul–Oct

Taxonomy—Class: Aves; Order: Charadriiformes; Family: Scolopacidae.

Identification—Nearly as large as long-billed curlew but long bill (orange at base, black at tip) is slightly upturned. Underparts unbarred buffy with cinnamon wing linings showing in flight; upper parts mottled with brown and buff. Tail barred cinnamon and black. Legs long and blackish. Utters a loud "godwit" with accent on second note.

Natural history—Found on sandbars of the river channel and in shallow waters along pond edges in small or larger flocks. Species' diet consists of invertebrates and seeds of aquatic plants.

Status—Occasional during spring and fall migration.

Gordon French

Western Sandpiper (*Calidris mauri*)

Mar, APR–MAY, Jun, JUL–SEP, Oct

Taxonomy—Class: Aves; Order: Charadriiformes; Family: Scolopacidae.

Identification—Sparrow-size sandpiper (1 of 5 so-called peeps, 4 of which occur in bosque). Sexes alike. Legs black (least sandpiper has yellowish or greenish legs); compared to both semipalmated and least sandpipers, black bill is notably longer and thicker at base, with slightly drooping tip. Otherwise nearly identical to semipalmated sandpiper (rarest of the 4 peeps found in the bosque; not described in this guide) in nonbreeding plumage (gray above and white below). Breeding plumage: rusty crown and ear patch and some rust on scapulars; heavily streaked breast. Utters a high-pitched "cheep."

Natural history—Found in flocks in river channel and along shores of ponds. Also in inundated fields adjacent to bosque.

Status—Widespread and uncommon to locally common during spring and fall migration. Uncommon (but not known to breed) at Bosque del Apache NWR during summer. Absent in winter.

Robert Shantz

Least Sandpiper   (*Calidris minutilla*)

Jan, FEB–APR, May–Jul, AUG–SEP, Oct–Dec

Taxonomy—Class: Aves; Order: Charadriiformes; Family: Scolopacidae.

Identification—Smaller than other "peeps" with more slender bill, yellowish or greenish (instead of black) legs, browner upper parts, and lightly spotted brown breast (other peeps have white breasts, spotted in breeding plumage). Utters a high "kreet."

Natural history—In flocks during migration. Occurs at ponds and wetlands and along the river. Also found in inundated fields adjacent to bosque.

Status—Occurs mainly during spring and fall migration, when widespread and uncommon to locally common. Occasional (but not known to breed) during summer and rare in winter at Bosque del Apache NWR.

Robert Shantz

Baird's Sandpiper   (*Calidris bairdii*)

APR, May, JUL–SEP, Oct

Taxonomy—Class: Aves; Order: Charadriiformes; Family: Scolopacidae.

Identification—Walks holding its body horizontal with wings extending beyond tail, unlike western and least sandpipers. Straight black bill; dark legs. In nonbreeding plumage (photo) adults are gray-brown above; throat white; breast buffy, lightly streaked, or dotted; belly white. Juveniles in fall are much brighter, with dark back and wings edged in white creating a scaled pattern; breast is quite buffy. In flight utters a low "kreep."

Natural history—Occurs mainly at ponds; also in river channel and along agricultural edges of bosque in flooded fields. Eats invertebrates.

Status—Uncommon spring and fall migrant (first fall migrants seen in July).

Robert Shantz

Long-billed Dowitcher (*Limnodromus scolopaceus*)

Jan, FEB–MAY, Jun–Sep, OCT–NOV, Dec

Taxonomy—Class: Aves; Order: Charadriiformes; Family: Scolopacidae.

Identification—Snipelike shorebird with long, straight bill, whitish eyebrow, and tail barred black and white. In breeding plumage (photo), upper parts are black with rufous and white edges; underparts are orange with small black spots on throat and breast and black bars on sides. In winter plumage, grayish brown above with white belly. In flight, white of rump extends up as stripe along midback. Sexes similar but female somewhat larger. Typical call is a high, sharp "keek" (short-billed dowitcher nearly identical and possible along Middle Rio Grande but utters a mellow "tu-tu-tu" instead).

Natural history—Forages in shallow waters and on mudflats at ponds and wetlands and in the river channel; also in adjacent, inundated fields. Diet consists largely of aquatic invertebrates (insect larvae, crustaceans, and mollusks); also plant material. Feeds with sewing-machine-like motions.

Status—Widespread; common as spring and fall migrant, overall rare to occasional in winter and summer.

Doug Brown

Wilson's Snipe (*Gallinago delicata*)

JAN–APR, May–Aug, SEP–DEC

Taxonomy—Class: Aves; Order: Charadriiformes; Family: Scolopacidae. Formerly known as common snipe.

Identification—Stocky with very long straight bill, boldly striped head and back, short legs, and short rusty tail. Zigzagging flight. When flushed utters a scratchy "skaip."

Natural history—Solitary and secretive. Found near water. Insects and aquatic invertebrates make up most of species' diet.

Status—Widespread. Uncommon to locally common during spring and fall migration. Uncommon in winter. Rare to occasional (with no breeding record) in summer.

Gordon French

Wilson's Phalarope   (*Phalaropus tricolor*)

APR–MAY, Jun, JUL–SEP, Oct–Nov

Taxonomy—Class: Aves; Order: Charadriiformes; Family: Scolopacidae.

Doug Brown

Identification—Tall shorebird with needlelike dark bill slightly longer than head. Sexes alike in winter (photo) with light gray upper parts, dark wings, white rump, and white unstreaked underparts. Female in breeding plumage has black eye stripe that merges into black neck stripe, white face, blue-gray top of head, orange foreneck, gray back striped with red, and white underparts. Male duller with some cinnamon on sides of neck. In all plumages phalaropes can be identified by habit of swimming in circles; in contrast to other phalaropes, Wilson's lacks wing stripes. Utters a nasal "wurk."

Natural history—Forages in and at edge of water. Eats small aquatic invertebrates.

Status—Uncommon to common during spring and fall migration. Rare into November.

Franklin's Gull   (*Larus pipixcan*)

MAR–MAY, Jun, Aug–Sep

Taxonomy—Class: Aves; Order: Charadriiformes; Family: Laridae.

Gordon French

Identification—Slender gull. Adults in breeding plumage (photo) have black head; red bill; broken white eye ring; white neck, breast, belly, and tail (underparts can also be pink due to diet); ashy gray back; black wing tips separated from gray upper wings by white band; and white trailing edge of wings. Adults in nonbreeding plumage have dark bill and smudgy half hood that doesn't include forehead. Immature resembles wintering adult but with broad black band across white tail. Call, a nasal, laughing "ha ha ha ha" similar to that of the laughing gull found mostly in coastal regions.

Natural history—Found at ponds and wetlands and along river channel; also in plowed fields adjacent to bosque, searching for insects. Generally found in small numbers but can occur in flocks of more than 100 birds.

Status—Widespread, uncommon spring migrant typically from late March to early May; occasional to rare during fall migration.

Ring-billed Gull   (*Larus delawarensis*)

JAN–MAY, Jun–Jul, AUG–DEC

Taxonomy—Class: Aves; Order: Charadriiformes; Family: Laridae.

Identification—Adults have white underparts and head, yellow bill with complete black ring near tip, and silvery wings that have black outer primaries with white spots at tip. Legs are yellowish or greenish (in summer). In winter, head is speckled with brown and legs may be gray. First winter plumage: gray back, wing coverts speckled with brown, pink bill with black tip, white tail with black subterminal band. Distinguishing from several other gull species, uncommon in the bosque, is tricky. Utters a high-pitched "high-er."

Natural history—Often found in and along the river channel, especially in urban areas. Flocks may forage on sandbars and in shallow waters. Gulls are known for their propensity to feed on garbage.

Status—Widespread and uncommon to locally common or abundant in fall, winter, and spring. Only rare to occasional in summer until mid-August. See also section on Elephant Butte Reservoir.

Forster's Tern   (*Sterna forsteri*)

APR–MAY, Jul, AUG–SEP, Oct

Taxonomy—Class: Aves; Order: Charadriiformes; Family: Laridae.

Identification—Slender tern with long deeply forked tail. Sexes similar. Pale gray back and wings and white underparts. In nonbreeding plumage (photo) has a white crown, long black eye mask, and black bill. In breeding plumage has black cap, orange-red bill with black tip, and whitish primaries. Calls include a grating, nasal "kyarr."

Natural history—Eats flying insects captured on the wing. Species' diet also includes fish and aquatic invertebrates.

Status—Widespread, occasional to uncommon spring and fall migrant.

Rock Pigeon   (*Columba livia*) ✳ ✳ [INT]

JAN–DEC

Taxonomy—Class: Aves; Order: Columbiformes; Family: Columbidae.

Identification—Much variation in plumage but typically blue-gray with white rump, 2 black bars on secondaries, and broad black band at tip of tail. Head is darker than body with iridescent green, copper, and purple on neck. Has pointed wings. Utters "coo-a-roo," repeated frequently.

Natural history—Marginal to bosque but nests on ledges under river and ditch bridges in urban settings (in some years nesting begins in early February). From bridges or power lines flies over cottonwood woodland, even perching in cottonwoods along levee roads. Swift flyer. Predators feeding on pigeons in the bosque include great horned owl.

Status—Restricted to urban or rural edges and, in bosque proper, to the vicinity of bridges. Common year-round.

Jean-Luc Cartron

Eurasian Collared-dove   (*Streptopelia decaocto*) [INT]

JAN–DEC

Taxonomy—Class: Aves; Order: Columbiformes; Family: Columbidae.

Identification—Medium-size turtle dove with gray body (with darker cinnamon gray wash on back); thin, short black bill; dark red irises; and narrow black half collar on hind neck. Tail long and square tipped with blackish base; blackish primaries; red legs. Song a monotonous "koo-koo-kook," with an accent on the second note. Also utters a nasal falsetto, "krreeeew," often before taking flight.

Natural history—Associated with open or semi-open habitats, often near human activity. Usually solitary or in pairs. Broad diet includes seeds, waste grain, and insects.

Status—Originally from Asia. Introduced to the Bahamas in the mid-1970s, it spread to Florida and is now rapidly expanding its range west and north across North America. Increasingly common along Middle Rio Grande.

Lisa Spray

White-winged Dove   (*Zenaida asiatica*) ✳✳

JAN–DEC

Taxonomy—Class: Aves; Order: Columbiformes; Family: Columbidae.

Identification—Sexes similar. Unmistakable with its white wing patches (at lower edge of closed wings when perched). Gray-brown above with conspicuous blue eye ring and small black mark on lower cheek. Rounded tail has broad white corners. Cooing is a hoarse, drawn-out "Who cooks for you?"

Natural history—Found in open cottonwood woodland near ponds and in moist open areas with scattered mature trees. Nests in cottonwoods.

Status—Local rather than widespread occurrence in the bosque. Where present, however, the species can now be common, reflecting a recent, spectacular increase in numbers in central and northern New Mexico.

Doug Brown

Mourning Dove   (*Zenaida macroura*) ✳✳

JAN–DEC

Taxonomy—Class: Aves; Order: Columbiformes; Family: Columbidae.

Identification—Midsize buff-brown dove with a pointed tail and a black bill; midsides of neck can show iridescent light green or pinkish areas; median wing coverts have distinctive black spots. Graduated outer rectrices are white. Utters a mournful, low-pitched "coo-who-coo-coo-coo" with accent on the higher-pitched second syllable.

Natural history—Habitat generalist. Uses saltcedar stands and burned areas. Nesting is from April–July; may raise several broods. Nests in cottonwood trees, Russian olives, saltcedars, and elms and even on jetty jacks! The flimsy nest (made of crossed twigs or sticks) is built in the canopy or down to a height of 1.2 m (4 ft). Clutch size is 2. Often occurs in flocks outside the nesting season. Found primarily at feeders and in open areas in the winter. Foraging is typically on the ground.

Jean-Luc Cattron

Status—Widespread and common to abundant, especially during spring and summer.

Yellow-billed Cuckoo

(*Coccyzus americanus*) ✳ ✳

Apr–Sep

Taxonomy—Class: Aves; Order: Cuculiformes; Family: Cuculidae.

Identification—Gray-brown above with rufous primaries; white below except for dark tail underneath, which also shows white spots in flight. Bill slender and down curved, mostly yellow (upper part is black); tail long and rounded. Song is a long, descending staccato ending with drawn-out notes. Also utters a hoarse "towp towp towp towp."

Natural history—Occurs in cottonwood woodland and in willows along ditches. Nesting recorded in cottonwood trees, Russian olives, and Goodding willows.

Status—Widespread; generally rare to occasional. One of the latest summer residents to arrive, typically in mid-May (but species recorded as early as late April); also departs early on its fall migration (most have left by early September). Conservation-sensitive species.

Robert H. Doster

Greater Roadrunner

(*Geococcyx californianus*) ✳ ✳

JAN–DEC

Taxonomy—Class: Aves; Order: Cuculiformes; Family: Cuculidae.

Identification—Unmistakable owing to both its morphology (large size, crested head, heavy beak, and long white-tipped tail) and behavior (rarely flies; typically is seen running rapidly and in zigzags with tail trailing on the ground). Bare skin patch behind eye can be a brilliant blue and red during breeding season. Dovelike call.

Natural history—Typically found along edges of cottonwood woodland with thick understory, saltcedar stands, and other dense vegetation. Roadrunners eat lizards, small rodents, and large invertebrates, all taken on the ground, as well as nestling birds. The shallow nest is built with sticks, usually at heights of 2.5–3.5 m (8–12 ft) above ground, on the low branch of a cottonwood or in a Russian olive.

Status—Widely distributed and generally common year-round except along the northernmost Middle Rio Grande, where it becomes uncommon.

John V. Brown

Barn Owl
(Tyto alba) ✳ ✳

JAN–DEC

Taxonomy—Class: Aves; Order: Strigiformes; Family: Tytonidae.

Identification—Unmistakable. Both sexes alike with heart-shaped white facial disk (often described as monkey faced), no ear tufts, and dark eyes. Legs long and feathered. Upper parts rusty with specks of gray; underparts white to cinnamon. Does not hoot but instead utters rasping hisses, screams, and clicks.

Natural history—Found in cottonwood woodland and in burned areas. Nests in large natural tree cavities. Hunts at night, roosts in trees during the day. Diet of barn owls consists mainly of small mammals.

Status—Widespread and found year-round. Uncommon.

Jean-Luc Cartron

Western Screech-owl
(Megascops kennicottii) ✳ ✳

JAN–DEC

Taxonomy—Class: Aves; Order: Strigiformes; Family: Strigidae.

Identification—Small owl with ear tufts ("horns") that can lay flat; irises are yellow; bill is black, as is ring around facial disk. Upper parts are gray with small blackish streaks. Underparts grayish with dark bold streaks and finer barring. Song is a bouncing-ball series of notes followed by a roll.

Natural history—Largely restricted to cottonwood woodland but also occurs in saltcedar thickets. Nocturnal species whose diet consists mainly of small rodents and invertebrates. Uses natural cavities or woodpecker holes in large cottonwood trees.

Status—Widely distributed and uncommon to common.

Doug Brown

Great Horned Owl   (*Bubo virginianus*) ✳ ✳

JAN–DEC

Taxonomy—Class: Aves; Order: Strigiformes; Family: Strigidae.

Identification—Large owl with yellow eyes and prominent ear tufts. Sexes alike but female slightly larger. Grayish brown body with typically white throat patch and dark crossbarring of the breast. Utters a series of deep hoots, "Hoo-hoo-hooo—hoo-hoo."

Natural history—During the breeding season uses old hawk or crow nests in cottonwood trees. Egg laying apparently occurs in February or March, and the young (often 2 or 3) typically fledge in late April or early May. Top predator of the bosque ecosystem with a very broad diet that includes muskrats, cottontails, and pheasants.

Status—Widely distributed and uncommon.

Jean-Luc Cartron

Lesser Nighthawk   (*Chordeiles acutipennis*)

Apr, MAY–SEP

Taxonomy—Class: Aves; Order: Caprimulgiformes; Family: Caprimulgidae.

Identification—Gray and brown with white mottling above; paler with dark barring below; long tail and long wings. Male has white throat; in flight shows white band on primaries and white subterminal tail band. Female has buff throat, lacks tail band, and in flight shows a smaller, buff wing band. Similar to common nighthawk but generally flies lower and with more fluttery wing beats; wing tips are rounded rather than pointed (though common nighthawk immatures may also show this feature); light band on primaries is closer to wing tip and plumage is overall more brownish than the grayer common nighthawk. Male utters a soft yodeling as well as mewing and whining notes. Calls include a very soft trilling, which can easily be mistaken for that of an insect.

Richard Ditch

Natural history—Insectivorous; forages over open areas and ponds and wetlands.

Status—Common only in the south, including at the Bosque del Apache NWR, north to southern Valencia County; listed as occasional at Rio Grande Nature Center during spring and fall migration. Not known to nest in the bosque proper.

Common Nighthawk   (*Chordeiles minor*)

MAY–AUG, Sep

Taxonomy—Class: Aves; Order: Caprimulgiformes; Family: Caprimulgidae.

Identification—Mainly dark brown spotted with gray. Throat is white in males (photo) and buffy in females. In flight both sexes show long slender wings and conspicuous, broad white wing bar across middle of primaries (similar lesser nighthawk has white bars closer to tips of wings); long notched tail has white bar near tip in males. Often flies high with quick or erratic wing beats. Utters nasal call, "peent."

Natural history—Typically observed flying over cottonwood woodland and open areas, catching flying insects with gaping mouth.

Doug Brown

Status—One of the latest migrants to arrive, typically starting the second week of May, and earliest to depart with very few seen after August. Widespread and common. Not known to nest in the bosque proper.

Black-chinned Hummingbird   (*Archilochus alexandri*) ✳ ✳

Mar, APR–OCT

Taxonomy—Class: Aves; Order: Apodiformes; Family: Trochilidae.

Identification—Small hummingbird. Male (photo) has dark face, white collar, and greenish sides and upper parts. Under right light, black throat (or gorget) presents a purple lower band. Females and immatures are gray and white below with greenish upper parts and tail feathers showing white tips. Utters a "teew."

Natural history—Occurs mainly in cottonwood woodland and along ditches with running water; also along open riverbanks and in burned areas. Nesting season mainly from May to July. Nests are placed low to high in the canopy of cottonwoods or as low as 1.3 m (4.5 ft) in shrubs such as saltcedar and especially Russian olive. Some nests appear white due to use of cotton as nesting material. Only female cares for eggs and nestlings. Throughout nesting season, males engage in display behavior consisting of U-shaped or pendulumlike swoops accompanied by obvious, low wing buzzes. Diet includes flower nectar and insects.

Doug Brown

Status—Widely distributed and abundant.

Calliope Hummingbird

(Stellula calliope)

Jul, AUG–SEP

Taxonomy—Class: Aves; Order: Apodiformes; Family: Trochilidae.

Identification—Smallest of the 4 hummingbird species in bosque. Bill and tail are both short for hummingbird. Male (photo) has green crown and green upper parts. Whitish below with very distinctive, elongated gorget streaked with red-magenta in right light. Female similar to female rufous and broad-tailed hummingbirds (green above, white below, and with buffy sides) but smaller.

Natural history—Often concentrates along ditches in areas with flowering annuals.

Status—Widespread and common to locally abundant fall migrant, seen mainly in August and early September.

Karen Krebbs

Broad-tailed Hummingbird

(Selasphorus platycercus)

APR–MAY, Jun–Jul, AUG–SEP, Oct

Taxonomy—Class: Aves; Order: Apodiformes; Family: Trochilidae.

Identification—Medium-size hummingbird. Adult male (photo) has green crown, back, and sides and white breast and midbelly. Gorget solid rose red (Calliope's gorget has streaks of magenta on white background); may look dark when not catching light (similar to black-chinned hummingbird) but look for narrow white chin above gorget. Tail green and blackish with some rufous. Adult female has green upper parts and cinnamon sides. Throat typically flecked with green, but some females have diminutive rose gorget (rose splodges). Immature much like adult female (green above with cinnamon sides). Throat of immature male spotted with variable amounts of rose spots. Male produces shrill wing trill.

Lisa Spray

Natural history—Often seen foraging in low to midcanopy of cottonwoods or visiting flowers in openings; found also at hummingbird feeders. Peak of spring migration through bosque varies annually and can be from mid-April to third week of May; peak of fall migration is in late August and early September.

Status—Widespread. Found from April to mid-October, mainly during spring and fall migration (but much more numerous during fall migration), and in small numbers throughout late spring and early summer. Does not breed in bosque.

Rufous Hummingbird   (*Selasphorus rufus*)

JULY–SEP, Oct

Taxonomy—Class: Aves; Order: Apodiformes; Family: Trochilidae.

Identification—Typical adult male (photo) unmistakable with rufous back, sides, and tail (but very small percentage of males have mostly or only green on back); red-orange gorget; green crown; white breast and midbelly stripe. Wings make a buzzing sound in flight. Female is green above with cinnamon-rufous sides and undertail coverts (darker and more contrasting than in broad-tailed hummingbird) and whitish breast and belly. Immature male and female largely like adult female.

Natural history—Mainly along ditches but also in cottonwood woodland. Present at hummingbird feeders, where it tends to be aggressive and dominate even the larger broad-tailed hummingbird.

Status—Widespread and uncommon to common "fall" migrant, mainly from mid-August to early September. Spring migration is generally along a different route, north through California and western Arizona.

Lisa Spray

Belted Kingfisher   (*Ceryle alcyon*) ✳ ✳

JAN–DEC

Taxonomy—Class: Aves; Order: Coraciiformes; Family: Alcedinidae.

Identification—Unmistakable with its large crested head and its thick, long, pointed black bill all contrasting with small body. Both sexes are blue-gray above and mostly white below with white collar and blue belt across breast. Female (photo) also has rufous sides and chestnut belt across belly. Call, a loud, rattling chatter.

Natural history—Typically seen along ditches, less often at ponds and in the river channel. Species' diet includes fish but also aquatic invertebrates, tadpoles, insects, lizards, small mammals, and berries. Dives from a perch or hovers in midair. Regurgitates pellets made of indigestible food such as fish bones.

Status—Widespread and uncommon to locally common year-round.

Robert Shantz

Ladder-backed Woodpecker   (*Picoides scalaris*) ✳ ✳

JAN–DEC

Taxonomy—Class: Aves; Order: Piciformes;
Family: Picidae.

Identification—About the size of a downy woodpecker. Alternate white and black barring on back and wings produces zebralike pattern. Outer tail feathers are white, barred with black; middle tail feathers are black. Face white with black eye stripe and black mustache often joining posteriorly in ringlike fashion. Underparts cream with black spots and bars along sides. Male (photo) has red cap and upper nape, whereas top of female's head is black. Call, single high-pitched, hoarse, or buzzy "peek" and descending, buzzy "chee-dee-dee-dee-dee-dee."

Natural history—Primarily in cottonwood woodland but recorded also in willow vegetation along ditches. Drills holes in cottonwood trees for nesting.

Status—Uncommon to common year-round north to about Bernardo; uncommon to occasional farther north.

Doug Brown

Downy Woodpecker   (*Picoides pubescens*) ✳ ✳

JAN–DEC

Taxonomy—Class: Aves; Order: Piciformes;
Family: Picidae.

Identification—In plumage resembles the hairy woodpecker, with black and white pied head, white underparts, white mid-back (ladder-backed woodpecker has no white stripe down the center of the back), and black wings showing some white spots. Only the male (photo) has a red nape patch (ladder-backed woodpecker male has a red crown patch instead). Notably smaller than hairy woodpecker with bill much shorter than length of head and black spots on white outer tail feathers. Utters a flat, clear, soft "pick." Also produces a clear, descending "whinny" call.

Natural history—Associated with cottonwood woodland with large, mature trees but also found occasionally along ditches. Males set up nesting territories in April. The nest cavity is in the branch of a cottonwood tree. Both the male and the female feed the nestlings.

Status—Widespread. Common year-round south to about Belen; uncommon farther south.

Patrick O'Brien

Hairy Woodpecker   (*Picoides villosus*) ✻ ✻

JAN–DEC

Taxonomy—Class: Aves; Order: Piciformes; Family: Picidae.

Identification—Much larger than downy woodpecker and with longer bill and unspotted white outer tail feathers. Otherwise very similar to downy woodpecker with black and white pied head, white underparts, white midback, and black wings showing white spots. Male (photo) has red nape. Utters a loud, high-pitched "peek!" and a loud rattle.

Natural history—Restricted to cottonwood woodland. Nests in cavities excavated by both the male and the female. Forages along tree trunks and branches in search of wood-boring insects.

Status—Widespread and present year-round but uncommon (not nearly as common as downy woodpecker).

Doug Brown

Northern Flicker   (*Colaptes auratus*) ✻ ✻

JAN–DEC

Taxonomy—Class: Aves; Order: Piciformes; Family: Picidae.

Identification—Brown crown; gray cheeks and throat; brownish back and upper wings barred with black; buff belly spotted with black; black crescent across the breast; white rump as well as reddish underwings and undertail revealed in flight. Only the male (photo) has red mustache. Undulating flight. Utters 2 loud calls, "klee-yer" and "wick-a? wick-a wick wick wick . . ."

Natural history—Typical habitat year-round is cottonwood woodland with mature to senescent trees. Also found in saltcedar stands, where it is one of the most common birds in winter. Begins nesting in April. Cavity nester; the holes it excavates in cottonwoods later serve as nest cavities for other bird species. Important part of diet in bosque consists of ants captured on the ground.

Status—Widespread and common year-round.

Doug Brown

Western Wood-pewee   (*Contopus sordidulus*) ✳ ✳

MAY–SEP

Taxonomy—Class: Aves; Order: Passeriformes; Family: Tyrannidae.

Identification—Sexes alike. Sparrow size (slightly larger than *Empidonax* flycatchers) and dusky with 2 narrow, whitish wing bars and no eye ring. Utters a harsh, nasal "peee-err" and makes clicking sound with its mandible when capturing insects.

Natural history—Builds its nest (made with mud and fibrous plant material) in cottonwoods or tall Russian olives, often on dead, horizontal branches. Many nests with nestlings in late June. Captures flying insects by sallying out acrobatically from perches, including along levee road or along small clearings. Peak migration is in mid- to late May and early September.

Status—Widespread; common as spring and fall migrant and common to abundant as summer breeding resident. Nest parasitism by brown-headed cowbird recorded in bosque.

Greg W. Lasley

Willow Flycatcher   (*Empidonax traillii*) ✳ ✳

Apr, MAY, Jun–Jul, AUG–SEP, Oct

Taxonomy—Class: Aves; Order: Passeriformes; Family: Tyrannidae.

Identification—Sexes alike. Dull olive-brown upper parts; whitish throat; slight yellowish wash on belly; 2 whitish wing bars; whitish eye ring is very thin or absent. Song is "fitz-bew"; call is "whit."

Natural history—As breeding summer resident arrives in May or early June. Pure saltcedar stands, dry soils, lack of understory are all unsuitable for breeding. Nests in flooded areas, primarily in Goodding's willow, less often saltcedar and Russian olive. Nestlings hatch in June and July and are fed a diet of insects. In migration associated with willow vegetation along ditches, cottonwood woodland, and even saltcedar stands. Peak migration is in late May (spring) and late August (fall).

Jean-Luc Cattron

Status—Widespread and common in migration. The subspecies breeding in the bosque, the southwestern willow flycatcher (*Empidonax traillii extimus*), is federally listed as endangered. Nests primarily near San Marcial but breeding also recorded at the Bosque del Apache NWR.

Hammond's Flycatcher

(Empidonax hammondii)

APR–MAY, AUG–SEP

Taxonomy—Class: Aves; Order: Passeriformes; Family: Tyrannidae.

Identification—Very similar to dusky and gray flycatchers. Back olive-brown; breast gray; 2 whitish wing bars; belly more yellow than dusky flycatcher's. Constantly flicks its tail up and down (in contrast to gray flycatcher). Call, "pik" or "peek."

Natural history—Occurs in willow vegetation along ditches, in cottonwood woodland, and in saltcedar associations; also along adjacent agricultural edges, especially in spring. Midpoint of migration through bosque in spring is in mid-May; midpoint of fall migration is mid- to late September.

Status—Widespread and occasional to uncommon during spring and fall migration.

David A. Rintoul

Gray Flycatcher

(Empidonax wrightii)

APR–MAY, AUG, Sep–Oct

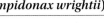

Taxonomy—Class: Aves; Order: Passeriformes; Family: Tyrannidae.

Identification—Pale gray above, whitish below with 2 pale wing bars and basal ⅔ of lower mandible pinkish yellow. Dips its tail gently (instead of flicking it like nearly identical dusky and Hammond's flycatchers). Call, "whit."

Natural history—Occurs in willow vegetation along ditches, in cottonwood woodland, and especially in saltcedar-dominated plant communities. Midpoint of migration through bosque in spring is in early May; midpoint of fall migration is during last week of August.

Status—Widespread, uncommon during spring and fall migration.

Greg W. Lasley

Dusky Flycatcher
(Empidonax oberholseri)

APR–MAY, AUG–SEP

Taxonomy—Class: Aves; Order: Passeriformes; Family: Tyrannidae.

Identification—Small and drab with narrow white eye ring and 2 wing bars. Gray upper parts with tinge of olive. Whitish underparts often with slight wash of yellow. Outer tail feathers have narrow white edge. Overall, identification of most *Empidonax* flycatchers down to the species level is tricky. Dusky flycatcher has longer tail and shorter wings than Hammond's flycatcher. Call, a soft "wit."

Natural history—Peak migration in the bosque in early to mid-May and in early September. Most strongly associated with saltcedar stands and with willows along ditches.

Status—Widespread and common (most abundant flycatcher during spring and fall migration).

Joseph V. Higbee

Black Phoebe
(Sayornis nigricans) ✳ ✳

JAN–DEC

Taxonomy—Class: Aves; Order: Passeriformes; Family: Tyrannidae.

Identification—Sexes alike. Nearly entirely black except for white belly (ending in an upside-down V in center of lower breast), undertail coverts, and wing edgings. Immature birds have cinnamon wing bars and edges to wing feathers. Most similar bird in bosque is dark-eyed junco, but black phoebe does not occur in flocks and stands erect on perch with flitting tail. Song, repetition of high-pitched, upward and downward "pitsee." Call, "tsip" or plaintive "chee."

Natural history—Typically along or above water, whether along ditches or river or at ponds. Catches insects during sallies into midair from low vegetation or bridge sides. Nest built with mud and plant material and typically secured to vertical surface under a bridge.

Status—Widespread and common.

Doug Brown

Say's Phoebe — *(Sayornis saya)* ✳ ✳

JAN–DEC

Taxonomy—Class: Aves; Order: Passeriformes; Family: Tyrannidae.

Identification—Sexes alike. Brown above with a darker crown, nape, and tail. No conspicuous wing bars. Rusty belly and vent are diagnostic as is the call, a descending, plaintive, soft "peeurr."

Natural history—Occurs in open areas along levee roads and bridges as well as along ditches and agricultural edges. Perches on low vegetation from which it darts into air or to ground to catch insects. Nests on ledges alongside bridges and buildings.

Status—Widespread and common year-round.

Doug Brown

Vermilion Flycatcher — *(Pyrocephalus rubinus)* ✳ ✳

JAN–DEC

Taxonomy—Class: Aves; Order: Passeriformes; Family: Tyrannidae.

Identification—Male (photo) has bright red underparts and crown with narrow, dark brown eye mask, dark brown upper parts, black bill. Female has white breast finely streaked with brown and salmon or pink belly and brown upper parts. Song, elated "pit-pit-pit-a-see" or "pit-a-see"; call, a sharp "pit."

Natural history—Occurs in open areas such as saltgrass meadows with scattered cottonwoods. Cup nest is in a cottonwood. Catches aerial insects during acrobatic sallies from low or high perch much like western wood-pewee.

Status—Found only in the south (Socorro and Sierra counties, including at Bosque del Apache NWR), where occasional to uncommon year-round.

Ralph Giles

Ash-throated Flycatcher

(*Myiarchus cinerascens*) ✳ ✳

APR–AUGUST, Sep

Taxonomy—Class: Aves; Order: Passeriformes; Family: Tyrannidae.

Identification—Sexes alike. Crown, brown and slightly crested; face, throat, and breast light gray; belly yellowish; back brown; wings brown with indistinct whitish bars; tail brown (both the tail and the wings have rufous highlights). Most characteristic call is a loud, rolling "pip-rrr," much like a police whistle.

Doug Brown

Natural history—Primarily associated with open cottonwood woodland and burned areas with some remaining trees or snags but also found along ditches and in stands of large saltcedars. Nesting is from May through mid-August. Usually builds its nest in a woodpecker hole either in a snag or in a dead branch of a live cottonwood; also uses nest boxes. Eats flying insects captured through aerial hawking (sallies into midair from perches).

Status—Widely distributed and common but migrates south early, and few birds are found after August.

Western Kingbird

(*Tyrannus verticalis*) ✳ ✳

APR–SEP, Oct

Taxonomy—Class: Aves; Order: Passeriformes; Family: Tyrannidae.

Identification—Large flycatcher with gray head, darkish area from bill to rear of eye, grayish olive upper parts, pale throat and upper breast, and yellow lower breast, belly, and under-tail coverts. The tail is blackish with white outer margins. The similar Cassin's kingbird (found in bosque during migration) has a buffy terminal tail band. Song, shrill "kit kit kit kiddle-dit"; call, a sharp "kit."

Lisa Spray

Natural history—Found mainly in open meadows with scattered trees, recently burned areas with snags, and drained ponds and along open banks of ditches bordering agricultural fields. Often perched on fences. Nests in mature or senescent cottonwoods and in snags (pairs often nest in close proximity to one another in adjacent trees). Along edges of bosque also nests on hardware equipment of utility poles. Aggressive around its nest toward birds of prey and crows. Diet composed largely of flying insects.

Status—Widespread and common summer breeding resident. Nearly all birds depart by end of September; stragglers possible until mid-October.

Loggerhead Shrike   (*Lanius ludovicianus*) ✳ ✳

JAN–DEC

Taxonomy—Class: Aves; Order: Passeriformes; Family: Laniidae.

Identification—Unmistakable. Gray above, white below. Head large with hooked bill and black eye mask. Wings largely black with conspicuous white patch. Tail black with white outer tail feathers. Song, a mix of repeated warbles and harsh squeaks. Calls include a harsh "shack shack."

Natural history—Associated with open saltcedar associations and other open areas. Also in fields adjacent to bosque. Preys on large insects as well as lizards, small birds, and mice. Known for impaling its prey on thorns of shrubs and trees and on barbed wire fences.

Status—Widespread and uncommon year-round.

Richard Ditch

Bell's Vireo   (*Vireo bellii*) ✳ ✳

APR–SEP

Taxonomy—Class: Aves; Order: Passeriformes; Family: Vireonidae.

Identification—Nondescript; sexes alike. Gray above, whitish or yellowish below. Faint whitish eyebrow and faint dark eye line; 1 or 2 whitish wing bars (if present the second wing bar is thin and narrow). Song, a harsh "needle needle me, needle needle you."

Natural history—Associated with shrubby thickets of Russian olives, willows, and some saltcedars but not with pure saltcedar stands. Diet consists of large and small insects.

Status—Uncommon summer breeding resident south of San Marcial. Reaches the Bosque del Apache NWR, where only occasional. Very rare farther north.

Greg W. Lasley

Plumbeous Vireo

(Vireo plumbeus) ✳

APR–MAY, Jun–Aug, SEP, Oct

Taxonomy—Class: Aves; Order: Passeriformes; Family: Vireonidae.

Identification—Gray upper parts and sides with 2 white wing bars and white spectacles. Underparts white. Similar vireos like Cassin's have greenish upper parts, while rare blue-headed vireo has a slate blue head contrasting sharply with white throat and greenish back. Call, a harsh "churr." Song is a series of warbled phrases, often sounding like questions and answers rising or falling at the end.

Natural history—Occurs in mature cottonwood woodland, along ditches, and in saltcedar-dominated communities (and also along agricultural edges). Nests in lower canopy of cottonwoods. Midpoint of spring migration through bosque is early to mid-May; midpoint of fall migration is around mid-September.

Status—Uncommon spring and fall migrant. Occasional during summer, with breeding recorded.

Warbling Vireo

(Vireo gilvus)

Apr, MAY, Jun–Jul, AUG–SEP

Taxonomy—Class: Aves; Order: Passeriformes; Family: Vireonidae.

Identification—Gray above, whitish below with a white eyebrow but no other head marking and no wing bars. Call, a harsh and rising "twee."

Natural history—Found in several habitat types, mainly ditch-side vegetation and, in fall especially, saltcedar; also along agricultural edges of bosque. Midpoint of spring migration through bosque is last week of May; midpoint of fall migration is mid- to late August. Mainly insectivorous.

Status—Common spring and fall migrant.

Western Scrub-jay

(Aphelocoma californica)

JAN–MAY, Aug, SEP–DEC

Taxonomy—Class: Aves; Order: Passeriformes; Family: Corvidae.

Identification—Crestless jay with blue head, hind neck, wings, rump, and tail. Face slightly darker. Throat is white with faint blue streaks, bordered below by dark streaky necklace. Back gray-brown; belly grayish. Call includes a loud series of harsh notes, "kwesh kwesh kwesh."

Natural history—Peak of spring migration in bosque is first week of May; peak of fall migration is during second half of September. Diet includes Russian olives.

Status—Widespread; rare to fairly common during migration and as winter visitor.

Doug Brown

American Crow

(Corvus brachyrhynchos) ✳ ✳

JAN–JUN, Jul–Sep, OCT–DEC

Taxonomy—Class: Aves; Order: Passeriformes; Family: Corvidae.

Identification—Sexes alike. Black all over with metallic violet gloss when catching the right light. Black bill is strong but not as heavy as that of larger Chihuahuan or common raven. In flight has squarish tail with rounded tip (tail is not wedge shaped like in common raven). May glide for up to 3 seconds but mostly flies with steady flapping of its wings and cannot soar like common raven. Call is "caw caw caw . . ."

Natural history—Occurs in large winter flocks in cottonwood woodland, where roosts in tall trees. Forages in nearby fields, along grassy edges of ponds, and on river sandbars; eats almost anything. Nest is in a cottonwood.

Status—Widespread. Common to locally abundant from late October through March; least common during summer but breeds in small numbers in bosque.

Bill Schmoker

Chihuahuan Raven   (*Corvus cryptoleucus*)

JAN–DEC

in air above

Taxonomy—Class: Aves; Order: Passeriformes; Family: Corvidae.

Identification—Similar to larger common raven, with glossy back plumage and heavy black bill. Under windy conditions, look for white at base of neck feathers (but note that common raven has light gray feathers at the base of its neck!). The 2 species are best distinguished by voice. Chihuahuan raven's only call is a flat, hoarse "kraaak" (common raven utters a variety of calls; "croonk, croonk" is lower pitched; "aack" higher pitched).

Natural history—Primarily a bird of arid, nonforested habitats, occurring in the bosque in open areas or flying overhead. Species' diet very diverse and includes insects, lizards, young of ground-nesting birds, and roadkills.

Status—Rare in the north; uncommon to common in the south.

Lee Zieger

Common Raven   (*Corvus corax*) ✳ ✳

JAN–DEC

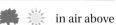

in air above

Taxonomy—Class: Aves; Order: Passeriformes; Family: Corvidae.

Identification—Sexes alike (but female smaller). Entirely glossy black with heavy black bill. In flight, tail appears wedge shaped and wings are pointed (smaller Chihuahuan raven appears similar in flight); can circle and soar like hawk. Utters several calls, including a low, deep "croonk, croonk."

Natural history—Often seen in pairs and flying over bosque. Nests in cottonwoods.

Status—Widespread; occasional to locally common. Breeds sparingly in bosque.

Doug Brown

Horned Lark   (*Eremophila alpestris*)

JAN–APR, May–Aug, SEP–DEC

Taxonomy—Class: Aves; Order: Passeriformes; Family: Alaudidae.

Identification—Brown above with some black streaking; mainly white below. Easily identified by black whisker contrasting with otherwise white face, black breast crescent, and white outer feathers of black tail. Male (photo) has 2 small horns. Call, "tsee-titi."

Natural history—Mainly a bird of agricultural areas, but winter flocks visit open areas of bosque and sandbars of river channel. Forages on the ground, relying for most of the year on seeds of weedy plants and on waste grain.

Status—Widespread. Uncommon to common during spring and fall migration and as winter resident, mainly in January and February and from September through December. Occasional in summer.

Doug Brown

Tree Swallow   (*Tachycineta bicolor*) ✳

MAR–MAY, Jun, JUL–OCT

 in air above

Taxonomy—Class: Aves; Order: Passeriformes; Family: Hirundinidae.

Identification—Sexes alike. Adults entirely metallic blue above, white below. Immatures brown above, white below. Tail notched. Distinguished from violet-green swallow by dark color reaching below eye and entirely dark rump. Call, a rapidly repeated "cheet" or "chi-veet." Song, a sweet and liquid twitter, "weet-trit-weet."

Natural history—Seen in flocks during migration. Often flies high, veering or circling back. Insectivorous. Nests in natural cavities or woodpecker holes near water. Nest site observed at Bosque del Apache NWR was woodpecker hole in willow snag in inundated area.

Status—Mainly observed during spring and fall migration, when widespread and common to abundant. Casual summer breeding resident.

Doug Brown

Violet-green Swallow (*Tachycineta thalassina*)

MAR–SEP, Oct

Taxonomy—Class: Aves; Order: Passeriformes; Family: Hirundinidae.

Identification—Sexes similar. Dark upper parts have violet-green gloss; underparts are white. Distinguished from tree swallow by white patches on sides of rump that almost merge in the middle and by white on face extending above and behind eyes. Notched tail. Utters a high, thin "chip." Song is sometimes compared to the noise of a high-tension wire.

Natural history—May occur in large flocks during migration, especially in spring along ditches. Eats flying insects captured on the wing.

Status—Widespread. Common spring and fall migrant. Rare to uncommon summer visitor but not known to nest in bosque.

Doug Brown

Northern Rough-winged Swallow (*Stelgidopteryx serripennis*) ✳✳

Feb, MAR–SEP, Oct

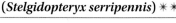

Taxonomy—Class: Aves; Order: Passeriformes; Family: Hirundinidae.

Identification—Grayish brown above; throat and breast pale brown (lacks clearly defined dark breast band of bank swallow); belly whitish; tail notched. Utters a raspy "brrrtt."

Natural history—Occurs mainly along agricultural edges of bosque but also often along ditches and among cottonwoods. Often solitary; may also occur in mixed flocks with other swallows. Eats aerial insects; nests in burrows along banks.

Status—Uncommon to common spring and fall migrant and summer resident. Widespread.

Doug Brown

Bank Swallow

(Riparia riparia) ✳ ✳

Mar, APR–SEP

Taxonomy—Class: Aves; Order: Passeriformes; Family: Hirundinidae.

Identification—Small swallow with brown upper parts. Sexes alike. White underparts with dark band across breast are diagnostic. Call very similar to northern rough-winged swallow's but somewhat harsher and usually given in a connected series "brrrrt, brrrrt, brrrrt, brrrrt."

Natural history—Nests in colonies in sand or mud banks along ditches. Male and female dig a burrow at the end of which they build the nest. Incubation of the eggs by both sexes. Eats flying insects.

Status—Widespread and uncommon as spring and fall migrant; rare to locally uncommon breeding summer resident in the Albuquerque area.

Greg W. Lasley

Cliff Swallow

(Petrochelidon pyrrhonota) ✳ ✳

MAR–SEP, Oct

Taxonomy—Class: Aves; Order: Passeriformes; Family: Hirundinidae.

Identification—Sexes alike. White forehead; dark blue crown, back, wings, and tail; chestnut face and throat; whitish underparts. Tail is squarish, not forked (see barn swallow). Immature has brown crown and back. Song, harsh creaks and gratings; calls include a soft "chur."

Natural history—Beginning in April, nests in colonies (up to 200 pairs) along the sides of main river bridges; smaller colonies alongside ditch bridges and in ditch culverts. The mud nest is enclosed with an entrance on side (barn swallow nest is an open cup). Foraging is conducted through glides and circles over river channel and along ditches. Diet composed of flying insects.

Status—Widespread and common during migration; locally common or abundant during nesting.

Richard Ditch

Barn Swallow

(Hirunda rustica) ✳ ✳

MAR–OCT

Taxonomy—Class: Aves; Order: Passeriformes; Family: Hirundinidae.

Identification—Unmistakable: glossy blue above and orange below (the throat and forehead are darker than the breast and the belly) with forked tail. White spots on tail. Female a little duller than male. Immature whitish below. Song, long and melodious twitter interspersed with gurgles. Calls include a soft "vit vit."

Natural history—Nests in small colonies under river bridges and under eaves of nearby buildings. Nest is built mainly with mud and plastered against vertical surface of supporting beam. Flies mainly over river, open riverbanks, and ponds and along ditches in pursuit of flying insects.

Status—Widespread. Uncommon to common during migration; common to abundant during nesting. Can occur in very large flocks in early October.

Doug Brown

Black-capped Chickadee

(Poecile atricapillus) ✳ ✳

JAN–DEC

Taxonomy—Class: Aves; Order: Passeriformes; Family: Paridae.

Identification—Diminutive bird with small bill. Cap and throat black, side of head below eye white (mountain chickadee has white line over eye). Olive-gray back with prominent white edges to secondaries on somewhat darker gray wings; white belly; buffy sides. Call is a well-enunciated "chick-a-dee-dee-dee"; song is a whistle, "fee-bee."

Natural history—Found in cottonwood woodland, often in family groups. Relies mainly on insects and spiders for its diet but also frequents bird feeders. Cavity nester.

Status—Common year-round in bosque in Bernalillo and Sandoval counties and, at least during nesting season, as far south as extreme northern Socorro County. Accidental farther south as far as Bosque del Apache NWR.

Doug Brown

Mountain Chickadee

(*Poecile gambeli*) ✳ ✳

JAN–MAR, Apr–Sep, OCT–DEC

Taxonomy—Class: Aves; Order: Passeriformes; Family: Paridae.

Identification—Similar to black-capped chickadee but with black eye line separated from black crown by white line over eye; also sides gray rather than buffy. Song resembles that of black-capped chickadee but with 1 additional whistled note; call raspier than in black-capped chickadee.

Natural history—Shares its habitat with black-capped chickadee, and hybridization occurs between the 2 species (bosque is one of a few places where this has been observed in the U.S.). May occur in flocks in winter. Cavity nester.

Status—Widespread. Uncommon to common winter resident; rare to occasional summer breeding resident in bosque in Bernalillo, Valencia, and northern Socorro counties.

Doug Brown

Verdin

(*Auriparus flaviceps*) ✳ ✳

JAN–DEC

Taxonomy—Class: Aves; Order: Passeriformes; Family: Remizidae.

Identification—Sexes similar. Very small with short, thin bill; light gray below, gray above with yellow face and throat and dark red patch at shoulder, often difficult to see. Juvenile lacks yellow and dark red markings; distinguished from bushtit by shorter tail. Call, a series of "chip" notes in rapid succession.

Natural history—Associated with mesquite vegetation outside the current floodplain. Marginal to the bosque ecosystem as defined here but found in willows along ditches. Builds conspicuous nests in mesquite stands for breeding and for roosting. Species' diet consists of invertebrates, fruit, and seeds.

Status—Found almost exclusively in the south, where an uncommon year-round resident. Very rare in southern Valencia County and north.

Patrick O'Brien

Bushtit

(Psaltriparus minimus) ✳ ✳

JAN–DEC

Taxonomy—Class: Aves; Order: Passeriformes; Family: Aegithalidae.

Identification—Very small, plain bird with tiny bill and long tail. Gray above with brown cheeks. Pale gray below. Females have yellow eyes; males (photo) dark eyes. Call is a weak, high "tsit," but groups will call often continually, becoming very noticeable.

Natural history—In winter occurs in straggling flocks of up to 30, flying from small tree to small tree. Nesting season begins in April. Nest is pendular bag hanging from lower, drooping terminal branch of cottonwood, partially concealed in cluster of leaves. Entrance is along 1 side near top. Parents may be assisted by non-breeding helpers. Eats mostly insects.

Status—Widespread and common in all seasons.

White-breasted Nuthatch

(Sitta carolinensis) ✳ ✳

JAN–DEC

Taxonomy—Class: Aves; Order: Passeriformes; Family: Sittidae.

Identification—Sexes alike. White face and underparts with varying amounts of rust on sides and undertail coverts; black eyes; black cap and nape; and blue-gray back. Call is a fast series of nasal notes.

Natural history—Strongly associated with stands of large cottonwood trees. Usually nests in a woodpecker hole or in a natural cavity in the dead branch of a live tree but also uses nest boxes. Both parents feed the young. Hunts for insects along tree trunks and large branches, often moving headfirst toward the ground. In fall and winter also visits bird feeders.

Status—Widely distributed and common in all seasons.

Brown Creeper

*(**Certhia americana**)* ✳

JAN–APR, May–Sep, OCT–DEC

Taxonomy—Class: Aves; Order: Passeriformes; Family: Certhiidae.

Identification—Sexes alike. Small, cryptically colored with thin, decurved bill. Brown upper parts streaked with white or buff; rump rufous; brown tail stiff and used as a prop when climbing trees; white underparts. White line above eye. Song, a high-pitched "Seeeee, now you see me." Call, "seep," high pitched and drawn out.

Natural history—Searches for insects moving up and in spirals around tree trunks and exploring underside of branches before flying to next tree, where it begins ascending again from near base of trunk. Nest may be in a woodpecker hole or under loose bark along a tree trunk.

Status—Widespread, uncommon during fall and winter; rare in mid- and late spring and in summer but breeding recorded.

Bewick's Wren

*(**Thryomanes bewickii**)* ✳ ✳

JAN–DEC

Taxonomy—Class: Aves; Order: Passeriformes; Family: Troglodytidae.

Identification—Medium-size wren with a slender, slightly decurved bill. Brown upper parts, white eyebrow, and white underparts. Wings and tail barred with black. Tail often held upright with outer tail feathers showing white between the black crossbars. Song varied but often a melodious and rapid "chip, chip, chip, de-da-a, teeeeee-dee" ("teeeeee" is a trill). Call is a harsh buzz.

Natural history—Found in highest densities in cottonwood woodland with an understory of saltcedar and usually observed on the ground or perched low in shrubs or in tangles of dead, fallen branches. Builds a cup nest in a woodpecker hole or in a natural cavity, most often in a cottonwood tree; also uses nest boxes or fallen logs. Nesting begins in March, and the first young may fledge in early to mid-May (but fledgling also recorded in early to mid-August). Nestlings are fed insects, including many crickets.

Status—Widespread and common year-round resident (breeding populations established themselves only recently and likely due in part to the spread of saltcedar).

House Wren
(Troglodytes aedon)

Jan–Apr, MAY, AUG–OCT, Nov–Dec

Taxonomy—Class: Aves; Order: Passeriformes; Family: Troglodytidae.

Identification—Small wren; brown above, medium to dark buff below. Note very indistinct buffy eyebrow and fine black barring on wings and tail, which is usually kept cocked up. Call, a sharp "chek."

Natural history—Most abundant along adjacent agricultural field edges but also in cottonwood woodland, among coyote willows along ditches, and in saltcedar. Eats insects. Midpoint of spring migration is mid-May; midpoint of fall migration is mid-September.

Status—Widespread. Common during spring and fall migration; rare in winter.

Greg W. Lasley

Marsh Wren
(Cistothorus palustris)

JAN–APR, May–Aug, SEP–DEC

Taxonomy—Class: Aves; Order: Passeriformes; Family: Troglodytidae.

Identification—Small with short, thin bill. Readily identified by combination of white eyebrow and black and white stripes on back. Wings, rump, and tail brown to rufous; crown black; underparts mostly white with pale brownish sides. Call, loud "check."

Natural history—Found primarily on ditch-side vegetation and at ponds and wetlands, especially among cattails. Also occurs in cottonwood woodland during migration. Eats insects.

Status—Widespread. Uncommon to locally common in fall, winter, and spring; rare in summer.

Greg W. Lasley

Ruby-crowned Kinglet

(Regulus calendula)

JAN–APR, SEP–DEC

Taxonomy—Class: Aves; Order: Passeriformes; Family: Regulidae.

Identification—Very small, with olive-gray upper body; white eye ring most pronounced at front and rear of eye; and 2 white wing bars (1 may be hidden). The male's (photo) red crown patch is often concealed. Call, a quick and scolding "ji-dit."

Natural history—Habitat generalist in bosque. Eats insects captured while hovering at twigs or during sallies from perches into midair. Diet also includes Russian olives.

Status—Widely distributed and uncommon to locally common during nonbreeding season.

Doug Brown

Blue-gray Gnatcatcher

(Polioptila caerulea)

Jan–Mar, APR–MAY, AUG–OCT, Nov–Dec

Taxonomy—Class: Aves; Order: Passeriformes; Family: Sylviidae.

Identification—Slender bird, blue gray above, white below. White eye ring. Tail long and black with white outer feathers, often wagged sideways or cocked like wren's. Call, a high nasal "pwee?"

Natural history—Midpoint of spring migration in bosque is late April; midpoint of fall migration is mid-September. Often perched in understory vegetation. Eats insects.

Status—Widespread. Uncommon spring and fall migrant; rare in winter.

Greg W. Lasley

Eastern Bluebird   (*Sialia sialis*) ✳ ✳

JAN–DEC

Taxonomy—Class: Aves; Order: Passeriformes; Family: Turdidae.

Identification—Male (photo) has bright blue upper parts; orange chin, throat, side of neck, and breast (male western bluebird has blue chin and an orange triangle in the back); and sharply contrasting white belly. Female similar but with blue-gray head and back. Juvenile is spotted. All birds often appear hunched when perched. Song is a melodious whistling, "cheer cheery charley"; call is a short, ringing "chir-lee."

Natural history—Found in cottonwood woodland and large openings (including burned areas) but only where an understory of shrubs is lacking. Nests in woodpecker holes in snags or live cottonwoods. Also uses nest boxes. Often seen fluttering to the ground from branch of cottonwood as it hunts insects. Diet also includes berries.

Status—Widespread and uncommon to common year-round. The species continues to expand westward and is a very recent addition to the Middle Rio Grande bosque fauna. Has greatly benefited from the occurrence of wild-fires and restoration projects leading to the removal of shrubs.

Doug Brown

Western Bluebird   (*Sialia mexicana*)

JAN–MAR, Apr–May, Jul–Sep, OCT–DEC

Taxonomy—Class: Aves; Order: Passeriformes; Family: Turdidae.

Identification—Male (photo) has blue head, throat, wings, and tail; rusty flanks and breast; and gray-ish belly (compare with eastern bluebird). Back has varying amount of blue and rust. Female has some blue in wings and tail; otherwise duller than male, grayish instead of blue and pale cinnamon instead of rusty. Immatures are grayish with speckled breast and some blue in tail and wings. Calls include a soft and short "phew."

Natural history—Often found along ditches lined with Russian olives and in cottonwood woodland visiting trees with mistletoe berries; also occurs in open areas.

Status—Widespread and uncommon to common in fall and winter. May also be seen in spring and summer, but not known to nest in the bosque.

Gordon French

Mountain Bluebird   (*Sialia currucoides*)

JAN–MAR, OCT–DEC

Taxonomy—Class: Aves; Order: Passeriformes; Family: Turdidae.

Identification—Male (photo) bright blue above, paler below with whitish belly. Female duller than male with blue rump and blue in wings; brown-gray throat, back, and head; and white eye ring. Immature similar to female but spotted below. Call, a low-pitched "chur."

Natural history—May occur as single birds or in very large flocks, including on sandbars of the river channel. Hunts insects by hovering low, then dropping to the ground, or by sallying out flycatcher-like from low branch into open air.

Status—Widespread and uncommon from late October to early March.

Doug Brown

Hermit Thrush   (*Catharus guttatus*)

JAN–MAY, SEP–DEC

Taxonomy—Class: Aves; Order: Passeriformes; Family: Turdidae.

Identification—Sexes alike. Brown above with narrow white eye ring and brown-spotted white breast. Rump and tail range in color from pronounced rufous to almost as brown as back. Often cocks, then lowers its tail. Tends to hide in underbrush, where most easily detected by call note, a low "chup."

Natural history—Favors thick, brushy areas with New Mexico or Russian olive. Peak migration in early to mid-May and mid-October.

Status—Widely distributed. Common during spring and fall migration; generally uncommon winter resident.

Patrick O'Brien

American Robin (*Turdus migratorius*) ✳ ✳

JAN–DEC

Taxonomy—Class: Aves; Order: Passeriformes; Family: Turdidae.

Identification—Relatively large with slender yellowish bill, dark gray-brown upper parts and face, white eye ring, orange breast, and white throat with dark stripes. Sexes are almost identical, but males are more richly colored. The breast of the immature is speckled or spotted with brown. Song is a series of clear and cheerful phrases rising and falling. Has several calls, including a "weep"; alarm call is a loud "squeet!"

Natural history—Associated with several habitat types including cottonwood woodland and, in winter especially, saltcedar-dominated vegetation. Often nests in lower canopy of cottonwoods (but density of breeding pairs generally lower than in adjacent urban areas). Invertebrates are essential part of the species' diet. In bosque also eats fruit of Russian olive, New Mexico olive, and mulberry.

Status—Widely distributed; common to locally abundant during spring and fall migration and in some years during the winter. Common during summer.

Gray Catbird (*Dumetella carolinensis*) ✳ ✳

Jan–Apr, MAY–SEP, Oct–Dec

Taxonomy—Class: Aves; Order: Passeriformes; Family: Mimidae.

Identification—Sexes alike. Uniformly slate gray with black cap and tail and chestnut undertail coverts. Bill slightly decurved. Call, a catlike "mew" somewhat descending. Song disjointed and variable. Can imitate other birds.

Natural history—Preferred nesting habitat is thick ditch-side vegetation, often with willow, and cottonwood woodland with a thick Russian olive understory; also recorded in migration in saltcedar-dominated plant communities. Typically nests in Russian olives. Midpoint of spring migration through bosque is late May; midpoint of fall migration is mid- to late September.

Status—Widespread. Uncommon spring and fall migrant and summer resident; rare in winter.

Northern Mockingbird

(Mimus polyglottos) ✳ ✳

Jan–Mar, APR–AUG, Sep–Dec

Taxonomy—Class: Aves; Order: Passeriformes; Family: Mimidae.

Identification—Sexes alike. Mainly gray above with dark tail; paler below. Slender, slightly curved bill. Large white patches on wings and white outer tail feathers revealed in flight. Imitates the songs of other species, repeating each musical phrase several times. Call, a loud "chak!"

Natural history—Particularly common in open areas with scattered young cottonwoods and in open salt-cedar associations. Less common in cottonwood woodland. Nest is placed low, often in a young cottonwood (also in New Mexico olive or in saltcedar). More difficult to see in fall and winter, when hides in brush. Eats insects and fruit.

Status—Widespread and common from April through July (north) or August (south). In fall and winter, nearly all birds withdraw south from Valencia County north and species is much more regular from Socorro County south.

European Starling

(Sturnus vulgaris) ✳ ✳ [INT]

JAN–DEC

Taxonomy—Class: Aves; Order: Passeriformes; Family: Sturnidae.

Identification—Sexes alike. During spring and summer (photo), black with iridescent green and purple gloss, some brown, and very small white spots; yellow bill. During winter, duller with black, green, and brown and heavily speckled with white. Short, square wings, triangular in flight. Juvenile resembles female cowbird with a long bill. Utters a chorus of whistles, clicks, warbles, and other sounds. Imitates the calls and songs of other birds.

Natural history—Uses all habitats but mainly found along edge of cottonwood woodland and along drains lined with cottonwoods, in both urban and farmland areas. Nests in natural cavities and old flicker holes in cottonwood trees. Competes for nest cavities with flickers and other native birds. Nesting birds usually fly to field or other open area outside the bosque to forage, then return to nest with food.

Status—Widespread and common to locally abundant year-round.

American Pipit
(Anthus rubescens)

JAN–APR, May, SEP–DEC

Taxonomy—Class: Aves; Order: Passeriformes; Family: Motacillidae.

Identification—Sparrow size, often confused for northern waterthrush. Gray-brown above; underparts buffy with streaking on breast and sides. White eye ring. White outer tail feathers revealed during flight, which is undulating. Walks with bobbing and wagging of tail and nodding of head. Call, "pi-pit."

Natural history—Occurs in flocks on river sandbars, along ditches, in open areas, and at ponds and wetlands; also in plowed fields adjacent to bosque. Searches for insects on the ground.

Status—Widespread and uncommon to common from late September through April.

Gordon French

Cedar Waxwing
(Bombycilla cedrorum)

JAN–MAY, Jun, Aug, SEP–DEC

Taxonomy—Class: Aves; Order: Passeriformes; Family: Bombycillidae.

Identification—Sexes similar. Conspicuous crest; short, slightly hooked bill; black forehead and eye mask bordered with white on brown face; brown back and breast; gray wings with red tips on secondaries; yellow belly; broad yellow tip on dark gray tail; white undertail coverts. Call, a high querulous (or wavering) "zeeeee."

Natural history—Occurs in flocks, often in the canopy of cottonwood trees. Feeds on fruit, including Russian olive and mulberry in bosque.

Status—Widespread. Numbers vary annually but overall uncommon to common; seen as late as May (early June) in spring.

Doug Brown

Phainopepla

(*Phainopepla nitens*) ✶ ✶

Jan–Apr, MAY–SEP, Oct–Dec

Taxonomy—Class: Aves; Order: Passeriformes; Family: Ptilogonatidae.

Identification—Male (photo) unmistakable: glossy black all over with red eyes, tall crest, long tail, and white wing patches revealed in flight. Female and juvenile gray with pale wing patches and no yellow band on tail (unlike waxwing). Song, complex, includes a whistled "wheeda-lay." Call, a low, rising "wurp?"

Natural history—Strongly tied to cottonwood woodland with abundant mistletoe and a native understory of New Mexico olives. Nests mostly in cottonwood trees, less often in saltcedars. Feeds on fruit of New Mexico olives and mistletoes.

Status—Primarily in the south, where locally common in spring and summer during most years (but numbers fluctuate from year to year) and rare in winter.

Lisa Spray

Orange-crowned Warbler

(*Vermivora celata*)

Jan–Mar, APR–MAY, AUG–OCT, Nov–Dec

Taxonomy—Class: Aves; Order: Passeriformes; Family: Parulidae.

Identification—Few distinctive features. Grayish olive upper parts; greenish yellow underparts. Head color can range from bright yellow to gray with darkish line through eye and yellowish line over eye. No wing bars. Orange crown patch larger in male (photo) than in female or immature, concealed except when crown feathers raised. Call is a soft "tsip."

Doug Brown

Natural history—Preferred habitat is ditch-side vegetation in spring, along with cottonwood woodland with an understory of Russian olive in late summer and fall (at that time also strongly associated with agricultural edges adjacent to bosque). Midpoint of spring migration is during first half of May; midpoint of fall migration is mid- to late September.

Status—Widespread. Common in spring migration, abundant during fall migration. Rare in winter.

Virginia's Warbler

(*Vermivora virginiae*)

APR–MAY, Jul, AUG–SEP

Taxonomy—Class: Aves; Order: Passeriformes; Family: Parulidae.

Identification—Small warbler, gray above, light below and easily identified by yellow rump and undertail coverts (similar Lucy's warbler has chestnut rump), yellow wash on breast, and conspicuous white eye ring. Chestnut patch on crown usually concealed. Female is duller than male, with smaller crown patch. Immatures similar to adult female but with more brown above. Call a metallic "chink."

Natural history—Found in willows along ditches, in cottonwood woodland, and in saltcedar. Also occurs along adjacent field edges. Midpoint of spring migration in bosque is early to mid-May; midpoint of fall migration is late August.

Status—Widespread and uncommon to common spring and fall migrant. Occasional during early summer.

Lucy's Warbler

(*Vermivora luciae*) ✳ ✳

MAR–SEP

Taxonomy—Class: Aves; Order: Passeriformes; Family: Parulidae.

Identification—Very small, with gray upper parts and whitish underparts. Rufous rump, light pinkish wash on sides, and thin white eye ring. Male (photo) has a red-brown crown patch (often hidden). Song, high and beginning with double notes, "whee-tee, whee-tee, chi, chi, chi." Call is a metallic "chink."

Natural history—Nests in natural cavities or woodpecker holes of cottonwood trees at heights of up to 9 m (30 ft). (Lucy's warbler is the only cavity nester among warblers of the western U.S.) Mostly insectivorous.

Status—Uncommon as spring and fall migrant and as summer breeding resident in the south. Found north to northern Socorro County and spreading north gradually.

Yellow Warbler
(Dendroica petechia) ✳ ✳

APR–SEP

Taxonomy—Class: Aves; Order: Passeriformes; Family: Parulidae.

Identification—Both male and female have bright yellow underparts and side of face and olive-yellow upper parts with yellow tail spots; wing feathers have some black in their centers. Dark eye obvious on face. Male (photo) has breast and sides streaked with reddish chestnut. Song is a loud "See-see-see-I'm-so-sweet." Call, a loud, sweet "chip."

Natural history—Mainly along ditch-side (willow) vegetation but also in cottonwood woodland, along agricultural edges, and in saltcedar associations (in spring). Nests appear to be in ditch-side willow thickets. Midpoint of spring migration through bosque is mid-May; midpoint of fall migration is late August. Insectivorous.

Status—Widespread and abundant during spring and fall migration; uncommon as summer breeding resident.

Robert Shantz

Yellow-rumped Warbler
(Dendroica coronata)

JAN–MAY, Aug, SEP–DEC

Taxonomy—Class: Aves; Order: Passeriformes; Family: Parulidae. Audubon warbler is the western race; myrtle warbler is the eastern race.

Identification—Yellow rump, crown spot, and sides of breast (less conspicuous in female and during winter) are diagnostic. In full plumage, male's upper parts are bluish gray with back streaked with black and black breast patch. Male of Audubon race (photo) has yellow throat and white wing patch. Male of myrtle race (generally not nearly as common) has white throat and 2 white wing bars (instead of wing patch). Female duller. Call, a soft, low-pitched "chuck."

Doug Brown

Natural history—Occurs in cottonwood woodland, along ditches lined with willows or Russian olives, and along agricultural edges. Also in saltcedar-dominated communities but only in the fall and not in high numbers. Peak migration in the bosque is late April to early May (spring migration) and late September to early October (fall migration).

Status—Widespread. One of the most abundant warblers during migration; especially common in fall. In winter uncommon but often the only warbler found north of Socorro County.

Townsend's Warbler   (*Dendroica townsendi*)

Apr–May, AUG–OCT

Taxonomy—Class: Aves; Order: Passeriformes;
Family: Parulidae.

Identification—Distinctive warbler with mostly yellow face, dark crown and cheek patch separated by broad yellow eyebrow, and small yellow crescent under eye; 2 white wing bars, yellow breast, and white belly with black streaks. Crown and cheek patch are black in adult male, dark green in female. Throat is black in male, yellow in female. Immature similar to adult female. Call is a loud, flat "chap." Male's song, a series of buzzy notes, "zee zee zee zee dee du dee," may be heard during spring migration.

Natural history—Seems more strongly associated with saltcedar stands and ditch-side willow vegetation in spring, cottonwood woodland in fall. Midpoint of fall migration is mid-September. Diet consists largely of insects.

Status—Occasional spring and uncommon fall migrant.

Northern Waterthrush   (*Seiurus noveboracensis*)

MAY, AUG–SEP

Taxonomy—Class: Aves; Order: Passeriformes;
Family: Parulidae.

Identification—Resembles small thrush. Sexes alike. Upper parts are brown with conspicuous tan eyebrow. Whitish underparts are streaked with dark. Legs are pink. Similar ovenbird (rare in bosque) lacks eyebrow but has orange crown patch edged by black lateral stripes. Often bobs its tail. Call, a loud, sharp "chink."

Natural history—Typically found on the ground along ditches and at the edge of small pools of water, where it hunts for insects. Midpoint of migration in spring is around mid-May; midpoint of fall migration is early September.

Status—Widespread; occasional to uncommon spring and fall migrant. Very rare in winter.

MacGillivray's Warbler (*Oporornis tolmiei*)

MAY, AUG–SEP

Taxonomy—Class: Aves; Order: Passeriformes; Family: Parulidae.

Identification—Male (photo) has slate gray hood (head, nape, and breast), partial white eye ring, yellow belly and undertail, olive back and upper tail, and pink legs. Female similar but hood not as conspicuous and tinged with brown above; paler below. Call is a loud "check."

Natural history—Often difficult to see as it forages in dense, shrubby vegetation. Found typically in cottonwood woodland (especially with an understory of Russian olive), in willow vegetation along ditches, and even in saltcedar communities; also along agricultural edges. Midpoint of spring migration through bosque is mid-May; midpoint of fall migration is early September.

Status—Abundant spring and fall migrant.

Common Yellowthroat (*Geothlypis trichas*) ✳ ✳

Jan–Mar, APR–OCT, Nov–Dec

Taxonomy—Class: Aves; Order: Passeriformes; Family: Parulidae.

Identification—Male (photo) olive above with black facial mask bordered above by broad white line, yellow throat and breast, and whitish belly. Female lacks black facial mask but otherwise similar. Easily identified by song, a repeated "witchity, witchity, witchity." Call, a sharp "chap."

Natural history—Secretive bird usually found along ponds and wetlands and on moist or seasonally flooded riverbanks. Nest is built very low, only about 30 cm (1 ft) above ground. Eats insects. Midpoint of spring migration is mid-May; midpoint of fall migration is early September.

Status—Widespread and common during migration and as breeding summer resident. Rare in winter as far north as Albuquerque.

Wilson's Warbler   (*Wilsonia pusilla*)

APR–MAY, JUL–OCT

Taxonomy—Class: Aves; Order: Passeriformes; Family: Parulidae.

Identification—Yellow underparts; greenish upper parts. Dark eye obvious on face. Adult male (photo) has black round cap. Female is a duller version of the male with olive replacing the black cap. Call, a sharp "tip" or "timp."

Natural history—Strongly associated with ditch-side willow vegetation during spring migration. More of a generalist during fall migration with increased use of cottonwood stands and agricultural edges. Males tend to migrate earlier than females, and stopover is typically short. Wilson's warbler is a foliage-gleaning insectivorous species.

Status—Widespread. One of the most abundant spring and fall migrants in the bosque, occurring in April and May and from late July through mid-October, mainly in May and September. Only 1 overwintering record.

Jean-Luc Cartron

Yellow-breasted Chat   (*Icteria virens*) ✴ ✴

APR–OCT

Taxonomy—Class: Aves; Order: Passeriformes; Family: Parulidae.

Identification—Sexes similar. Olive green above; yellow throat and breast; whitish belly. Curved bill, white "spectacles." Long tail. Song is medley of whistles, clucks, and other sounds, reminiscent of mockingbird. Call, a loud "chack."

Natural history—Secretive bird. Prefers willow and Russian olive thickets along riverbanks; occasionally also in dense saltcedar in mature cottonwood woodland. Nest is typically in a willow or a Russian olive at a height of 1.5 m (5 ft) or less. Eggs typically in June; nests frequently parasitized by brown-headed cowbird. Midpoint of spring migration is latter part of May, midpoint of fall migration is late August to early September.

Status—Widespread. Common from late April through early October (but may be difficult to detect in migration if not singing or calling).

Doug Brown

Summer Tanager (*Piranga rubra*) ✴✴

APR–SEP, Oct

Taxonomy—Class: Aves; Order: Passeriformes; Family: Thaupidae.

Identification—Male (photo) is rose red with pale thick bill and no crest. Female is olive above and yellow below. Most frequent and characteristic call is a "pih-ti-tuck." Song is a melodious warble similar to that of an American robin.

Natural history—Usually nests in the foliage of cottonwood trees (but nests in Russian olive and Goodding's willow also observed). Some nests are parasitized by brown-headed cowbird. Eats mostly insects but diet also includes Russian olives. Midpoint of spring migration through bosque is mid-May; midpoint of fall migration is late August.

Status—Widespread and common from late April to late September, with the last fall migrants observed in early October.

Jean-Luc Cartron

Western Tanager (*Piranga ludoviciana*)

MAY, Jun, JUL–SEP, Oct

Taxonomy—Class: Aves; Order: Passeriformes; Family: Thaupidae.

Identification—Male (photo) has deep orange-red head; yellow underparts and rump; and black back, wings, and tail. Wings have 2 wing bars, 1 yellow, the other white. Female is greenish above and yellow below; also has 2 wing bars on dark wings. Call, a slurred "per-dick."

Natural history—Primarily found in cottonwood woodland, where perches in canopy of trees; also along ditches and agricultural edges. Diet in bosque includes Russian olives.

Status—Widespread and common during spring and fall migration. Not known to nest in bosque despite sightings of this species during breeding season.

Doug Brown

Green-tailed Towhee

(Pipilo chlorurus)

Jan–Mar, APR–MAY, Aug, SEP, Oct–Dec

Taxonomy—Class: Aves; Order: Passeriformes; Family: Emberizidae.

Identification—Sexes alike. Rufous cap, gray face, black mustache, white throat, gray breast and sides, and olive green back and tail. Call, a short catlike "mew."

Natural history—Resembles its close relative the spotted towhee in its choice of habitats and in its behavior. Associated with shrubby ditch vegetation, cottonwood woodland, and saltcedar stands during spring and fall. Scratches the ground in search of worms and insects. Also eats seeds.

Status—Widespread and common as a spring and fall migrant. Occasional during winter.

Doug Brown

Spotted Towhee

(Pipilo maculatus) ✳ ✳

JAN–DEC

Taxonomy—Class: Aves; Order: Passeriformes; Family: Emberizidae.

Identification—Head and breast are black (male; photo) or dusty black (female); eyes red; sides rufous; wings, rump, and tail are black (male) or dusty black (female); white spots on the wings and back; white underparts and outer tail feathers. Song, "chup chup chup zeeeeeee." Call, a rising "weee."

Natural history—Found mainly in cottonwood woodland especially in association with understory thickets; also strongly associated with dense ditch-side vegetation. Typically perches on shrubs and on the ground, where it searches for worms and insects. Typical foraging technique is a backward rakelike scratching move among leaves. Seeds also a large component of the diet, especially during nonbreeding season. Nest is placed on the ground or in low, thick vegetation (e.g., wolfberry patch, saltcedar). Spotted towhee nests are often parasitized by the brown-headed cowbird.

Doug Brown

Status—Widespread and found year-round. One of the most abundant nesting species in suitable habitat; not as abundant in winter. With recent clearing of saltcedar and Russian olive the species may become less common, especially in summer.

Chipping Sparrow (*Spizella passerina*) ✳ ✳

Jan–Mar, APR–OCT, Nov–Dec

Taxonomy—Class: Aves; Order: Passeriformes; Family: Emberizidae.

Identification—Small sparrow best identified from other small sparrows by its black eye line. Also has bright rufous cap in breeding season, white eyebrow, and gray cheek. Brown back is streaked with black; grayish underparts are unstreaked. Fall plumage is highly variable. Immature birds plain brown, streaked all over. Call, "tsee-ip"; song, a fast-trilled "chip chip chip . . ." all given on same tone.

Natural history—In migration occurs mostly in saltcedar associations and ditch-side vegetation and in lower numbers also in cottonwood woodland. In fall favors agricultural edges rather than bosque itself. During summer found in cottonwood woodland, where a few nests recorded in Rocky Mountain juniper and Russian olive. Midpoint of spring migration through bosque is first week of May; midpoint of fall migration is mid-September.

Status—Widespread and common as spring migrant, abundant during fall migration. Occasional to locally uncommon summer resident. In winter, occasional to rare in southern areas.

Lark Sparrow (*Chondestes grammacus*) ✳ ✳

Mar, APR–SEP

Taxonomy—Class: Aves; Order: Passeriformes; Family: Emberizidae.

Identification—Sexes alike. Readily identified by dark central spot on whitish breast, white outer tail corners, and distinctive harlequin head pattern: chestnut crown with white median stripe at top, white line over eye, narrow black eye line, chestnut cheek, and black malar stripe. Juvenile similar to adult but has streaked breast. Song, with clear notes, buzzing, and trills and interrupted by pauses. Call, a sharp "tsip."

Natural history—Found mainly along agricultural edges of bosque but also in open grassy areas, along ditches, and more occasionally in cottonwood woodland. Nests near ground at the base of shrubs, including young saltcedars. Midpoint of spring migration through bosque is early May; midpoint of fall migration is late August.

Status—Widespread. Common during spring and fall migration and as breeding summer resident.

Savannah Sparrow   (*Passerculus sandwichensis*)

JAN–APR, Aug, SEP–DEC

Taxonomy—Class: Aves; Order: Passeriformes; Family: Emberizidae.

Identification—Sexes similar. Brown upper parts streaked with black; underparts whitish with dark streaks over breast and sides and possible central spot on breast; legs pink or flesh colored. Stripe over eye typically tinged with yellow and often with white stripe through top of crown. Call, "tsip."

Natural history—Often forages in small flocks; eats insects and seeds. Midpoint of spring migration is mid- to late April; midpoint of fall migration is around mid-October. Mainly in agricultural fields adjacent to bosque in fall.

Status—Widespread. Common during migration especially in fall; uncommon in winter.

Robert Shantz

Song Sparrow   (*Melospiza melodia*)

JAN–APR, May, SEP–DEC

Taxonomy—Class: Aves; Order: Passeriformes; Family: Emberizidae.

Identification—Plumage highly variable across multiple races of this species. Dark rusty line through eye; tail long and rounded; whitish breast coarsely streaked with dark, often with a conspicuous central dark spot. Many song sparrows in bosque in winter have gray and rufous face and are brown above with chestnut stripes along wings and tail. Call, a loud "chimp."

Natural history—Found in most habitat types but primarily in or at edge of dense vegetation near water. Forages on the ground and in shrubs often together with white-crowned sparrows. Eats seeds of grasses and weeds; visits bird feeders.

Status—Widespread; common to locally abundant from late September to April (highest numbers from October through March) with a few birds still observed in early May.

Doug Brown

Lincoln's Sparrow

(Melospiza lincolnii)

JAN–APR, May, SEP–DEC

Taxonomy—Class: Aves; Order: Passeriformes; Family: Emberizidae.

Identification—Sexes alike. Similar to song sparrow but white underparts are finely streaked with brown through a contrasting buffy breast band; also has buffy orange mustachial stripe. Gray-brown upper parts and rounded tail. Tiny white eye ring. Call during migration like that of junco ("chup"); also has a thin "zeeeee" call shared only with swamp sparrow.

Natural history—Most strongly associated with agricultural edges during spring and fall migration. Often found also among willows along ditches and in cottonwood woodland, especially stands with an understory of Russian olive or native vegetation, much less frequently saltcedar. Found in saltcedar-dominated associations in fall migration. Secretive species.

Status—Widepread. Most common during fall migration; uncommon during spring migration and as winter resident.

Swamp Sparrow

(Melospiza georgiana)

JAN–APR, OCT–DEC

Taxonomy—Class: Aves; Order: Passeriformes; Family: Emberizidae.

Identification—Medium-size sparrow with unstreaked underparts. Face, breast, and sides of neck gray. Often has a slightly orangish mustachial stripe. Whitish line over eye. Throat and belly whitish, contrasting with grayer breast. Back streaked with black, brown, white, and buff. Rufous shoulder patch. In nonbreeding plumage has streaked cap with gray central stripe. Call, a thin "zeeeee" and a louder "chup."

Natural history—Shy and found singly or in small groups. Associated with marshy vegetation, including cattail. Wades into shallow water searching for floating insects. Also eats seeds.

Status—Locally uncommon. Most easily found at La Joya.

White-throated Sparrow   (*Zonotrichia albicollis*)

JAN–APR, May, OCT–DEC

Taxonomy—Class: Aves; Order: Passeriformes; Family: Emberizidae.

Identification—Somewhat similar to white-crowned sparrow (black and white striped crown, gray cheeks and breast, and 2 white wing bars) but with dark bill and conspicuous yellow lores and white throat. Some adults have a crown striped with brown and tan (as pictured) instead of black and white. Immature may lack yellow on lores and has crown streaked with brown and tan, duller throat, and dull breast streaks. Calls include a high-pitched, slurred "tseet."

Natural history—Found mainly in dense cottonwood woodland, in shrubby thickets of Russian olive, and along ditches; also along agricultural edges of bosque. Occasionally in small groups of 3 to 8 individuals; often with flocks of white-crowned sparrows.

Status—Widespread and uncommon. Overall numbers fluctuate from winter to winter.

White-crowned Sparrow   (*Zonotrichia leucophrys*)

JAN–MAY, Jun, SEP–DEC

Taxonomy—Class: Aves; Order: Passeriformes; Family: Emberizidae.

Identification—Sexes alike. Adult has yellow, pink, or orange bill; broad white and black stripes across the crown (the lateral stripes are black, separated by a central white stripe); white eyebrow; black eye stripe; whitish throat; unstreaked gray breast; gray back and wings streaked with brown; and 2 thin white wing bars. Immature similar but the stripes of the crown are brown and pale tan. Call is a sharp "tseek" or "pink."

Natural history—Typically seen in small flocks along ditches and along the levee-side edge of the cottonwood woodland in bushes or on the ground. Also common in saltcedar. Winter diet includes seeds. Frequents bird feeders.

Status—Widely distributed and common to locally abundant as a spring and fall migrant and winter resident. Observed in the bosque until early May, more occasionally into early June.

Dark-eyed Junco (*Junco hyemalis*)

JAN–MAY, SEP–DEC

Taxonomy—Class: Aves; Order: Passeriformes; Family: Emberizidae.

Identification—Sparrowlike with conical pale bill, gray or black head (often giving hooded appearance), whitish belly, and conspicuous white outer tail feathers. Pink-sided (gray hood, brown back, and pinkish sides) and Oregon (photo; black hood and rusty back and sides) forms most common but other forms recorded, including gray-headed (mostly gray with chestnut triangular patch on back) and slate-colored (black and white much like black phoebe but generally in flocks with other juncos). Juveniles are streaked (can be mistaken for vesper sparrow, which has white outer tail feathers too). Call, a sharp "tik." Song, heard in late winter and spring, generally a melodious trill.

Natural history—Occurs in small flocks, typically on the ground along ditches and in cottonwood woodland. Eats seeds and Russian olives; frequents bird feeders.

Status—Widespread and common to locally abundant from October through April, with fewer birds also seen in September and early May.

Robert Sivinski

Black-headed Grosbeak (*Pheucticus melanocephalus*) ✳ ✳

APR–SEP

Taxonomy—Class: Aves; Order: Passeriformes; Family: Cardinalidae.

Identification—Males (top) have black heads often with orange line extending above and behind cheek; orange breasts, collars, sides, and rumps; yellow on belly extending onto center of breast. The black tail and wings have white patches (male spotted towhee shares some of the same color patterns but lacks heavy conical bill and has red eyes and black breast). Females (bottom) are largely brown above with a conspicuous white eyebrow and underparts washed in ocher. Female red-winged blackbirds also have the white eyebrow but have heavily streaked breasts and a thinner bill. The song is a loud and varied, melodious warble reminiscent of an American robin's. Calls include a loud "wheet."

Natural history—Associated with cottonwood woodland and coyote willow or coyote willow–Russian olive thickets along riverbanks. Nesting is from May to July. The nest is bulky and loosely built with twigs placed high in the canopy or in the understory. Some nests are parasitized by the brown-headed cowbird. Species' diet consists of seeds, fruits (including mulberries in the bosque), and insects.

Status—Widespread and common.

Photographs: Doug Brown

Blue Grosbeak · (*Passerina caerulea*) ✳ ✳

MAY–SEP, Oct

Taxonomy—Class: Aves; Order: Passeriformes; Family: Cardinalidae.

Identification—Male (photo) is deep blue with 2 brownish bands on wings; female is brown. Thick, silvery beak. Song, a series of sweet warbles. Call is a loud "chink."

Natural history—Associated with most habitat types, especially along edges (e.g., along levee roads) and on open riverbanks with shrubs. The nest is a cup typically built 1 m (3 ft) above ground or lower in a shrub (e.g., coyote willow, Russian olive); more occasionally higher, in a cottonwood. The bluish eggs are found in June, July, and August. Nests are frequently parasitized by the brown-headed cowbird.

Status—Widespread and common. Among the latest summer residents to arrive.

Greg W. Lasley

Lazuli Bunting · (*Passerina amoena*) ✳ ✳

APR–SEP

Taxonomy—Class: Aves; Order: Passeriformes; Family: Cardinalidae.

Identification—Small finchlike bird with triangular bill. Male (photo) has turquoise blue upper parts and throat, orange breast, white belly, and 2 conspicuous white wing bars. Female brown with blue highlights in wings and tail and 2 pale wing bars (female indigo bunting does not have any conspicuous wing bars). Song is series of high-pitched warbles. Call, similar to indigo bunting's, a short "brrzzt."

Natural history—Observed nests have been in saltcedar and Chinese tree of heaven at heights of about 1.8 m (6 ft). Seed eater.

Status—Widespread and uncommon to common spring (April–May) and fall (August–September) migrant. Uncommon to locally common summer breeding resident, almost exclusively in Sandoval County.

Lisa Spray

Indigo Bunting   (*Passerina cyanea*) ✳ ✳
Apr, MAY–AUG, Sep

Taxonomy—Class: Aves; Order: Passeriformes; Family: Cardinalidae.

Identification—Small finchlike bird with triangular bill. Plumage of male (photo) is entirely blue without the male blue grosbeak's chestnut wing bars (no other bird is blue all over). Female: brown upper parts; buffy underparts with breast showing faint darker streaks. Females and immature birds distinguished from lazuli bunting by presence of darker streaks on breast. Song is high pitched, nearly identical to lazuli bunting's. Call is a short "brrzzt" similar to lazuli bunting's.

Natural history—Nests in saltcedar and seep-willow at heights of up to 3 m (10 ft). Some nests likely parasitized by the brown-headed cowbird. Occasionally hybridizes with lazuli bunting in the bosque. Seed eater.

Status—Widely distributed but uncommon as spring and fall migrant and summer breeding resident.

Jean-Luc Cartron

Red-winged Blackbird   (*Agelaius phoeniceus*) ✳ ✳
JAN–DEC

Taxonomy—Class: Aves; Order: Passeriformes; Family: Icteridae.

Identification—Males (photo) are black with distinctive red wing patches bordered in yellow; females (often confused with sparrows by beginning birders but overall much larger) have brown upper parts with darker streaks, a light stripe over the eye, and streaked underparts. Song, a loud and gurgling "oak-a-lee." Calls include a dry "chek."

Natural history—Occurs in wetlands (including seasonally inundated riverbanks and wetlands along ditches), in ponds, and on small vegetated islands. The nest is placed near or over water, low in emergent aquatic vegetation (rushes, cattail), a young cottonwood, or a coyote willow. Males aggressively defend their nest territories against intruders. Some males have 2 mates and defend both nests. Often occurs in large flocks when not breeding; especially in winter these flocks are single sex only.

Status—Year-round resident; locally common to abundant.

Ralph Giles

Western Meadowlark   (*Sturnella neglecta*) ✳ ✳

JAN–DEC

Taxonomy—Class: Aves; Order: Passeriformes; Family: Icteridae.

Identification—Brown, speckled upper parts. Yellow under-parts with black V across the breast. White eyebrow with some yellow. White outer tail feathers show in flight and when perched. Flight reminiscent of a quail's. Nearly iden-tical to eastern meadowlark but yellow extends onto cheek and song a flutelike, gurgling "too tee too tiddleyou."

Natural history—Mainly in grasslands or agricultural fields along edges but also in bosque proper in open saltcedar associations and saltgrass meadows. Nest is placed on the ground, hidden in grass.

Status—Common to locally abundant resident.

Yellow-headed Blackbird   (*Xanthocephalus xanthocephalus*)

JAN–APR, May–Jun, JUL–DEC

Taxonomy—Class: Aves; Order: Passeriformes; Family: Icteridae.

Identification—Male (photo) easily identified by yellow head and breast with rest of body black and conspicuous white patch on wing. Female smaller and brown above, identified mainly by yellow eyebrow, throat, and breast. Call is a hoarse croak.

Natural history—Found mostly outside bosque in adja-cent agricultural fields (often perched in mixed flocks with red-winged blackbirds on utility poles). In bosque proper occurs mainly at ponds and wetlands and less often along ditches. Fall migration begins in July but midpoint is late August.

Status—Common spring and fall migrant; during winter, uncommon in the south, more occasional northward.

Brewer's Blackbird

(*Euphagus cyanocephalus*)

JAN–MAY, SEP–DEC

☀ in air above

Taxonomy—Class: Aves; Order: Passeriformes; Family: Icteridae.

Identification—Male has black head with purple iridescence, black body with greenish iridescence, and pale yellow eyes. Female is grayish brown below with darker brown upper parts and dark eyes (female great-tailed grackle has yellow irises and is much larger with a longer bill). Call, a harsh "shack."

Natural history—Often in flocks. Species' diet consists of insects and seeds. Forages on the ground.

Status—Common but local spring and fall migrant; common winter resident in the south.

Robert Shantz

Great-tailed Grackle

(*Quiscalus mexicanus*) ✳ ✳

JAN–DEC

Taxonomy—Class: Aves; Order: Passeriformes; Family: Icteridae.

Identification—Unmistakable due to its large rudderlike tail. Male (photo) is black with a gloss of purple and blue-green. Female smaller with smaller tail; dark brown above and buffy below. Irises in both sexes yellow.

Natural history—Often seen flying in flocks over open bosque areas or foraging and roosting near water, including in cattail marshes. Nests in Russian olive thickets and other dense vegetation along ditches and at edge of ponds. Competes for nest sites with red-winged blackbirds. Bulk of diet consists of invertebrates.

Status—Widespread and common.

Doug Brown

Brown-headed Cowbird   (*Molothrus ater*) ✳✳

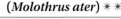 

Jan–March, APR–SEP, Oct–Dec

Taxonomy—Class: Aves; Order: Passeriformes; Family: Icteridae.

Identification—Male shiny black with brown head; female uniformly gray-brown. Sparrowlike bill. Song, a bubbly and squeaking "bubble-lee come seee." Flight call is a high-pitched "weee teetee."

Natural history—Lays eggs (whitish with brown specks and blotches mostly at large end) in the nests of other bosque species such as yellow warbler, blue grosbeak, yellow-breasted chat, and spotted towhee, typically 1 egg per nest. Host species provides all care for egg and nestling. Forages in agricultural fields adjacent to bosque, often near cattle. Eats both plant food and insects. In fall, often in large flocks with other blackbirds. Midpoint of spring migration is late May, fall migration late August.

Status—Widespread and common during spring and summer. Rare to occasional in fall and winter.

Doug Brown

Bullock's Oriole   (*Icterus bullockii*) ✳✳

APR–SEP

Taxonomy—Class: Aves; Order: Passeriformes; Family: Icteridae.

Identification—Male (photo) is mostly orange below with black chin and black central stripe on throat; upper parts are largely black with conspicuous white patch on wing. Combination of orange cheek, black line through eye, and black crown is diagnostic. Female has olive green upper parts and whitish belly contrasting with yellowish breast and undertail coverts. Call is a rapid chatter, "cha-cha-cha-cha." Song, loud whistles.

Natural history—Likes open cottonwood stands. Nest is an oval woven bag built in a cottonwood or an elm. Diet composed mostly of insects and worms but also berries. Midpoint of spring migration in late May, fall migration in mid-August.

Status—Widespread and uncommon to common.

Robert Shantz

House Finch
(Carpodacus mexicanus) ✳ ✳

JAN–DEC

Taxonomy—Class: Aves; Order: Passeriformes; Family: Fringillidae.

Identification—Typical male (photo) has red forehead, eyebrow, chin, breast, and rump with brown streaks over white belly; eye stripe, back, wings, and tail brown. In some males the red is replaced with yellow to orange. Female is brown above, whitish below with brown streaking of breast and belly. Song is a loose, musical warble with rapidly alternating low and high frequencies, often ending on a nasal, down-slurred "jeer." Call, "weet."

Natural history—Most typically found along ditches (winter) and edges and in the more open areas of the bosque. Nesting begins in April. Nests are in cottonwoods and other trees. Diet in bosque includes mulberries, Russian olives, and sunflower seeds. In winter occurs in small flocks and frequents bird feeders.

Status—Widespread and common to abundant year-round.

Pine Siskin
(Carduelis pinus)

JAN–JUN, SEP–DEC

Taxonomy—Class: Aves; Order: Passeriformes; Family: Fringillidae.

Identification—Sexes alike. Small finch with thin, sharply pointed bill; bold dusky streaks on brownish upper parts and underparts; faint yellow in wings and notched tail. Several calls, including "clee-up" and long, rising "shreeeee."

Natural history—Species often found in erratic wandering flocks during migration and in winter. Associated with cottonwood woodland and adjacent agricultural fields. Eats mostly seeds; especially likes wild sunflowers. Peak of fall migration is early October.

Status—Widespread spring and fall migrant and winter resident. Most common in fall and early winter. Numbers vary widely from year to year.

Lesser Goldfinch · (*Carduelis psaltria*) ✳ ✳

JAN–DEC

Taxonomy—Class: Aves; Order: Passeriformes; Family: Fringillidae.

Identification—Male (photo) yellow below with olive green or black back (breeding male American goldfinch has bright yellow back), black cap, black tail, and white undertail coverts. Black wings with white patch useful to differentiate from warblers. Female light yellow below with olive green back and dull black tail and wings (white on wings less conspicuous than in male). In all plumages distinguished from American goldfinch by yellow undertail coverts. Utters plaintive notes, rising "tee-yee, then falling "tee-yer." Song incorporates imitations of many other birds.

Natural history—Found typically in cottonwood woodland and along ditches lined with willows as well as along agricultural edges. Nests in cottonwoods, less often saltcedars; builds a round cup nest using cotton as material for the outer wall. Nesting often timed with periods of high rainfall. Seed eater; often seen outside nesting season in small groups on sunflowers. Midpoint of spring migration through bosque is early June; midpoint of fall migration is mid- to late September.

Status—Widespread. Common all along Middle Rio Grande from April through October; uncommon winter resident in southern half of bosque, rare to occasional farther north.

American Goldfinch · (*Carduelis tristis*)

JAN–MAY, Jun–Aug, SEP–DEC

Taxonomy—Class: Aves; Order: Passeriformes; Family: Fringillidae.

Identification—Male in spring and summer is bright yellow with black cap and tail and with conspicuous white bars and edgings on black wings. In winter (photo) has grayish brown upper parts but throat remains yellow and wings and tail mostly unchanged. Female in summer yellow below, olive above, with dark tail and 2 white bars on dark wings; in winter largely similar to male. In all plumages white undertail coverts distinguish American from lesser goldfinch. Note notched tail and conical bill (many warblers have some yellow but have thin, needle-pointed bills). Call, given in flight, "per-chik-o-ree."

Natural history—In fall and winter mainly in open areas and along agricultural edges of bosque, where they often occur in small flocks perched on stalks of sunflowers, eating the seeds. Flocks travel in deeply undulating (roller-coaster) flights. In spring mainly along ditches.

Status—Widespread. Uncommon to locally common from September through May; rare in June and July, with no nesting recorded in bosque. August sightings are becoming more frequent.

House Sparrow

(Passer domesticus) ✳ ✳ [INT]

JAN–DEC

Taxonomy—Class: Aves; Order: Passeriformes; Family: Passeridae.

Identification—Male (photo) has gray crown, white cheeks, chestnut patch from behind eyes to nape, black chin, and in summer black bib. Back and upper wings brown, streaked with black; grayish underparts. Female duller, mostly brown above, paler below, with whitish streak over eye. Immature birds or adult males with odd bibs may be confused with immature Harris's sparrow. Call, "chir-rup"; no true song but "chereep," repeated.

Natural history—Mostly along agricultural and urban edges of the bosque. Nests alongside bridges in old cliff swallow nests (but brings in twigs as additional nesting material), typically over land rather than above water. Nesting for this species may begin as early as late February!

Status—Locally common.

Jean-Luc Cartron

Mammals

Mammals all share three distinguishing characteristics: a body covered with hair, mammary glands for producing milk (in females), and three middle ear bones transmitting vibrations of the tympanic membrane (eardrum) to the inner ear. Most mammals also have a four-chambered heart, well-differentiated teeth, and a well-developed brain. They are divided into three subclasses, the Prototheria (monotremes, or egg-laying mammals), Metatheria (marsupials), and Eutheria. Most species—including all those described in this field guide—are members of the latter group, or placental mammals. The developing young or fetus is carried inside the female's uterus until fully developed and nourished via a placenta. Most placental mammals are rodents and bats.

The 35 species described in the following pages represent a large proportion of all the mammals documented or possible in the bosque and approximately one-fourth of all mammals known to occur in New Mexico. Many of the 35 species are difficult to see. Some are rare, but others such as the white-footed mouse (*Peromyscus leucopus*) are common or even abundant. They easily escape detection because they are nocturnal, live under cover of dense vegetation, or both. The few species frequently encountered during the day and throughout most of the bosque are the desert cottontail (*Sylvilagus audubonii*), rock squirrel (*Spermophilus variegatus*), common muskrat (*Ondatra zibethicus*), common porcupine (*Erethizon dorsatum*), and coyote (*Canis latrans*). Also widely distributed but less easily seen are the American beaver, long-tailed weasel, and common raccoon. The mule deer is a highly visible species at the Bosque del Apache NWR but not in many other areas of the bosque. Because many mammals are difficult to see, learning to recognize their tracks is important.

Common raccoon

Common porcupine

American beaver

Long-tailed weasel

Striped skunk

Gray fox

Bobcat

Coyote

Elk

Black bear

Mountain lion

Mule deer

Illustration: Jane Mygatt

Desert Shrew

(Notiosorex crawfordi) ✳ ✳

Jan–Mar, APR–OCT, Nov–Dec

Taxonomy—Class: Mammalia; Order: Soricomorpha; Family: Soricidae.

Identification—Unlike mice, shrews have long, conical muzzles, tiny eyes, 5 toes per foot (mice have 4 toes on forefeet), and ears hidden along sides of head. Desert shrew is grayish, with musk glands along flanks. Distinguished from other shrews by dentition: 30 teeth total, with 3 unicuspids in each maxillary tooth row.

Natural history—Inhabits moist and/or more densely vegetated habitat types, particularly cottonwood woodland and marshy areas but also ditch banks and saltcedar associations. Like all other shrews eats mainly invertebrates such as insects and spiders. Active through at least early November and probably on warm winter days.

Status—Only shrew species in the bosque. Widespread and possibly among the most common mammals in the bosque, though rarely detected.

Dale and Marian Zimmerman

Yuma Myotis

(Myotis yumanensis) ✳ ✳

MAY–OCT

Taxonomy—Class: Mammalia; Order: Chiroptera; Family: Vespertilionidae.

Identification—Medium-size bat with medium-length ears. Body yellowish or dull brown above, whitish below. No keel. Very difficult to distinguish from Arizona myotis but ears and wing membranes paler in Yuma myotis.

Natural history—Like all bats in the bosque, Yuma myotis is nocturnal, becoming active at dusk, and uses echolocation to catch insects. Maternity roosts in cavities in dead cottonwoods, in crevices under concrete bridges, or in buildings along human-inhabited edges of bosque. Individuals at roosts can range in number from a few to over 100. Forages low over water along ditches and over the Rio Grande, ponds, and wetlands. Hibernates.

Status—Widespread and common to locally abundant.

Scott Altenbach

Arizona Myotis
(*Myotis occultus*) ✳ ✳

MAY–OCT

Taxonomy—Class: Mammalia; Order: Chiroptera; Family: Vespertilionidae. Populations of this species in New Mexico—including in the bosque—were formerly assigned to the little brown myotis (*M. lucifugus*).

Identification—Medium-size bat with broad face and medium-length, rounded ears. Sagittal crest present on skull. Small upper premolars often missing or crowded out of alignment. Dorsal pelage reddish brown or auburn, whereas ventral fur is tan in color. Can be easily confused with Yuma myotis, but ears and wing membranes are darker in Arizona myotis.

Natural history—Active at dusk and during night. Forages over water surfaces, including ditches, ponds, wetlands, and river. Diet is varied in bosque but consists mainly of hard-bodied insects such as beetles. In spring, up to 500 gravid females or more may congregate at maternity roosts, where young are born and grow. Solitary and colony maternity roosts found in natural tree cavities, under exfoliating bark, in buildings, or under wooden bridges. Roosts often shared with other species such as Yuma myotis, Townsend's big-eared bat (not described in this guide), pallid bat, or Brazilian free-tailed bat. Hibernates, likely in nearby montane areas.

Status—Widespread and common near permanent sources of water.

Long-legged Myotis
(*Myotis volans*)

MAY–OCT

Taxonomy—Class: Mammalia; Order: Chiroptera; Family: Vespertilionidae.

Identification—Medium-size myotis bat with short ears rounded at tip, relatively long tail, long tibias, well-furred underside of wing and interfemoral membranes out to line joining elbow to knee, and keeled calcar. Uniformly brown with little bicoloration in dorsal and ventral pelage. Can be confused with Arizona and Yuma myotis, but these 2 species lack a keel and have relatively longer ears.

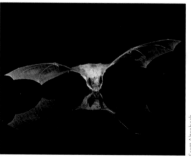

Natural history—Recorded over ponds and wetlands at Bosque del Apache NWR. However, this is not a water-surface forager like the previous 2 species and instead relies more on back and forth pursuit of aerial insects over open areas.

Status—Not known to breed in bosque.

Fringed Myotis   (*Myotis thysanodes*)

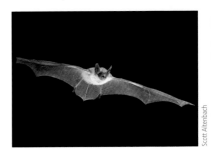

MAY–OCT

Taxonomy—Class: Mammalia; Order: Chiroptera; Family: Vespertilionidae.

Identification—Medium-size bat with long ears and no keel. Trailing edge of tail membrane both above and below has conspicuous fringe of short, stiff hairs. Reddish brown or brown above, paler below.

Natural history—Belongs to the category of hovering gleaners: tends to fly slowly and picks insects from trees, shrubs, and rocks or from the ground.

Status—Not known to breed in bosque.

Hoary Bat   (*Lasiurus cinereus*)

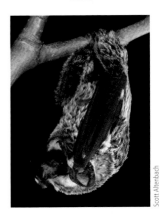

MAY–JUN, SEP–OCT

Taxonomy—Class: Mammalia; Order: Chiroptera; Family: Vespertilionidae.

Identification—Large bat with tips of fur frosted with grayish white (hence the name hoary), a yellowish throat, and short, rounded, furred ears rimmed with naked black skin. Tail membrane is furred and brown above.

Natural history—Uses river as flyway during migration. Tends to be solitary. Probably roosts in trees as is general habit of this species. Flies over water (along ditches and at ponds) in search of insects; feeds mostly on moths.

Status—Spring and fall migrant.

Big Brown Bat   (*Eptesicus fuscus*)

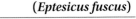

MAY–OCT

Taxonomy—Class: Mammalia; Order: Chiroptera; Family: Vespertilionidae.

Identification—Large bat with pelage brown to dark brown dorsally, light brown or tan ventrally. Ears, wings, and inter-femoral membrane black without fur. Face broad with relatively short ears and blunt tragus. No small upper premolars behind canines (myotis bats have 1 to 2 small upper premolars behind the canines). Calcar keel.

Natural history—Tends to be a habitat generalist. Recorded in cottonwood woodland and flying over ponds and wetlands at dusk and probably occurs in other habitat types. Catches flying insects.

Status—Widespread. Not known to breed in bosque.

Pallid Bat   (*Antrozous pallidus*) ✳ ✳

MAY–OCT

Taxonomy—Class: Mammalia; Order: Chiroptera; Family: Vespertilionidae.

Identification—Large bat with piglike face, very large pale ears, and large eyes. Body cream to beige above, white below. Wings and interfemoral membrane nearly bare. No keel. Utters audible high-pitched sounds, including an insectlike buzz.

Natural history—Pregnant and lactating females may roost singly or in small colonies, typically near or along urban edges of the bosque (rather than in the bosque proper). Maternity roosts observed in buildings (including a church in Corrales) and in crevices along rocky cliffs. Swoops down on large ground arthropods and catches flying insects over land or open water.

Status—Widespread.

Scott Altenbach

Brazilian Free-tailed Bat   (*Tadarida brasiliensis*) ✳ ✳

May–Oct

Taxonomy—Class: Mammalia; Order: Chiroptera; Family: Molossidae.

Identification—Medium-size bat with naked tail extending well beyond tail membrane (thus name free-tailed bat). Ears are broad and not joined at base but almost meet along midline of forehead. Body dark brown or dark gray above, paler below.

Natural history—Emerges at sunset to hunt for flying insects along ditches and at ponds and wetlands. Maternity colonies tend to be very large. One maternity roost documented in a church in Corrales along urban edge of bosque. Other maternity roosts under bridges over river and probably also in caves near bosque.

Status—Widespread, common-to-abundant migrant and summer resident. Most migrate south to central and southern Mexico for the winter.

Scott Altenbach

Black-tailed Jackrabbit
(Lepus californicus)

JAN–DEC

Taxonomy—Class: Mammalia; Order: Lagomorpha; Family: Leporidae.

Identification—Much larger than cottontail rabbits. Easily recognized by its very large ears tipped with black. Fur gray, peppered with black above. Tail striped with black above. Scat, round pellets about 1.3 cm (½ in) in diameter.

Natural history—Associated with dry open saltcedar associations, burned areas, and edges. Likes to eat alfalfa (grown in some fields adjacent to bosque). Important prey species for many predators, including coyotes and bobcats.

Status—Widespread and uncommon year-round; somewhat marginal.

Patrick O'Brien

Desert Cottontail
(Sylvilagus audubonii) ✱✱

JAN–DEC

Taxonomy—Class: Mammalia; Order: Lagomorpha; Family: Leporidae. Only the desert cottontail has been recorded in the bosque, but mountain and eastern cottontails are possible.

Identification—Medium size; gray above with buffy brown or yellow wash, white below with large ears and cottonball-like short, fluffy tail. Scat, piles of pellets, often left on logs and stumps.

Natural history—Found in most habitat types, where it is active during day and at night year-round. Uses burrows; has several litters of young year-round. Herbivorous species.

Status—Widespread and common.

Richard B. Forbes

Rock Squirrel (*Spermophilus variegatus*) ✳ ✳

Jan–Feb, MAR–OCT, Nov–Dec

Taxonomy—Class: Mammalia; Order: Rodentia; Family: Sciuridae.

Identification—Large ground squirrel, gray-brown above, becoming more brown toward rump. Pale below. Long, bushy, narrow tail. Conspicuous white eye ring.

Natural history—Preferred habitat is along edges, including along ditches and levee roads, and in the more open stands of cottonwood woodland. Active during the day. Often scampers along logs and climbs trees, including Russian olive (for its fruit). Also feeds on seeds under bird feeders (at Rio Grande Nature Center). Makes its den in a burrow.

Status—Widespread and common in spring, summer, and early fall. In winter, active aboveground during spells of warmer weather.

Botta's Pocket Gopher (*Thomomys bottae*) ✳ ✳

Jan–Mar, APR–OCT, Nov–Dec

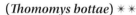

Taxonomy—Class: Mammalia; Order: Rodentia; Family: Geomyidae.

Identification—Resembles a rat but with adaptations to fossorial life: tiny eyes and ears, forefeet with long digging claws. Genus *Thomomys* characterized by lack of conspicuous grooves on upper incisors.

Natural history—Associated with deep, sandy soils in cottonwood woodland where tree density is low to moderate. Also often associated with coyote willow and with river channel during periods of low flow. Mostly solitary except during breeding season. Builds burrow complex, emerging aboveground only occasionally. When constructing tunnel pushes loose dirt up to surface, sealing temporary opening before retreating underground but leaving behind mound. Eats mostly underground parts of plants.

Status—Common and widespread. Active year-round but least likely to be found outside its burrow in winter.

Silky Pocket Mouse   (*Perognathus flavus*) ✴ ✴

Jan–Mar, APR–OCT, Nov–Dec

Taxonomy—Class: Mammalia; Order: Rodentia; Family: Heteromyidae.

Identification—Very small, sharply bicolored rodent: tan above with many black hairs on back, white below. Conspicuous buff-colored patches behind ears. Cheek pouches appear as folds of skin on either side of mouth, used to hold and carry food in. Small hind feet. No long hairs on tail.

Natural history—Nocturnal. Avoids more mesic areas. Mostly in open saltcedar stands at the edge of the riparian zone but also encountered in cottonwood woodland with little or no shrub layer. Sandy soil usually present. Eats mainly seeds and other plant material; may store some food in burrow, which is small and has tiny opening. Probably enters torpor during spells of cold winter weather.

Status—Widespread and uncommon.

Richard B. Forbes

Ord's Kangaroo Rat   (*Dipodomys ordii*) ✴ ✴

JAN–DEC

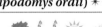

Taxonomy—Class: Mammalia; Order: Rodentia; Family: Heteromyidae.

Identification—Short body with long, powerful hind limbs adapted for jumping and contrasting with short forelimbs; long tail with tufted tip; 5 toes per hind foot (similar-looking Merriam's kangaroo rat, found in New Mexico but not in bosque, has only 4). Upper parts cinnamon brown with some black on back, white underparts. Patches of white above eye and below ear.

Natural history—Nocturnal. Strongly associated with dry, open areas with friable sandy soils and herbaceous cover. Found in open saltcedar communities, less often open cottonwood woodland and clearings; rare along ditches. Digs burrows (burrow mounds not as conspicuous as those of banner-tailed kangaroo rats). Seeds essential part of diet; are transported in cheek pouches and stored in caches. Predators in the bosque include great horned owls and most likely also coyotes and snakes.

Jon Dunnum

Status—Widespread and locally common year-round in preferred habitat. Somewhat marginal species (found largely at edge of riparian zone).

American Beaver   (*Castor canadensis*) ✳ ✳

JAN–DEC

Taxonomy—Class: Mammalia; Order: Rodentia; Family: Castoridae.

Identification—Large aquatic rodent covered with dark brown fur and flattened, paddle-shaped tail. Head rounded with small ears and eyes and large incisors. Hind feet are webbed. When swimming, young beavers may be mistaken for muskrats but do not hold their backs and tails partially above water like muskrats do. Webbed hind feet leave track twice as long as forefeet and wider. Gnawed tree trunks are sign of local beaver activity.

Natural history—Occurs at ponds, along ditches and riverbanks, and in cottonwood woodland. Most beavers in the bosque build burrows, including along banks of ditches. Some build dams, for example at the Rio Grande Nature Center. Diet includes the cambial tissue under the bark of cottonwood and willow.

Status—Widespread and common, but beavers of the bosque have had to adapt to dramatic changes to their natural environment. Prior to flow regulation, the river had multiple channels that were narrow enough for beavers to build dams and lodges. Today the single river channel is too wide for them, and they have shifted their habits and become "bank beavers." Legally protected in New Mexico since 1897, whereas before the species had been severely impacted by commercial trapping.

Western Harvest Mouse   (*Reithrodontomys megalotis*) ✳ ✳

JAN–DEC

Taxonomy—Class: Mammalia; Order: Rodentia; Family: Cricetidae.

Identification—Tiny mouse, brown above and pale below. Ears medium size; tail bicolored (pale below); grooves on anterior surface of upper incisors.

Natural history—Prefers moist areas with thick, grassy vegetation but found across all habitat types, especially in association with some ground cover. Very prolific breeder (reproduction likely occurs throughout most of the year and females may bear litters after only 3 months of life) but life span less than a year. Builds a woven nest aboveground. Diet (not studied in bosque) presumably includes a lot of insects in summer but mostly seeds in fall and winter.

Status—Widespread and common to locally abundant (second most abundant small mammal in bosque after white-footed mouse).

White-footed Mouse

(Peromyscus leucopus) ✴ ✴

JAN–DEC

Taxonomy—Class: Mammalia; Order: Rodentia; Family: Cricetidae. North American deer mouse (*Peromyscus maniculatus*) possible in bosque but not nearly as common. The 2 species are very difficult to differentiate based on appearance.

Identification—Darker above than below and white footed (like other *Peromyscus* species). Sharply bicolored tail measures nearly half total body length.

Natural history—Nocturnal and semi-arboreal (ability to climb vegetation allows species to escape flooding events). Found in all habitat types of the bosque but prefers more densely vegetated areas. Species' diet generally consists of seeds, nuts, fruits, and invertebrates. Food may be stored near nest.

Status—Widespread and active year-round. Most abundant mammal in bosque.

David Lightfoot

Hispid Cottonrat

(Sigmodon hispidus) ✴ ✴

JAN–DEC

Taxonomy—Class: Mammalia; Order: Rodentia; Family: Cricetidae.

Identification—Grizzled dark brown or blackish fur with stiff guard hairs, whitish or gray below. Ears large but partially concealed in fur. Tail scaly and nearly naked, less than half of total length.

Natural history—Mainly nocturnal. Adept swimmer. Prefers very dense herbaceous vegetation such as found in wet meadows and at edge of cattail marshes; also in weedy areas and within stands of saltcedar where cover is dense. Species' diet includes mainly green plants but also some insects and the eggs and nestlings of ground-nesting birds. Builds runways radiating from nest, which is under protective cover of vegetation or just below the ground. Very prolific breeder.

Status—Widespread and uncommon to locally abundant.

Richard B. Forbes/ASM

Tawny-bellied Cottonrat

(*Sigmodon fulviventer*) ✳✳

JAN–DEC

Taxonomy—Class: Mammalia; Order: Rodentia; Family: Cricetidae.

Identification—Very similar to hispid cottonrat except for tawny ventral coloration. Dark brown or blackish above, tail brownish black all around.

Natural history—Associated with undisturbed mesic environments, mainly wetlands with perennial bunch-grass, sedges, and often also cocklebur. Builds runways similar to hispid cottonrat.

Status—Species highly restricted to fragmented wetland habitat in the Middle Rio Grande Valley between Cochiti Dam and Los Lunas. Loss of habitat, and possibly competition with hispid cottonrat, likely caused this species to experience precipitous population decline. Found year-round but numbers can fluctuate greatly over time.

White-throated Woodrat

(*Neotoma albigula*) ✳✳

JAN–DEC

Taxonomy—Class:Mammalia;Order:Rodentia; Family: Cricetidae. Populations east of the Rio Grande have been assigned to the species *N. leucodon*; boundaries between the 2 species are unclear.

Identification—Sharply bicolored body with long tail, large naked ears, and large eyes. Gray or gray brown above, white below (including feet and underside of tail). Unlike other woodrats, patch of fur on throat has hairs that are white from base to tip (elsewhere on underparts base of hairs is gray).

Natural history—Mainly nocturnal. Associated with cottonwood woodland with accumulations of downed woody debris, probably used for making their bulky nests. Female bears several litters of 2. Eats plants and some invertebrates. Uses hind foot drumming for communication.

Status—Widespread and rare to locally common.

Common Muskrat   (*Ondatra zibethicus*) ✳✳

JAN–DEC

Taxonomy—Class: Mammalia; Order: Rodentia; Family: Cricetidae.

Identification—Similar in appearance to beaver but much smaller and with a long, scaly tail. Glossy brown fur; partially webbed hind feet, small eyes and ears. Highly aquatic, not often seen out of water. Swims showing head, back, and tail.

Natural history—Capable of staying underwater up to about 15 minutes. Builds a lodge amid aquatic vegetation, which is also staple diet (known to eat cattail shoots and roots at Bosque del Apache NWR). Predators in the bosque include great horned owl and probably also raccoon, coyote, and even domestic dog.

Status—Widespread and common year-round.

Tom Kennedy

House Mouse   (*Mus musculus*) ✳✳ [INT]

JAN–DEC

Taxonomy—Class: Mammalia; Order: Rodentia; Family: Muridae.

Identification—Small, grayish brown or dark brown mouse with nearly hairless scaly tail. Key to identification are the upper incisors, ungrooved but with notch on cutting surface. Most have a dark belly, but some in bosque are white or gray bellied.

Natural history—Species is largely commensal, living near humans, often around houses. In bosque found mainly in moist, grassy areas such as along riverbanks, ditch banks, and the periphery of wetlands. Very prolific breeder (females may begin reproducing 1 month after birth!). Typically lives in groups. Eats seeds and other plant material as well as arthropods. Hawks, great horned owls, snakes, and skunks likely among main predators.

Richard B. Forbes

Status—Perhaps the most populous mammal on earth after humans. Originally from Asia, spread throughout Europe, then arrived in North America on board ships of explorers and settlers. Often considered a pest in agricultural areas and can spread bubonic plague and other diseases but also have beneficial effects (diet includes seeds of weeds). Widespread and common to abundant in suitable bosque habitat.

New Mexico Meadow Jumping Mouse   (*Zapus hudsonius luteus*) ✳ ✳

APR–OCT

Taxonomy—Class: Mammalia; Order: Rodentia; Family: Dipodidae.

Identification—Brown back, yellowish sides, and white belly. Very long tail, long hind feet, naked soles, deeply grooved incisors, and no external fur-lined cheek pouches.

Natural history—Associated with thick, tall grasses and sedges in wet areas. Spends winter hibernating in a burrow, relying on accumulated body fat reserves. Eats plant material (especially seeds) and insects. When startled, capable of spectacular leaps.

Status—Exact population status uncertain. Populations at Isleta Marsh and the Bosque del Apache NWR appear to be isolated. Was likely more common and widespread before channelization of the river and construction of dams.

Jennifer Frey

Common Porcupine   (*Erethizon dorsatum*) ✳ ✳

JAN–DEC

Taxonomy—Class: Mammalia; Order: Rodentia; Family: Erethizontidae.

Identification—Unmistakable, with heavy body covered with long guard hairs in the front and quills on the rump and tail. The face and legs are black, the back is high arching, and the tail is rounded. Scat variable but overall similar to deer's. Tracks are inward facing.

Natural history—Solitary and primarily nocturnal in all seasons, resting during the day high up in cottonwood trees. Species' diet consists of plant material, including the inner bark of trees. Breeds in the fall. A single young is born in the spring and stays with the adult female until late summer or fall. If attacked lowers its head and defends itself with its quills erect and its tail lashing out. On contact, the quills can become embedded in the predator's skin. Natural enemies of the porcupine include the great horned owl and the coyote.

Patty Hoban

Status—Widely distributed and generally common, though recent decline in number of sightings at the Bosque del Apache NWR.

Coyote

(*Canis latrans*) ✳ ✳

JAN–DEC

Taxonomy—Class: Mammalia; Order: Carnivora; Family: Canidae.

Identification—Larger than a fox; generally resembles a medium-size domestic dog with pointed, erect ears but has black-tipped, bushy tail that is held straight out and below back when running. Coat long and a mix of gray, buffy, and black above, whitish below. Barks and howls but also utters yelps and yip notes. Scat, long and twisted, often with hair, bones, and berries. Tracks doglike.

Natural history—Typically observed singly but may form small packs. Diet in the bosque includes cottontails and other mammals as well as berries (Russian olive fruit). In adjacent farmlands also relies on truck crops. Habits not well studied in the bosque but generally known to dig up its den or take over burrows of other mammals. Mating is in late winter. Gestation period lasts about 2 months.

Status—Widespread and common.

Gray Fox

(*Urocyon cinereoargenteus*) ✳

JAN–DEC

Taxonomy—Class: Mammalia; Order: Carnivora; Family: Canidae.

Identification—Silvery gray above with white throat and underside. Lower sides, chest, and legs rusty. Top and tip of tail black. Scat narrow and tending to cylindrical, typically tapered at 1 end. Tracks may reveal 4 nonretractile claws.

Natural history—Mainly crepuscular and nocturnal. Very adept at climbing trees. Diet very diverse, includes invertebrates, small vertebrates, eggs, and berries. Breeding is in late winter and early spring. Social unit consists of adult pair and young.

Status—Widespread and uncommon to fairly common.

Black Bear (*Ursus americanus*)

APR–OCT

Taxonomy—Class: Mammalia; Order: Carnivora; Family: Ursidae.

Identification—Unmistakable (only bear species in New Mexico). Large with round head and ears. Coat of fur typically black but can also be brown. Scat, doglike. Hind tracks and front tracks are paired on both sides. Broad footprints; hind footprints up to 2.3 cm (9 in) long.

Natural history—Omnivorous. Known to eat berries in the bosque. Adult female may be accompanied by cubs (typical litter size is 2), born in winter. Bears are normally not aggressive toward people but should not be approached, especially when foraging or if cubs around.

Status—Widespread but rare nonbreeding visitor to bosque.

Diana Doan-Crider

Common Raccoon (*Procyon lotor*) ✳ ✳

JAN–DEC

Taxonomy—Class: Mammalia; Order: Carnivora; Family: Procyonidae.

Identification—Stocky with grayish coat, black mask, and tail ringed with black and tan. Legs short. Scat, variable. Tracks, flat footed with claws showing on all 5 toes.

Natural history—Active mostly at night. Occurs on sandbars and along banks of river channel, along drains, at ponds and wetlands, and in cottonwood woodland (where it may be seen up in trees). Diet in the bosque includes Russian olive fruit, crawfish, and fish. Also lifts up the lid of bird feeders to eat seeds (at Rio Grande Nature Center), depredates nest boxes, and feeds on garden produce in semirural or rural habitats adjacent to bosque.

Status—Widespread and common year-round.

Rick and Nora Bowers

Long-tailed Weasel

(*Mustela frenata*) ✳ ✳

JAN–DEC

Taxonomy—Class: Mammalia; Order: Carnivora; Family: Mustelidae. The subspecies represented in the bosque is *M. frenata neomexicana.*

Identification—Long bodied with long tail but small face and short legs. Upper body is light brown contrasting with white underparts. Form present in the bosque may show conspicuous black face mask surrounded by white fur (top) or no face mask (bottom). Due to black mask, long-tailed weasel in lowland New Mexico is often erroneously misidentified as black-footed ferret, but it has brown instead of black feet and it is more sharply bicolored. Scat, long and slender. Tracks, foreprint slightly wider than hind print.

Natural history—Active both at night and during the day. Mostly terrestrial but capable of also climbing trees. Bulk of local diet probably consists of small rodents, rock squirrels, and cottontail rabbits. Crushes prey's skull with canines. When startled may release a fetid musk. Does not hibernate.

Status—Widespread and fairly common.

Striped Skunk

(*Mephitis mephitis*) ✳ ✳

JAN–DEC

Taxonomy—Class: Mammalia; Order: Carnivora; Family: Mephitidae.

Identification—Black and white and cat size. Back black in the middle, flanked by 2 wide white stripes that meet at the shoulders. Nape white; head mostly black with a narrow white stripe along forehead. Lower sides are black. Tail long and bushy, black and white. Scat, variable. Tracks, front and hind feet have both 5 toes; hind feet larger but with smaller space between claw marks and toes; hind feet placed just behind front feet.

Natural history—Tracks often observed in cottonwood woodland, along ditches and levees, and on sandbars. Eats small vertebrates, insects, and plants. For defense against predators sprays a foul-smelling musk that can temporarily blind (if makes contact with eyes). Good climber. Young fully grown at age of 3 months.

Status—Widespread and common (although seldom seen). Often observed as roadkill.

Mountain Lion

(*Felis concolor*)

JAN–DEC

Taxonomy—Class: Mammalia; Order: Carnivora; Family: Felidae.

Identification—Large unspotted cat, usually tawny above, whitish below. Small head, long legs, large paws, and long, black-tipped tail. Cubs are spotted. Produces screams, growls, hisses, and purrs. Scat variable. Round tracks with 4-toe paw prints showing no claws and measuring 10 cm (4 in) long.

Natural history—Solitary except for female with cubs. Ranges over very large area. Good climber and capable of leaping 6 m (20 ft). Mountain lion deer kills observed at Bosque del Apache NWR; diet otherwise unknown in bosque but elsewhere also includes rabbits, large rodents, birds, even raccoons and coyotes. Avoids humans but can also attack and should not be approached if detected.

Status—Rarely encountered in bosque but exact status unknown.

Rick and Nora Bowers

Bobcat

(*Felis rufus*) ✳

JAN–DEC

Taxonomy—Class: Mammalia; Order: Carnivora; Family: Felidae.

Identification—Large version of the domestic cat with indistinct black spots and bars on orange-brown or grayish fur coat. Tail short and stubby, tipped above with black. Ears slightly tufted and largely black on back side. Scat similar to that of domestic dog. Tracks, front edge of heel pad is concave.

Natural history—Mainly nocturnal. Apparently prefers dense brushy vegetation. Species' diet includes mammals, birds, and reptiles (but diet in bosque not known). Waits for small prey to approach, then pounces on it; often stalks larger animals. Excellent climber (occasionally seen up in cottonwood trees); can swim. Female raises litters of up to 7 kittens.

Status—Mostly in the south, where there is less development. Probably not rare and possibly breeding but exact status in bosque unknown.

Ralph Giles

Elk   (*Cervus elaphus*) ✳✳

JAN–DEC

Taxonomy—Class: Mammalia; Order: Artiodactyla; Family: Cervidae.

Identification—Larger than mule deer. Has long head, thick neck, and slender legs. Brown above with darker head, neck, and legs; large rump patch and very short tail appear white at a distance. Male (bull; photo) larger than female (cow); has dark brown mane on throat and typically grows wide, 6-pointed antlers on each side. During breeding season, bull utters "bugles," beginning as low bellows, then turning into loud whistles. Scat, dark pellets or flattened chips; tracks larger and rounder than those of mule deer. Male also leaves marks on bark of trees where it rubs its antlers.

Doug Brown

Natural history—Forages in open areas and wetlands; also in alfalfa fields adjacent to bosque. Uses dense shrubby vegetation for cover. Besides herbaceous plants, diet includes woody vegetation. Bulls bugle and establish harems during breeding season, which in New Mexico begins in late August and peaks in September and October. Bull sheds antlers in late winter or in spring. Calves are born in late May or June.

Status—Small herd present year-round in bosque from Bernardo south to the Bosque del Apache NWR, including at La Joya. Apparently breeding (calves observed).

Mule Deer   (*Odocoileus hemionus*) ✳✳

JAN–DEC

Taxonomy—Class: Mammalia; Order: Artiodactyla; Family: Cervidae.

Identification—Medium-size deer named for its large mulelike ears, nearly always in motion and swiveling independently. Upper parts gray-brown or brown, rump whitish, tail white at base and on underside with black tip. Male (photo) grows dichotomously branched antlers that do not extend backward over back as in elk. Scat, dark, hard, cylindrical pellets. Tracks, foreprints and hind prints resemble "split hearts" with forward-facing end narrow and pointed.

Jean-Luc Cartron

Natural history—Usual social group consists of a doe with her fawns of 1 or 2 years. Such groups may be seen foraging along ditch banks and in open areas while using willow thickets and cottonwood woodland for cover. Mating season generally in late fall or early winter with single male temporarily joining a doe and her family group. Fawns are born in early summer. Males shed their antlers after mating season, growing new ones in late summer.

Status—Most likely to be seen at Bosque del Apache NWR, where common year-round.

GLOSSARY OF VERTEBRATE TERMS

Arboreal: Living in trees.

Bib: In some birds, band across the throat and breast in the form of a bib.

Bicolored: Having two colors. Typically *ventral* coloration is paler than *dorsal* coloration.

Calcar keel: In bats, cartilaginous flap protruding posteriorly from trailing edge of tail membrane and attaching to the ankle bone on both legs.

Call: In birds, vocalization other than a song. Calls are less complex and shorter than songs.

Canines: In mammals, pointed teeth for tearing and puncturing, present in the jaw between the incisors and the molars.

Cap: In birds, top of the crown.

Carapace: In turtles, dorsal part of the shell.

Carnivorous: Feeding on flesh.

Caruncle: In the wild turkey, wartlike projection from the forehead.

Cere: In birds, featherless area at the base of the beak and enclosing the nostrils.

Chick: Young bird.

Chorus: In toads and frogs, cluster of singing males.

Cornified: Thick and compacted by the accumulation of keratin, a specialized protein, in the dead upper layer of the skin.

Coverts: Feathers covering the base of flight feathers on the tail and the wings.

Covey: In quails, flock of 12 individuals or more.

Crepuscular: Active around dawn and dusk.

Crest: In birds, tuft of elongated feathers rising from the crown.

Crown: In birds, top part of the head.

Decurved bill: In birds, bill that curves downward from the base toward the tip.

Dorsal: Along the top (or back) side of an animal.

Dorsolateral: Toward the sides of the dorsal surface of the body.

Echolocation: In bats, ability to emit high-frequency sounds and navigate and locate prey from the reflected sound waves.

Facial disk: In owls, circular area surrounding the eyes and helping to funnel sound into the ears.

Flank: In birds, area of the body that is lateral to the back and posterior to the side and extends to the base of the tail.

Fledging: Time at which nestlings are able to leave the nest.

Fledgling: Young bird that has fledged but is not yet capable of surviving on its own and still receives parental care.

Flight feathers: In birds, feathers on the wings and tail used during flight for lift and maneuverability; wing flight feathers are attached to the bones of the wing and include primaries and secondaries.

Forewing: In birds, part of the wing that holds the ulna and radius and the secondaries.

Fossorial: Adapted for burrowing or digging.

Gills: In the larvae of amphibians, organs used for breathing underwater.

Gorget: On the throat of hummingbirds, patch of iridescent feathers changing color with different light angles.

Guard hairs: Coarse hairs forming the outer coat of a mammal.

Gular fold: In some lizards, fold of skin across the throat.

Harem: Group of two or more breeding females controlled and defended by one male.

Hatch-year bird: Young bird less than a year old.

Herbivorous: Feeding on plants.

Hibernaculum: Place where a snake or bat spends the winter.

Hibernation: Extended form of *torpor* lasting up to several months during which an animal becomes inactive and allows its body temperature to fall.

Hinge: In some turtles, flexible joint between *scutes* of the *plastron*, allowing the shell to partially close.

Hybridization: Interbreeding between two different species.

Immature: In birds, juvenile that has gone through its first molt but has not acquired the adult plumage yet.

Incisors: In mammals, front teeth on both jaws adapted for cutting or gnawing.

Insectivorous: Feeding on insects.

Interfemoral membrane (or uropatagium): In bats, skin membrane extending between both legs.

Iris: Colored portion of the eye.

Keel (bats): See *calcar keel*.

Keel (turtles): On the carapace, longitudinal, linear ridge.

Keeled scales (reptiles): Scales with a narrow ridge running along the middle from front to rear and giving a rough feel to the skin.

Larva: Immature stage (amphibians).

Lore: In birds, area of the face between the bill and the eye.

Malar stripe: See *mustache*.

Mandible: Lower jawbone. In birds, the upper and lower parts of the bill are often referred to as upper and lower mandibles.

Maxilla/Maxillary: Upper jawbone.

Metamorph: Amphibian newly transformed to the adult stage.

Metamorphosis: Transformation from the larval to the adult stage (amphibians).

Mid-dorsal: Along the middle of the back.

Migrant: A bird or bat that migrates; spring and fall migrants are birds or bats that neither breed nor overwinter locally but simply pass through during spring and fall migration.

Morph: One of several distinct types of plumage in a bird and unrelated to sex or age.

Musk gland: Scent-producing gland for recognition or for defense against predators.

Mustache: In birds, stripe on each side of the chin and extending down onto the throat; also called malar stripe.

Nape: Back (or upper) side of neck.

Nest parasitism: In birds, act of laying eggs in the nests of other birds; parental care is left to the host species.

Nocturnal: Active at night.

Omnivorous: Eating plant and animal food.

Parotoid glands: In some toads, large, prominent glands on either side of the neck; bufotoxins produced by parotoid glands are used for defense against predators.

Parthenogenesis: In some lizards and other vertebrates, reproduction without male fertilization. All individuals are females.

Pelage: Coat of a mammal, consisting of hair, fur, or wool.

Pit organ: In rattlesnakes, heat-sensing organ for detecting prey.

Plastron: In turtles, ventral portion of the shell.

Plumage: All of a bird's feathers.

Plume: In birds, long, showy feather displayed by males for attracting a mate.

Poult: Young turkey.

Precocial birds: Birds that hatch with their eyes open and their body covered with down and can leave the nest almost immediately.

Premolars: In mammals, teeth between the canines and molars, designed for grinding.

Primaries: Outermost flight feathers of birds, long, stiff, and attached to bones of the "hand."

Quills: Specially modified, stiff hairs with needle-sharp tips covering most of a porcupine's body.

Rectrices: Flight feathers of the tail; rectrices are long, stiff feathers.

Rookery: Breeding colony of birds.

Rump: In birds, area of the body between the upper-tail coverts and the back.

Sagittal crest: Bony ridge at the juncture between the two parietal bones on the skull. The parietal bones form the top and sides of the skull behind the frontal bone (forehead).

Scalation: Size and arrangement of scales on a reptile's body.

Scale: Small platelike structure forming the external covering of reptiles. Keeled scales have longitudinal ridges, giving them a rough feel; smooth scales lack ridges.

Scapulars: In birds, short feathers covering the area of the body where the back and wing join.

Scat: Fecal pellet or dropping.

Scute: Scale modified and enlarged into a horny (or keratinous) plate on the shell of a turtle.

Secondaries: In birds, wing flight feathers attached to the forearm; secondaries are long, stiff feathers.

Sexually dimorphic: Showing differences in size and/or appearance between the male and the female.

Side: In birds, part of the body between the belly, wing, and back; the side is anterior to the flank.

Song: In birds (mainly passerines), series of musical notes or phrases often repeated and used during the breeding season for advertising territoriality and for courtship. Typically only the male sings.

Spade: Keratinized metatarsal tubercle (or outgrowth) found on the hind foot of spadefoot toads and used for burrowing. Metatarsals are bones in the feet.

Spectacle: In birds, combination of an eye ring and a line above the *lore*.

Speculum: In some duck species, brightly colored wing patch on the *secondaries.*

Subadult: In eagles, individual largely similar to adult but not yet capable of breeding.

Suture: In turtles, seam between *scutes.*

Tibia: One of the two bones in the hind limb between the knee and ankle.

Torpor: State of inactivity during which an animal allows its body temperature to fall to reduce metabolic requirements during cold weather and times of reduced food supplies.

Tragus: Cartlilaginous projection in front of the external opening of the ear.

Transplant: Animal (or plant) transported from one area to another.

Underparts: *Ventral* side of the body; in a bird in flight, part of the body that is visible from below.

Undertail: Underside of the tail.

Undertail coverts: Feathers covering the underside base of the tail.

Underwing: Underside of the wing on a flying bird. On a perched bird, the underwing is tucked against the body.

Unicuspid: Tooth with a single cusp.

Upper parts: Dorsal side of the body; in a bird in flight, part of the body that is visible from above.

Upper tail: Upper side of tail.

Upper wings: Upper side of the wing on a flying bird.

Vent: In birds, opening of the cloaca, the terminal chamber into which the intestine and urogenital ducts discharge.

Ventral: Along the underside of an animal.

Vocal sac: Inflatable, resonating pouch of skin on the throat of male toads and frogs.

Wattle: Fleshy appendage hanging from a turkey's chin.

Wing coverts: In birds, wing feathers covering the bases of the flight feathers.

BIRDING AT ELEPHANT BUTTE RESERVOIR

Elephant Butte Reservoir is the largest lake in New Mexico. Its southern shore lies less than 5 miles northeast of Truth or Consequences in Sierra County. With 200 miles of shoreline, the reservoir pool—the lake at full capacity—extends 40 miles northward, reaching into Socorro County. Elephant Butte Reservoir derives its name from an island in the lake, a flat-topped, eroded volcanic core in the shape of an elephant.

A man-made lake, Elephant Butte Reservoir is impounded by Elephant Butte Dam and can hold 2,065,010 acre-feet of water. The northern and southern parts of the reservoir pool are divided by the Narrows, a pinch point between two escarpments. At full capacity, both parts hold water. Due to prevailing drought conditions, however, water levels have declined dramatically since the mid-1990s, and in recent years the reservoir pool has held water well below 50% of capacity. As a result, the current lake is confined to the southern section of the

Robert H. Doster

Elephant Butte Reservoir.

reservoir pool. The northern section is no longer underwater. It has been reveg-etated by lush riparian vegetation dominated by Goodding's willow, Rio Grande cottonwood, saltcedar, and Russian olive and also has extensive cattail marshes. Upland vegetation is typical of the Chihuahuan Desert and consists largely of creosote, yucca, prickly pear cactus, and mesquite.

Elephant Butte Reservoir is part of Elephant Butte Lake State Park, established in 1964 with lands leased from the Bureau of Reclamation. With its marinas, camp-sites, picnicking areas, and beaches, Elephant Butte Lake State Park is an impor-tant recreational destination in New Mexico. Fishing, waterskiing, jet skiing, and bird watching are all popular activities. The birds mentioned in this section are those of the current lake (south of the Narrows).

BIRDS TO SEE

Elephant Butte Reservoir is very large, and many birds may be far offshore, out of reach with simple binoculars. For this reason, a spotting scope is essential. From north to south, North Monticello Point, South Monticello Point, Three Sisters, Long Point, Rock Canyon Marina, Hot Springs Cove, Lion's Beach, Marina del Sur, and Dam Marina are all locations overlooking the current lake and acces-sible to the public. Among all of those sites, however, North Monticello Point is generally the most rewarding for bird watching at the lake. The well-graded gravel road to that point is accessed by taking exit 89 or exit 92 off Interstate 25. The best period of the year for bird watching is from September to April, although fall migration for many shorebirds occurs in July and August.

White pelicans off North Monticello Point.

Elephant Butte is known primarily for its waterbirds and shorebirds. Clark's and western grebes, American pelicans, double-crested cormorants, great blue herons, American coots, and killdeer all occur year-round (or nearly so) at the lake. In winter, the Clark's and western grebes are impossible to miss. They number in the thousands, with both species present in approximately equal numbers. The large concentrations of these two wintering grebes have earned Elephant Butte Lake State Park its designation as an Important Bird Area (IBA). Other wintering birds to look for in the lake include many duck and goose species. Gadwalls, American wigeons, green-winged teals, lesser scaups, and ruddy ducks occur at times in good numbers, while northern shovelers, northern pintails, and mallards are also typically present. With more luck, snow geese, Ross's geese, Canada geese, canvasbacks, redheads, ring-necked ducks, buffleheads, and common and red-breasted mergansers can be seen as well. Besides Clark's and western grebes, pied-billed grebes are usually present. Horned grebes are more occasional, while the red-necked grebe, a rare bird in New Mexico, was spotted once recently at Elephant Butte Reservoir. Although not as numerous as ring-billed gulls, herring gulls may be observed in winter, and additional rare gulls include mew and Thayer's gulls. A small number of bald eagles overwinter at Elephant Butte Reservoir. Sandhill cranes are occasional.

Elephant Butte receives an influx of shorebirds, gulls, and terns during migration. Some of the migrating shorebirds include willets and marbled godwits (both in flocks) as well as black-bellied, snowy, and semipalmated plovers; American avocets; greater and lesser yellowlegs; and spotted, western, and least sandpipers. Franklin's, Bonaparte's, and California gulls—the latter species can also be seen at the lake in winter—as well as Forster's tern (the most common tern) are also regularly seen. Baird's sandpipers and black terns may be seen during fall migration. Rare but possible spring and fall migrants are additional gull and tern species, including the Caspian tern.

Summer visitors or residents at Elephant Butte Lake include the great and snowy egrets. Turkey vultures are common overhead. The osprey is primarily a spring and fall migrant at Elephant Butte Lake, but a pair nested here recently.

BIBLIOGRAPHY

Alden, P., B. Cassie, P. Friederici, J. D. W. Kahl, P. Leary, A. Leventer, and W. B. Zomlefer. 1999. *National Audubon Society field guide to the southwestern states.* New York: Knopf.

Allen, T. J., J. P. Brock, and J. Glassberg. 2005. *Caterpillars in the field and garden.* New York: Oxford University Press.

Allred, K. W. 2005. *A field guide to the grasses of New Mexico.* 3rd ed. Las Cruces: New Mexico Agricultural Experimental Station.

———. 2007. *A working index of New Mexico vascular plant names.* spectre.nmsu.edu/dept/docs/rsh/working%20index.pdf.

American Ornithologists' Union. 1998. *Check-list of North American birds.* 7th ed. McLean, VA: American Ornithologists' Union.

Arnett, R. H., and R. L. Jacques. 1981. *Simon and Schuster's guide to insects.* New York: Simon and Schuster.

Benson, L. 1982. *The cacti of the United States and Canada.* Stanford: Stanford University Press.

Biggs, K. 2004. *Common dragonflies of the Southwest.* Sebastopol, CA: Azalea Creek.

Borror, D. J., and R. E. White. 1970. *A field guide to the insects of America north of Mexico.* Boston: Houghton Mifflin.

Brock, J. P., and K. Kaufman. 2003. *Kaufman focus guides: Butterflies of North America.* New York: Houghton Mifflin.

Brown, D. E., ed. 1982. Biotic communities of the American Southwest United States and Mexico. *Desert Plants* 4:1–342.

Carter, J. L. 1997. *Trees and shrubs of New Mexico.* Boulder, CO: Mimbres.

Correll, D. S., and H. B. Correll. 1972. *Aquatic and wetland plants of southwestern United States.* Vols. 1 and 2. Stanford: Stanford University Press.

Crawford, C. S., A. C. Cully, R. Leuthauser, M. S. Sifuentes, L. H. White, and J. P. Wilber. 1993. Middle Rio Grande ecosystem: Bosque biological management plan. Biological Interagency Team, U.S. Fish and Wildlife Service, Albuquerque, NM.

Crawford, C. S., L. M. Ellis, and M. C. Molles Jr. 1998. The Middle Rio Grande Bosque: An endangered ecosystem. *New Mexico Journal of Science* 36:277–299.

Crother, B. I., ed. 2000. Scientific and standard English names of amphibians and reptiles of North America north of Mexico, with comments regarding confidence in our understanding. SSAR Herpetological Circular 29:1–82.

Degenhardt, W. G., C. W. Painter, and A. H. Price. 2006. *Amphibians and reptiles of New Mexico.* Albuquerque: University of New Mexico Press.

Dick-Peddie, W. A. 1993. *New Mexico vegetation: Past, present and future.* Albuquerque: University of New Mexico Press.

DiTomaso, J. M., and E. A. Healy. 2003. Aquatic and riparian weeds of the West. Publication 3421, University of California, Oakland: Agriculture and Natural Resources.

Dunkle, S. W. 2000. *Dragonflies through binoculars*. New York: Oxford University Press.

Eaton, E. R., and K. Kaufman. 2007. *Kaufman field guide to insects of North America*. New York: Houghton Mifflin.

Evans, A. V. 2007. *Field Guide to Insects and Spiders of North America*. National Wildlife Federation. Sterling Publishing Co., Inc. New York.

Findley, J. S. 1987. *The natural history of New Mexican mammals*. Albuquerque: University of New Mexico Press.

Findley, J. S., A. H. Harris, D. E. Wilson, and C. Jones. 1975. *Mammals of New Mexico*. Albuquerque: University of New Mexico Press.

Finch, D. M., J. C. Whitney, J. F. Kelly, and S. R. Loftin. 1999. Rio Grande ecosystems: Linking land, water and people: Toward a more sustainable future for the Middle Rio Grande Basin. USDA Forest Service Rocky Mountain Research Station, RMRS-P-7, Albuquerque, NM.

Flora of North America Editorial Committee. 1993. *Flora of North America: North of Mexico*. New York: Oxford University Press.

Glassberg, J. 2001. *Butterflies through binoculars: The West*. New York: Oxford University Press.

Hink, V. C., and R. D. Ohmart. 1984. Middle Rio Grande Biological Survey. Final report submitted to the U.S. Army Corps of Engineers, Albuquerque, NM. Contract No. DACW47-81-C-0015.

Ivey, R. D. 2003. *Flowering plants of New Mexico*. 4th ed. Albuquerque: R. D. Ivey.

Levi, H. W., and L. R. Levi. 2002. *Spiders and their kin*. New York: St. Martin's.

Ligon, J. S. 1961. *New Mexico birds and where to find them*. Albuquerque: University of New Mexico Press.

Martin, W. C., and C. R. Hutchins. 1981. *A flora of New Mexico*. Vols. 1 and 2. Vaduz, Germany: J. Cramer.

Milne, L. J., and M. J. G. Milne. 1980. *The Audubon Society field guide to North American insects and spiders*. New York: Knopf.

New Mexico Rare Plant Technical Council. 1999. New Mexico rare plants. Albuquerque, NM. nmrareplants.unm.edu.

Pearson, D. L., C. B. Knisley, and C. J. Kazilek. 2006. *A field guide to the tiger beetles of the United States and Canada*. New York: Oxford University Press.

Ricketts, T. H., E. Dinerstein, D. M. Olson, C. J. Loucks, W. Eichbaum, D. DellaSala, and K. Kavanagh, et al. 1999. *Terrestrial ecoregions of North America: A conservation assessment*. Washington, DC: World Wildlife Fund, Island Press.

Scurlock, D. 1998. From the Rio to the Sierra: An environmental history of the Middle Rio Grande Basin. USDA Forest Service Rocky Mountain Research Station, General Technical Report RMRS-GTR-5, Fort Collins, CO.

USDA Natural Resources Conservation Service. Plants database. plants.usda.gov/.

Werner, F., and C. Olson. 1994. *Learning about and living with insects of the Southwest*. Tucson, AZ: Fisher Books.

White, R. E. 1983. *A field guide to the beetles of North America*. Boston: Houghton Mifflin.

Yong, W., and D. M. Finch. 2002. Stopover ecology of landbirds migrating along the Middle Rio Grande in spring and fall. USDA Forest Service Rocky Mountain Research Station, General Technical Report RMRS-GTR-99, Ogden, UT.